12.50

D1483321

Curriculum Theorizing

THE
RECONCEPTUALISTS

William Pinar

University of Rochester

EDITOR

McCutchan Publishing Corporation
2526 Grove Street
Berkeley, California 94704

copyright 1975 by McCutchan Publishing Corporation
all rights reserved
Library of Congress catalogue card number: 74-12821
ISBN: 0-8211-1513-8
printed in the United States of America

For P. K.

Contents

Credits

Chapter 1.   James B. Macdonald, "Curriculum Theory," *Journal of Educational Research* 64, no. 5 (January 1971): 196-200.

Chapter 2.   Lawrence A. Cremin, "Curriculum Making in the United States," *Teachers College Record* 73, no. 2 (December 1971): 207-220.

Chapter 3.   Herbert M. Kliebard, "Persistent Curriculum Issues in Historical Perspective," *Educational Comment* (1970): 31-41.

Chapter 4.   Herbert M. Kliebard, "Bureaucracy and Curriculum Theory," in *Freedom, Bureaucracy, and Schooling*, 1971 Yearbook, ed. Vernon Haubrich (Washington, D.C.: Association for Supervision and Curriculum Development, 1971), pp. 74-93. Reprinted with permission of the Association for Supervision and Curriculum Development and Herbert M. Kliebard. Copyright 1971 by the Association for Supervision and Curriculum Development.

Chapter 5.   Herbert M. Kliebard, "Reappraisal: The Tyler Rationale," *School Review* (February 1970): 259-72. Published by the University of Chicago Press. Copyright 1970 by the University of Chicago.

Chapter 6.   Herbert M. Kliebard, "Metaphorical Roots of Curriculum Design," *Teachers College Record* 74, no. 3 (February 1972): 403-4.

Chapter 7.   Michael W. Apple, "The Hidden Curriculum and the Nature of Conflict," *Interchange* 2, no. 4 (1971): 27-40.

Chapter 9.   John S. Mann, "Curriculum Criticism," *Curriculum Theory Network* 2 (Winter 1968-69): 2-14.

Chapter 10.   John S. Mann, "A Discipline of Curriculum Theory," *School Review* 76, no. 4 (December 1968): 359-78. Published by the University of Chicago Press. Copyright 1968 by the University of Chicago. The research was supported in its initial phase by a faculty grant awarded to the author. Current support is being provided by the Center for the Study of Social Organization of Schools under a grant from the U.S. Office of Education, U.S. Department of Health, Education, and Welfare Grant No. OEO-2-7-061610-0207.

Chapter 12.   Ross L. Mooney, "The Researcher Himself," in *Research for Curriculum Improvement*, 1957 Yearbook (Washington, D.C.: Association for Supervision and Curriculum Development, 1957), pp. 154-86. Reprinted with the permission of the Association for Supervision and Curriculum Development and Ross L. Mooney. Copyright 1957 by the Association for Supervision and Curriculum Development.

Chapter 13.   Dwayne Huebner, "Curricular Language and Classroom Meanings," in *Language and Meaning*, ed. James B. Macdonald and Robert R. Leeper (Washington, D.C.: Association for Supervision and Curriculum Development, 1966), pp. 8-26. Reprinted with permission of the Association for Supervision and Curriculum Development and Dwayne Huebner. Copyright 1966 by the Association for Supervision and Curriculum Development.

Chapter 14.   Dwayne Huebner, "Curriculum as Concern for Man's Temporality," *Theory Into Practice* 6, no. 4 (October 1967): 172-79.

Chapter 18.   Maxine Greene, "Curriculum and Consciousness," *Teachers College Record* 73, no. 2 (December 1971): 253-69.

Chapter 19.   Philip Phenix, "Transcendence and the Curriculum," *Teachers College Record* 73, no. 2 (December 1971): 271-83.

Chapter 20.   William J. Murphy and William F. Pilder, "Alternative Organizational Forms, Cultural Revolution, and Education," *Viewpoints* 48, no. 3 (May 1972): 57-66. Published by the School of Education, Indiana University.

Chapter 25.   George Willis, "Curriculum Theory and the Context of Curriculum," *Curriculum Theory Network* 6 (Winter 1970-71).

Preface

I look at this book in two ways. First, I see it as the presentation of work of major contemporary curriculum theorists. These theorists are not well known to many of you associated with the curriculum field, but they represent an avant-garde whose significance for the field will make itself more and more obvious as time passes. Second, I see the collection as a report of a movement just under way, an example of "work-in-progress," the theme and function of which at first challenge and then supplant traditional curriculum writing.

Before I continue, let me clarify what I mean by "traditional curriculum writing." I mean the work of Professor Tyler, and all the work that falls under his considerable shadow, e.g., Hilda Taba's famous book, Saylor and Alexander's, the Smith-Stanley-Shores volume, and so on. This genre constitutes the heritage of the contemporary curriculum field, and it is a field characterized by the pragmatic, by the concrete ever-changing tasks of curriculum development, design, implementation, and evaluation. The bulk of this writing has one essential purpose; it is intended as guidance for those who work in the schools.[1] Understandably, this writing has been largely atheoretical; being directed at school people who want to know "how-to," it has had to be "practical." Of course, given our astonishingly changing circumstances, both in schools and out, such handbooks have rapidly become dated, and new editions of the old ones and new handbooks appear unceasingly. While it is true that themes of these books differ—from "humanizing" the curriculum, to organizing it around the structures of disciplines—the function of these books is basically the same. They are intended to guide practitioners. Probably 60 to 80 percent of university and college professors of curriculum belong to this group.

There is a second, much smaller group (perhaps 15 to 20 percent of curricularists) whose work differs from the traditionalists, often both in theme and function. This group tends to be steeped in the theory and practice of present-day social science. Professor Beauchamp's *Curriculum Theory* is one attempt to apply ideas of theory development in the social sciences to the formulation of theory in curriculum. Another example of this sort is the 1967 essay by professors Duncan and Frymier given at that year's Ohio State University Curriculum Theory Conference. Other "conceptual empiricists" forgo the question of theory and use the methodology of the social sciences to investigate curriculum "phenomena." Professors Decker Walker of Stanford University, Ian Westbury of the University of Illinois, Mauritz Johnson of the State University of New York at Albany, and William T. Lowe of the University of Rochester are members of this group. Professor Edmund Short of the Pennsylvania State University reviews the work of many such curricularists in a recent issue of the *Review of Educational Research*.[2] It is true that there are wide thematic variations among these researchers; there is however little functional difference. Like most work in contemporary social and behavioral science it investigates "phenomena" empirically, with an eye to the goal of prediction and control of behavior.

The final 3 to 5 percent of the curriculum field are the subject of this book. Their importance for the field far exceeds their number. This importance lies in both the theme and function of their writing. The purpose of this work is not to guide practitioners, as it is with the traditionalists, and to some extent with the conceptual empiricists. Nor is it to investigate phenomena with the methods and aims of behavioral and social science as they are understood today. The function of this work would appear to be, to understand, and this understanding is of the sort aimed at and sometimes achieved in the humanities. The humanities fields that have been influential thus far are history, philosophy, and literary criticism. Hence the dominant modes of inquiry for this group have been historical, philosophical, and literary. Further, the primary "objects" of study have not been observable and measurable behavior—as they tend to be for the conceptual empiricists—or the tasks of the practitioner—as they tend to be for the traditionalist. Rather, the reconceptualists tend to concern themselves with the internal and existential experience of the public world. They tend to study not "change in behavior" or "decision making in the classroom," but matters of temporality, transcendence, consciousness, and politics. In brief, the reconceptualist attempts to understand the nature of educational experience.

This attempt at understanding has led to two functionally different kinds of work. One kind serves as criticism of the old, e.g., the traditionalists and the conceptual empiricists. Professors Apple, Kliebard, and Mann are important critics of a reconceptualist sort. The second subgroup of reconceptualists, whom I have characterized as "postcritical," also tends to be critical of what is; however, the work of this group begins to shift from criticism of the old to creation of the new.

In general terms, this process of reconceptualization has three stages. First, a tradition accumulates, and many initiates accept uncritically the values of that tradition. Their work is that of application, and occasionally the extension of that work theoretically. Essentially this work is of a technical sort; it is carrying the load of others. To surpass this condition, which becomes one of atrophy, the critic is required. His task is complicated and often thankless. It involves learning the language of the heritage, of the masters, in order to be understood. This learning nearly always occurs because the critic comes of age in the tradition; it is through his own usually painful self-education that he comes to realize the difficulties with accepted tradition. Only then does he begin to criticize in hope of rectifying the situation. While the criticism is consciously aimed at his colleagues, the real target lies within him, placed there by his early acculturation. So the effects of criticism are as discomforting to the critic as to those who are criticized. Yet this second stage is necessary for the third to begin.

The final stage has just begun in the curriculum field. Some of us have begun to turn our attention from the past (the Tyler tradition and present-day social science) and begun to look to the present and to the future. This stage has meant introducing existentialism and phenomenology to the field, in order to provide conceptual tools by which we can understand human experience of education. It has also entailed a sensitivity to contemporary historical and cultural developments: the political events of the sixties and the rise of the counterculture. The intellectual foundations of continental philosophy and the experience of life in the United States (specifically in the schools) in this last third of the twentieth century are the two primary "ingredients" of the curriculum field reconceived. At its most ambitious, the field will attempt to become a synthesis of contemporary social science and the humanities. It will attempt a marriage of two cultures: the scientific and the artistic and humanistic. Fairly clearly this is the next step in the West's intellectual evolution, and the field of curriculum (because it is so theoretically loose and hence has less to let go of) may be one of the places where it first occurs. But this is still some time off; let us look at where the movement is now.

Let me briefly introduce the sections by which the collection is organized. In the first I deviate from the general plan, which is to organize around both the individual writer and the function of his writing. This first section is Professor Macdonald's "Curriculum Theory," which raises the very important matter of function. Because this idea seems so important and because I have used the idea to organize the book, I have set it off by itself, to provide a further introduction. The next section is "History and Criticism." Both traditionalists and conceptual empiricists tend to be ahistorical, a deficiency Professor Kliebard has pointed out. I include two of his historical studies, his interesting arrangement of curriculum metaphors, and his criticism of the Tyler rationale. Also included in this section is Professor Cremin's "Curriculum Making in the United States." While obviously Mr. Cremin's distinguished work lies not in the curriculum field and so he cannot be called a reconceptualist, this article does function as revisionist, and so I have included it. Professor Apple's and Professor Mann's important work functions as criticism, and criticism in both political and methodological veins, and it forms the next section along with Professor Mooney's "The Researcher Himself." Concluding the volume is a section of writing that begins to be postcritical in function; these articles point the way to the future of the curriculum field.

Notes

1. See Professor Macdonald's "Curriculum Theory" in this volume (chapter 1).
2. *Review of Educational Research* 43, no. 3 (Summer 1973).

part one

State of the Field

Professor Macdonald's initial differentiation in "Curriculum Theory" is functional in nature; many orderings of the field tend to be thematic. This is important; one begins to dwell less on the specific themes of scholarly work and more on its function. Yet this matter of function is complex. For example, one may write to report on work-in-progress; such writing is essentially journalism. Or one may write to persuade others to accept a certain viewpoint. Other writing is exploratory and experimental. These are usually conscious aims of one's work, but there are others, often less conscious and examined.

For example, what is the psychological function of an essay? That is, how does the work affect your psychological state? Does it steady you with its own formality and self-assurance; does it move you with its mood as well as its argument? What does one's own writing mean psychologically? How does it reflect one's psychological condition and assumptions regarding human being? What does it express symbolically? Other functions come to mind. What is the political function of one's work? Does it tend to endorse established political and economic arrangements? Is it a defense, perhaps in a disguised way, of one's social and economic class? Does the author use a tone of authority to command respect for his views regardless of their inherent reasonableness; or does he allow the argument to stand on its own? Other functions are present—the esthetic, the ethical, the religious. The matter is complicated and important; I am grateful to Professor Macdonald for raising it.

James B. Macdonald

One of the more important aspects (and the least revealed) of what people write is why they write it. "Publish or perish" may help explain some or even much of what appears on the printed page; yet it is not a satisfactory explanation for the material gathered together in this book.

Personally, my own work in the field in retrospect is best explained to myself as an attempt to combine my own personal growth with a meaningful social concern that has some grounding in the real world of broader human concerns. Thus, education has served as a societal pivotal point to explore myself and the broader human condition in a meaningful context.

Hidden in the whole process are personal and social values which only emerge from a tacit state over a lengthy period of time. It is in other words easier to come to know what one values through one's writing than to write from our values as rational beginning points.

Looking back I can see that two major value themes have appeared and reappeared over the years. One has been expressed in a desire to construct intellectually satisfying conceptual maps of the human condition which were educationally meaningful and personally satisfying. The second has been expressed in a utopian hope that somehow people could improve the quality of their existence, specifically through educational processes and generally through broader social policy.

It is apparent to me that the first theme appeared earlier in my own cognitive professional interest. For it was during this earlier period that I was much enamored with taxonomics, general systems theory, and technical schemes such as the "Tyler rationale and behavioral objectives." This period of some ten years was spent being engaged in a great deal of empirical research and technical developmental work.   That it met a need for me that paralleled some educational needs, there can be no doubt.

But life seems to move in circles and somewhere from my past the utopian impulse, perhaps best experienced and later expressed in terms of justice, equality, fairness, etc., pressed into my professional consciousness.   At this point education became a moral enterprise rather than simply a set of technical problems to be solved within a satisfying conceptual scheme.   And with this shift a concern for quality became a dimension that was not the same as, though still related to, the quantity of problems "solved," or outputs measured.

It is clear to me now that when we speak of education we speak in the context of a microscopic paradigm of a macroscopic human condition, a paradigm that holds all of the complexities in microcosm of the larger condition.

Thus, the struggle for personal integration, educational integrity, and social justice go on, necessitating the constant reevaluation of oneself, one's work and one's world—with the hope that whatever creative talent one may possess will lead toward something better that we may all share, each in his own way.

1

Curriculum Theory

Curriculum theory and theorizing may be characterized as being in a rather formative condition, for essentially there are no generally accepted and clear-cut criteria to distinguish curriculum theory and theorizing from other forms of writing in education. The present situation may be summarized by saying that curriculum theory and theorizing exists because a fair number of thoughtful and respected professional persons say they do it and that it exists. Still others refer to the work of these persons as theorizing and their efforts as theories. A reasonably knowledgeable look at the curriculum "situation" readily reveals some of the problems which create the present confusion.

To begin with, one would suspect that theory would be focused upon a clearly identified realm of phenomena. Unfortunately, this is not so in curriculum for the definitions of curriculum are as narrow as "the subject matter to be learned" and as broad as "all the experiences students have in school." Thus, writings called curriculum theory have varied on one pole from essentially epistemological statements to the other pole of statements of a "philosophy of living."

There is also some disagreement among "theorizers" about the purpose of theorizing. Among those few who give much thought to this problem there appear to be three major camps. One group (by far the largest) sees theory as a guiding framework for applied curriculum development and research and as a tool for evaluation of curriculum development.

Thus, theory becomes a springboard for prescribing and guiding practical activity in relation to curriculum. Theory in this sense functions like a philosophy in that it is not directly thought of as open to empirical validation. That this approach is not called curriculum philosophy may perhaps be so primarily because the persons who engage in it are not usually trained philosophers regardless of the fact that much of it is a form of philosophizing.

A second "camp" of ofttime younger (and far fewer) theorizers is committed to a more conventional concept of scientific theory. This group has attempted to identify and describe the variables and their relationships in curriculum. The purpose of this theory is primarily conceptual in nature, and research would be utilized for empirical validation of curriculum variables and relationships, rather than as a test of the efficiency and effectiveness of a curriculum prescription.

A third group of individuals look upon the task of theorizing as a creative intellectual task which they maintain should be neither used as a basis for prescription or as an empirically testable set of principles and relationships. The purpose of these persons is to develop and criticize conceptual schema in the hope that new ways of talking about curriculum, which may in the future be far more fruitful than present orientations, will be forthcoming. At the present time, they would maintain that a much more playful, freefloating process is called for by the state of the art.

A further interesting and sometimes complicating factor is that individuals who theorize may well operate in all three realms upon different occasions as specific professional pressures and tasks appear. Thus, any piece of curriculum theory must be looked at carefully as a specific piece of theorizing in order to assess its intent.

Huebner[1] offers an analysis of theoretical statements which is of considerable interest here. Curriculum theory he proposes can be categorized in terms of the various uses of language by theorists. Thus, he finds that there are six kinds of language used: (1) descriptive, (2) explanatory, (3) controlling, (4) legitimizing, (5) prescriptive, and (6) affiliative.

If we accept this analysis it becomes clear that "curriculum theory" varies with the intentions of theorists, as witnessed by their use of language, in any particular time and place. This may appear to be unusual in relation to the history of scientific theory at first glance, but a little reflection shows that there are similar varieties of theory in many fields. The problem that variety creates for curriculum is perhaps of a different order. It would appear that the variety is less troublesome than the confusion among theorists about the variety and of the intentions of other theorists. The result has been something like a series of theoretical exchanges which have often been at cross purposes, together with an essential lack of historical development. Instead, the historical state of the field looks much more like a set of out-of-phase cycles. It is suggested from this that curriculum theory is much in need of historical study, with the goal of untangling what Huebner referred to as the different uses of curricular language.

Kliebard[2] offers an insightful perspective on the history of curriculum issues. He highlights the idea that curriculum has been essentially plagued by "an ahistorical posture," an "ameliorative orientation," and a lack of definition. He concludes that "our basic framework and our intellectual horizons have been severely limited." He further suggests that "the task of the future is the development of alternative modes of thinking to the dominant 'production model' of the past 50 years."

The production model Kliebard speaks of is that associated with Bobbit[3] and others in the early part of the 20th century and later with the Tyler[4] rationale. In Huebner's terms this is variously a "controlling" and "prescriptive" use of language. But even here the elements of control and prescription are fundamentally grounded in a technological rationale rather than in philosophical and/or scientific theory.

This technical model has been developed to its greatest sophistication by vocational education workers. An excellent recent "state of the art" review was edited by Smith and Moss[5] who summarize the process as: (1) specifying the role for which training is to be provided, (2) identifying the specific tasks that comprise the role, (3) selecting the tasks to be taught, (4) analyzing each of the tasks, (5) stating performance objectives, (6) specifying the instructional sequence, (7) identifying conditions of learning, (8) designing an instructional strategy, (9) developing instructional events, and (10) creating student and curriculum evaluative procedures and devices.

For all intents and purposes this has been what has passed for the prevailing "theory" of most curriculum workers (with variations and alterations for different areas). Many curriculum theorists, however, have not found this to be a satisfactory model for a variety of reasons; perhaps most fundamentally because the technical process begins with an acceptance of contemporary social values (thus eliminating the value question of what to teach).

The Concerns of Curriculum Theory

Philosophies of education, according to Frankema[6] are either analytical or normative. That is, they are essentially attempting to describe, discriminate, and establish meanings for terms, or they are essentially sets of statements about what should or should not be included in education and what should or should not be done during the educational process.

Curriculum theorists have found such neat categories difficult to parallel, since the concerns of curriculum at some times must be related to what is learned by persons. Thus, curriculum always has action implications with a broad directional concern for outcomes. Under these circumstances, one is always involved in assumptions and implicit (if not explicit) statements which could be classified at various times and places as ontological; axiological, and epistemological. Concern for the nature of human "being," value theory, and the nature of knowledge are intricately interwoven in action contexts. But in many ways curriculum theorizing can be conveniently categorized as oriented toward statements about knowledge, statements about the curriculum realities, and statements about valued activity.

Knowledge-Oriented Statements

Undoubtedly, the most prolific group of curriculum thinkers in the past decade have been those persons concerned with knowledge. This is a reasonable and important development since the curriculum has a substance which is drawn from the accumulated cultural development of a civilization. It is indeed quite difficult to comprehend the justification of schooling outside this context. (Although whether the school is the best place to learn about it has been challenged.)

In some ways, the recent concern for knowledge has been a reactive phenomena to critics' perceptions of education as life adjustment and broad social pressures to keep up with the Russians. Whatever the motivational source of the energy in the process, a sizable number of academically talented persons have entered the curriculum arena.

Bruner[7] sounded the clarion call for the movement toward reconceptualizing the subject matter of the schools around the structure of the disciplines and the modes of disciplined inquiry. This has been picked up by persons from many disciplines and has resulted in a veritable landslide of curriculum revisions, new programs, revised and/or new materials, and in-service programs for teachers.

Essentially, as Brownell and King[8] so ably state, the rationale for the priority of disciplines lies in the assertion that man's essential nature is most reasonably fulfilled by his symbolic capacities with priority on general ideas and especially those most teachable and learnable. Thus, the curriculum needs to be fundamentally grounded in a conception of those general structures of symbolic systems which can be most communicated to and learned by others.

Schwab[9] and Phenix[10] have also been in the forefront of this general approach. Schwab has provided a fundamental analysis of the organizational, substantive, and syntactical structures of the disciplines. Phenix contributed a conceptual reorganization of the fields of knowledge with the intention of facilitating learning and use of knowledge. Vandenberg[11] edited a useful volume of readings in which he presented selected articles by a variety of persons, which help put the theory of knowledge into educational perspective.

As far as the new impetus for the disciplines and structure have moved us, there are still a sizable number of theorists who feel epistemology or knowledge is too limited a base for an adequate curriculum theory. Questions about the relevance of social, human, and personal qualities would appear to lead to broader vistas in order to cope comfortably with curriculum decisions.

Reality-Oriented Statements

At the risk of misusing the concept of ontology and in a heuristic spirit, there are a number of theoretical statements which talk about the "nature of things" as they are relevant to the consideration of the curriculum. Principally, these attempts focus upon the social, cultural, and personal context and fabric which is interwoven into a complex mosaic of living and being. The curriculum thus becomes primarily a focal point for a much more fundamental concern about reality which when conceptualized can be utilized to look at curriculum.

Goodlad[12] characterized the curriculum picture in terms of two eras, the progressive era and the discipline-centered era. He noted that major proponents of these eras have been heard selectively. Thus, Jerome Bruner as a major figure in the recent disciplines era has many secondary propositions which are directly corollary with concerns of the progressives; and John Dewey (as representative of progressives) warned about the tendency of some progressives to forget the disciplines. This, of course, suggests that political forces may be quite important in influencing the perceptions of scholarly work in eras of curriculum theory development.

Mann[13] made an initial foray into the relationship of politics to curriculum theory. He focused primarily upon student unrest and politics in relation to curriculum. As noteworthy as his contribution is, much more thought needs to be given and analysis needs to be carried on of the nature of the influence of changing climates of broad social and political circumstances as they impinge upon the development of curriculum theory and the selectivity of perceptions of curriculum developers when encountering this theory.

The significance of this concern should be clear. The question of whether an adequate curriculum theory can be formulated without a sophisticated awareness of political phenomena provides a dimension to theorizing that has only been noted in passing, hinted at, or broadly sketched in the past. Some theorists are beginning to wonder if these political influences may not be far more important than they generally have been thought to be.

Goodlad and Richter[14] have presented the most elaborate contemporary model for curriculum. They identify four levels of decision making: social, ideological, institutional, and instructional.

This model is predicated upon the process of rational decision making and is an extension of the Tyler[15] rationale. However, contrary to Tyler they assume that values are beginning points, not only screens to be introduced after analysis of society, learners, and subject matter, thus avoiding one of the major criticisms of the work of Tyler.[16]

The intent of this conceptual model is clearly to control, explain, and describe. However, limiting a conceptual model to rational decision-making processes may well rule out important descriptive and explanatory phenomena, such as that discussed by Mann, and thus weaken the long-range usefulness of the model for more short-term needs for control of the curriculum processes.

Macdonald[17] proposed a conceptual model which views "actions" as the central unit of curriculum theory (rather than the decisions of the Tyler-Goodlad variety). The attempt here was to explain the activity found in relevant contexts of schooling and to describe the various levels of activity that go on and at least hint at their relationships.

Johnson[18] pointed out some conceptual confusion in this model between curriculum and curriculum development. The criticism was well put and his modifications were an important clarification of the intended meaning of the conceptualization. He went on to spell out the flow of activity between curriculum development and instruction and to provide a schema for curriculum.

Again, however, it is clear that the intentions of theorists differ. Johnson clearly is seeking the kind of control that Goodlad and Richter are after, whereas Macdonald's attempt was not predicated upon a control factor in terms of specific output.

Huebner[19] has been exploring at a different level. His approach has dealt with language systems and the ways in which language shapes the process of building conceptual models and/or facilitating processes and decisions in curriculum. Thus, the technical, scientific, political talk is noted in many models; but one may imply from Huebner's discourse that the ethical and aesthetic talk about schooling has been limited, inconsistent, and of much lower priority.

It would appear then, that one central concern of theorists is identifying the fundamental unit of curriculum with which to build conceptual systems. Whether this be rational decisions, action processes, language patterns, or any other potential unit has not been agreed upon by the theorizers.

Further, it seems clear that the intentions of theorizers influence the selection of the unit. In Huebner's[20] terms, it would make sense to suggest that the intent to control predisposes selection of scientific and technical language, and the conceptual system which develops reflects this initial bias. Thus, the value question has not been transcended by the curriculum models that are presently available.

Value-Oriented Statements

Curriculum designs are value-oriented statements. The literature is replete with suggested designs. Designs, in contrast to epistemological theories or reality-oriented statements, attempt to project a theoretically based pattern of experiences as desirable.

It should be noted that curriculum designs are implicit and sometimes explicit in other kinds of models. Yet the intention of designs is clearly to prescribe, legitimize, and win advocates rather than simply describe, explain, and/or control.

Over the years we have witnessed a succession of designs, from the subject-centered, to broad fields, to problems of living and the child-centered approach. Other prominent forms have been called the "activity curriculum," the "core curriculum," and the "emerging needs curriculum." Johnson,[21] in an article on design, mentions that there appear to be from three to a half dozen current designs.

Designers, however, have not escaped the problem of the conceptual modelers. In fact, Herrick[22] suggested that in the end the designers may well be faced with the task of theorizing at the same level. There is still the problem of the basic unit around which designs are built; and the value commitment, perhaps at a different level, is central to design.

Just as rational decisions have been the predominant unit for conceptual models, designs have often utilized learning experiences as a basic unit. Other units frequently proposed have been instructional objectives, learning tasks, and functional social roles and skills.

Value priorities have generally been set in one of the basic referents of curriculum. Designers have generally opted for priority on subject matter, social phenomena, or people (learners). As arguable as this either-or position appears on a philosophical level it is extremely difficult to avoid on a practical design level since the nature of rational thought is linear and it does make a difference which one of the three one begins with. This is frequently so because the choice of priority often implies a value position about a referent that makes the definition of this referent different from what its definition would be if it came later in the set of priorities.

The problems of design are, in fact, what fostered the current interest in curriculum theory. It is reasonable to suggest that as crucial as designs are in terms of the exigencies of practical decision making, the curriculum theorist needs to do much more work before many of the design problems can be solved.

Conclusion

One may conclude that we have only touched upon the area of curriculum theory here, certainly excluding more than has been included. It is a difficult task to formalize such a diverse and wide-ranging field. Yet it is an exciting venture for persons whose dispositions lead them in this direction. There is an article of faith involved which is analogous to Dewey's comment that educational philosophy was the essence of all philosophy because it was "the study of how to have a world." Curriculum theory in this light might be said to be the essence of educational theory because it is the study of how to have a learning environment.

Notes

1. Dwayne Huebner, "The Tasks of the Curriculum Theorist," mimeographed (New York: Teachers College, Columbia University, 1968).
2. Herbert Kliebard, "Persistent Curriculum Issues in Perspective," in *A Search for Valid Content for Curriculum Courses*, ed. Edmund Short (Toledo, Ohio: College of Education, The University of Toledo, 1970), pp. 31-41.
3. Franklin Bobbit, *The Curriculum* (Boston: Houghton Mifflin, 1918).
4. Ralph Tyler, *Basic Principles of Curriculum and Instruction* (Chicago: University of Chicago Press, 1950).
5. Brandon B. Smith and Jerome Moss, Jr., "Process and Techniques of Vocational Curriculum Development," (Minneapolis, Minn.: Research Coordinating Unit for Vocational Education, University of Minnesota, April 1970).
6. William R. Frankema, "A Model for Analyzing a Philosophy of Education," *High School Journal* 2 (October 1966).
7. Jerome Bruner, *The Process of Education* (Cambridge, Mass.: Harvard University Press, 1961).
8. John A. Brownell and Arthur King Jr., *The Curriculum and the Discipline of Knowledge* (New York: Wiley, 1966).
9. Joseph J. Schwab, "Structure of the Disciplines: Meanings and Significance" in *The Structure of Knowledge and the Curriculum*, ed. Ford and Pugno (Chicago: Rand McNally, 1964), pp. 1-30.
10. Phillip Phenix, *Realms of Meaning* (New York: McGraw-Hill, 1965).
11. Donald Vandenberg, ed., *Theory of Knowledge and Problems of Education* (Urbana: University of Illinois Press, 1969).
12. John Goodlad, "Curriculum: A Janus Look," *Journal of Curriculum Studies* 1, no. 1 (November 1968): 34-46.
13. John Mann, "Politics and Curriculum Theory: An Informal Inquiry," *Curriculum Theory Network* 5 (Spring 1970).
14. John Goodlad and Maurice Richter, "The Development of a Conceptual System for Dealing with Problems of Curriculum and Instruction," Cooperative Research Project No. 454, ED 010 064 (Washington, D.C.: U.S. Department of Health, Education and Welfare, 1966).
15. Tyler, *Basic Principles*.
16. See, for example, Herbert Kliebard, "The Tyler Rationale," *School Review* 78 (February 1970): 259-72.
17. James B. Macdonald, "Structures in Curriculum," Proceedings of the Conference on Curriculum Leadership (Madison, Wis.: Wisconsin State Department of Public Instruction, 1966), pp. 28-46.
18. Mauritz Johnson, "Definition and Models in Curriculum Theory," *Educational Theory* 17 (April 1967): 127-40.
19. Dwayne Huebner, "Curriculum Language and Classroom Meanings," *Language and Meaning* (Washington, D.C.: ASCD, 1966).
20. Ibid.
21. Mauritz Johnson, "On the Meaning of Curriculum Design," *Curriculum Theory Network* 3 (Spring 1969): 3-9.
22. Virgil E. Herrick, "Curriculum Structure or Design," mimeographed (School of Education: University of Wisconsin).

part two

History and Criticism

Sartre, referring to American sociology, wrote: "Hyper-empiricism —which on principle neglects connection with the past—could arise only in a country whose History is relatively short." He could have been remarking as well on American psychology or on the curriculum field. Professor Kliebard has made similar observations of the field; therefore, in attending to this neglect of the past, I am pleased to include two of his historical studies (as well as two other essays) and a piece by the distinguished Professor Cremin.

I am not at all sure that one can justify historical study by the famous argument that knowing the past helps avoid repetition of it, although Mr. Cremin does appear to be making that very point. It seems to me, admittedly not a historian, that social, economic, and political conditions differ sufficiently to make replication of a situation unlikely if not impossible. But it is possible, I suppose, for structure (ethical issues, psychic conditions) to remain the same while content (external conditions) differs. If so, then historical study that acknowledges this distinction might well have a guiding function. Probably Professor Cremin would not disagree.

I am convinced that the study of history—whether educational, psychological, or political—is necessary, if not to help us avoid the errors committed in the past, then definitely to help us understand the present. If we have learned anything from psychoanalysis it is that the past dwells in the present. It is as if the past were a transparent veil over the present, fine enough to be overlooked, but consequential enough to skew our perception not only of the present but also of the future and the past. I am almost awed by the lengths to which we Americans (perhaps it is all of us in the Western Hemisphere, as Sartre's remark suggests) go to avoid facing the past. We continually, if not compulsively, alter our environmental conditions, and we ascribe considerable power to the influence of environments. In doing so we tend to forget the power and presence of the past. As Jung noted, however, "forgetting" is not the same as "getting rid of." The past remains present, whether we are aware of it or not. Let us work to be aware of it.

Lawrence A. Cremin

I attended the Townsend Harris High School and the College of the City of New York between 1938 and 1946 (with a period out for military service) and received in those institutions a solid grounding in the social sciences and the humanities. That grounding stood me in good stead when I went on to Columbia University to study with George S. Counts, John L. Childs, R. Freeman Butts, Henry Steele Commager, Harry J. Carman, and Ralph Linton. They taught me that education and politics are inextricably intertwined, that one cannot discuss the ends and means of education apart from the most fundamental questions of value, and that education proceeds through a variety of institutions of which the school is only one. They also led me to John Dewey (whom I had the pleasure of knowing personally) and got me to read him systematically and intelligently. And while they were doing that, my fellow student Martin S. Dworkin introduced me to critical philosophy in general and Morris R. Cohen in particular, thereby helping me to develop a perspective from which to consider Dewey.

During the quarter-century that I have taught and written in the field of education I have been blessed with superlative colleagues. Among those who have influenced my thinking most profoundly have been Philip H. Phenix, Robert K. Merton, and the late Richard Hofstadter at Columbia, Bernard Bailyn and Israel Scheffler at Harvard, and Merle L. Borrowman at the University of California at Berkeley. The discussions of the Committee on the Role of Education in American History, on which I served during the early

17

1960s, were also immensely valuable to me, both in confirming the particular approach to education that I had begun to take in my work and in helping me to develop the historiographical techniques that would be most appropriate to that approach.

Lawrence A. Cremin
Teachers College
Columbia University
June, 1974

2

Curriculum Making
in the United States

Curriculum in its English usage is a comparatively recent term, dating from the nineteenth century, if one accepts the examples in *The Oxford English Dictionary* as authoritative. The word seems first to have been used to describe formal courses of study in the schools and universities, for example, the high school curriculum or the medical curriculum, and it doubtless served to distinguish between such courses and the particular subjects they comprised, that is, reading or arithmetic or anatomy or physiology. In its very nature the term carries a variety of connotations, such as coherence, sequence, and articulation, for a course of any kind has a beginning. a middle, and an end. But interest in these values long antedates the term itself, going back at least to the time of the Sophists and perhaps even earlier.

Not surprisingly, sustained concern with curriculum emerged in the United States during the early decades of the Progressive Era, when for good reason and bad the schools and colleges found themselves teaching an astonishing variety of subjects to an immensely heterogeneous clientele. Elementary schools had added nature study, drawing, music, manual training, and physical education to the traditional core of reading, writing, arithmetic, history, and geography; high schools were teaching natural sciences, social studies, and a host of trade and vocational subjects alongside the older fare of languages and mathematics; and the colleges were offering all manner of literary, scientific, and professional instruction under the twin banners of equal opportunity and public service. Inexorably expansionist about the role and function of schooling, progressives of every persuasion pressed for including their favorite subjects in programs of study; relentlessly rationalistic about the nature and management of institutions, they pressed as vigorously for a rethinking of that program as a whole. The result was the modern curriculum movement, with all its infinite diversity and with all its prodigious influence.

The story begins in earnest with the efforts of William Torrey Harris, superintendent of the St. Louis school system during the 1870s. The leading figure of a postwar generation of schoolmen that included Barnabas Sears and Albert P. Marble of Massachusetts, James Pyle Wickersham of Pennsylvania, F. Louis Soldan of Missouri, William Henry Ruffner of Virginia, and James M. Greenwood of Kansas, Harris has been portrayed as a staunchly conservative, or at best confusingly "transitional" figure whose Hegelian metaphysics buttressed a half-century of antiprogressive thought. Yet in his own time Harris was generally perceived as a reformer, and the difficulty of a proper appraisal may lie less in the character of his contribution than in the categories and definitions we have used to judge it. In the last analysis, though, whether Harris himself was a progressive may be less important than the characteristic solution he and his generation developed for the seemingly intractable problem of universal schooling in an increasingly urban society, namely, the rationalizing of the school system along bureaucratic and industrial lines. For that solution was widely adopted by the most influential segments of the progressive movement, with incalculable significance for the curriculum.[1]

Education, Harris once explained in a brief statement of his pedagogical creed, is a process "by which the individual is elevated into the species," or alternatively, a process by which a self-active being is enabled to become privy to the accumulated wisdom of the race. And it is the task of the curriculum to make that accumulated wisdom economically and systematically available. "The question of the course of study—involving as it does the selection of such branches as shall in the most effective manner develop the substantial activity as well as the formal activity of the child, is the most important question which the educator has before him." And the only defensible course of study is one that "takes up in order the conventionalities of intelligence." Those "conventionalities" include the two great provinces of thought, nature and spirit, and it is the duty of the school to lead the child sequentially through those provinces in as coherent a manner as possible, viz.:

District or Common School

Topics Relating to Nature:
  Inorganic—arithmetic, oral lessons in natural philosophy;
  Organic or Cyclic—geography, oral lessons in natural history.
Topics Relating to Man; or "The Humanities":
  Theoretical (Intellect)—grammar (reading, writing, parsing and analyzing);
  Practical (Will)—history (of United States);
  Esthetical (Feeling and Phantasy)—reading selections from English and American literature, drawing.

High School or Preparatory School

Topics Relating to Nature:
  Inorganic—algebra, geometry, plane trigonometry, analytical geometry, natural philosophy, chemistry;
  Organic or Cyclic—physical geography, astronomy (descriptive), botany or zoology, physiology.
Topics Relating to Man; or "The Humanities":
  Theoretical (Intellect)—Latin, Greek, French or German, mental and moral philosophy;
  Practical (Will)—history (universal), Constitution of the United States;
  Esthetical (Feeling and Phantasy)—history of English literature, Shakespeare or some standard author (one or more whole works read), rhetoricals (declamation and composition), drawing.

College or University

Topics Relating to Nature:
  Inorganic—analytical geometry, spherical trigonometry, differential and integral calculus, physics, chemistry, astronomy, (etc., electives);
  Organic or Cyclic—anatomy and physiology, botany, zoology, meteorology, geology, ethnology, (etc., electives).
Topics Relating to Man; or "The Humanities":
  Theoretical (Intellect)—Latin, Greek, French or German, comparative philology, logic, history of philosophy, Plato or Aristotle, Kant or Hegel, (or a representative of ancient philosophy and also one of modern philosophy);
  Practical (Will)—philosophy of history, political economy and sociology, civil and common law, constitutional history, natural theology and philosophy of religion;

Esthetical (Feeling and Phantasy)—philosophy of art, history of literature, rhetoric, the great masters compared in some of their greatest works; Homer, Sophocles, Dante, Shakespeare, Goethe, Phidias, Praxiteles, Skopas, Michelangelo, Raphael, Mozart, Beethoven, etc.

The instrument of the process would be the textbook, which Harris saw as the pedagogical tool par excellence in a newspaper civilization where public opinion ruled and where the entire community needed access to similar facts and arguments if harmony was to be achieved. The energizer of the process would be the teacher, who would use the recitation to get the pupil to deliberate over what he had read and to relate it to his own life. And the monitor of the process would be the examination, whereby pupils could be frequently classified and then moved individually through a carefully graded system.[2]

Now, the particulars of Harris' course of study need not concern us for the moment, though it is significant that in comprehensiveness, detail, and theoretical coherence it was unique for its time. What is of special interest is rather the analytical paradigm. There is the learner, self-active and self-willed by virtue of his humanity and thus self-propelled into the educative process; there is the course of study, organized by responsible adults with appropriate concern for priority, sequence, and scope; there are materials of instruction which particularize the course of study; there is the teacher who encourages and mediates the process of instruction; there are the examinations which appraise it; and there is the organizational structure within which it proceeds and within which large numbers of individuals are enabled simultaneously to enjoy its benefits. All the pieces were present for the game of curriculum making that would be played over the next half-century; only the particular combinations and the players would change.

Burgeoning Literature

Whatever the adequacy of Harris' solution—and his contemporaries argued endlessly over the details (Should manual training be included? Should history be the organizing core?)—the problems of universal schooling sharpened drastically after the 1880s, with the result that the concern for curriculum became the leitmotif of the progressive movement. There were the recommendations of the immensely influential committees of the National Education Association—the Committee of Ten (on secondary schooling, 1893), the Committee of Fifteen (on elementary schooling, 1895), the Committee on College Entrance Requirements (1899), the Committees on Economy of Time (on elementary schooling, 1915-1919), and the Commission on the Reorganization of Secondary Education (1918)—and there were those of the more specialized committees established by such organizations of scholars and teachers as the American National Council of Teachers of Mathematics. There were the innovations within particular schools or school systems aimed at developing or demonstrating a specific approach to curriculum—witness the Gary Plan or the Winnetka Plan or the Montessori Method (the Deweys reported on some of these in *Schools of To-Morrow* (1915), stressing the inextricable ties between social need, educational theory, curriculum content, and pedagogical process). And there were the innumerable formulations of individual theorists, the Deweys, the Bobbitts, the Charterses, the Bonsers, the Bagleys, and the Judds.

Several works have attempted to assess the meaning and influence of these efforts, among them Isaac Kandel's *American Education in the Twentieth Century* (1957), Edward Krug's *The Shaping of the American High School* (1964), and my own book *The Transformation of the School* (1961). There was, to be sure, an extraordinary richness and diversity about the discussion, including as it did a range of ideas that went from Marietta Johnson's preoccupation with the spontaneous activities of the child to W.W. Charters' argument that the "life activities" of adults should be the sole determinant of curriculum content, from Maria Montessori's stress on youthful independence to William Wirt's emphasis on youthful socialization, from William Heard Kilpatrick's abhorrence of "subject-matter-laid-out-in-advance" to John Dewey's insistence on a multiplicity of carefully conceived curricula, from George S. Counts' urging that the curriculum deliberately criticize the social order to Isaac Kandel's questioning whether it ever really could. But for all its variety, there was an undeniable drift of the argument in the direction of expansion, election, activity, and utility in the curriculum. Indeed, by the 1930s the body of writings on curricular reform was so large and the array of alternatives proposed so broad that there began to emerge a secondary literature cataloguing and evaluating the writings themselves.

Some Central Ideas

Once again, my interest for the moment is not in the substance of the alternatives, as fascinating as that may be, but rather in certain characteristics of the movement as a whole. Two points in particular stand out. In the first place, most of the discussion accepted both the structure and the components of Harris' paradigm, seeking either to multiply the number and range of possible curricula or to alter the content and character of individual standardized curricula. I missed this fact some years ago in an article I wrote on the revolution in American secondary education between 1893 and 1918. Comparing the report of the Committee of Ten with the report of the Commission on the Reorganization of Secondary Education, I pointed to a radical change in the concept of schooling, in the prevailing idea of what could and should be its primary goals and responsibilities. Whereas the earlier report had viewed schooling as a preparation "for the duties of life" via the systematic study of a curriculum enlarged to include the sciences and modern languages, the later report had talked of developing in each individual "the knowledge, interests, habits, and powers whereby he will find his place and use that place to shape both himself and society toward ever nobler ends" and had then set forth seven primary objectives of schooling at all levels, namely, health, command of fundamental processes, worthy home membership, vocation, citizenship, worthy use of leisure, and ethical character. In the contrast, I argued, most assuredly lay a pedagogical revolution.[3]

No one, of course, would deny the extent of change during the quarter-century separating the two reports: the schools were indeed transformed. But one gains a better sense of the character of the transformation if he goes beyond the summary reports to the individual recommendations of the several subject matter committees involved in the work. Thus if we take the social sciences as an example, we discover that the conference on history, civil government, and political economy held under the auspices of the Committee of Ten during the last days of 1892 celebrated the role of the social studies in broadening and cultivating the mind and then went on to be quite specific about curricular topics (for example, "the Puritan movement of the seventeenth century"), textbooks, and related teaching materials. Similarly, the committee on social studies associated with the Commission on the Reorganization of Secondary Education, which reported in 1916, announced its commitment to social efficiency as the "keynote of modern education" and then went on to be equally specific about curricular topics (for example, the "attitudes of the Puritans toward recreation"), textbooks, and related teaching materials. The effort here is not to gloss over immensely significant differences in the suggestions of the two reports regarding the substance, materials, methods, and goals of social science instruction; it is merely to indicate that there were fairly detailed proposals, subject by subject, which preceded the general summary documents, and that however much "cultivation of the mind" may differ from development of "social efficiency," the Puritans remained in the curriculum.[4]

In the second place, with the rapid growth of professional training for educators during the progressive period, the burgeoning literature of curriculum making became the substance of a distinct field of study in which those preparing to lead in the development or coordination of public school curricula could concentrate their academic efforts. The roots of this movement toward professionalization doubtless go all the way back to Harris, whose work was widely studied in schools and departments of education; but the movement itself dates from the second decade of the twentieth century, when Frederick Taylor's concept of scientific management swept not only industry but education as well, leaving in its wake certain characteristic notions of economy and efficiency. Raymond Callahan has documented the profound influence of Taylorism on the general management of schooling; in the field of curriculum development, its influence is manifest in the work of Franklin Bobbitt and W.W. Charters, both of whom tended to analogize from the world of the factory to the world of the school, conceiving of the child as the raw material, the ideal adult as the finished product, the teacher as the worker, the supervisor as the foreman, and the curriculum as the process whereby the raw material was converted into the finished product. To the extent that the characteristics of the raw material, the finished product, and the conversion process could be quantitatively defined, rationally dealt with, and objectively appraised, curriculum making could become a science; to the extent that the workers and the foremen could engage together in the scientific determination and rational pursuit of curriculum objectives, teaching could become an applied science, a form of educational engineering.[5]

Such ideas were central in the reports of the Committees on Economy of Time between 1915 and 1919; and they were central in the widely publicized program of curriculum revision that Jesse

Newlon introduced at Denver in 1922, probably the first in which classroom teachers participated significantly in a systemwide effort at reform. Once the Denver pattern caught on, it was obvious that specialists other than the superintendent would be needed to manage the process, and it was for the purpose of training such specialists that the curriculum field was created. Beginning initially as a subfield of educational administration in some universities, of elementary education in others, and of secondary education in still others, the study of curriculum gradually came into its own, achieving academic independence with the organization of the Society for Curriculum Study in 1932 and establishment of a full-fledged department of curriculum and teaching at Columbia's Teachers College six years later.

Professionalization served many purposes, not the least of which was preparation of knowledgeable practitioners to assume an emergent role within school systems committed to curricular innovation. What it also did, willy-nilly, was to demarcate the analysis and development of the curriculum as the special preserve of a definable group of specialists working within the schools and trained within the education faculty of the university. The consequences of this staking out were prodigious with respect to who would "make" curricula from that time forward and to the assumptions under which curriculum making would proceed.

Striking Similarities

I have argued elsewhere the extent of continuity between the curriculum movement of the 1950s and 1960s and its counterpart during the Progressive Era, in that both aimed ultimately at humanizing knowledge so that it could be popularized. What is also increasingly clear, however, as we gain a measure of historical distance from the later movement, are the striking similarities in the assumptions of the two movements regarding the connotations of the term "curriculum" and the general province of curriculum reform.

Consider, by way of example, the paradigm developed by Jerrold Zacharias and his colleagues on the Physical Sciences Study Committee during the decade following 1956. They began with a given, the high school physics course (usually a year in duration), and with a hypothesis, namely, that the best way to improve high school physics would be to gather together able scholars in the physical sciences and able high school physics teachers and offer them the time, money, and technical resources (writers and moviemakers) to work out syllabi and instructional materials designed to introduce students as engagingly and efficiently as possible to the leading concepts and methods of the field of physics. As the effort proceeded, they discovered that whether syllabi and materials were engaging and efficient could be determined only in actual instructional situations, so they added the insistence that syllabi and materials be tested and refined during the course of their development. And as soon as the syllabi and materials became available and ready for use, they learned that there could be no successful introduction of the courses unless teachers were trained to teach them; hence they also added provision for the retraining of in-service teachers, with the materials themselves as the basis of the retraining. In the interaction of these hypotheses and discoveries lay the essence of what came to be known as the curriculum reform movement of the late 1950s and early 1960s. As Zacharias noted in a 1964 essay entitled "The Requirements for Major Curriculum Revision," curriculum revision signified "the entire process of the preparation of educational materials for use in the formal school system, or in direct association with the formal school system"; and at least four distinct components could be identified as necessary to any program of curriculum revision:

(a) The process of determining the precise boundaries of the educational system unit that will be treated; (b) the process of identifying the subject matter which is to be dealt with within the educational unit; (c) the embodiment of that subject matter in material form, as text, laboratory or classroom materials, and other learning aids; and (d) the preparation of teachers in the new subject matter and in the use of the materials. Of these four components, the first is likely to precede the rest; the determination of subject matter, its embodiment, and the preparation of teachers must however be carried on to a large degree simultaneously.[6]

By the time Zacharias wrote his essay, the reform movement was well under way in the natural sciences and mathematics and was slowly spreading to the humanities and the social sciences. Indeed, Zacharias himself, working through the quasi-public curriculum development organization known as Educational Services Incorporated, had broadened his concern to the whole course of study at every level, suggesting as a conceptual model a box graph, with the entire range of subject fields as one axis and the several school levels from kindergarten through twelfth grade (though not, significantly, through the sixteenth grade—or the nineteenth) as the other. By that time, too, Jerome Bruner had articulated certain leading principles of the curriculum reform movement in *The Process of Education* (1960), using concepts like "structure" to characterize the canon of curricular selection, "discovery" to describe the approach to curricular method, and "spiraling" to express the view of curriculum sequence; and Zacharias was widely citing the Bruner book as the statement of pedogogical theory that would lend coherence to the graph once the various boxes had been filled in.

For all the criticisms one could level against such a scheme—I suggested a number in *The Genius of American Education* (1965)—one could also elaborate it into a far fuller and richer approach to curriculum reform, involving, for example, representatives of the public, who might be more likely to look beyond the academicism of the model than the academics themselves, or specialists from anthropology, sociology, philosophy, psychology, and other related disciplines who might contribute a far more sophisticated concept of the pedagogical process and the ways in which its outcomes might be appraised. But again, my intent is neither to criticize nor to embroider but rather to stress the extent to which curriculum reformers of the 1950s and 1960s accepted a fairly traditional paradigm of curriculum making. They did increase the number of options available within selected subject areas; and they did break the increasingly exclusive hold of professionalized curriculum makers on the direction and control of the process. But it is not without irony that Zacharias' boxes, when filled, call to mind Harris' much older curriculum. Seeking to rid himself of the pedagogical preoccupations of the Progressive Era by avoiding the literature of education, Zacharias ended up accepting the paradigm of curriculum making that had prevailed for three-quarters of a century. And in avoiding the literature, he and others like him inevitably impoverished the character of educational discussion. Insistently eschewing the past, the curriculum reformers of the fifties and sixties eventually became its captive: like Lord Keynes' practical men, they ended up the victims of academic scribblers who had written in very different places and at very different times.[7]

Definition of Education

Let us return for a moment to Harris' definition of education as a process "by which the individual is elevated into the species," or alternatively, by which a self-active human being is enabled to become privy to the accumulated wisdom of the race. Now, Harris was incisive enough to recognize that the process is by no means confined to the school, and indeed he discussed at many points in his writing the respective domains and responsibilities of the family, the state, the church, civil society (whose most important educative

	English	Mathematics	Social Sciences	Natural Sciences	Arts	Physical Education
k						
1						
2						
3						
4						
5						
6						
7						
8						
9						
10						
11						
12						

function is "organization of the industry of man in the form of division of labor"), and the school. On some occasions, Harris' effort was to establish a sequence among the agencies: thus the discussion in the *Psychologic Foundations of Education* (1898), in which, using the metaphor of widening concentric circles, Harris indicated a sequence of familial education, schooling, the education of one's special vocation, the education of political participation, and the education of religion (which transcends all the others). On other occasions his effort was rather to establish a principle of interaction among the agencies: thus the discussions of moral education in his early reports as superintendent of schools in St. Louis, in which he attempted to relate the school's efforts to those of families and churches; and thus too the discussion in "Education in the United States" (1893), in which the textbook is seen as the vehicle par excellence for "preparation of a people for a newspaper civilization—an age wherein public opinion rules." Yet discussions of this sort were almost always formalistic in Harris' writings, and the fact is that he rarely extended them sufficiently to indicate what a curriculum of instruction in all the chief educative institutions might look like or how the curriculum of the school might reflect an awareness of other curricula. The result is that when Harris considered the course of study, he occupied himself almost exclusively with schooling, acknowledging other domains only in his insistence that the teaching of trades be a concern primarily of civil society and the teaching of religion a concern primarily of the church.[8]

This pattern of acknowledging other domains of education and then proceeding to ignore them became characteristic during the Progressive Era. To take but two examples, Dewey began his analysis in *Democracy and Education* (1916) with a discussion of the distinction between the broad educational process inherent in the very idea of social life and "a more formal kind of education—that of direct tuition or schooling"; but he proceeded to confine his attention to schooling, the initial discussion apparently intended not to introduce a consideration of the educative process in its entirety but to ensure that the subsequent treatment of schooling would be seen as essentially continuous with the larger educative process of living. Similarly, Franklin Bobbitt distinguished in *The Curriculum* (1918) between two quite different definitions of curriculum: (1) the entire range of experiences, both directed and undirected, concerned in unfolding the abilities of the individual and (2) the series of consciously directed training experiences that the schools use for completing and perfecting the unfoldment. "Our profession uses the term usually in the latter sense," Bobbitt explained. "But as education is coming more and more to be seen as a thing of experiences, and as the work and play experiences of the general community life are being more and more utilized, the line of demarcation between directed and undirected training experience is rapidly disappearing. Education must be concerned with both, even though it does not direct both." Yet the "profession" to which Bobbitt alluded was a profession of schoolmen, and it is not surprising that, like Dewey, he too went on to deal almost entirely with the problems of schooling. By the end of World War I the drift was unmistakable, with the curriculum being most commonly conceived over the quarter-century that followed as a sequence of planned experiences taking place entirely in or under the auspices of the school.[9]

What if we were to go back to Harris' definition of education and consider the curriculum as the accumulated widsom of the race, to be made available to individuals through a variety of institutions in a variety of modes? And what if we were to conceive of education as the effort to define that wisdom in the large and then assist individuals in the business of sharing it more comprehensively, more economically, more self-consciously, and more critically. Several perspectives would immediately change. In the first place, we would be forced to contend with the question of how what is taught and learned in one institution relates to what is taught and learned in another. Walter Lippmann dealt with the problem in *Public Opinion* (1922) when he asked the schools to prepare their pupils to deal in a much more critical manner with the "information" presented to them in the press. And Martin Dworkin dealt with it recently in a discussion of "visual literacy," speaking not only of the "image curriculum" presented via the several media of mass communication but also of the "image curricula" presented in the schools by teachers who have been the unwitting students of the media. Similarly, Robert Lynn and others have been asking how a reconceived religious education program under the aegis of the churches might relate to what the media are teaching on the one hand and what the schools are teaching on the other. And Israel Scheffler and Thomas F. Green have been raising the more general question of how the character and efficacy of teaching in any one of these institutions differ from and relate to the character and efficacy of teaching in all the others.[10]

In the second place, we would be forced to a conception of a radically individualized educative process. Dewey once described the child and the curriculum as two limits which define a single process. "Just as two points define a straight line, so the present standpoint of the child and the facts and truths of the studies define instruction. It is continuous reconstruction, moving from the child's present experience out into that represented by the organized bodies of truth we call studies." But as Dewey pointed out again and again in his writings, the child is always a particular child with a particular experience, not some abstraction in the curriculum maker's mind. And that child from the moment of his birth is in continuing interaction with many curricula in many educative institutions, or, if one prefers, with an extended curriculum taught and learned (and mistaught and mislearned) in a variety of situations. The various segments of the process are as often conflicting as they are complementary, as often random as they are sequential, and as often confusing as they are meaningful. And the very nature of a free and complicated society precludes our ever wholly ordering or rationalizing them—or, I would argue, wanting to. But they can at least be viewed in their full range and complexity whenever we contemplate instruction. And to do so would be to move us in several directions. It would press us to prescribe modes and sequences of instruction for particular individuals rather than for age-groups or other equally artificial categories—thus the promise of the Cronbach-Snow paradigm of aptitude-treatment interaction. It would focus our concern on the results of instruction in those particular individuals and not merely on the design of the substance presented. And it would dramatize the necessity for developing far more effective means of self-appraisal, one critical mark of maturity in a pluralistic educational situation being a growing ability to diagnose and prescribe for oneself (such self-appraisal, incidentally, would supplement rather than supplant societal examination of individuals and groups for purposes of selection or certification). None of these points, of course, would deny the need to hold some larger conception of a desirable curriculum (or curricula) constantly in mind; but that larger conception can never take the place of an equally necessary understanding of the diverse processes by which individuals come to share the knowledge, values, skills, and sensibilities embodied in such a curriculum.[11]

In the third place, we would be forced to acknowledge the diversity of curricula being defined and taught at any given time by a variety of groups, more or less professional in character, and the need to call such groups to a measure of public responsibility. The staff of the *Book of Knowledge* has a curriculum; the staff of the Children's Television Workshop has a curriculum; the staff of the Boy Scouts of America has a curriculum; the staff of the New York City public school system has a curriculum; and the staff of the *New York Review of Books* has a curriculum. So too do the advertising agencies that serve the American Tobacco Company and the American Cancer Society; so too do the public relations counsels that serve the Democratic and the Republican parties. Charles Silberman recognized these phenomena as clearly as anyone in the early sections of *Crisis in the Classroom* (1970) and then proceeded ably to explore the bearing of his analysis on one institution and the professions that operate it. The other institutions desperately need the same critical scrutiny from the standpoint of education, not merely to call their activities to public attention, but to call their activities to the attention of one another. I should add emphatically, however, that by public attention I do not mean governmental attention, but rather the attention implicit in open, vigorous discussion.

Finally, we would be forced to recognize that in a pluralistic society marked by a pluralistic education, it becomes a matter of the most urgent public concern to look at all these curricula in their various interrelations and to raise insistent questions of definition, scope, and priority. Philosophers since Plato have told us that education is more than a succession of units, courses, and programs, however excellent, and that serious considerations of curriculum must call into play the most fundamental questions of value, belief, and loyalty. Philosophers today seem to have turned away from such questions, thinking, perhaps, that their historic responsibility to ask them carries a corresponding obligation to come up with timeless answers. I for one would hope they return to the charge, for if they do not others will, only less thoughtfully, less systematically, and less responsibly.

Notes

1. The critique of the traditional historiography on Harris suggested here is based on Martin Dworkin's forthcoming volume in the *Classics in Education* series entitled *William Torrey Harris on Education.* For bureaucratization as a characteristic progressive response to the problems of urban schooling during the last decades of the nineteenth century, see Michael Katz, "The Emergence of Bureaucracy in Urban Education: The Boston Case, 1850-1884," *History of Education Quarterly* 8 (1968): 155-88, 319-57; David Tyack, "Bureaucracy and the Common School: The Example of Portland, Oregon, 1851-1913," *American Quarterly* 19 (1967): 475-98; and David Conrad Hammack, "The Centralization of New York City's Public School System, 1896: A Social Analysis of a Decision" (Master's thesis, Columbia University, 1969).
2. William T. Harris, "My Pedagogical Creed," *The School Journal* 54 (1897): 813; *Fourteenth Annual Report of the Board of Directors of the St. Louis Public Schools, 1868* (St. Louis: George Knapp, 1869), p. 94. The curricula itself, taken from William T. Harris, "A Course of Study from Primary School to University," *The Western,* n.s. 2 (1876): 521-38, is reproduced in Carl Lester Byerly, *Contributions of William Torrey Harris to Public School Administration* (Chicago: n.p., 1946).
3. Lawrence A. Cremin, "The Revolution in American Secondary Education, 1893-1918," *Teachers College Record* 56 (1955): 295-308.
4. *Reports of the Conferences on Secondary Education, Held December 28-30, 1892* (n.p.: printed for the use of the Committee of Ten, n.d.), p. 94 and *passim*; and Arthur William Dunn, "The Social Studies in Secondary Education: Report of the Committee on Social Studies of The Commission on the Reorganization of Secondary Education of the National Education Association," United States Bureau of Education Bulletin no. 28 (Washington, D.C.: Government Printing Office, 1916), p. 34 and *passim.* Once one has properly comprehended the reports, of course, there remains the difficult task of ascertaining what was actually taught in classrooms, by what methods, and in what spirit.

5. Raymond E. Callahan, *Education and the Cult of Efficiency* (Chicago: University of Chicago Press, 1962); Franklin Bobbitt, "Some General Principles of Management Applied to the Problems of City-School Systems," *Twelfth Yearbook of the National Society for the Study of Education, Part I* (Chicago: University of Chicago Press, 1913), and *The Curriculum* (Boston: Houghton Mifflin, 1918); W.W. Charters, *Curriculum Construction* (New York: Macmillan, 1923); Mary Louise Seguel, *The Curriculum Field: Its Formative Years* (New York: Teachers College Press, 1966); and Arno A. Bellack, "History of Curriculum Thought and Practice," *Review of Educational Research* 39 (1969): 283-92.

6. Jerrold R. Zacharias and Stephen White, "The Requirements for Major Curriculum Revision," *New Curricula*, ed. Robert W. Heath (New York: Harper & Row, 1964). See also Paul E. Marsh and Ross A. Gortner, *Federal Aid to Science Education: Two Programs* (Syracuse, N.Y.: Syracuse University Press, 1963); William Wooton, *SMSG: The Making of a Curriculum* (New York: Yale University Press, 1965); and the other essays in the Heath anthology. As is well known, Bruner worked closely with Zacharias on the various projects of Educational Services Incorporated, and the formulations of *The Process of Education* (Cambridge, Mass.: Harvard University Press, 1960) derived in part from a conference at Woods Hole Massachusetts in 1959, attended by persons active in the curriculum reform movement.

7. In pointing to certain specific similarities between the curriculum making paradigms of the progressives and those of the later reformers, I do not mean to disparage by omission the several schools of curriculum reform that simply went in other directions, contending that the central problem was not the reordering or reconstituting of subject matter but rather the revitalizing and redirecting of individual schools and teachers. See, for example, Alice Miel, *Changing the Curriculum* (New York: Appleton-Century, 1946); and Hollis L. Caswell et al., *Curriculum Improvement in Public School Systems* (New York: Teachers College, Columbia University, 1950). An appraisal of those schools of thought and an analysis of their influence on classroom practice would properly be the subjects of another paper.

8. William T. Harris, *Psychologic Foundations of Education* (New York: Appleton, 1898); *Seventeenth Annual Report of the Board of Directors of the St. Louis Public Schools, 1871* (St. Louis, Mo.: Plate, Olshausen, 1872); and William T. Harris, "Education in the United States," in *The United States of America*, ed. Nathaniel Southgate Shaler, (New York: Appleton, 1894).

9. John Dewey, *Democracy and Education* (New York: Macmillan, 1916) and Bobbitt, *The Curriculum*.

10. Walter Lippmann, *Public Opinion* (New York: Harcourt Brace, 1922); Martin S. Dworkin, "Toward an Image Curriculum: Some Questions and Cautions," *The Journal of Aesthetic Education* 4 (1970): 129-32; Special Joint Committee on the Church and Public Education of the Board of Christian Education, Presbyterian Church in the United States, and the Board of Christian Education, The United Presbyterian Church in the United States of America, *An Open Letter: The Public and Its Education* (Philadelphia: Board of Christian Education, The United Presbyterian

Church, U.S.A., 1969); Israel Scheffler, *The Language of Education* (Springfield, Ill.: Charles C. Thomas, 1960); and Thomas F. Green, *The Activities of Teaching* (New York: McGraw-Hill, 1971).

11. John Dewey, *The Child and the Curriculum* (Chicago: University of Chicago Press, 1902). The Cronbach-Snow paradigm is the basis of a series of experiments on instruction at the USOE Research Center at Stanford University. The "classic" article is Lee J. Cronbach, "The Two Disciplines of Scientific Psychology," *The American Psychologist* 12 (1957): 671-84. The recent research is summarized in Lee J. Cronbach and Richard E. Snow, *Final Report: Individual Differences in Learning Ability as a Function of Instructional Variables* (Stanford, Calif.: Stanford University Press, 1969); and Glenn H. Bracht, "Experimental Factors Related to Aptitude-Treatment Interactions," *Review of Educational Research* 40 (1970): 627-45.

Herbert M. Kliebard

Herbert M. Kliebard is presently a professor in the Department of Curriculum and Instruction and chairman of the Department of Educational Policy Studies at the University of Wisconsin-Madison. He received his doctorate from Teachers College, Columbia University. Professor Kliebard's early research involved intensive studies of classroom behavior in collaboration with Arno A. Bellack of Teachers College. These studies were essentially descriptive in character and designed to establish a theoretical and empirical base for the study of teaching. In general, these studies did not have as their primary focus the establishment of relationships between classroom variables and learning outcomes, but were directed instead toward establishing a means for analyzing classroom behavior through the language of teachers and students. Articles on this research appeared in the Journal of Teacher Education *as well as in the book,* The Language of the Classroom *(Teachers College Press, 1966). The book has now been translated into Japanese and German.*

Much of Professor Kliebard's writing in the area of curriculum theory has sought to bring an historical perspective to bear on the persistent problems and issues of the field. His interest in history has not been directed toward exalting the wisdom of early curriculum workers, but toward trying to understand the origins of present curriculum thought. The articles which appear here mainly represent efforts to consider present curricular issues in the light of their roots in an earlier period. In particular, Professor Kliebard has sought to explore the development of a technological rationale in curriculum thinking as well as in educational research.

3

Persistent Curriculum Issues in Historical Perspective

In a series of essays on the role of the past in the development of philosophical ideas, John Herman Randall reviewed the ways in which philosophers continually reconstruct and criticize their past as an integral part of their work.[1] This involvement with the past need not be construed as formal historical writing, but rather as a kind of dialogue across generations about the basic concerns of the field. By engaging in such a dialogue, present-day practitioners are at least aware of the ideas and the forces that have helped shape their field and their thinking.

The values associated with viewing complex questions from an historical vantage point are not always clear-cut or easy to state. Frequently, however, such an approach does serve to provide some sense of continuity and direction, and, for me at least, offers a broad perspective on the state of the curriculum field generally and on certain curriculum issues in particular.

The State of the Field

There is some justification for dating the emergence of the curriculum field as a self-conscious field of specialization from around the year 1918. That is the year when several influential works in the curriculum field were published including Franklin Bobbitt's *The Curriculum*[2] and Clarence Kingsley's *Cardinal Principles of Secondary Education*.[3] It is followed in the 1920s by a period of feverish activity directed toward curriculum reform. The tenor of the times was a melange of post-World War I nationalism, a drive for the "Americanization" of immigrants, a faith in the methods of science, and a concern for the uplift of the masses. To a large extent the curriculum field seems to have been shaped by this atmosphere and a reaction against what was believed to be a kind of education that was static, irrelevant to modern life, and nonfunctional. The reformers proposed a school program that was perpetually innovative, directly related to the ongoing world of affairs, and supremely utilitarian in orientation. The curriculum reformers almost totally rejected previously established procedures and practices, which they generally associated with the discredited doctrine of mental discipline. To this day, the picture we have of the once vital and exciting theory of mental discipline is by and large the caricature that was drawn in the early days of the curriculum reform movement. The essentially metaphorical use of a term like "faculties of the mind" is taken literally, and positions are ascribed to the mental disciplinarians which were at best products of a kind of intellectual underworld (e.g., phrenology). This tendency to denigrate the past in favor of an enlightened and inspired present has had several important consequences for the development of the curriculum field.

An Ahistorical Posture

The most immediate consequence of the impulse to reject the past is the simple lack of knowledge that prevails even among our most articulate spokesmen as to the basic facts in recent curriculum history. Certain myths are perpetuated (like the myth about mental discipline) because they tend to support or at least make plausible certain ideological convictions that are being promoted. One widespread instance is that of the speaker or writer who wishes to proclaim the inappropriateness of such "college-entrance" subjects as algebra or foreign languages as being too academically rigorous for the present high school population. Frequently, one segment of the school population is specified such as the disadvantaged or the "non-college-bound" or the low socioeconomic classes. To support his argument, he will usually cite the "fact" that high school students around the turn of the century (or the first decade or two after that) were overwhelmingly college bound and that since the high school now serves a diverse population it must correspondingly adapt its curriculum. The evidence of course is to the contrary—that probably a higher percentage of high school graduates now go on to college than at any time in the period since 1900 and probably before. All this is also quite apart from the question of whether probable destination is an appropriate justification for teaching a subject like algebra to all, some, or none of the high school population.

Another possible consequence of the ahistorical posture in the field of curriculum is the singular lack of dialogue that exists between present day practitioners in the field and their professional forebears. It is not surprising, for example, to find university graduate programs, sometimes leading to a Ph.D. in curriculum, where the student has no opportunity to study the ideas of the men who shaped and gave direction to the field of curriculum. This is not to say, of course, that the writings of men like Bobbitt and Charters and Snedden represent the supreme wisdom in the field of curriculum. We may want to study the work of these men only to rid ourselves of their unseen influence. It is as if advanced graduate students in sociology would study only Parsons and Merton and knew nothing of Weber and Durkheim. Generally speaking, the foremost scholars in other fields of study continually engage in a kind of dialogue with their ancestral counterparts—rejecting, revising, or refining the early formulations and concepts. No such cumulative approach to the content of the curriculum field has yet emerged, and this has had a telling effect on the relative permanence of curriculum thinking. Issues tend to arise *de novo,* usually in the form of a bandwagon and then quickly disappear in a cloud of dust. Sometimes these issues have their counterparts in an earlier period, but this is rarely recognized. The field in general is characterized by an uncritical propensity for novelty and change rather than funded knowledge or a dialogue across generations.

The Ameliorative Orientation

Apart from its generally ahistorical posture, the curriculum field is also characterized by an overwhelmingly ameliorative orientation. This is not to imply that some ultimate good in terms of classroom practices and procedures is an inappropriate direction or outcome of curriculum study and research. An ameliorative component is clearly present in many fields of study. In the curriculum field, however, the urge to do good is so immediate, so direct, and so overwhelming that there has been virtually no toleration of the kind of long-range research that has little immediate value to practitioners in the field, but which may in the long run contribute significantly to our basic knowledge and understanding.

There seem to be at least two reasons for this predominantly ameliorative orientation. One is that the origin of the curriculum field is associated with a reform movement, one that took the form essentially of a drive toward a supremely functional curriculum largely oriented toward socially useful knowledge and skills. The curriculum field, therefore, is at least in one sense a movement, a drive to topple old gods and to replace them with new ones. Until quite recently, one's acceptance into the curriculum field was practically contingent on holding certain convictions. One had to uphold democratic interaction, abhor lectures, speak deprecatingly of "subject matter specialists," and use functional criteria in judging the value of school subjects. The major research in the field, such as the Eight-Year Study, are basically efforts to establish the primacy of the forces of good over the forces of wickedness and reaction. There were, of course, bitter and savagely fought battles within the movement over the past fifty years or so; but these tended to be fought within a rather limited area. They are much like the internecine battles that take place between political or religious groups that are only a hair apart in doctrine. It is also true that there has been over the past ten or twelve years a kind of frontal attack on many of the most hallowed tenets of the curriculum field, but these attacks were launched essentially from outside the professional curriculum community. Insofar as the curriculum field is a reform movement rather than a field of study, it is seriously threatened with disintegration by these outside forces. Movements—drives for a special cause—rise to prominence, then fade and die; fields of study adapt, change and grow.

Apart from its origins in a reform movement, there is one other possible explanation for the strongly ameliorative stance that pervades the curriculum field: it rests with the huge constituency of teachers, school administrators, and supervisors who exert continual pressure on those who conduct research for answers to such practical questions as, how can I improve my teaching, which are the best programs, and how can I recognize and reward a good teacher. These are perfectly natural questions, but they are probably unanswerable in their present form; at any rate, our simplistic approach to them has not been rewarding. The huge body of research on teacher effectiveness is a case in point. Much of it, dating back to the early decades in this century, is based on the assumption that certain specific acts or behaviors in the classroom could be correlated with certain criteria of success in teaching, usually a supervisor's positive rating or a score on an achievement test. These specific behaviors ranged from asking "good" questions to placing one's thumbs in one's suspenders. Research of this kind has been inconclusive or contradictory. Part of the problem, I think, is the value-laden orientation. Immediate emphasis on "good" and "bad" practices frequently leads to circular propositions which take the form of "good teachers do good things in the classroom." In a larger sense, the problem revolves around the effort to develop a kind of technology of teaching leading to the performance of certain presumably effective behaviors in the absence of any fundamental understanding or conception of what kind of activity teaching is. B. O. Smith's dictum in 1956 that "Knowledge of what teaching is in fact is prerequisite to its systematic improvement,"[4] combined with his subsequent research as well as the research of others in this vein, has served to modify somewhat the earlier simplistic approach in favor of a more sophisticated research tradition. Nevertheless, the pressure remains understandably strong for practical answers to immediately practical questions.

The Lack of Definition

Along with the questions of the ahistorical posture and the ameliorative orientation, there is probably one other issue relating to the state of the field of curriculum which deserves attention. It is the paucity of ordered conceptions of what the curriculum field is and its relationships to cognate fields. This question is perhaps so broad as to incorporate the other two but deserves some attention on its own. In part, this problem involves a clarification of the chaotic state of curriculum terminology, a problem alluded to by many leaders in the curriculum field since the 1920s. A variety of widely differing programs, for example, have been proposed and implemented under the names of the activity curriculum or the experience curriculum. [5] The approach to the problem, however, need not take the form of simply attempting to legislate the use of certain terms in certain ways. It involves the broader and more difficult task of critically analyzing the concepts we use as a way of clarifying the nature of our enterprise. Fortunately, some momentum seems to be building in this area as a result of the efforts of analytically oriented philosophers of education. There is little evidence, however, that the considerable insight that Peters, for example, has shown on the question of curricular objectives has permeated curriculum thinking and practice in this country. A typically rigid and pervasive "party line" has developed with respect to the specification of curricular objectives which brooks very little opposition.

The question of definition in the curriculum field extends also to the question of where the boundaries of the curriculum field leave off and where others begin. As one example, one might consider the use of the term *experiences* as the basic unit element in the curriculum. Franklin Bobbitt in the first book ever written on the curriculum defined the curriculum as a "series of experiences which children and youth must have by way of attaining . . . objectives," [6] and various definitions of curriculum have used the term *experiences* ever since. Consider, for example, the following definitions of curriculum:

1. "a series of experiences as a result of which the child's personality is continuously modified" [7]
2. "the whole of interacting forces of the total environment provided for pupils by the school and the pupil's experiences in that environment" [8]
3. "a sequence of potential experiences . . . set up in the school for the purpose of disciplining children and youth in group ways of thinking and acting" [9]
4. "the experiences that a learner has under the guidance of the school" [10]

Definitions such as these clearly extend the notion of curriculum beyond the commonsense notion of the subjects of study, and yet where it ends is not quite clear. Is the definition of curriculum preactive or interactive? [11] Is it to be found in the action system involving a teacher, pupils, and a classroom? If so, then the notion of teaching is somehow subsumed in the definition of curriculum, a conception which violates at least my sense of how these terms are used in ordinary language. If, on the other hand, curriculum and teaching are different concepts, then how are they different and how can we conceive of the relationship that exists between them? In general, the notion of an experience is to me so intimate, so vague and so subjective a concept as to be untenable as a unit element in the curriculum.

Persistent Issues

To my knowledge, controversies exist in all fields of study on the nature of the field and on what constitutes the basic components and orientation of a discipline. In the curriculum field, however, this controversy is viewed from an unusually narrow perspective, one where the issues are not well defined. I have tried to clarify these issues in my own mind at least by reviewing the development of certain central issues in the field over the past half century or so. I shall try to outline briefly two of these: the role of curricular objectives and the question of curriculum differentiation.

The Role of Curricular Objectives

The broad question of what education is for or what is a good education is one that pervades all of the field of education and is not particularly distinctive to the curriculum field. The narrower question, however, of the role of objectives in the planning and development of school programs is a central one in the field and has been since the field emerged as an identifiable entity. Our basic model of a curriculum specialist, Franklin Bobbitt, for example, was one of the principal early advocates of the notion that the first task of curriculum development is the stipulation in minute detail of numerous, specific, and "particularized" objectives. He argued that this task is central; what follows are the essentially pedestrian tasks of providing the learning "experiences" that will achieve the objectives and then undertaking some evaluation in terms of whether those objectives have been achieved or not. As a matter of fact, Bobbitt devoted a major portion of his most influential book, *How to Make a Curriculum*, to the listing of numerous objectives.[12] Included are such objectives as, "The ability to use general principles in analyzing and considering economic, political, and other social problems,"[13] "Ability to entertain one's friends, and to respond to entertainment by one's friends,"[14] and "Ability to sharpen, adjust, clean, lubricate, replace worn or broken parts, and otherwise keep household and garden tools and appliances in good order and good working condition."[15] These objectives are perhaps lacking in the pseudo precision of "Given a list of 35 chemical elements, the learner must be able to recall and write the valences of at least 30,"[16] but the principle is essentially the same. About all we have done on the question of the role of objectives in curriculum development since Bobbitt's day is, through some verbal flim-flam, convert Bobbitt's "ability to" into what are called behavioral or operational terms and to enshrine the whole process into what is known as the "Tyler rationale."

The essence of the "Tyler rationale" is not, it seems to me, the curriculum planning steps that are frequently associated with it, but the embodiment of a production model of how the process of teaching and learning proceeds. In applying the model, we are asked in effect to state certain design specifications for how we want the learner to behave, and then we attempt to arrive at the most efficient methods for producing that product quickly and, I suppose, cheaply. A curricular objective in this sense is only a way of stating what someone will do or behave like once we get through with him. We are even urged to state objectives in the most precise terms in order to make it easier to tell whether we have succeeded or not. Despite the significant efforts of a few curriculum theorists, such as Huebner and Macdonald, major alternatives to the "design specification" view of the role of curricular objectives have not emerged. As a matter of fact, the production model along with efficiency as the criterion of success has achieved new prominence and popularity under the influence of the burgeoning educational technology.

Of some importance, however, is the existence of a modern philosophical tradition in education running from Dewey to R. S. Peters which explicitly rejects such a view of objectives. "Ends, objectives of conduct," Dewey says,

are those foreseen consequences which influence present deliberation and which finally bring it to rest by furnishing an adequate stimulus to overt action. Consequently ends arise and function within action. They are not, as current theories too often imply, things lying beyond activity at which the latter is directed. They are not strictly speaking ends or termini of action at all. They are terminals of deliberation, and so turning points *in* activity.[17]

Putting the idea of an aim in its natural context of shooting or throwing, Dewey says, "Men do not shoot because targets exist, but they set up targets in order that throwing and shooting may be more effective and significant."[18] In other words, hitting a bull's-eye is not an objective for which the activity of shooting was designed; the idea of a target emerges out of the activity of shooting and adds a dimension to it. If one were to accept this view, it would be hard to imagine how one could set up objectives in advance of teaching. R. S. Peters puts the matter even more strongly:

Education . . . can have no ends beyond itself. Its value derives from principles and standards implicit in it. To be educated is not to have arrived at a destination; it is to travel with a different view. What is required is not feverish preparation for something that lies ahead, but to work with precision, passion and taste at worthwhile things that lie to hand.[19]

To my way of thinking, such a view places the emphasis where it belongs—on the quality and worthwhileness of the educational activity itself. In the curriculum field, however, we have not been able to rid ourselves of the persistent notion that teaching and learning are somehow unpleasant or at least neutral activities to be disposed of quickly and efficiently on the way to achieving an appropriate external objective. That notion is imbedded in the formulations of Bobbitt and other early curriculum leaders as well as the most sophisticated systems analysis approach today.

Curriculum Differentiation

Another persistent issue that had its origins more or less in the early beginnings of the curriculum field is the question of differentiated curricula for different identifiable groups in the school population. This is perhaps where the impact of the measurement movement following World War I was most strongly felt. The heart of the question lies not so much in the obvious fact of individual differences or in our ability to measure those differences but in the curricular implications we attach to those differences. Does, for example, a difference in I.Q. of ten or twenty or thirty points dictate a different set of school subjects or at least radically modified content in those subjects? Or, to use a different criterion, is the program of studies controlled by one's probable destination insofar as it can be determined? In other words, to what extent is the design of the curriculum in elementary and secondary schools determined by our guess as to whether someone is to become a lawyer, a salesman, or a taxidermist?

The long-standing emphasis on each differentiation in the field of curriculum seems to be at least in part a reflection of a utilitarian framework for legitimizing school subjects. Put in the context of the Cardinal Principles Report, for example, subjects find their justification in their contributions to the external aims of health, vocation, worthy use of leisure, and so on. Once we accept that framework, it becomes normal and natural to want to know what actual and practical activities men will perform, determine what knowledge and skills one will need to perform them, and then to label both our students and our subjects. It is presently quite possible, for example, to refer to both a student and a school subject such as physics as being "college-entrance." In the school setting, such a process becomes a vast bureaucratic machinery for labeling, stamping, and tracking students into different curriculum patterns. While some subjects find their obvious justification in terms of future or present utility, problems arise when the utilitarian criterion is applied to all school subjects and made the basis of curriculum differentiation.

The alternatives to the utilitarian justification of school subjects and their subsequent orientation toward different groups of students are even less clear-cut than in the case of curricular objectives. Part of the problem is that utility is probably the only really public criterion we have. As such, we are frequently reduced to explaining to parents or to students that we study French so that we can some day order from a French menu or that geometry is useful in determining square footage when fertilizing a suburban lawn. As a last resort, we can always say French and geometry are "college-entrance" subjects.

One alternative seems to lie in the tradition of a liberal education especially as it is creatively redefined by Paul Hirst. As Hirst describes it,

Knowledge . . . must never be thought of merely as vast bodies of tested symbolic expressions. These are only the public aspects of the ways in which human experience has come to have shape. They are significant because they are themselves the objective elements round which the development of mind has taken place. To acquire knowledge is to become aware of experience as structured, organized and made meaningful in some quite specific way, and the varieties of human knowledge constitute the highly developed forms in which man has found this possible.[20]

For such a conception to be implemented, at least some portion of the curriculum would have to be protected from the vicissitudes of the ulitarian justification. As Krug express this position in explicating his concept of intellectual play as a deliberate function of the schools, "To foster intellect as play will not require in the schools the neglect of intelligence for practical ends, but it will mean an end to the demand that subjects be evaluated *only* in those terms."[21] Perhaps some day the conventional labels we now apply to school subjects such as "college-entrance" and "non-college-entrance" will be replaced by the "playful" and the "useful" with students of widely different abilities, different destinations, and different social classes tasting freely of both. Strangely enough, this brings us back to Bobbitt. Of all the early curriculum leaders, he explicitly tried to make the case for "play-level" activities as opposed to the "work-level," "the serious duties of life."[22] Even those activities which bear no direct relationship to practical affairs, he argued, should be pursued as part of the curriculum. "Learning things because of curiosity without reference to the use of knowledge," he said, "is really one of the largest normal activities of man."[23] This aspect of his curriculum theory, however, has been largely forgotten.

Conclusion

Perhaps the most obvious conclusion that could be drawn from viewing curriculum issues in the perspective of the past fifty years or so is that our basic framework and our intellectual horizons have been severely limited. The production model and the utilitarian criterion applied to all school subjects as they have evolved over the past half century will constitute our fundamental frame of reference. The coming of modern technology, rather than freeing us from the earlier formulations, has served instead only to reinforce them or restrict them further. The task of the next fifty years in the curriculum field is essentially one of developing alternatives to the mode of thinking and the limited framework that have so clearly dominated our first fifty years.

Notes

1. John Herman Randall, Jr., *How Philosophy Uses Its Past* (New York: Columbia University Press, 1963).
2. Franklin Bobbitt, *The Curriculum* (Boston: Houghton Mifflin Co., 1918).
3. Commission on the Reorganization of Secondary Education, *Cardinal Principles of Secondary Education* (Washington, D.C.: Government Printing Office, 1918).
4. B. Othanel Smith, "On The Anatomy of Teaching," *Journal of Teacher Education* 7 (December 1956): 339.
5. Max Wingo, "Methods of Teaching," in *Encyclopedia of Educational Research*, ed. Chester W. Harris (New York: Macmillan, 1960), p. 852.
6. Bobbitt, *The Curriculum*, p. 42.
7. John K. Norton and Margaret Alltucker Norton, *Foundations of Curriculum Building* (Boston: Ginn, 1936), p. 548.
8. Vernon Anderson, *Principles and Procedures of Curriculum Improvement* (New York: Ronald Press, 1956), p. 9.
9. B. Othanel Smith, William O. Stanley, and J. Harlan Shores, *Fundamentals of Curriculum Development* (Yonkers-on-Hudson, N.Y.: World Book, 1957), p. 3.
10. Nolan C. Kearney and Walter W. Cook, "Curriculum," in *Encyclopedia of Educational Research*, ed. Harris, pp. 359-60.
11. The use of this terminology is developed in: Philip W. Jackson, "The Way Teaching Is," in *The Way Teaching Is* (Washington, D.C.: ASCD, 1966), pp. 7-27.
12. Franklin Bobbitt, *How to Make a Curriculum* (Boston: Houghton Mifflin, 1924), pp. 1-43.
13. Ibid., p. 17.
14. Ibid., p. 20.
15. Ibid., p. 28.
16. Robert F. Mager, *Preparing Instructional Objectives* (Palo Alto, Calif.: Fearon, 1962), p. 30.
17. John Dewey, *Human Nature and Conduct* (1922; reprint ed., New York: Modern Library, 1930), p. 223.
18. Ibid., p. 226.
19. R. S. Peters, *Education as Initiation* (London: George G. Harap, 1964), p. 47.
20. Paul H. Hirst, "Liberal Education and the Nature of Knowledge," in *Philosophical Analysis and Education*, ed. Reginald D. Archambault (New York: Humanities Press, 1965), p. 124.

21. Edward Krug, "Whose Anti-Intellectualism Should We Be Against?" *Teachers College Record* 67 (February 1966): 408.
22. Bobbitt, *The Curriculum*, p. 18.
23. Ibid., p. 10.

4

Bureaucracy and Curriculum Theory

Historians of education agree that American education went through a kind of metamorphosis after the turn of this century, but the nature and effect of the changes are in some dispute. In the popular mind, the reforms that were wrought during that period—indeed the whole first half of the twentieth century—have become associated with a broad and loosely defined "progressive education" movement. John Dewey is seen as the dominant force in American educational practice with an undisciplined child-centered pedagogy dubiously ascribed to him. Even a cursory examination of the work of educational reformers during this period, however, indicates that influential leaders differed widely in the doctrines they espoused and in the pedagogical reforms they advocated. Clearly, the educational ideas of a David Snedden or a Franklin Bobbitt differed enormously from those of a John Dewey or a Stanwood Cobb. There is no doubt that this was a period of ferment in education, with new ideas filling the void being created by the steadily declining theory of mental discipline.

The picture that emerges from the apparently frenetic educational activity during the first few decades of this century seems to be one of growing acceptance of a powerful and restrictive bureaucratic model for education which looked toward the management techniques of industry as its ideal of excellence and source of inspiration. The dominant metaphor for educational theory in the early twentieth century was drawn not from the educational philosophy of John Dewey or even from romantic notions of childhood, but from corporate management. As Ellwood Cubberley explicated that model in 1916,

Every manufacturing establishment that turns out a standard product or a series of products of any kind maintains a force of efficiency experts to study methods of procedure and to measure and test the output of its works. Such men ultimately bring the manufacturing establishment large returns, by introducing improvements in processes and procedure, and in training the workmen to produce larger and better output. Our schools are, in a sense, factories in which the raw products (children) are to be shaped and fashioned into products to meet the various demands of life. The specifications for manufacturing come from the demands of twentieth-century civilization, and it is the business of the school to build its pupils according to the specifications laid down. This demands good tools, specialized machinery, continuous measurement of production to see if it is according to specifications, the elimination of waste in manufacture, and a large variety in the output.[1]

Children, in other words, were to become the "standard products" which would be fashioned according to the design specifications set forth by the social world. The institution of schooling was simply that vast bureaucratic machinery which transforms the crude raw material of childhood into a socially useful product. A redesigned curriculum, stripped of the playful and wasteful, was to be the chief instrument in effecting the change.

Scientific Management

The context for the bureaucratization of the school curriculum that was to take place in the twentieth century was manifest in the general social and intellectual climate of American society at the turn of the century. The late nineteenth century saw the breakdown of a community-centered society and with it the ideal of the individual as the unit element in social life. The press of corporate expansion and urbanization made the individual merely a cog in a great machine. Whereas the individual retained a measure of recognition in a community-centered society, the vast new social and economic units robbed him of his identity. Responses to this fundamental change in American society ranged from the economic radicalism of Henry George to the utopian socialism of Edward Bellamy. But "the ideas that filtered through and eventually took the fort," according to Wiebe, "were the bureaucratic ones peculiarly suited to the fluidity and impersonality of an urban-industrial world."[2]

The particular response that captured the imagination of Americans at the turn of the century was a form of idealized bureaucracy known widely as scientific management. Its principal spokesman was Frederick W. Taylor, and its watchword was efficiency. Taylorism differs from classical conceptions of bureaucracy (for example, Weber) in its emphasis on sheer practical efficiency rather than analysis of complex lines of power and influence within organizations. Under Taylor's concept of scientific management, productivity is central, and the individual is simply an element in the production system. Basic to Taylor's conception of scientific management was the assumption that man is motivated by economic gain and would sacrifice much in the way of job satisfaction and physical ease in order to achieve such gain. Yet scientific principles had to be applied to the workman as well as to the work, and this involved careful study of the workman's "own special abilities and limitations" in an effort "to develop each individual man to his highest state of efficiency and prosperity"[3] (anticipating, in a way, the modern guidance movement in schools).

One of Taylor's proudest accomplishments was to inveigle a man he called Schmidt into increasing his handling of pig iron at a Bethlehem Steel plant from 12½ tons a day to 47 tons. Schmidt was selected after careful observation and study of seventy-five men, partly because he was observed to trot home in the evening about as fresh as when he trotted into work in the morning and partly because inquiries revealed that he was "close with a dollar." Taylor even gives an extended verbatim account of his discussion with Schmidt:

"Schmidt, are you a high-priced man?"

"Vell, I don't know vat you mean."

"Oh, yes you do. What I want to know is whether you are a high-priced man or not."

"Vell, I don't know vat you mean."

"Oh, come now, you answer my questions. What I want to find out is whether you are a high-priced man or one of these cheap fellows here. What I want to find out is whether you want to earn $1.85 a day or whether you are satisfied with $1.15, just the same as all those cheap fellows are getting."

"Did I vant $1.85 a day? Vas dot a high-priced man? Vell, yes, I vas a high-priced man."

"Oh, you're aggravating me. Of course you want $1.85 a day—everyone wants it! You know perfectly well that that has a very little to do with you being a high-priced man. For goodness' sake answer my questions, and don't waste any more of my time. Now come over here. You see that pile of pig iron?"[4]

Using this economic motivation, Taylor proceeded to instruct Schmidt in the efficient performance of every stage of the operation. Schmidt's step must have been a little heavier as he trotted home that night.

Thus, the individual under Taylorism was not ignored; on the contrary, he was made the subject of intense investigation, but only within the context of increasing product output. Through time and motion studies, the worker's movements were broken down into minute operations and then standards of efficiency were developed for each of the operations. The rules of scientific management and psychological principles were then applied to the worker to bring him up to the appropriate level of efficiency. As Mouzelis summarizes the individual's role under Taylorism, "The organisation member was conceived as an instrument of production which can be handled as easily as any other tool (provided that one knows the laws of scientific management)."[5] The essence of scientific management was the fragmentation and analysis of work and its reordering into the most efficient arrangement possible.

One of the attractions of Taylorism was that it carried with it an ethical dimension which bore a superficial resemblance to some of the tried and true virtues of the nineteenth century. Taylor's first professional paper, for example, delivered in 1895 at a meeting of the American Society of Mechanical Engineers, made the case for a "piece-rate system" partly on moral grounds. The minimum time for each operation would be computed and the worker would be paid for his performance relative to that fixed performance level. In this way, the workman's interest would coincide with that of his employer and "soldiering" (loafing on the job) would be eliminated. Once the work load was broken down into elementary operations, an "honest day's work" could be scientifically computed.[6] "If a man won't do what is right," Taylor argued, "*make* him."[7] Since scientific rate fixing could be used to outline the dimensions of virtuous activity, industry could be rewarded and sloth punished.

The appeal of Taylor's doctrine of scientific efficiency was not limited to an elite corps of business leaders. The rising cost of living in the early twentieth century was a matter of great concern to the broad American middle class, and scientific management promised lower prices through increased efficiency. The wide publicity given the Eastern Rate Case of 1910-11 also drew much popular attention to the cause of efficiency. Railroads were asking an increase in freight rates, and, arguing against their position, Louis Brandeis claimed that scientific management could save the railroads a million dollars a day. In support of this contention, he brought forward a series of witnesses in the form of efficiency experts. As Haber summarized the effect of their testimony, "The Eastern Rate Case was transformed into a morality play for up-to-date middle-class reformers,"[8] which eventually culminated in an orgy of efficiency affecting millions of Americans. The effect on the schools was not long in coming.

Bureaucratic Efficiency in School Management and Curriculum Theory

The bureaucratic model for curriculum design had a rather unremarkable birth. School administrators simply reacted to the influence of the scientific management movement in industry by extrapolating those methods to the management of schools. Managers of schools patterned themselves after their counterparts in industry and took pride in adapting the vocabulary and techniques of industry to school administration.[9] Cost accounting and maximum utilization of school plants were among their paramount concerns. The period, in fact, may be regarded as one in which the "transition of the superintendent of schools from an educator to a business manager" took place.[10]

The efficiency movement, however, was to affect more than just the administration of schools. Its most profound effect was on curriculum theory itself. Among the early prophets of the new efficiency in school administration was the man who later was to become the preeminent force in curriculum reform, and, indeed, the man who gave shape and direction to the curriculum field, John Franklin Bobbitt.

Bobbitt's early work essentially followed the main line of adapting business techniques for use in schools. In 1912, for example, Bobbitt took as his model of efficiency the operation of the Gary Indiana schools. "The first principle of scientific management," he announced, "is to use all the plant all the available time."[11] Although the typical school plant operates at 50 percent efficiency, the "educational engineer" in Gary set as his task the development of a plan to operate at 100 percent efficiency during school hours. Although a relatively high level of efficiency of school plant operation was achieved by creating regular and special periods of activity, perfect efficiency was thwarted by the fact that the school plant was used only five days a week. "That an expensive plant should lie idle during all of Saturday and Sunday while 'street and alley time' is undoing the good work of the schools," Bobbitt complained, "is a further thorn in the flesh of the clear-sighted educational engineer."[12] He also mourned the closing of the school plant during the summer, "a loss of some 16 percent, no small item in the calculations of the efficiency engineer."[13]

Bobbitt's second principle of scientific management, "to reduce the number of workers to a minimum by keeping each at the maximum of his working efficiency,"[14] reflected the need for division of labor and job specialization in the school. His third principle simply involved the elimination of waste. Here, Bobbitt commented on the wasteful concomitants of "ill-health and lowered vitality" and commended Superintendent Wirt's efforts to provide appropriate recreational facilities for the students in the Gary schools.

Bobbitt's fourth principle of general scientific management made the leap from the areas of simple plant and worker efficiency into the realm of educational theory itself:

> Work up the raw material into that finished product for which it is best adopted. Applied to education this means: Educate the individual according to his capabilities. This requires that the materials of the curriculum be sufficiently various to meet the needs of every class of individuals in the community; and the course of training and study be sufficiently flexible that the individual can be given just the things he needs.[15]

This extrapolation of the principles of scientific management to the area of curriculum made the child the object on which the bureaucratic machinery of the school operates. He became the raw material from which the school-factory must fashion a product drawn to the specifications of social convention. What was at first simply a direct application of general management principles to the management of schools became the central metaphor on which modern curriculum theory rests.

"Educate the individual according to his capabilities" has an innocent and plausible ring; but what this meant in practice was that dubious judgments about the innate capacities of children became the basis for differentiating the curriculum along the lines of probable destination for the child. Dominated by the criterion of social utility, these judgments became self-fulfilling prophecies in the sense that they predetermined which slots in the social order would be filled by which "class of individuals." Just as Taylor decided that "one of the first requirements for a man who is fit to handle pig iron as a regular occupation is that he shall be so stupid and phlegmatic that he more nearly resembles in his mental makeup the ox than any other type,"[16] so it was the schools that now were to determine (scientifically, of course) what biographical, psychological, or social factors in human beings fit them to be the hewers of wood and the drawers of water in our society. Although still in undeveloped form, this conception of the work of the school in relation to the child and his studies became a central element in Bobbitt's influential curriculum research and theory a decade or so later. The ramifications of this central production metaphor in educational theory are now widely felt.

Through the first quarter of the twentieth century, Bobbitt continued to take the lead in reforming the administration of public schools along the lines of scientific management advocated by Taylor. One such recommendation, for example, took the Harriman railroad system as the model of efficiency. Bobbitt pointed out how that massive enterprise had been divided into thirty autonomous divisions, each with its own specialized staff, resulting in a high rate of efficiency. Extrapolating from this and other examples, Bobbitt went on to comment on the functions of specialized supervisors in schools in determining "the proper methods" and "the determination of more or less definite qualifications for the various aspects of the teaching personality."[17] The supervisor of instruction occupied that middle-management function roughly comparable to the foreman in industry.

Increasingly, however, Bobbitt was moving from the mere translation of general principles of scientific management to the management of schools into the domain of curriculum theory. As a kind of quality control, Bobbitt advocated that "definite qualitative and quantitative standards be determined for the product."[18] In the railroad industry, he pointed out, each rail "must be thirty feet in length, and weigh eighty pounds to the yard. It must be seven and three-eighths inch in height, with a head two and one-sixty-fourth of an inch in thickness and five inches deep, and a base five inches wide."[19]

Based on studies by Courtis and others and using standard scores, Bobbitt concluded that:

> The third-grade teacher should bring her pupils up to an average of 26 correct [arithmetic] combinations per minute. The fourth-grade teacher has the task, during the year that the same pupils are under her care, of increasing their addition speed from an average of 26 combinations per minute to an average of 34 combinations per minute. If she does not bring them up to the standard 34, she has failed to perform her duty in proportion to the deficit; and there is no responsibility upon her for carrying them beyond the standard 34.[20]

Two years later, Bobbitt was to apply principles of cost accounting in business organizations to school subjects. This brought the heart of the school curriculum, the subjects, into the orbit of bureaucratic efficiency. Bobbitt continued to be impressed by standardization in relation to efficiency in railroad administration.

He pointed out, for example, that railroad companies know that "locomotive repair-cost should average about six cents per mile-run" and that "lubricating oils should cost about eighteen cents per hundred miles for passenger locomotives, and about twenty-five cents for freight locomotives."[21] Using cost per 1,000 student-hours as his basic unit, Bobbitt was able to report, in terms comparable to those of industry, that the cost of instruction in mathematics in his sample of twenty-five high schools ranged from $30 to $169 and that Latin instruction was, on the average, 20 percent more expensive than mathematics instruction. The implications of such an accounting procedure were developed later by Bobbitt, his colleagues, and his present-day intellectual heirs.

Standardization and the Worker

The great bane of bureaucracy is uncertainty. The inevitable course of the bureaucratization of the curriculum, therefore, was in the direction of predictability. As in industry, this was accomplished mainly through the standardization of activity or work units and of the products themselves. In the curriculum field, vague conceptions of the purposes of schooling became intolerable, and "particularization" of educational objectives became a byword. "An age of science is demanding exactness and particularity," announced Bobbitt in the first modern book on curriculum.[22] The curriculum became something progressively to be discovered through the scientific analysis of the activities of mankind. Just as scientific management became associated with virtue, so the incipient field of curriculum looked to scientific curriculum making as the source of answers to the great value questions that govern the purposes of education.

The process had a commonsensical appeal. "The curriculum-discoverer will first be an analyst of human nature and human affairs."[23] He would go out into the world of affairs and discover the particular "abilities, attitudes, habits, appreciations, and forms of knowledge" that human beings need. These would become the objectives of the curriculum. When these multitudinous needs are not filled by "undirected experiences," then "directed experiences" would be provided through the curriculum. Bobbitt set forth the basic principle: "The curriculum of the directed training is to be discovered in the shortcomings of individuals after they have had all that can be given by undirected training."[24] The curriculum was the mechanism for remedying the haphazard effects of ordinary living, for achieving the standard product which undirected socialization achieved so imperfectly.

One major concomitant of such a conception of the curriculum was the broadening of its scope into the boundless domain of human activity. Instead of being merely the repository of man's intellectual inheritance, the curriculum now embraced the gamut of human experience, "the total range of habits, skills, abilities, forms of thought, valuations, ambitions, etc., that its members need for the effective performance of their vocational labors, likewise, the total range needed for their civic activities; their health activities; their recreational activities; their language; their parental, religious, and general social activities."[25] The standard product would be designed and particularized in every detail.

A lonely voice of opposition to the "blight of standardization" was that of the president emeritus of Harvard University and the chief architect of the Committee of Ten report, Charles W. Eliot. Eliot, then eighty-nine years old, pointed out that while standardization of the worker's movements in industry may have resulted in increased productivity, "the inevitable result was the destruction of the interest of the workman in his work." Standardization, he argued, was also having the same effect in education. What is more, it was antithetical to the true process of education as he saw it. "The true educational goal," he said, "is the utmost development of the individual's capacity or power, not in childhood and adolescence alone, but all through life. Fixed standards in labor, in study, in modes of family life, are downright enemies of progress for the body, mind, and soul of man."[26] Clearly, the temper of the time would not support such an anachronistic conception of education.

Standardization of Product Diversification

Apart from its implications for the individual as producer, the production metaphor in curriculum theory carries with it important implications for the individual as product. By the 1920s, a massive effort was under way to reform the curriculum through product standardization and predetermination. As usual, Bobbitt set the tone:

In the world of economic production, a major secret of success is predetermination. The management predetermines with great exactness the nature of the products to be turned out, and in relation to the other factors, the quality of the output. They standardize and thus predetermine the processes to be employed, the quantity and quality of raw material to be used for each type and unit of product, the character and amount of labor to be employed, and the character of the conditions under which the work should be done. . . . The business world is institutionalizing foresight and developing an appropriate and effective technique.

There is a growing realization within the educational profession that we must particularize the objectives of education. We, too, must institutionalize foresight, and, so far as conditions of our work will permit, develop a technique of predetermination of the particularized results to be obtained.[27]

The technique that Bobbitt referred to, the analysis of man's activities into particular and specialized units of behavior, came to be known as activity analysis.

By the 1920s, Bobbitt had been joined in his campaign to reform the curriculum by such extraordinarily influential education leaders as W. W. Charters and David Snedden. In the main, the reform in the 1920s took the form of using activity analysis to strip away the nonfunctional, the "dead wood" in the curriculum. Increasingly, this was being done with reference to particular groups in the school. "The curriculum situation has become acute," Charters declared in 1921. "The masses who send their children to school are growing restive under what they consider to be the useless material taught in the grades."[28]

Besides his concern for the masses, Charters went on to show how a curriculum could be developed for another identifiable group, women. He developed a curriculum particularly for women as part of the famous study he conducted for Stephens College of Columbia Missouri. Charters' task was to develop a program which would provide "specific training for the specific job of being a woman."[29] What constitutes being a woman, of course, was determined through activity analysis. Women all over the country were asked to write a complete statement of what they did for a week, and 95,000 replies were received. The replies were then analyzed into about 7,300 categories such as food, clothing, and health. Using these activities as his base, Charters developed the curriculum for Stephens College.

Just as Taylor found it necessary to identify discrete units of work, so were the educational leaders of the period embarking on the task of identifying the units of all human activity as the first step in curriculum planning. As Charters expressed it, the job is one of "finding out what people have to do and showing them how to do it."[30] The possibilities were limitless. Once women were identified and trained to be women, so could almost any other identifiable group in our society be trained for its role. To be sure, all persons would be trained to perform some activities in common, such as some of those involved in maintaining physical efficiency, but their differentiated roles in society could be programmed as well. As in current proposals, such programs could be advertised under the slogans of curriculum flexibility and individualized instruction.

Paradoxically, the effort to diversify the product along the lines of probable destination called for an even greater effort to standardize the units of work than before. Product diversification was not to be accomplished by diversifying work and creating variety in school activity, but by arranging the standard units of work into the most efficient arrangement for manufacturing the particular products. The man who took the lead in this aspect of the social efficiency movement was David Snedden. In 1921, Snedden had written that, "By 1925, it can confidently be hoped, the minds which direct education will have detached from the entanglements of our contemporary situation a thousand definite educational objectives, the realization of which will have demonstrable worth to our society."[31] Snedden devoted the next few years to the realization of that prediction, and also differentiating the curriculum so that the right objectives were applied to the right "case groups."

Case groups were defined as "any considerable group of persons who in large degree resemble each other in the common possession of qualities significant to their school education."[32] Objectives, therefore, would not be applied indiscriminately, but only with reference to the raw material. This was a particular problem, according to Snedden, in the junior high school where "differences of abilities, of extra-school conditions, and of prospects will acutely manifest themselves, forcing us to differentiate curricula in more ways, probably, than as yet suspected."[33] Such a division of the school population into appropriate case groups, in Snedden's mind at least, required sustained attention to the standardization and atomizing of the curriculum. His smallest curriculum unit, the "peth," is probably best illustrated by a single spelling word.[34]

Peths, however, had to be assembled in relation to "strands," classifications of "adult life performance practices" such as "health conservation through habitual safeguarding practices" for which Snedden estimated 50 to 100 peths, and "moral (including fellowship) behaviors" for which the same number was estimated. The vocational participations strand, however, necessitated differentiated numbers of peths, a streetcar motorman requiring only 10 to 20 while a farmer or a homemaker would call for 200 to 500 peths, a "lotment," in turn, was "the amount of work that can be accomplished, or ground covered, by learners of modal characteristics (as related to the activity considered) in 60 clock hours."[35] Thus, as in Taylorism, standards of efficiency were set for individual units of work in line with idealized performance levels. Actually, much of Snedden's work parallels the work of one of Taylor's major disciples, Frank Gilbreth, who identified eighteen units of motion which he called "therbligs," thereby immortalizing his name in reverse.[36]

Yet the quaint obscurity of the educational terminology of the period tends to mask the underlying serious implications of the bureaucratic model applied to curriculum theory. The schoolchild became something to be molded and manipulated on his way to filling his predetermined social role. Guidance departments probed his inner resources in order to determine which of his potentialities were worth mining. Usually, these policies were followed in the name of bringing the outmoded academic curriculum into line with the new high school population, now dominated by the great unwashed. The curriculum was simply being made more democratic; but as Ellul has pointed out, the individual potentialities that were identified tended to coincide, as if by magic, with the needs of modern industrial society.[37] As the raw material was processed through the curriculum on its way to its ultimate state, simple efficiency dictated a differentiated curriculum in order to achieve the diversification of human labor that a modern industrial society demanded.

Snedden's ideal curriculum of minute standardized work units organized into the most efficient combinations for distinctive case groups was, of course, never achieved. The influence of such a conception of the curriculum was, nevertheless, widely felt. As early as 1923-24, when George S. Counts was conducting his classic study of the high school curriculum, the multiplication of different types of curricula designed for different population groups within the schools was evident. Of the fifteen city school systems studied, only two, Detroit and Kansas City, used a system of constants and electives in their high school programs rather than a series of labeled curricula. Los Angeles, where Bobbitt's influence was undoubtedly strong in this period, maintained eighteen different curricula in its high schools. Newton, Massachusetts, for example, listed the following fifteen differentiated curricula:[38] Classical, Scientific, General, Business, Stenographic, Clerical, Household Arts, Agriculture, Printing, Electricity, Machine Work, Cabinet and Pattern Making, Drafting, Automobile, and Carpentry. The principle of predetermination was in this way applied to differentiated vocational roles in addition to one's role as a citizen, parent, church member, and so on.

In the 1923-24 school year, also, the Lynds found in Middletown a "manifest concern . . . to dictate the social attitudes of its young citizens."[39] This was in part reflected in a host of required courses in civic training designed to support "community solidarity against sundry divisive tendencies."[40] The inculcation of appropriate civic attitudes was second only in emphasis to vocational preparation. Upon entering high school, the Middletown student chose among twelve courses of study, eight of which were distinctly vocational. Education in Middletown was clearly becoming specific preparation for certain community-sanctioned adult roles.

By the mid to late 1920s signs began to appear of a decline in efficiency as the predominant educational ideal and social control as a major function of the schools. Bobbitt's contribution to the influential Twenty-Sixth Yearbook of the National Society for the Study of Education represents a curious denial of some of the basic curriculum tenents he had proposed in his most popular book, published only two years before. In *How To Make a Curriculum*, Bobbitt set forth, as one of his major premises that, "Education is primarily for adult life, not for child life. Its fundamental responsibility is to prepare for the fifty years of adulthood, not for the twenty years of childhood and youth."[41] It was on this fundamental assumption that Bobbitt based his case for the analysis of adult activities as the source of curriculum objectives. The efficient performance of adult activities of all kinds was the ideal toward which the whole curriculum was directed. In 1926, however, Bobbitt was to declare: "Education is not primarily to prepare for life at some future time. Quite the reverse; it proposes to hold high the current living, making it intense, abundant, fruitful, and fitting it firmly in the grooves of habit. . . . In a very true sense, life cannot be 'prepared for.' It can only be lived."[42]

Such a declaration can only mean a rejection of the production model of curriculum theory, since it denies such central concepts as predetermination and predictability. When, in 1934, Bobbitt was asked to prepare a statement summarizing his curriculum theory, his rejection of his former work was clearly evident and nearly complete.[43] In the 1930s, the ideal of social efficiency in education and the production metaphor as the basis for curriculum theory were obviously in a period of decline, a decline which, however, proved to be only temporary.

The Contemporary Revival

Just as the first great drive toward standardization, predetermination, and fragmentation in the school curriculum came about in the aftermath of the first industrial revolution, so the renewal of those curriculum tendencies has come about in the aftermath of the second one—what is sometimes called the electronic or technological revolution. To be sure, some differences are evident. In the first place, the theory of behaviorism has been raised to the status of canon law in the social sciences, and so we are admonished to state the design specifications which set forth how a student will turn out in terms of observable behaviors. Second, the 1920s doctrine of social efficiency has been overlaid with a thin veneer of academic respectability, and so the modern design specifications tend to call for a student to identify certain points on a map or to reel off the valences of a set of chemical elements instead of emphasizing practical, nonacademic activities.

Given these qualifications, Snedden's bureaucratic ideal of a thousand educational objectives to be used as a blueprint for shaping the educational product is now closer to realization than ever before. Teachers may now order from a catalog 96 objectives in language arts 7-9 for $3.00, or 158 objectives in social science (geography) K-9 for $4.00, or 25 objectives in English literature 10-12 for $3.00[44] Snedden would have considered these a bargain at twice the price. These new objectives, furthermore, are evidently being formulated with such precision and wisdom that one major proponent of the new bureaucracy was led to observe of the period preceding the present millennium: "American educators have generally engaged in the same level of discourse regarding the specification of educational goals that one might derive from the grunts of a Neanderthal."[45] "One can only sympathize," he reflected, "with the thousands of learners who had to obtain an education from an instructional system built on a muddle-minded conception of educational goals."[46]

One can avoid muddle-mindedness, apparently, by overcoming a preoccupation with means or process in favor of a focus on outcomes.[47] Current curriculum practice seems to take the form of drawing up endless lists of minute design specifications in behavioral terms and then finding the right "media mix" by which the product can be most efficiently manufactured. "Judgments about the success of an instructional procedure," we are told, "are made exclusively on the basis of results, that is, the changes in learner behavior which emerge as a consequence of instruction. Only if the hoped-for changes in learner behavior have been attained is the instructional process considered successful."[48] The efficient achievement of the end product becomes the criterion by which the means are selected.

Such a sharp dichotomy between ends and means is precisely what resulted from the introduction of the assembly line in the first industrial revolution. Work became important only insofar as it was instrumental in achieving the desired product. The success of the assembly line depends on the fact that it reduces the process of production to units so simple that the predicted outcome is assured. The worker's movements are made so elementary and routine that the product inevitably emerges independent of the will or conscious desire of the worker. John McDermott has observed about the assembly line effect: ".... since each operation uses only a small fraction of a worker's skill, there is a very great likelihood that the operation will be performed in a minimally acceptable way. Alternately, if each operation taxed the worker's skill there would be frequent errors in the operation, frequent disturbance in work flow, and a thoroughly unpredictable quality to the end product."[49] To ensure predictability and efficiency in education, the techniques of industry are introduced with the same effect. Work loses any organic relationship with the end product.

Take, for example, the much publicized program, Individually Prescribed Instruction. Teachers prepare prescriptions—directions for what the child must accomplish. The child, after receiving his prescription, places a recorded disk on some playback equipment, and a disembodied voice asks, "Hello, how are you today?" (Pause for response.) "Today we are going to learn the sounds of the letters. Do you have a pencil?" The child responds and then is directed in the performance of certain tasks. If the child is able to perform these tasks with 85 percent accuracy, he is rewarded with a new prescription. If he fails, he is given remedial training until he meets the performance standard.[50] His progress is carefully plotted by a computer as he passes through the standard work units. Individuality, here, refers to the speed by which one makes his way through the standard work units. Of course, just as corporate management can make the tedium of the assembly line tolerable by scheduling a scientifically determined number of coffee breaks, so can the modern technologist make school work bearable by building into his system an appropriate schedule of other activities. But this would go about as far to create delight in intellectual activity as coffee breaks have in restoring the dignity of work.

In education, as in industry, the standardization of the product also means the standardization of work. Educational activity which may have an organic wholeness and vital meaning takes on a significance only in terms of its contribution to the efficient production of the finished product. As in industry, the price of worship at the altar of efficiency is the alienation of the worker from his work—where the continuity and wholeness of the enterprise are destroyed for those who engage in it. Here, then, is one great threat that the production metaphor governing modern curriculum theory poses for American education.

The bureaucratic model, along with its behavioristic and technological refinements, threatens to destroy, in the name of efficiency, the satisfaction that one may find in intellectual activity. The sense of delight in intellectual activity is replaced by a sense of urgency. The thrill of the hunt is converted into an efficient kill. The wonder of the journey is superseded by the relentless pursuit of the destination. And to condition the victim to enjoy being conditioned is certainly less humane than open coercion or bribery.

The tragic paradox of the production metaphor applied to curriculum is that the dehumanization of education, the alienation of means from ends, the stifling of intellectual curiosity carry with them very few compensations. In the corporate structure, the worker who has become a cog in a vast bureaucracy is at least rewarded with an improved financial status and opportunity for leisure. The megamachine in ancient Egypt, where the autonomy of human beings was sacrificed in the great cause of the building of the pyramids, at least produced some measure of increased agricultural production and flood control.[51] What comparable benefits accrue from a corresponding regimentation in education? The particularization of the *educational* product, it turns out, is tantamount to its trivialization. A case in point is what happens to history as it is particularized in the highly regarded and liberally financed ES '70s project. One of the more than fifty pilot schools lists among its educational products the following typical examples in the form of items on a computer-printed individual student progress report (formerly known as a report card):

> Given a list which includes Sibley, Colonel Snelling, Father Galtier, J. J. Hill, Ramsey, Fur Traders, Missionaries, soldiers, and settlers of Minnesota and several true statements about their contributions, the student is able to match the listed people with the proper true statements.
>
> Given several statements describing early and present day lumbering in Minnesota, the student is able to identify lumbering in Minnesota by writing E -early lumbering-, P -present day lumbering-, or B -both- in front of the applicable statements.

Educational products manufactured at such a level of particularity, even if multiplied a millionfold, could only be trivial.

History (assuming that history is the discipline represented by these performance outcomes) simply is not the accurate recitation of bits and pieces of information. Nor is any discipline a specific finite assemblage of facts and skills. So to define it *is* to trivialize it.

This is not to say that instructional objectives, in and of themselves, are useless. They can add a dimension to educational activity; but they have no meaning outside the context of the means toward their achievement. There are, certainly, a variety of ways to consider the complex interrelationships between means and ends.[52] But the creation of a sharp dichotomy between means and ends or the consideration of means only in the context of efficiency is, pedagogically speaking, a travesty. From an educational point of view, behavior, in and of itself, is of little significance. It is, on the other hand, critically important to know how one comes to behave as he does; whether, for example, a given act derives from mere conditioning or from rational decision-making processes.

Modern curriculum theory, currently being influenced by systems analysis, tends to regard the child simply as input inserted into one end of a great machine from which he eventually emerges at the other end as output replete with all the behaviors, the "competencies," and the skills for which he has been programmed. Even when the output is differentiated, such a mechanistic conception of education contributes only to man's regimentation and dehumanization, rather than to his autonomy.

The mechanistic conception of man, the technology-systems analysis approach to human affairs, the production metaphor for curriculum design all share a common perspective. They represent a deterministic outlook on human behavior. The behavior of human beings is controlled in an effort to make people do the particular things that someone wants them to do. This may take the form of getting people to vote every election day, to buy the latest miracle detergent, or to recite on cue the valences of thirty out of thirty-five chemical elements. As Von Bertalanffy put it, "stimulus-response, input-output, producer-consumer are all the same concepts, only expressed in different terms. . . . people are manipulated as they deserve, that is, as overgrown Skinner rats."[53]

Notes

1. Ellwood P. Cubberley, *Public Administration* (Boston: Houghton Mifflin, 1916), p. 338.
2. Robert H. Wiebe, *The Search for Order 1877-1920* (New York: Hill and Wang, 1967), p. 145.

3. Frederick Winslow Taylor, *The Principles of Scientific Management* (New York: Harper, 1911), p. 43.
4. Ibid., pp. 44-45.
5. Nicos P. Mouzelis, *Organisation and Bureaucracy: An Analysis of Modern Theories* (Chicago: Aldine, 1967), p. 85.
6. Cited in Samuel Haber, *Efficiency and Uplift: Scientific Management in the Progressive Era 1890-1920* (Chicago: University of Chicago Press, 1964), pp. 1-3.
7. Frank Barkeley Copley, *Frederick Winslow Taylor: Father of Scientific Management* (New York: Harper, 1923). Quoted in Haber, ibid., pp. 2-3.
8. Haber, *Efficiency and Uplift*, p. 54.
9. The administration aspect of the bureaucratization of the schools has been ably interpreted by Raymond E. Callahan, *Education and the Cult of Efficiency: A Study of the Social Forces That Have Shaped the Administration of the Public Schools* (Chicago: University of Chicago Press, 1962).
10. Ibid., p. 148.
11. John Franklin Bobbitt, "The Elimination of Waste in Education," *The Elementary School Teacher* 12, no. 6 (February 1912): 260.
12. Ibid., p. 263.
13. Ibid., p. 264.
14. Ibid.
15. Ibid., p. 269.
16. Taylor, *Principles of Scientific Management*, p. 59.
17. Franklin Bobbitt, "Some General Principles of Management Applied to the Problems of City-School Systems," *Twelfth Yearbook of the National Society for the Study of Education, Part I* (Chicago: University of Chicago Press, 1913), p. 62.
18. Ibid., p. 11.
19. Ibid.
20. Ibid., pp. 21-22.
21. J. F. Bobbitt, "High School Costs," *The School Review* 23, no. 8 (October 1915): 505.
22. Franklin Bobbitt, *The Curriculum* (Boston: Houghton Mifflin, 1918), p. 41.
23. Ibid., p. 43.
24. Ibid., p. 45.
25. Ibid., p. 43.
26. Letter to *The New York Times* 72, no. 23,946 (August 17, 1923). Copyright 1923 by The New York Times Company. Reprinted by permission.
27. Franklin Bobbitt, "The Objectives of Secondary Education," *The School Review* 28, no. 10 (December 1920): 738.
28. W. W. Charters, "The Reorganization of Women's Education," *Educational Review* 62, no. 3 (October 1921): 224.
29. W. W. Charters, "Curriculum for Women," *University of Illinois Bulletin* 23, no. 27 (March 8, 1926): 327.
30. Ibid., p. 328.
31. David Snedden, *Sociological Determination of Objectives in Education* (Philadelphia: J. B. Lippincott, 1921), p. 79.

32. David Snedden, " 'Case Group' Methods of Determining Flexibility of General Curricula in High Schools," *School & Society* 17, no. 429 (March 17, 1923): 290.
33. David Snedden, "Junior High School Offerings," *School & Society* 20, no. 520 (December 13, 1924): 740.
34. David Snedden, "Planning Curriculum Research, I," *School & Society* 22, no. 557 (August 29, 1925): 259-65.
35. Snedden, "Junior High School Offerings," p. 741.
36. Gilbreth's other brush with immortality was Clifton Webb's portrayal of him as the superefficient father in the film, *Cheaper by the Dozen*.
37. Jacques Ellul, *The Technological Society* (New York: Vintage Books, 1964), pp. 358-63.
38. George S. Counts, *The Senior High School Curriculum* (Chicago: University of Chicago Press, 1926), pp. 12-14.
39. Robert S. Lynd and Helen Merrell Lynd, *Middletown* (New York: Harcourt Brace, 1929), p. 197.
40. Ibid., p. 196.
41. Franklin Bobbitt, *How To Make A Curriculum* (Boston: Houghton Mifflin, 1924), p. 8.
42. Franklin Bobbitt, "The Orientation of the Curriculum-Maker," in *The Foundations of Curriculum-Making*. Twenty-Sixth Yearbook of the National Society for the Study of Education, Part II (Bloomington, Illinois: Public School Publishing, 1926), p. 43.
43. Franklin Bobbitt, "A Summary Theory of the Curriculum," *Society for Curriculum Study News Bulletin* 5, no. 1 (January 12, 1934): 2-4.
44. Instructional Objectives Exchange, W. James Popham, Director, Center for the Study of Evaluation, University of California, Los Angeles.
45. W. James Popham, "Objectives and Instruction," American Educational Research Association Monograph on Curriculum Evaluation (Chicago: Rand McNally, 1969), pp. 32-33.
46. Ibid.
47. W. James Popham, "Focus on Outcomes: A Guiding Theme for ES '70 Schools," *Phi Delta Kappan* 51, no. 4 (December 1969): 208-10.
48. Ibid., p. 208.
49. John McDermott, "Technology: The Opiate of the Intellectuals," *New York Review of Books* 13, no. 2 (July 31, 1969): 34.
50. "Individually Prescribed Instruction," in *Education USA* (Washington, D.C.: National School Public Relations Association, 1968), p. 4.
51. Lewis Mumford, *The Myth of the Machine* (London: Secker & Warburg, 1967), p. 12.
52. See, for example, D. S. Shwayder, *The Stratification of Behavior* (New York: Humanities Press, 1965), pp. 144-64.
53. Ludwig Von Bertalanffy, *Robots, Men, and Minds: Psychology in the Modern World* (New York: George Braziller, 1967), p. 12. Reprinted with the permission of the publisher. Copyright 1967 by Ludwig Von Bertalanffy.

5

Reappraisal: The Tyler Rationale

One of the disturbing characteristics of the curriculum field is its lack of historical perspective. New breakthroughs are solemnly proclaimed when in fact they represent minor modifications of early proposals, and, conversely, anachronistic dogmas and doctrines maintain a currency and uncritical acceptance far beyond their present merit. The most persistent theoretical formulation in the field of curriculum has been Ralph Tyler's syllabus for Education 360 at the University of Chicago, *Basic Principles of Curriculum and Instruction*, or, as it is widely known, the Tyler rationale.[1] Tyler's claims for his rationale are modest, but, over time, his proposal for rationally developing a curriculum has been raised almost to the status of revealed doctrine. In the recent issue of the *Review of Educational Research* devoted to curriculum, Goodlad, commenting on the state of the field, reports that "as far as the major questions to be answered in developing a curriculum are concerned, most of the authors in [the] 1960 and 1969 [curriculum issues of the *Review*] assume those set forth in 1950 by Ralph Tyler." Later, he concludes with obvious disappointment, "General theory and conceptualization in curriculum appear to have advanced very little during the last decade."[2] Perhaps the twentieth anniversary of the publication of the Tyler rationale is an appropriate time to reexamine and reevaluate some of its central features.

Tyler's rationale revolves around four central questions which Tyler feels need answers if the process of curriculum development is to proceed:

1. What educational purposes should the school seek to attain?
2. What educational experiences can be provided that are likely to attain these purposes?
3. How can these educational experiences be effectively organized?
4. How can we determine whether these purposes are being attained?[3]

These questions may be reformulated into the familiar four-step process by which a curriculum is developed: stating objectives, selecting "experiences," organizing "experiences," and evaluating.[4] The Tyler rationale is essentially an elaboration and explication of these steps. The most crucial step in this doctrine is obviously the first since all the others proceed from and wait upon the statement of objectives. As Tyler puts it, "If we are to study an educational program systematically and intelligently we must first be sure as to the educational objectives aimed at."[5]

The Selection of Educational Objectives

Tyler's section on educational objectives is a description of the three sources of objectives: studies of learners, studies of contemporary life, and suggestions from subject matter specialists, as well as an account of how data derived from these "sources" are to be "filtered" through philosophical and psychological "screens." The three sources of educational objectives encapsulate several traditional doctrines in the curriculum field over which much ideological blood had been spilled in the previous several decades. The doctrines proceeded from different theoretical assumptions, and each of them had its own spokesmen, its own adherents, and its own rhetoric. Tyler's proposal accepts them all, which probably accounts in part for its wide popularity.

While we are aware that compromise is the recourse frequently taken in the fields of diplomatic or labor negotiation, simple eclecticism may not be the most efficacious way to proceed in theorizing. When Dewey, for example, identified the fundamental factors in the educative process as the child and the "values incarnate in the matured experience of the adult," the psychological and the logical, his solution was not to accept them both but "to discover a reality to which each belongs."[6] In other words, when faced with essentially the same problem of warring educational doctrines, Dewey's approach is creatively to reformulate the problem; Tyler's is to lay them all out side by side.

Subject Matter as a Source of Objectives

Of the three "sources"—studies of the learners themselves, studies of contemporary life, and suggestions about objectives from subject matter specialists—the last one seems curiously distorted and out of place. Perhaps this is because Tyler begins the section by profoundly misconceiving the role and function of the Committee of Ten. He attributes to the Committee of Ten a set of objectives which, he claims, has subsequently been followed by thousands of secondary schools. In point of fact, the notion of objectives in the sense that Tyler defines the term was not used and probably had not even occurred to the members of the Committee of Ten. What they proposed were not objectives, but "four programmes": Classical, Latin-Scientific, Modern Languages, and English. Under each of these rubrics is a listing of the subjects that constitute each of the four courses of study. This recommendation is followed by the reports of the various individual committees on what content should be included and what methods should be used in the various subject fields. Unless Tyler is using the term ''objectives'' as being synonymous with "content" (in which case it would lose all its importance as a concept), then the use of the term "objectives" in the context of the report of the Committee of Ten is erroneous. Probably the only sense in which the term "objective" is applicable to the Committee of Ten report is in connection with the broad objective of mental training to which it subscribes.

An even more serious error follows:

"It seems clear that the Committee of Ten thought it was answering the question: What should be the elementary instruction for students who are later to carry on much more advanced work in the field. Hence, the report in history, for example, seems to present objectives [*sic*] for the beginning courses for persons who are training to be historians. Similarly the report in mathematics outlines objectives [*sic*] for the beginning courses in the training of a mathematician."[7]

As a matter of fact, one of the central questions that the Committee of Ten considered was, "Should the subject be treated differently for pupils who are going to college, for those who are going to a scientific school, and for those, who, presumably, are going to neither?"[8] The committee decided unanimously in the negative. The subcommittee on history, civil government, and political economy, for example, reported that it was "unanimously against making such a distinction"[9] and passed a resolution that "instruction in history and related subjects ought to be precisely the same for pupils on their way to college or the scientific school, as for those who expect to stop at the end of grammar school, or at the end of the high school."[10] Evidently, the Committee of Ten was acutely aware of the question of a differentiated curriculum based on probable destination. It simply rejected the doctrine that makes a prediction about one's future status or occupation a valid basis for the curriculum in general education. The objective of mental training, apparently, was conceived to be of such importance as to apply to all, regardless of destination.

Tyler's interpretation of the Committee of Ten report is more than a trivial historical misconception. It illustrates one of his fundamental presuppositions about the subjects in the curriculum. Tyler conceives of subjects as performing certain "functions." These functions may take the form of a kind of definition of the field of study itself such as when he sees a function of science to be enabling the student to obtain a "clearer understanding of the world as it is viewed by the scientist and man's relation to it, and the place of the world in the larger universe"; or the subject may perform external functions such as the contribution of science to the improvement of individual or public health or to the conservation of natural resources. The first sense of function is essentially a way of characterizing a field of study; in the second sense of function, the subject field serves as an instrument for achieving objectives drawn from Tyler's other two sources. Tyler's apparent predisposition to the latter sense of function seems to be at the heart of his misreading of the Committee of Ten report. To Tyler, studying history or algebra (as was universally recommended by the Committee of Ten), if they are not meeting an obvious individual or social need, is a way of fulfilling the vocational needs of a budding historian or mathematician. Otherwise, how can one justify the existence of mathematics qua mathematics in the curriculum? As such, "suggestions from subject matter specialists" is really not a source in the sense that the other two are. Subject matter is mainly one of several means by which one fulfills individual needs such as vocational aspirations or meets social expectations.

Needs of the Learner as a Source of Objectives

The section on the "learners themselves as a source of educational objectives," although it is less strained and more analytical than the one on subject matter, is nevertheless elliptical. Tyler proceeds from the assumption that "education is a process of changing behavior patterns of people."[11] This notion, of course, is now widely popular in this country, but, even if one were to accept such a view, it would be important to know the ways in which education would be different from other means of changing behavior, such as hypnosis, shock treatment, brainwashing, sensitivity training, indoctrination, drug therapy, and torture. Given such a definition, the differences between education and these other ways of changing behavior are not obvious or simple.

Tyler proceeds from his basic definition of education to a consideration of the reason for wanting to study the learner: "A study of the learners themselves would seek to identify needed changes in behavior patterns of the students which the educational institution should seek to produce."[12] There follows an extended discussion of "needs," how they are determined, and how they contribute to the determination of educational objectives. The notion of needs as a basis for curriculum development was not a new one when Tyler used it in 1950. It had been a stable element in the curriculum literature for about three decades.[13] When tied to the biological concept of homeostasis, the term "needs" seems to have a clear-cut meaning. Hunger, for example, may be conveniently translated into a need for food when one has in mind a physiological state of equilibrium. Need becomes a much trickier concept when one speaks of the "need of a haircut" or the "need for a good spanking." These needs involve rather complex social norms on which good men and true may differ sharply. Tyler astutely recognized that the concept of need has no meaning without a set of norms, and he described the kind of study he envisioned essentially as a two-step process: "first, finding the present status of the students, and second, comparing this status to acceptable norms in order to identify the gaps or needs."[14] This formulation is virtually identical to what Bobbitt referred to as "shortcomings" in the first book written exclusively on the curriculum, published in 1918.[15] The key term, in Tyler's version, of course, is "acceptable norms." They are neither self-evident nor easy to formulate.

One of Tyler's illustrations of the process he advocates is a case in point: A "discovery" is made that 60 percent of ninth-grade boys read only comic strips. The "unimaginative" teacher, Tyler says, might interpret this as suggesting the need for more attention to comic strips in the classroom; the imaginative teacher uses the data as a justification "for setting up objectives gradually to broaden and deepen these reading interests."[16] What is the acceptable norm implicit in Tyler's illustration? Apparently, it is not a statistical norm since this could imply that the 40 percent minority of boys should be encouraged to emulate the 60 percent majority. The norm seems to be the simple conviction that having broader and deeper reading interests is better than limiting oneself to the reading of comic strips. The question is what does the 60 percent figure contribute to the process of stating educational objectives. What difference would it have made if the figure were 80 percent or 40 percent? The key factor seems to be the nature and strength of the teacher's conviction as the acceptable norm, toward which the status study contributes very little.

The whole notion of need has no meaning without an established norm, and, therefore, it is impossible even to identify "needs" without it. As Archambault put it, "An objective need can be discovered, but only within a completely defined context in which the normal level of attainment can be clarified."[17] Furthermore, even when a genuine need is identified, the role of the school as an institution for the remediation of that or other needs would have to be considered. Even the course that remediation should take once the need and the responsibility have been established is an open question. These serious value questions associated with the identification and remediation of needs make the concept a deceptively complex one whose advantages are more apparent than real. Komisar, for example, had described this double use of need, "one to report deficiencies and another to prescribe for their alleviation," as so vague and elusive as to constitute a "linguistic luxury."[18]

As already mentioned, Tyler is acutely aware of the difficulties of "deriving" educational objectives from studies of the child. His last word on the subject in this section is to suggest to his students that they compile some data and then try using those data as the basis for formulating objectives. He suggests this exercise in part to illustrate the difficulty of the process. Given the almost impossible complexity of the procedure and the crucial but perhaps arbitrary role of the interpreter's value structure or "philosophy of life and of education," one wonders whether the concept of need deserves any place in the process of formulating objectives. Certainly, the concept of need turns out to be of no help in relation to avoiding central value decisions as the basis for the selection of educational objectives, and without that feature much of its appeal seems to disappear. As Dearden concluded in his analysis of the term:

The concept of 'need' is an attractive one in education because it seems to offer an escape from arguments about value by means of a straightforward appeal to the facts empirically determined by the expert. But . . . it is false to suppose that judgments of value can thus be escaped. Such judgments may be assumed without any awareness that assumptions are being made, but they are not escaped.[19]

Studies of Contemporary Life as a Source of Objectives

Tyler's section on studies of contemporary life as a source of curricular objectives follows the pattern set by the section on the learner. His conception of the role that such studies play in determining objectives is also similar in many respects to that of his spiritual ancestor, Franklin Bobbitt, who stimulated the practice of activity analysis in the curriculum field. Like Bobbitt, Tyler urges that one "divide life" into a set of manageable categories and then proceed to collect data of various kinds which may be fitted into these categories. One of Tyler's illustrations is especially reminiscent of Bobbitt:

Students in the school obtain [ed] from their parents for several days the problems they were having to solve that involved arithmetic. The collection and analysis of this set of problems suggested the arithmetic operations and the kinds of mathematical problems which are commonly encountered by adults, and became the basis of arithmetic curriculum.[20]

Tyler tends to be more explicitly aware than Bobbitt of the traditional criticisms that have been directed against this approach. Bode, for example, once pointed out that "no scientific analysis known to man can determine the desirability or the need of anything." The question of whether a community with a given burglary rate needs a larger police force or more burglars is entirely a question of what the community wants.[21] Tyler's implicit response to this and other traditional criticism of this approach is to argue that in his rationale studies of contemporary life do not constitute the sole basis for deriving objectives, and, of course, that such studies have to be checked against "an acceptable educational philosophy."[22] In this sense, the contemporary life source is just as dependent on the philosophical screen as is the learner source.

The Philosophical Screen

Tyler's treatment of the section on the learner and on contemporary life as sources of educational objectives are roughly parallel. In each case, Tyler is aware of the serious shortcomings of the source but assumes that they can be overcome, first, by not relying exclusively on any one of them—in a sense counting on his eclecticism to blunt the criticism. And second (and probably more important), he appeals to philosophy as the means for covering any deficiencies. This suggests that it is philosophy after all that is the source of Tyler's objectives and that the stipulated three sources are mere window dressing. It is Tyler's use of the concept of a philosophical screen, then, that is most crucial in understanding his rationale, at least insofar as stating the objectives is concerned.

Even if we were to grant that people go through life with some kind of primitive value structure spinning around in their heads, to say that educational objectives somehow flow out of such a value structure is to say practically nothing at all. Tyler's proposal that educational objectives be filtered through a philosophical screen is not so much demonstrably false as it is trivial, almost vacuous. It simply does not address itself in any significant sense to the question of which objectives we leave in and which we throw out once we have committed ourselves to the task of stating them. Filtering educational objectives through a philosophical screen is simply another way of saying that one is forced to make choices from among the thousands or perhaps millions of objectives that one can draw from the sources that Tyler cites. (The number of objectives is a function of the level of specificity.) Bobbitt was faced with the same predicament when he was engaged in his massive curriculum project in Los Angeles in 1921-23. Bobbitt's solution was to seek "the common judgment of thoughtful men and women,"[23] an appeal to consensus. Tyler's appeal is to divine philosophy, but the effect is equally arbitrary as long as we are still in the dark as to how one arrives at a philosophy and how one engages in the screening process.

Take, for example, one of Tyler's own illustrations of how a philosophy operates:

> If the school believes that its primary function is to teach people to adjust to society it will strongly emphasize obedience to present authorities, loyalty to the present forms and traditions, skills in carrying on the present techniques of life; whereas if it emphasizes the revolutionary function of the school it will be more concerned with critical analysis, ability to meet new problems, independence and self-direction, freedom, and self-discipline. Again, it is clear that the nature of the philosophy of the school can affect the selection of educational objectives.[24]

Although Tyler appears elsewhere to have a personal predilection for the latter philosophy, we really have no criterion to appeal to in making a choice. We are urged only to make our educational objectives consistent with our educational philosophy, and this makes the choice of objectives precisely as arbitrary as the choice of philosophy. One may, therefore, express a philosophy that conceives of human beings as instruments of the state and the function of the schools as programming the youth of the nation to react in a fixed manner when appropriate stimuli are presented. As long as we derive a set of objectives consistent with this philosophy (and perhaps make a brief pass at the three sources), we have developed our objectives in line with the Tyler rationale. The point is that, given the notion of educational objectives and the necessity of stating them explicitly and consistently with a philosophy, it makes all the difference in the world *what* one's guiding philosophy is since that consistency can be as much a sin as a virtue. The rationale offers little by way of a guide for curriculum making because it excludes so little. Popper's dictum holds not only for science, but all intellectual endeavor:

Science does not aim, primarily, at high probabilities. It aims at high informative content, well backed by experience. But a hypothesis may be very probable simply because it tells us nothing or very little. A high degree of probability is therefore not an indication of "goodness"—it may be merely a symptom of low informative content.[25]

Tyler's central hypothesis that a statement of objectives derives in some manner from a philosophy, while highly probable, tells us very little indeed.

Selection and Organization of Learning Experiences

Once the crucial first step of stating objectives is accomplished, the rationale proceeds relentlessly through the steps of the selection and organization of learning experiences as the means for achieving the ends and, finally, evaluating in terms of those ends. Typically, Tyler recognizes a crucial problem in connection with the concept of a learning experience but passes quickly over it: The problem is how can learning experiences be *selected* by a teacher or a curriculum maker when they are defined as the *interaction* between a student and his environment. By definition, then, the learning experience is in some part a function of the perceptions, interests, and previous experience of the student. At least this part of the learning experience is not within the power of the teacher to select. While Tyler is explicitly aware of this, he nevertheless maintains that the teacher can control the learning experience through the "manipulation of the environment in such a way as to set up stimulating situations—situations that will evoke the kind of behavior desired."[26] The Pavlovian overtones of such a solution are not discussed.

Evaluation

"The process of evaluation," according to Tyler, "is essentially the process of determining to what extent the educational objectives are actually being realized by the program of curriculum and instruction."[27] In other words, the statement of objectives not only serves as the basis for the selection and organization of learning experiences, but the standard against which the program is assessed. To Tyler, then, evaluation is a process by which one matches initial expectations in the form of behavioral objectives with outcomes. Such a conception has a certain commonsensical appeal, and, especially when fortified with models from industry and systems analysis, it seems like a supremely wise and practical way to appraise the success of a venture. Actually, curriculum evaluation as a kind of product control was set forth by Bobbitt as early as 1922,[28] but product control when applied to curriculum presents certain difficulties.

One of the difficulties lies in the nature of an aim or objective and whether it serves as the terminus for activity in the sense that the Tyler rationale implies. In other words, is an objective an end point or a turning point? Dewey argued for the latter: "Ends arise and function within action. They are not, as current theories too often imply, things lying outside activity at which the latter is directed. They are not ends or termini of action at all. They are terminals of deliberation, and so turning points *in* activity."[29] If ends arise only *within* activity it is not clear how one can state objectives before the activity (learning experience) begins. Dewey's position, then, has important consequences not just for Tyler's process of evaluation but for the rationale as a whole. It would mean, for example, that the starting point for a model of curriculum and instruction is not the statement of objectives but the activity (learning experience), and whatever objectives do appear will arise within that activity as a way of adding a new dimension to it. Under these circumstances, the process of evaluation would not be seen as one of matching anticipated consequences with actual outcomes, but as one of describing and of applying criteria of excellence to the activity itself. This view would recognize Dewey's claim that "even the most important among all the consequences of an act is not necessarily its aim,"[30] and it would be consistent with Merton's important distinction between manifest and latent functions.[31]

The importance of description as a key element in the process of evaluation has also been emphasized by Cronbach:

> When evaluation is carried out in the service of course improvement, the chief aim is to ascertain what effects the course has. . . . This is not to inquire merely whether the course is effective or ineffective. Outcomes of instruction are multidimensional, and a satisfactory investigation will map out the effects of the course along these dimensions separately.[32]

The most significant dimensions of an educational activity or any activity may be those that are completely unplanned and wholly unanticipated. An evaluation procedure that ignores this fact is plainly unsatisfactory.

Summary and Conclusion

The crucial first step in the Tyler rationale on which all else hinges is the statement of objectives. The objectives are to be drawn from three sources: studies of the learner, studies of society, and suggestions from subject matter specialists. Data drawn from these sources are to be filtered through philosophical and psychological screens. Upon examination, the last of the three sources turns out to be no source at all but a means of achieving objectives drawn from the other two. Studies of the learner and of society depend so heavily for their standing as sources on the philosophical screen that it is actually the philosophical screen that determines the nature and scope of the objectives. To say that educational objectives are drawn from one's philosophy, in turn, is only to say that one must make choices about educational objectives in some way related to one's value structure. This is to say so little about the process of selecting objectives as to be virtually meaningless. One wonders whether the long-standing insistence by curriculum theorists that the first step in making a curriculum be the specification of objectives has any merit whatsoever. It is even questionable whether stating objectives at all, when they represent external goals allegedly reached through the manipulation of learning experiences, is a fruitful way to conceive of the process of curriculum planning. Certainly, the whole concept of a learning experience requires much more analysis than it has been given. Finally, the simplistic notion that evaluation is a process of matching objectives with outcomes leaves much to be desired. It ignores what may be the more significant latent outcomes in favor of the manifest and anticipated ones, and it minimizes the vital relationship between ends and means.

One reason for the success of the Tyler rationale is its very rationality. It is an eminently reasonable framework for developing a curriculum; it duly compromises between warring extremes and skirts the pitfalls to which the doctrinaire are subject. In one sense, the Tyler rationale is imperishable. In some form, it will always stand as the model of curriculum development for those who conceive of the curriculum as a complex machinery for transforming the crude raw material that children bring with them to school into a finished and useful product. By definition, the production model of curriculum and instruction begins with a blueprint for how the student will turn out once we get through with him. Tyler's version of the model avoids the patent absurdity of, let us say, Mager's by drawing that blueprint in broad outline rather than in minute detail.[33]

For his moderation and his wisdom as well as his impact, Ralph Tyler deserves to be enshrined in whatever hall of fame the field of curriculum may wish to establish. But the field of curriculum, in its turn, must recognize the Tyler rationale for what it is: Ralph Tyler's version of how a curriculum should be developed—not *the* universal model of curriculum development. Goodlad once claimed that "Tyler put the capstone on one epoch of curriculum inquiry."[34] The new epoch is long overdue.

Notes

1. Ralph W. Tyler, *Basic Principles of Curriculum and Instruction* (Chicago: University of Chicago Press, 1950). Note differences in pagination in 1969 printing.
2. John I. Goodlad, "Curriculum: State of the Field," *Review of Educational Research* 39 (1969): 374.
3. Tyler, *Basic Principles*, pp. 1-2.
4. I have argued elsewhere that the characteristic mode of thought associated with the field of curriculum frequently manifests itself in enumeration and particularization as a response to highly complex questions. Herbert M. Kliebard, "The Curriculum Field in Retrospect," in *Technology and the Curriculum*, ed. Paul W. F. Witt (New York: Teachers College Press, 1968), pp. 69-84.
5. Tyler, *Basic Principles*, p. 3.
6. John Dewey, "The Child and the Curriculum," in *John Dewey on Education*, ed. Reginald D. Archambault (1902; reprint ed., New York: Random House, 1964), pp. 339-40.
7. Tyler, *Basic Principles*, p. 17.
8. National Education Association, *Report of the Committee on Secondary School Studies* (Washington, D.C.: Government Printing Office, 1893), p. 6.
9. Ibid., p. 203.
10. Ibid., p. 165.
11. Tyler, *Basic Principles*, p. 4.

12. Ibid., pp. 4-5.
13. See, e.g., H. H. Giles, S. P. McCutchen, and A. N. Zechiel, *Exploring the Curriculum* (New York: Harper & Bros., 1912); V. T. Thayer, Caroline B. Zachry, and Ruth Kotinsky, *Reorganizing Secondary Education* (New York: Appleton Century, 1939). The former work was one of the volumes to come out of the Progressive Education Association's Eight-Year Study. Tyler was closely associated with that research. The latter volume was published under the auspices of the Progressive Education Association's Commission on Secondary School Curriculum. Tyler was also a member of the committee that prepared the NSSE yearbook on needs. Nelson B. Henry, ed., *Adapting the Secondary School Program to the Needs of Youth*, Fifty-second Yearbook of the National Society for the Study of Education, Part 1 (Chicago: University of Chicago Press, 1953). An early statement of needs in relation to curriculum organization appeared in *The Development of the High-School Curriculum*, Sixth Yearbook of the Department of Superintendence (Washington, D.C.: Department of Superintendence, 1928). Needs as the basis for the curriculum in English was mentioned by E. L. Miller as early as 1922. North Central Association of Colleges and Secondary Schools, *Proceedings of the Twenty-seventh Annual Meeting of the North Central Association of Colleges and Secondary Schools* (Cedar Rapids, Iowa: Torch Press, 1922), p. 103.
14. Tyler, *Basic Principles*, p. 6.
15. Franklin Bobbitt, *The Curriculum* (Boston: Houghton Mifflin, 1918), p. 45 ff.
16. Tyler, *Basic Principles*, p. 10.
17. Reginald D. Archambault, "The Concept of Need and Its Relation to Certain Aspects of Educational Theory," *Harvard Educational Review* 27 (1957): 51.
18. B. Paul Komisar, " 'Need' and the Needs Curriculum," in *Language and Concepts in Education*, eds. B. O. Smith and Robert H. Ennis (Chicago: Rand McNally, 1961), p. 37.
19. R. F. Dearden, " 'Needs' in Education," *British Journal of Educational Studies* 14 (1966): 17.
20. Tyler, *Basic Principles*, pp. 16-17.
21. Boyd H. Bode, *Modern Educational Theories* (New York: Macmillan, 1927), pp. 80-81.
22. Tyler, *Basic Principles*, p. 13.
23. Franklin Bobbitt, *Curriculum-making in Los Angeles*, Supplementary Educational Monographs no. 20 (Chicago: University of Chicago, 1922), p. 7.
24. Tyler, *Basic Principles*, p. 23.
25. Karl Popper, "Degree of Confirmation," *British Journal for the Philosophy of Science* 6 (1955): 146.
26. Tyler, *Basic Principles*, p. 42.
27. Ibid., p. 69.
28. Franklin Bobbitt, "The Objectives of Secondary Education," *School Review* 28 (1920): 738-49.
29. John Dewey, *Human Nature and Conduct* (New York: Random House, 1922), p. 223.
30. Ibid., p. 227.

31. Robert K. Merton, "Manifest and Latent Functions," in *Social Theory and Social Structure* (Glencoe, Ill.: Free Press, 1957), pp. 19-84.
32. Lee J. Cronbach, "Evaluation for Course Improvement," *New Curricula*, ed. Robert W. Heath (New York: Harper & Row, 1964), p. 235.
33. Robert F. Mager, *Preparing Instructional Objectives* (Palo Alto, Calif.: Fearon, 1962).
34. John I. Goodlad, "The Development of a Conceptual System for Dealing with Problems of Curriculum and Instruction," U.S. Department of Health, Education, and Welfare, Office of Education Cooperative Research Project no. 454 (Los Angeles: Institute for the Development of Educational Activities, UCLA, 1966), p. 5.

6

Metaphorical Roots of Curriculum Design

In simplicity or in sophistication man tends to think in metaphors, intuitively drawn from his social and personal experience—J. H. Plumb.

The Metaphor of Production

The curriculum is the means of production, and the student is the raw material which will be transformed into a finished and useful product under the control of a highly skilled technician. The outcome of the production process is carefully plotted in advance according to rigorous design specifications, and when certain means of production prove to be wasteful, they are discarded in favor of more efficient ones. Great care is taken so that raw materials of a particular quality or composition are channeled into the proper production systems and that no potentially useful characteristic of the raw material is wasted.

The Metaphor of Growth

The curriculum is the greenhouse where students will grow and develop to their fullest potential under the care of a wise and patient gardener. The plants that grow in the greenhouse are of every variety, but the gardener treats each according to its needs, so that each plant comes to flower. This universal blooming cannot be accomplished by leaving some plants unattended. All plants are nurtured with great solicitude, but no attempt is made to divert the inherent potential of

84

the individual plant from its own metamorphosis or development to the whims and desires of the gardener.

The Metaphor of Travel

The curriculum is a route over which students will travel under the leadership of an experienced guide and companion. Each traveller will be affected differently by the journey since its effect is at least as much a function of the predilections, intelligence, interests, and intent of the traveller as it is of the contours of the route. This variability is not only inevitable, but wondrous and desirable. Therefore, no effort is made to anticipate the exact nature of the effect on the traveller; but a great effort is made to plot the route so that the journey will be as rich, as fascinating, and as memorable as possible.

part three

Political and Methodological Criticism

In this section we further explore the heart of the attack on tradition. In the last section we saw Professor Kliebard's "Reappraisal: The Tyler Rationale," which stands as one of the most damaging volleys fired. The essays of Professor Apple are commensurately powerful. In fact, if I were asked to name one of the two or three most important critics at work in the curriculum field today, I would answer, Michael Apple. While it is true his work has been influenced by Professor Kliebard, currently his colleague, and by Professor Huebner, with whom he studied, he has taken this influence and is making of it an original contribution.

Professor John Steven Mann is the other name that comes to mind when I reflect on important critics in the field. Recently Professor Mann's work has been primarily political, and while his views are not my own, I respect and appreciate them. His earlier work focuses on the methodological, and it is impressive; in fact, I think it is fair to recognize his "Curriculum Criticism" as the source of later interest in literary criticism as a model for curriculum criticism.

Professor Mooney's article is an important one; perhaps extraordinarily so, although the language is dated. "The Researcher Himself" was printed in the 1957 ASCD yearbook, which helps explain the language and makes his insight all the more astonishing. For Professor Mooney has identified some profound errors in the accepted view of educational research, errors still very much with us.

But Professor Mooney has also pointed the way toward inquiry that is postcritical in nature. He distinguishes the basic modes of attitude toward educational research; one must look for their origins in North American capitalism and perhaps in the structure of the Western personality. Because these modes are so fundamental, there is danger of viewing them as commonplace. If, however, one dwells on the distinction between the consumptive and the productive, one will see it reflected not only in educational research, but also in the dominant theoretical models of American psychology, business, and education generally: in nothing less than the North American's way of being-in-the-world. It is a paper to be taken very seriously.

Michael W. Apple

*Statements of personal stances are difficult, both to write and no
doubt to read. They are hard to write because most of us never
attempt to set down on paper a position that is usually held only
semiconsciously. They are probably just as hard to read because each
paragraph, often single sentences, and even individual words have to
stand for twenty paragraphs, sentences, and words. Each written
point is a tortuous summary of yet another summary, condensed
into language that leaves both the writer and reader discontented. I
am dissatisfied with those points penned here, but not as dissatisfied
as I am about the state of things that continually go on in our institutions, among them schools. The latter agony seems more important
than the former.*

*I would like to begin by affirming the fact of being an educator
but by rejecting the comforting illusion that the types of questions
that are commonly being asked by curriculum workers and other
educators are fruitful. In fact, it seems to me that many of the
modes of activity, the forms of language, the basic ideologies, even
the things we do that supposedly "help" kids are in need of radical
(in the sense of going to the very root of an issue) rethinking. For
one thing, there is no educational poetry, no disciplined esthetic
sense; yet we misconstrue education if we think of it as engineering
(though part of it is, to be sure). Furthermore, the influencing by
one group of another group of individuals—here, younger ones—is
ultimately a moral activity. As such it cannot be understood without
recourse to, and thus must be held accountable to, ethical principles
and obligations of justice and responsibility to other persons.*

*The usual questions that school people are so fond of asking—
better management systems, behavioral objectives pro and con,
"affective" education, and so forth—are ultimately false issues. Their
roots lie in ideological rules that are dialectically related to social and*

economic forms. That is, the absence of, say, "affect" in schools and the attempts to add it on through the addition of exercises in value clarification, sensitivity training, etc., simply ignore the absence of any significant community within schools (something Dewey recognized as being fundamental to any serious educational endeavor) and the relationship between what goes on in schools and what goes on outside of them in a basically manipulative society. In this way, schools are not mirrors of society, they are society.

For example, the dominant consciousness in advanced industrial societies is centered on a vulgar instrumentality—a logical structure that places at its foundation the search for certainty, order, the cooptation of significant social dissent, process/product reasoning, therapy to treat surface symptoms rather than basic structural change, and the search for even more efficient instrumentality. It, thereby, vitiates or redefines into less potent issues the political, ethical, and even esthetic questions of any moment. Hence, politics and manipulation become coequal; education and the guaranteeing of certainty in human interaction become synonymous.

Thus, it should be clear that educators are not simply members of a community of other school people. More important is the fact that they are members of a larger collectivity whose values provide the fundamental framework for their thought and action. This fact cuts two ways. First, it means that any critical act in an educational sense is by necessity an act that is critical of the dominant normative structure of the larger society. Educational criticism, hence, becomes cultural, political, and economic criticism as well. Without the latter, the former is impotent. Second, the setting of educators within a more basic social group means that extensive investigations are required to demonstrate to other educators and a concerned citizenry the concrete linkages between personal, social, and economic injustice and education's models of inquiry, of talking about schooling, of "helping" children, and so forth. That is, the sense that education is always moral and political activity in some degree must be the constitutive framework from which any committed educator can act.

Here, I am not speaking of new ways of talking, but, if I may borrow from Wittgenstein, of new forms of life, new ways of being with students, with each other. New ways of talk can only emerge from the dialectic of language and the generation of altered community. And this can only be generated if the negativity of the existing community is shown. We cannot limit ourselves to more sloganizing of the type that dominated the sixties both in educational institutions and elsewhere. That kind of language has little potency *any longer. This requires at least two things—alternative visions that will emerge from ones* bearing witness *to the negativity of existing patterns of interaction and knowledge to give this critique more power. But the knowledgeable critique, the standing in witness, is the prior act.*

Thus any cogent critique of the "quality of life" within schools must also be a critique of the quality of life outside of schools. By this, I do not wish to focus only on the educational structure of society, but on a critique of the ways in which meanings are created and how they are distributed in society—a society's unequal economic structure, its dominant fantasies, esthetics, imagination (or abasement of it), its reductive language, the forms of knowledge (impersonal) which are dominant, its authoritarian personality structures, its limited forms of personal interaction, and the growing sense of powerlessness, to name just a few of them. The role of the school in reinforcing and distributing these forms of meaning must be illuminated.

Yet, having said this, I realize that there is a certain caughtness involved in calling oneself an educator. Not only does one "care" for individuals and groups whose pasts, presents, and futures have been and will continue to be unduly dominated, but one also "cares" for traditions, for forms of meaning that enable personal and political power to make sense. It is this caring for meaning in all its forms that enables poetry to emerge, that shows the openness to experience that characterizes education rather than indoctrination or training. Present modes of institutional domination that create misshapen images of the uses of tradition and the difficult search for personal and interpersonal meaning are attempts to reduce both of these concerns to mere instrumentality.

All of this is indicative of a lack of poetry in our encounters with others, our inability to do more than flatten the complexity of the human condition, our failure to create institutions that "cause" what Camus calls "style" and even dignity to be lived rather than played at much like the masques of an old French passion play.

But there are ways of transcending these collective failures, art and esthetic consciousness being a primary mode of recapturing the sensitivity that modern consciousness has conspired to stain. This is one reason that my making of films and experimenting with filmic art with kids is so important to me, not only for the pure exhilaration of the means, of the here and now, but also as a way of increasing the ways in which kids can build and transform their meanings and hence their world.

I do not wish, however, to make a strong distinction between esthetic and political meanings and actions, for poetics and politics are actually nearly one and the same. Both seek to create forms of communication that explore the potential of inherited institutions or, finding them wanting, seek to illuminate the problematics of accepted forms and thus to break out of the unwarranted domination of common sense. Ultimately, each finds its meaning in the creation of new linguistic and political institutions which themselves will and must be made responsive to human sentiment. In fact, there is little difference between linguistic institutions and social ones, for both of them are essentially historically evolving ways of organizing the symbolic interaction among people. Some types of organizing lead to non-repressive interaction and communication, while others contribute to the increasing rationalization of men's and women's relationships to others and their environment and thus must be recreated.

The possibility of such a recreation, though, remains just that—a possibility, something that cannot be guaranteed. Yet we can point to one thing; it will not be brought significantly closer by a community of educators that repeatedly denies the complex issues— political, economic, and cultural—that need to be confronted honestly if educators are to do more than serve existing institutional regularities and the flattening of reality that results.

Because of this complexity, I must reject any false posturing of certainty. "Do these things and it will lead invariably to 'freedom' " is to me a dishonest statement. None of us knows the specific steps to "freedom," "meaningfulness," and so on, educational or otherwise. What we can do is be guided by an insight of Marx in arguing that specific steps will become clearer only when the ways are illuminated that institutions now function to deny "freedom," to destroy or degrade meaning, to unduly dominate the intersubjective and intrasubjective relations of a society. From this negation can emerge a positive vision.

Finally, I must admit not to a cynicism but to a pessimism (defined as optimism without illusion, holding out the hope for substantive change, knowing it may not occur or, if it does, it may be repressive as well). It seems to me that no matter how noncommitted one is on the topic of schools and their relationship to other institutions which may deny people the values they most prize, one is taking a tacit stance. I would prefer that my position be a conscious choice, one based on the realization of the close connection between the subtle repression in schools and the subtle and not so subtle repression found in the larger society, on the sentiment that poetics and politics must be joined in educational activity if it is to have real substance, and on the affirmation that one, thus, has no choice but to be committed.

Michael W. Apple
Associate Professor
Department of Curriculum and Instruction
University of Wisconsin at Madison

7

The Hidden Curriculum and the Nature of Conflict

There has been, so far, little examination of how the treatment of conflict in the school curriculum can lead to political quiescence and the acceptance by students of a perspective on social and intellectual conflict that acts to maintain the existing distribution of power and rationality in a society. This paper examines two areas—social studies and science—to indicate how an unrealistic and basically consensus-oriented perspective is taught through a "hidden curriculum" in schools. The argument centers around the fundamental place that forms of conflict have had in science and the social world and on the necessity of such conflict. The paper suggests that a greater emphasis in the school curriculum upon the ideal norms of science, e.g., organized skepticism, and on the uses of conflict could counterbalance the tacit assumptions being taught.

Conflict and the Hidden Curriculum

The fact that schools are usually *overtly* insulated from political processes and ideological argumentation has both positive and negative qualities. The insulation has served to defend the school against whims and fads that can often have a destructive effect upon educational practice. It also, however, can make the school rather unresponsive to the needs of local communities and a changing social order. The pros and cons of the school as a "conservative" institution have been argued fervently for the last ten years or so, at least. Among the most articulate of the spokesmen have been Edgar Z. Friedenberg and the late Jules Henry. The covert teaching of an achievement and marketplace ethic and the probable substitution of a "middle-class" and often "schizophrenic" value system for a student's own biographical meanings are the topics most usually subject to analysis. A good deal of the focus has been on what Jackson (1968) has so felicitously labeled the "hidden curriculum"—that is, on the norms and values that are implicitly, but effectively, taught in schools and that are not usually talked about in teachers' statements of ends or goals. Jackson (pp. 3-37), for instance, deals extensively with the way students learn to cope with the systems of crowds, praise, and power in classrooms: with the large amount of waiting children are called upon to experience, with the teacher as a child's first "boss," and how children learn to falsify certain aspects of their behavior to conform to the reward system extant in most classrooms.

These critiques of the world view being legitimated in the schools have been incisive, yet they have failed to focus on a prevailing characteristic of current schooling that significantly contributes to the maintenance of the same dominant world view. There has been, so far, little examination of how the treatment of *conflict* in the school curriculum can lead to political quiescence and the acceptance by students of a perspective on social and intellectual conflict that acts to maintain the existing distribution of power and rationality in a society. The topic of conflict is crucial for two reasons. How it is dealt with helps to posit a student's sense of the legitimate means of gaining recourse within industrial societies. This is particularly important, and will become more so, in urban areas. It may be rather imperative that urban students develop positive perspectives toward conflict and change, ones that will enable them to deal with the complex and often repressive political realities and dynamics of power of their society in a manner less apt to preserve current institutional modes of interaction (cf. Eisinger 1970). Also, there may well be specific programmatic suggestions that can be made and instituted fairly readily in ongoing school programs that may alleviate some of the problems.

We can learn a bit about the importance of tacit or hidden teaching from the literature on political socialization. It is beginning to be clear that "incidental learning" contributes more to the political socialization of a student than do, say, civics classes or other forms of deliberate teaching of specific value orientations (Sigel 1970, p. xiii). Children are taught how to deal with and relate to the structures of authority of the collectivity to which they belong by the patterns of interaction they are exposed to to a certain extent in schools.

Obviously, it is not only the school that contributes to a student's "adjustment to authority." For instance, peer groups and especially the family, through its child-rearing practices and its style of interpersonal interaction, can profoundly affect a child's general orientation to authority (Sigel, p. 105). However, there is a strong suggestion in recent research that schools are rather close rivals to the family as significant agents of political socialization. As Sigel (p. 316) puts it:

> [There] is probably little doubt that the public schools are a choice transmission belt for the traditional rather than the innovative, much less the radical. As a result, they facilitate the political socialization of the mainstream young and tend to equip them with the tools necessary for the particular roles they are expected to play in a given society. One may wish to quarrel with the differential roles the government and the schools assign to students, but it would probably be considerably more difficult to deny the school's effectiveness.[1]

It should be stated that the negative treatment given to the uses of conflict goes far beyond the way with which it is overtly dealt in any one subject, say, social studies, the area in which one usually finds material on and teaching about conflict situations. Rather, the negative and quite unrealistic approach seems endemic to many areas, and especially to science, the area usually associated with objectivity and noninterpersonal conflict.

It has become increasingly evident that history books and social studies texts and materials have, over the years, presented a somewhat biased view of the true nature of the amount and possible use of internecine strife in which groups in this country and others have engaged. Our side is good; their side is bad. "We" are peace loving and want an end to strife; "they" are warlike and aim to dominate. The list could be extended considerably, especially in racial matters (Gibson 1969; Willhelm 1970). Yet, we must go beyond this type of analysis, often even beyond the work of the revisionist historians, political scientists, students of political socialization, and educators to get at many of the roots of the teaching of this dominant orientation. We examine here two specific areas—social studies and science. In so doing, we point out that the presentation of these two areas (among others) in schools both mirrors and fosters an ideology that is oriented to a static perspective: in the social studies, on the positive and even essential functions of social conflict; and in science, on the nature of scientific work and argumentation and on what has been called "revolutionary" science. The view presented of science, especially, in the schools is particularly interesting since it is essentially an archetype of the ideological position on conflict we wish to illuminate.

The tacit assumptions seem to be prominent in teaching and in curricular materials. The first centers around a negative position on the nature and uses of conflict. The second focuses on man as a recipient of values and institutions, not on man as a creator and recreator of values and institutions. These assumptions act as basic guidelines that order experiences.

Basic Rules and Tacit Assumptions

Fundamental patterns in society are held together by tacit assumptions, rules if you will, which are not usually conscious. These rules serve to organize and legitimate the activity of the many individuals whose interaction makes up a social order. Analytically it is helpful to distinguish two types of rules—constitutive or basic rules and preference rules (McClure and Fischer 1969). Basic rules are like the rules of a game; they are broad parameters in which action takes place. Preference rules, as the name suggests, are the choices one has within the rules of the game. Take chess, for instance. There are basic ground rules (which are not usually brought to a level of awareness) that make chess different from, say, checkers or other board games or even nonboard games. And, within the game of chess, one has choices of the moves to make within this constitutive framework. Pawns' choices involve moving forward (except in "taking" an opponent), rooks move forward or side to side, and so forth. If an opponent's pawn were to jump over three men to put you in check, then he obviously would not be following the "rules of the game"; nor would he be following the tacitly accepted rules if he, say, swept all your men from the board and shouted "I win!"

On the very broadest level, one of the constitutive rules most predominant in our society involves the notion of trust. When we drive down the street, we trust that the car approaching from the opposite direction will stay in its lane. Unless there is some outward manifestation of deviance from this rule, we never even bring to a level of conscious awareness how this basic rule of activity organizes our lives.[2] A similar rule is the one that posits the legitimate bounds of conflict. The rules of the game implicitly set out the boundaries of the activities people are to engage or not to engage in, the types of questions to ask, and the acceptance or rejection of other people's activities.[3] Within these boundaries, there are choices among a range of activities. We can use the courts, but not bomb; we can argue, but not duel; and so forth. A basic assumption seems to be that conflict among groups of people is inherently and fundamentally bad and we should strive to eliminate it within the established framework of institutions.

Clearly, my critique is not an attempt to impugn the motives or integrity of schools. Some of the better schools and classrooms are alive with issues and controversy. However, the controversies usually exhibited in schools concern choices *within* the parameters of implicitly held rules of activity. Little attempt is made to focus on the parameters themselves.

The hidden curriculum in schools serves to reinforce basic rules surrounding the nature of conflict and its uses. It posits a network of assumptions that, when internalized by students, establishes the boundaries of legitimacy. This process is accomplished not so much by explicit instances showing the negative value of conflict, but by nearly the total absence of instances showing the importance of intellectual and normative conflict in subject areas. The fact is that these assumptions are *obligatory* for the students, since at no time are the assumptions articulated or questioned. By the very fact that they are tacit, their potency is enlarged.[4]

The potent relationship between basic assumptions dominant in a collectivity and the hidden curriculum of school is examined by Dreeben (1968). He argues that students tacitly learn certain identifiable social norms mainly by coping with the day-to-day encounters and tasks of classroom life. The fact that these norms that students learn penetrate many areas of later life is critical since it helps document how schooling contributes to individual adjustment to an ongoing social, economic, and political order. Schooling, occupation, and politics in the United States are well integrated for Dreeben (pp. 144-45). The former acts as a distributor of a form of rationality that, when internalized by the student, enables him to function in and, often, accept "the occupational and political institutions which contribute to the stability of an industrial society."

Social studies and science as they are taught in the large majority of schools provide some of the most explicit instances of the hidden teaching. We have chosen these areas for two reasons. First, there has been built up a rather extensive and important literature concerned with the sociology of the disciplines of scientific endeavor. This literature deals rather insightfully with the "logic in use" of scientists (that is, what scientists seem actually to do) as opposed to the "reconstructed logic" of scientists (that is, what philosophers of science and other observers say scientists do) that is normally taught in schools (Apple 1972). Second, in social studies the problems we discuss can be illuminated rather clearly by drawing upon selected Marxian notions (ideas, not necessarily dogma) to show that the commonsense views of social life often found in the teaching of social studies are not inevitable. Let us examine science initially. In so doing, we propose an alternate or, rather, a broader view of scientific endeavor that should be considered by educators and, especially, curriculum workers, if they are, at the very least, to focus on the assumptions inherent in much that is taught in our educational institutions.

Conflict in Scientific Communities

One of our basic theses is that science, as it is presented in most elementary and a large proportion of secondary classrooms, contributes to the learning by students of a basically unrealistic and essentially conservative perspective on the usefulness of conflict. Scientific domains are presented as bodies of knowledge ("thats" and "hows"), at best organized around certain fundamental regularities as in the many discipline- and inquiry-centered curricula that evolved after the "Brunerian revolution," at worst as fairly isolated data one masters for tests. Almost never is it seriously examined as a personal construction of human beings. Let us examine this situation rather closely.

A science is not "just" a domain of knowledge or techniques of discovery and formulating justifications; it is a *group* (or rather, groups) of individuals, a *community* of scholars in Polanyi's (1964) terms, pursuing projects in the world. Like all communities, it is governed by norms, values, and principles that are both overtly seen and covertly felt. By being made up of individuals and groups of scholars, it also has had a significant history of both intellectual and interpersonal struggle. Often the conflict is generated by the introduction of a new and usually quite revolutionary paradigm that challenges the basic meaning structures that were previously accepted by the particular body of scientists, often, thereby, effectively dividing the scholarly community. These struggles have been concerned with the modes of gaining warranted knowledge, with what is to be considered properly scientific, with the very basic foundations upon which science is based. They have also been concerned with such situations as conflicting interpretations of data, with who discovered what first, and many more.

What can be found in schools, however, is a perspective that is akin to what has been called the "positivist ideal" (Hagstrom 1965, p. 256). In our schools, scientific work is tacitly always linked with accepted standards of validity and is seen (and taught) as always subject to empirical verification with no outside influences, either personal or political. "Schools of thought" in science do not exist, or, if they do, "objective" criteria are used to persuade scientists that one side is correct and the other wrong. Just as is evident in our discussion of social studies instruction, children are presented with a *consensus theory of science*, one that underemphasizes the serious disagreements over methodology, goals, and other elements that make up the paradigms of activity of scientists. By the fact that scientific consensus is continually exhibited, students are not permitted to see that without disagreement and controversy science would not progress or would progress at a much slower pace. Not only does controversy stimulate discovery by drawing the attention of scientists to critical problems (Hagstrom, p. 264), but it serves to clarify conflicting intellectual positions. More is mentioned about this point later in our discussion.

A point that is also quite potent is that it is very possible that the standards of "objectivity" (one is tempted to say "vulgar objectivity") being exhibited and taught in school may often lead to a detachment from political commitment. That is, it may not be neutrality as it is overtly expressed, but it may mirror a rather deep fear of intellectual, moral, and political conflict (Gouldner 1970, pp. 102-3) and the personally intense commitment that coheres with the positions taken (Polanyi 1964). The focus in educational institutions on the student scientist (who is often a passive observer in many classrooms despite the emphasis being placed on inquiry by theorists and curriculum specialists) as an individual who objectively and rationally tests or deduces warranted assumptions or makes and checks hypotheses or what have you critically misrepresents the nature of the conflicts so often found between proponents of alternative solutions, interpretations, or modes of procedure in scientific communities. It cannot enable students to see the political dimension of the process by which one alternative theory's proponents win out over their competitors. Nor can such a presentation of science do more than systematically neglect the power dimension involved in scientific argumentation.

Not only is the historical and continuing conflict between competing theories in scientific domains ignored, but little or no thought has evidently been given to the fact that hypothesis testing and the application of *existing* scientific criteria are *not sufficient* to explain how and why a choice is made between competing theories. There have been too many counterinstances that belie this view of science (Kuhn 1962).[5] It is much more perceptive to note that science itself is not necessarily cumulative, nor does it proceed according to a basic criterion of consensus, but that it is riven by conceptual revolutions that cause groups of scientists to reorganize and reconceptualize the models by which they attempt to understand and manipulate the world. "The history of science has been and should be [seen] as a history of competing research programs (or, if you wish 'paradigms'), but it has not been and must not become a succession of periods of normal science: the sooner competition starts the better for progress." (Lakatos 1970, p. 155).[6]

We are not trying to make a case here for a view of science that states that "objectivity" and "neutrality," hypothesis-testing and inquiry procedures are not of paramount importance. What we are saying is that scientific argumentation and counterargumentation are a major part of the scientific enterprise and that the theories and modes of procedure ("structures of disciplines," if you will) act as norms or psychological commitments that lead to intense controversy between groups of scientists (Apple 1972; Mulkay 1969). This controversy is central to progress in science, and it is this continuing conflict that is hidden from students.

Perhaps this point can be made clearer by delving a bit more deeply into some of the realistic characteristics of scientific disciplines often hidden from public view and almost never taught in schools. We have been discussing conflict in scientific domains, yet it is difficult to separate conflict from competition.[7] One of the more important oversights in schools is the lack of treatment whatsoever of the "problem" of competition in science. Competition over priority and recognition in new discoveries is a characteristic of *all* established sciences (Hagstrom 1965, p. 81). One need only read Watson's (1968) lively account of his race with Linus Pauling for the Nobel Prize for the discovery of the structure of DNA to realize how intense the competitiveness can be and how very human are scientists as individuals and in groups.

Competition also can be seen quite clearly between specialties in a discipline (Hagstrom 1965, p. 130), not necessarily on the "frontiers" of knowledge as in Watson's case. Here, as in football, the "commodity" (if I may speak metaphorically) is top-notch students who can be recruited to expand the power and prestige of an emerging specialty. There is continuous, but usually covert, competition among subdisciplines in science for what seem to be limited amounts of prestige available. The conflict here is crucial. Areas whose prestige is relatively high tend to recruit members with the most talent. Relatively lower prestige areas can have quite a difficult time gaining adherents to their particular interests. Realistically a prime factor, if not the most important factor, in high quality scientific research is the quality of student and scientific "labor" a specialty can recruit. Prestige has a strong influence in enticing students and the competition over relative prestige can be intense, therefore, because of these consequences (Hagstrom, p. 173).

My point here is decidedly not to denigrate competition in science, nor is it to present a demonic view of the scientific enterprise in all its ramifications. Rather it is to espouse a more realistic perspective on this enterprise and the *uses of conflict among its practitioners.* Conflict and competition themselves are quite functional. They induce scientists in each area to try to establish a domain of competence in their subjects that is specifically theirs. Competitive pressures also help to assure that less popular research areas are not neglected. Furthermore, the strong competitive element in the scientific community encourages members to take risks, to outdistance their competitors, in effect, thereby increasing the possibility of new and exciting discoveries (Hagstrom 1965, pp. 82-83).

Conflict is also heightened by the very normative structure of the scientific community itself. In fact, it may be a significant contributing agent in both conflict and competition. Among the many norms that guide the behavior of scientists, perhaps the most important for our discussion here is that of organized skepticism. Storer (1966, pp. 78-79) defines it as follows:

> This norm is directive, embodying the principle that each scientist should be held individually responsible for making sure that previous research by others on which he bases his work is valid. He cannot be excused if he has accepted a false idea and then pleads innocence "because Dr. X told me it was true," even if privately we cannot accuse him of willfully substituting error for truth; he should have been properly sceptical of Dr. X's work in the first place . . . .
>
> The scientist is obligated also by this norm to make public his criticisms of the work of others when he believes it to be in error. . . . It follows that no scientist's contribution to knowledge can be accepted without careful scrutiny, and the scientist must doubt his own findings as well as those of others."

It is not difficult to see how the norm of organized skepticism has contributed to the controversies within scientific communities.

Other examples of conflict abound. Perhaps the one most important for our own topic is the existence of "rebellious" subgroups in scientific communities. Specialties that revolt against the goals and/or means of a larger discipline are quite common within the scientific tradition. These rebellious groups of researchers are alienated from the main body of current scientific discourse in their particular areas and sparks may very well fly because of the argumentation between the rebels and the traditionalists. Here, often added to this situation, even the usual arguments that we associate with science—that is, arguments among groups and individuals over substantive issues such as warranted knowledge and the like—blend with arguments over goals and policies (Hagstrom 1965, pp. 193-94).[8] Even more importantly today, it is becoming quite common (and in my view, happily so) for there to be heated discussion and dissension over the political stance a discipline should take and over the social uses of its knowledge.

So far we have been documenting the rather important dimension of conflict in scientific communities. We have been making the point that scientific knowledge as it is taught in schools has, in effect, been divorced from the structure of the community from which it evolved and which acts to criticize it. Students are "forced," because of the very absence of a realistic picture of how communities in science apportion power and economic resources, to internalize a view that has little potency for questioning the legitimacy of the tacit assumptions about interpersonal conflict that govern their lives and their own educational, economic, and political situations. Not only are they presented with a view of science that is patently unrealistic, but, what is more important for our own position, they are not shown how critical interpersonal and intergroup argumentation and conflict have been for the progress of science. When this situation is generalized into a basic perspective on one's relation to the economic and political paradigms of activity in a society, it is not difficult to see how it can serve to reinforce the quiescence of students or lead them into "proper channels" for changing these structures.

Conflict in Society

The second area of schooling in which one finds hidden curricular encounters with and tacit teaching of constitutive assumptions about conflict, and that we have chosen to explicitly focus upon, is that of social studies. As in our discussion of science, in delving into this area we propose an alternative or broader view on conflict in society. We also document some of the social uses of intellectual and normative conflict, uses that are ignored in most of the curricular encounters found in schools.

An examination of much of the literature in social studies points to an acceptance of society as basically a cooperative system. Observations in classrooms over an extended period of time reveal a similar perspective. The orientation stems in large part from the (perhaps necessarily unconscious) basic assumption that conflict, and especially social conflict, is not an essential feature of the network of social relations we call society (Dahrendorf 1959, p. 112). More often than not, a social reality is pictured that tacitly accepts "happy cooperation" as the normal if not the best way of life. Now it must be made clear that the truth value of the statement that society is a cooperative system (if only everyone would cooperate) *cannot* be determined empirically. It is essentially a value orientation that helps determine the questions that one asks or the educational experiences one designs for students. And the educational experiences seem to emphasize what is fundamentally a conservative perspective.

The perspective found in schools leans heavily upon how all elements of a society, from the postman and fireman in first grade to the partial institutions in civics courses in high school, are linked to each other in a functional relationship, each contributing to the ongoing *maintenance* of society. Internal dissension and conflict in a society are viewed as inherently antithetical to the smooth functioning of the social order. *Consensus* is once more a pronounced feature. This orientation is also evident in the implicit emphasis upon students (and man in general) as value-transmitting and value-receiving persons rather than as value-creating persons in much of their school experience (Gouldner 1970, p. 193).

The fact that there are a number of paradigmatic ways one can perceive the social world has long been noted. However, it is also important to note that each posits a certain logic of organization upon social activity and each has certain, often strikingly different, valuative assumptions that underlie it. The differences between the Durkheimian and the more subjectivistic Weberian perspectives offer a case in point. The recent analysis of structural-functional social theories, especially those of Parsons, by Gouldner offers a more current example. His examination, one that has a long intellectual history in the sociology of knowledge, raises intriguing questions about the social and political consequences of contemporary social thought—that much of its background of assumptions is determined by the personal and class existence of the thinker, that it presents a "very selective, one-sided picture of American society," one geared to "the avoidance of political tensions" and aimed at a notion that political stability, say, "would be achieved if efforts at social change prudently stopped short of changing established ways of allocating and justifying power" (Gouldner 1970, p. 48). In short the underlying basis of such a social "paradigm" used to order and guide our perceptions is fundamentally oriented to the legitimation of the existing social order. By the very fact that it seeks to treat such topics as social equilibrium and system maintenance, for example, there is a strong tendency toward conformity and a denial that there need be conflict (pp. 210-18).

Opposed to the structural-functional type of reasoning, Gouldner advocates a different "paradigm," one that is rooted in the individual's search to transform himself and his activity, and one that sets not existing society as measure but rather the possibility of basic structural change through an individual's passionate commitment and social involvement. The question of legitimation, hence, becomes less a process of studying how institutional tensions evolve and can be "settled," and more an attempt to link institutions with their historical development and their need for transformation according to explicitly chosen principles based on political and moral argumentation. The perspective on conflict of the latter position is quite different from that of the school of thought Gouldner criticizes.

In its analysis of the background assumptions of Parsonian social thought, for example, Gouldner's examination documents the place of moral argumentation and value conflict, which are at the heart of the human sciences and their understanding of society. He thereby considerably expands the boundaries of possible conflict. This situation is perhaps most evident in his criticism of the inordinate place Parsons gives to a socialization process that implicitly defines man as primarily a recipient of values (Gouldner 1970, p. 206). He censures functionalist social theories for being incapable of dealing with "those who oppose social establishments actively and who struggle to change its rules and membership requirements." Gouldner opposes this view with a focus upon human beings as engaged in a dialectical process of receiving, creating, and recreating values and institutions (p. 427; Berger and Luckmann 1966). The continual recreation of values in a society is a difficult process and often involves conflict among those of disparate valuative frameworks. It is this type of conflict, among others, to which Gouldner attempts to give a place.

By their very nature, social "paradigms" themselves are constantly changing. In fact, Gouldner's recent work can be seen to mirror and be a part of this change. However, they leave behind reifications of themselves found in both elementary and high school curricula. This may be particularly true in the case of the models of understanding of social life we find in schools today.

There is, perhaps, no better example of the emphasis upon consensus, order, and the absence of any conflict in social studies curricula than that found in one of the more popular sets of educational materials, Science Research Associates' economics "kit," *Our Working World*. It is designed to teach basic concepts of disciplined economics to elementary school students. The primary grade course of study subtitled "Families at Work" is organized around everyday social interaction, the likes of which children would be familiar with. Statements such as the following pervade the materials. "When we follow the rules, we are rewarded; but if we break the rules, we will be punished. So you see, dear, that is why everyone does care. That is why we *learn* customs and rules, and why we *follow* them. Because if we do, we are all rewarded by a nicer and more orderly world" (Senesh 1964, p. 22).

The attitude exhibited toward the *creation* of new values and customs and the value placed on an orderly, nonconflicting world seem to be indicative of a more constitutive set of assumptions concerning consensus and social life. When one realizes that students are inundated with examples of this type throughout the day, ones in which it is rather difficult to find any value placed upon disorder of any significant sort, it makes one pause.

Even most of the inquiry-oriented curricula, though fruitful in other ways to be sure, show a signal neglect of the efficacy of conflict and the rather long and deep-seated history it has held in social relationships. For example, the basic assumptions that conflicts are to be "resolved" within accepted boundaries and that continuing change in the framework and texture of institutional arrangements is less than desirable can be seen in the relatively sophisticated discipline-centered social science curricula that are being developed currently. One of these curricula (Center for the Study of Instruction 1970) overtly offers a "conceptual schemes" approach that puts forward a hierarchy of generalizations that, ideally, are going to be internalized by the student through his active participation in role playing and inquiry. These levels of generalizations range from rather simple to fairly complex and are subsumed under a broad "descriptive" generalization or "cognitive scheme." For example, subsumed under the organizing generalization "Political organization (government) resolves conflicts and makes interactions easier among people" are the following subgeneralizations. They are listed in ascending complexity.

1. The behavior of individuals is governed by commonly accepted rules.
2. Members of family groups are governed by rules and law.
3. Community groups are governed through leadership and authority.
4. Man's peaceful interaction depends on social controls.
5. The pattern of government depends upon control by participation in the political system.
6. Stable political organization improves the quality of life shared by its citizens. (p. T-17)[9]

Coupled with these "descriptive" generalizations, which the students are to be led up to, are such "supporting concepts" as "Rules help to maintain order" and "Rules help protect health and safety" (p. T-26). Now, few will quarrel with these statements. After all, rules do help. But, like the assumptions prevalent in the economics material, children are confronted with a tacit emphasis once again on a stable set of structures and on the maintenance of order.

What is intriguing is the nearly complete lack of treatment of or even reference to conflict as a social concern or as a category of thought in most available social studies curricula or in most classrooms observed. Of the more popular materials, only those developed under the aegis of the late Hilda Taba refer to it as a key concept. However, while the Taba Social Studies Curriculum overtly focuses on conflict, and while this focus in itself is a welcome sight, its orientation is on the serious consequences of sustained conflict rather than on the many positive aspects also associated with conflict itself. Conflict again is viewed as "dysfunctional," even though it is pictured as being ever present (Durkin, Duvall, and McMaster 1969, p. v).

As we noted previously, to a large extent society as it exists, in *both* its positive and negative aspects, is held together by implicit commonsense rules and paradigms of thought. Social studies materials such as this (and there are many others to which we have not referred) can contribute to the reinforcing and tacit teaching of certain dominant basic assumptions and, hence, a proconsensus and antidissension belief structure.

This view is being countered somewhat by a portion of the content now being taught under the rubric of Black Studies. Here, struggle and conflict on a communal basis are often explicitly and positively focused upon (Hare 1969; Wilcox 1969, pp. 20-21). While many curriculists may find such overt espousal of community goals somewhat antithetical to their own inclinations, the fact that there has been an attempt to present a comparatively realistic outlook on the significant history and uses of conflict in the progress of social groups, through the civil rights and black power movements for instance, must be recognized. Even those who would not applaud or would applaud only a rather safe or conservative view on this subject should realize the potency and positive value of just such a perspective for developing a group consciousness and a cohesiveness not heretofore possible. This point is made again in our more general discussion of the uses of conflict in social groups.

To say, however, that most Black Studies curricula exhibit this same perspective would be less than accurate. One could also point to the by now apparent presentation of black historical material where those blacks are presented who stayed within what were considered to be the legitimate boundaries (constitutive rules) of protest or progressed in accepted economic, athletic, scholarly, or artistic fields. Usually, one does not find reference to Malcolm X, Marcus Garvey, or others who offered a potent critique of existing modes of activity. However, it is the *massiveness* of the tacit presentation of the consensus perspective that must be stressed, as well as its occurrence in the two areas examined in this paper.

It is not sufficient, though, for our purposes to "merely" illuminate how the hidden curriculum obligates students to experience certain encounters with basic rules. It is essential that an alternative view be posited and that the uses of social conflict that we have been mentioning be documented.

It is possible to counter the consensus orientation with a somewhat less consensus-bound set of assumptions, assumptions that seem to be as empirically warranted, if not more so, as those to which we have raised objections. For instance, some social theorists have taken the position that "society is not primarily a smoothly functioning order of the form of a social organism, a social system, or a static social fabric." Rather, continuous change in the elements *and* basic structural form of society is a dominant characteristic. Conflicts are the systematic products of the changing structure of a society and by their very nature tend to lead to progress. The "order" of society, hence, becomes the regularity of change. The "reality" of society is conflict and flux, not a "closed functional system" (Dahrendorf 1959, p. 27). It has been stated that the most significant contribution to the understanding of society made by

Marx was his insight that a major source of change and innovation is internal conflict. This crucial insight can be appreciated without the necessity of accepting his metaphysical assumptions (Walker 1967, pp. 217-218). In essence, therefore, conflicts must be looked at as a basic and often beneficial dimension of the dialectic of activity we label society.

An examination of positions within and closely allied with this general orientation can help to illuminate the importance of conflict. One of the more interesting perspectives points to its utility in preventing the reification of existing social institutions by exerting pressure upon individuals and groups to be innovative and creative in bringing about changes in institutional activities. Coser (Dahrendorf 1959, p. 207) puts it well:

> Conflict within and between groups in a society can prevent accommodations and habitual relations from progressively impoverishing creativity. The clash of values and interests, the tension between what is and what some groups feel ought to be, the conflict between vested interests and new strata and groups demanding their share of power, have been productive of vitality.

Yet one is hard pressed to find anything akin to this orientation in most of the materials and teaching exhibited in schools. The basic rules of activity that govern our perception tend to cause us to picture conflict as primarily a negative quality in a collectivity. However, "happy cooperation" and conflict are the two sides of the societal coin, neither of which is wholly positive or negative. This outlook is forcefully put by Coser (1956, p. 31):

> No group can be entirely harmonious for it would then be devoid of process and structure. Groups require disharmony as well as harmony, dissociation as well as association; and conflicts within them are by no means altogether disruptive factors. Group formation is the result of both types of processes. The belief that one process tears down what the other builds up, so that what finally remains is the result of subtracting the one from the other, is based on a misconception. On the contrary, both "positive" and "negative" factors build group relations. Conflict as well as cooperation has social functions. Far from being necessarily dysfunctional, a certain degree of conflict is an essential element in group formation and the persistence of group life.

The basic rule of activity that constitutes the unconscious negative value associated with conflict tends to lead to the designing of experiences that focus on the "law or rule breaking" dimension of conflict, yet it should be made clear that conflict leads not "merely" to law breaking but, in effect, law *creating* as well (Coser 1956, p. 126). [10] It performs the considerable task of pointing to areas of needed redress. Furthermore, it brings into conscious awareness the more basic rules that govern the particular activity over which there is conflict but that were hidden from view. That is, it performs the unique function of enabling individuals to see the hidden imperatives built into situations that act to structure their actions, thereby partially freeing individuals to create relevant patterns of actions to an extent not usually possible. These law-creating and expanding-awareness properties of conflict situations offer, in combination, a rather positive effect. Since conflict brings about inherently new situations that to a large degree are undefined by previous assumptions, it acts as a stimulus for the establishment of new and possibly more flexible or situationally pertinent norms of activity. By literally forcing conscious attention, issues are defined and new dimensions can be explored and made clear (Coser, pp. 124-215).

Documentation of the positive effects of conflict would not be even nearly adequate if a major use were to go unmentioned, especially given our own commitment to making urban education, in particular, more responsive to the needs of the community it serves. Here we are speaking of the importance of conflict for both creating and legitimating a conscious and specifically ethnic experience. It is now well known that one of the primary ways groups define themselves is by perceiving themselves as struggling with other groups and that such struggle both increases members' participation in group activities and makes them more conscious of the bonds that tie them together (Coser 1956, p. 90). That the black and other ethnic communities have, to a significant extent, defined themselves along these in-group/out-group lines is of no small moment since it enables a greater cohesiveness among the various elements within their respective communities. By drawing upon "primordial sentiments" such as race a communal meaning structure is created that makes plausible an individual's and a group's continued and separate existence (Berger 1967, pp. 24-25; Geertz 1963, p. 118). Just as conflict seems to be a primary means for the establishment of individual autonomy and for the full differentiation of personality from the outside world (Coser, p. 33),[11] so too it is effective for the full differentiation of community autonomy. Respect for pluralistic societies may require a greater acceptance of this perspective.

We have been proposing an alternative outlook on the presence and uses of conflict in social groups. It is feasible for it to be used as a more objective foundation for designing curricula and guiding teaching so that the more static hidden curriculum students encounter can be counterbalanced to some extent. The explicit focusing on conflict as a legitimate category of conceptualization and as a valid and essential dimension of collective life could enable the development by students of a more viable and potent political and intellectual perspective from which to perceive their relation to existing economic and political institutions. At the least, such a perspective gives them a better understanding of the tacit assumptions that act to structure their own activity.

Programmatic Considerations

There are a number of programmatic suggestions that can be made that could at least partially serve to counterbalance the hidden curriculum most evident in science and social studies. While these are by their very nature still rather tentative and only partial, they may prove important.

A more balanced presentation of some of the espoused values of science is essential, especially that relating to organized skepticism. The historical importance to the scientific communities of the overriding skeptical outlook needs to be recognized and focused upon.

The history of science can be seen as a continuing dialectic of controversy and conflict between advocates of competing research programs and paradigms, between accepted answers and challenges to these "truths." As such, science itself could be presented with a greater historical orientation documenting the conceptual revolutions necessary for significant breakthroughs to occur.

Rather than adhering to a view of science as truth, the balanced presentation of science as "truth until further notice," a process of continual change, could prevent the crystallization of attitudes (Apple and Popkewitz 1971). In this connection also, the study of how conceptual revolutions in science have proceeded would contribute to a less positive perspective on consensus as the only mode of progress.

To this point can be added a focus upon the moral uses and dilemmas of science. For example, personalizing the history of science through cases such as Oppenheimer, Watson, and, intriguingly, the controversy surrounding the Velikovsky case (cf. Mulkay 1969), would indeed be helpful. When taken together, these suggestions would help to eliminate the bias of present curricula by introducing the idea of personal and interpersonal controversy and conflict.

In the social studies, a number of suggestions can be made. The comparative study of revolution, say the American, French, Russian, and Chinese, would serve to focus upon the properties of the human condition that cause and are ameliorated by interpersonal conflict. This suggestion is made more appropriate when coupled with the fact that in many countries revolution is the legitimate (in a quite real sense of the word) mode of procedure for redressing grievances.

A more realistic appraisal and presentation of the uses of conflict in the civil rights movement of blacks, Indians, and others would no doubt assist in the formation of a perspective that perceives these and similar activities as legitimate models of action. The fact that laws *had* to be broken and were then struck down by the courts later is not usually focused upon in social studies curricula. Yet, it was through these types of activities that a good deal of progress was and is made. Here community and "movement" studies by urban students of how changes have been effected is an interesting process, one that should prove of considerable moment.

Finally, the comparison of different paradigmatic views on social life and the differing value assumptions of each would be helpful. While the normative implication of many paradigms of social thought may serve to limit their usefulness as models of action, and in fact may make them totally unacceptable on occasion, the presentation and analysis of alternative conceptions to those now dominant could still be effective.

Beyond these suggestions for specific programmatic changes, one further area should be noted. Sociological "paradigms" also attempt to account for the commonsense reality in which students and teachers dwell. Schools are integrally involved in this reality and its internalization. It might be wise to consider engaging students in the articulation and development of paradigms of activity within their everyday lives at school. Such involvement could enable students to come to grips with and amplify crucial insights into their own conditionedness and freedom. Such insights could potentially alter the original paradigm and the commonsense reality itself. It would also make possible to a greater degree a concrete and meaningful educational encounter for students with the process of value and institutional recreation.

Conclusions

Research on political socialization of children seems to indicate the importance of the president and policeman as points of contact between children and the structures of authority and legitimacy in a society (Easton and Dennis 1969, p. 162). For instance, there is a strongly personal initial bond between the child and these representatives of the structures of authority. As the child matures, these very personal ties are transferred to more anonymous institutions such as a congress or to political activities such as voting. The tendency to lift impersonal institutions to high esteem may be quite an important source of the relative stability and durability of the structures of authority in industrial societies (pp. 271-76).

Yet it is not quite certain that this formulation really answers the questions one could raise concerning political and social stability. The foundation of political (broadly conceived) leanings and relations to political and social structures is in a belief system that itself rests upon basic patterns of assumptions. Such rules for activity (and thought as a fundamental form of this activity) are probably more important to a person's relation to his life-world than we realize. We have been examining one of these constitutive assumptions.

It is our contention that the schools systematically distort the functions of social conflict in collectivities. The social, intellectual, and political manifestations of this distortion are manifold. They may contribute significantly to the ideological underpinnings that serve to fundamentally orient individuals.

Students in most schools and in urban centers in particular are presented with a view that serves to legitimate the existing social order since change, conflict, and man as creator as well as receiver of values and institutions are systematically neglected. We have pointed to the massiveness of the presentation. Now something else must be stressed once again—the fact that these meaning structures are obligatory. Students receive them from persons who are "significant others" in their lives, through their teachers, other role models in books and elsewhere. To change this situation, students' perceptions of to whom they are to look as holders of "expert knowledge" must be radically altered. In ghetto areas, a partial answer is, perhaps, instituting a more radical perspective in the schools. This change can be carried out only by political activity. It may very well be that to divorce an educator's educational existence from his political existence is to forget that as an act of influence, education is also an inherently political act.

One of the primary tasks of this analysis has been to present lenses that are alternatives to those that normally legitimate many of the activities and encounters curriculists design for students. The curriculum field has limited its own forms of consciousness so that the political and ideological assumptions that undergird a good deal of its normal patterns of activity are as hidden as those that students encounter in schools (Huebner 1962, p. 88). We have pointed to the possibilities inherent in a more theoretically realistic approach to the nature of conflict as one alternative "form of consciousness." Yet when all has been said, it is still possible to raise the question of whether such theoretical investigations are either heuristically, politically, or programmatically helpful.

One of the difficulties in seeking to develop new perspectives is the obvious and oft-pointed-to distinction between theory and practice or, to put it in common-sense language, between "merely" understanding the world and changing it. This distinction is rooted in our very language. Yet it is crucial to remind ourselves that while, say, Marx felt that the ultimate task of philosophy and theory was not merely to "comprehend reality" but to change it, it is also true that according to Marx revolutionizing the world has as its very foundation an adequate understanding of it. (After all, Marx spent most of his lifetime writing *Das Kapital*—Avineri 1968, p. 137.)

The significant danger is not that theoretical thought offers no mode of critiquing and changing reality, but that it can lead to quietism or a perspective that, like Hamlet, necessitates a continuing monologue on the complexity of it all, while the world tumbles down around us. It would seem important to note that not only is an understanding of existing reality a necessary condition for changing it (Avineri 1968, p. 148), but it is a major (and perhaps the major) step in actually effecting this reconstruction. However, with this understanding of the social milieu in which curriculists operate, there must also be a continual attempt to bring to a conscious level those hidden epistemological and ideological assumptions that help to structure the decisions they make and the environments they design (Heubner 1962).[12] These fundamental assumptions can have a significant impact on the hidden curriculum in which students tacitly dwell.

Without an analysis and greater understanding of these latent assumptions, educators run the very real risk of continuing to let values work through them. A conscious advocacy of a more realistic outlook on and teaching of the dialectic of social change would, no doubt, contribute to preparing students with the political and conceptual tools necessary to deal with the dense reality they must face. I do not think it is necessary to enumerate the possible consequences if this self-evaluation should not occur.

Notes

1. Such a statement is both realistic and rather critical. In a way, critics of the schools (and the present author to a large extent) are caught in a bind. It is rather easy to denigrate existing "educational" structures (after all, everyone seems to do it); yet, it is not quite as easy to offer alternative structures. The individual who attempts to ameliorate some of the more debilitating conditions runs the risk of actually helping to shore up and perpetuate what may very well be an outmoded set of institutional arrangements. Yet, not to try to better conditions in what are often small and stumbling ways is to neglect those real human beings who now inhabit the schools for most of their preadult lives. Therefore, one tries to play both sides of the battle often. One criticizes the fundamental assumptions that undergird schools as they exist today and, at the same time, paradoxically attempts to make these same institutions a bit more humane, a bit more educative. It is an ambiguous position, but, after all, so is one's total situation. Our discussion of the fundamental glossing over of the nature and necessity of conflict and the tacit teaching that accompanies it shows this ambiguity. However, if urban education in particular is to make a difference (and here we should read politically and economically), then concrete changes must be effected now *while* the more basic criticisms are themselves being articulated. One is not an excuse for the other.
2. The language of "rules of activity" is less analytically troublesome than the distinction often made between thought and action, since it implies that the distinction is somewhat naive and enables action, perceptual, conceptual, and bodily, to be the fundamental category of an individual's response to his situation. While we often use rules of activity and assumptions interchangeably, the point should be made that assumptions usually connote a less inclusive category of phenomena and are actually indicative of the existence of these socially sedimented rules and boundaries that seem to affect even our very perceptions. Further work on such rules can be found in the ethnomethodological literature (Garfinkel 1967) and, of course, in the later Wittgenstein (1958).
3. In essence, the "system" that many individuals decry is *not* an ordered interrelationship of institutions, but a framework of fundamental assumptions that are prior to and act in a dialectical relationship with these institutions.
4. The questions we are posing can obviously lead to a circular type of controversy. Do the children learn, say, political quiescence and acceptance in school and then transfer these to life in general, or do the schools "merely" reinforce constitutive rules learned elsewhere? This is not the point (though it is, no doubt, quite important). What is more important is to at least begin to ask *how* the schools may function, through the hidden curriculum, to obligate and reinforce the learning by children of a certain perspective.
5. Kuhn's seminal work is subjected to rather acute analysis, and discussed with rebuttal and counterrebuttal in Lakatos and Musgrave (1970). The entire volume is devoted to the issues, epistemological and sociological, raised by Kuhn's book.

6. Normal science refers to that science that has agreement (consensus) on the basic paradigms of activity to be used by scientists to interpret and act on their respective fields. See Kuhn (1962; 1970) for an intensive analysis of normal and revolutionary science.
7. It is important to distinguish between conflict and competition, however. While conflict seems to stem from a number of the conditions we have examined or will examine—new paradigms, disagreements over goals, methodology, etc.—competition seems to have its basis in the exchange system of science. See, for example, Storer's (1966) interesting examination of the place of professional recognition and commodity exchange in the scientific community.
8. Statistics is an interesting example.
9. It is questionable whether many blacks in the ghettos of the United States would support this "description."
10. Perhaps the best illustration of material on the law-breaking dimension of conflict is a primary grade course of study, "Respect for Rules and Law" (New York State Bureau of Elementary Curriculum Development 1969). One set of curricular materials does take some interesting and helpful steps in allowing for a more honest appraisal of conflict. See Oliver and Newmann (1968).
11. This is perhaps one of Piaget's most fruitful insights.
12. The commonsense assumptions that seem to posit a rather static logic upon curriculum design also seem to cohere with a type of bureaucratic rationality that has had a long tradition in curriculum thought. For an excellent analysis of this tradition, see Kliebard (1971).

References

Apple, M. W. "Community, Knowledge, and the Structure of Disciplines." *The Educational Forum* 37, no. 1 (1972): 75-82.
———, and Popkewitz, T. S. "Knowledge, Perspective and Commitment: An Essay Review of Thomas Kuhn and Alvin Gouldner." *Social Education* 35 (1971): 935-37.
Avineri, S. *The Social and Political Thought of Karl Marx.* New York: Cambridge University Press, 1968.
Berger, P. L. *The Sacred Canopy.* New York: Doubleday, 1967.
———, and Luckmann, T. *The Social Construction of Reality.* New York: Doubleday, 1966.
Center for the Study of Instruction. *Principles and Practices in the Teaching of the Social Sciences: Teacher's Edition.* New York: Harcourt, Brace and World, 1970.
Coser, L. *The Functions of Social Conflict.* New York: Free Press, 1956.
Dahrendorf, R. *Class and Class Conflict in Industrial Society.* Stanford, Calif.: Stanford University Press, 1959.
———. *Essays in the Theory of Society.* London: Routledge & Kegan Paul, 1968.
Dreeben, R. *On What Is Learned in School.* Reading, Mass.: Addison-Wesley, 1968.
Durkin, M. C.; Duvall, A.; and McMaster, A. *The Taba Social Studies Curriculum: Communities around Us.* Reading, Mass.: Addison-Wesley, 1969.

Easton, D., and Dennis, J. *Children in the Political System*. New York: McGraw-Hill, 1969.

Eisinger, P. K. "Protest Behavior and the Integration of Urban Political Systems." Unpublished paper, Madison, Wis.: Institute for Research on Poverty, University of Wisconsin, 1970.

Garfinkel, H. *Studies in Ethnomethodology*. Englewood Cliffs, N.J.: Prentice-Hall, 1967.

Geertz, C. "The Integrative Revolution: Primordial Sentiments and Civil Politics in the New States." In *Old societies and New States*, edited by C. Geertz, pp. 105-57. New York: Free Press, 1963.

Gibson, E. F. "The Three D's: Distortion, Deletion, Denial." *Social Education* 33 (1969): 405-9.

Gouldner, A. W. *The Coming Crisis of Western Sociology*. New York: Basic Books, 1970.

Hagstrom, W. O. *The Scientific Community*. New York: Basic Books, 1965.

Hare, N. "The Teaching of Black History and Culture in the Secondary Schools." *Social Education* 33 (1969): 385-88.

Huebner, D. "Politics and the Curriculum." *In Curriculum Crossroads*, edited by A. H. Passow, pp. 87-95. New York: Teachers College Press, 1962.

Jackson, P. *Life in Classrooms*. New York: Holt, Rinehart & Winston, 1968.

Kliebard, H. M. "Bureaucracy and Curriculum Theory." In *Freedom, Bureaucracy and Schooling*, edited by V. Haubrick, pp. 74-93. Washington, D.C.: ASCD, 1971.

Kuhn, T. S. *The Structure of Scientific Revolutions*. Chicago: University of Chicago Press, 1962.

——. *The Structure of Scientific Revolutions*. 2d ed. Chicago: University of Chicago Press, 1970.

Lakatos, I. "Falsification and the Methodology of Scientific Research Programmes." In *Criticism and the Growth of Knowledge*, edited by I. Lakatos and A. Musgrave, pp. 91-195. New York: Oxford University Press, 1970.

——, and Musgrave, A., eds. *Criticism and the Growth of Knowledge*. New York: Oxford University Press, 1970.

McClure, H., and Fischer, G. "Ideology and Opinion Making: General Problems of Analysis." Unpublished paper. New York: Bureau of Applied Social Research, Columbia University, July 1969.

Mulkay, M. "Some Aspects of Cultural Growth in the Natural Sciences." *Social Research* 36 (1969): 22-52.

New York State Bureau of Elementary Curriculum Development. *Respect for Rules and Law*. Albany: New York State Dept. of Education, 1969.

Oliver, D., and Newmann, F. *Harvard Social Studies Project: Public Issues Series*. Columbus, Ohio: American Education Publications, 1968.

Polanyi, M. *Personal Knowledge*. New York: Harper & Row, 1964.

Senesh, L. "Recorded Lessons." In *Our Working World: Families at Work*, edited by L. Senesh. Chicago: Science Research Associates, 1964.

Sigel, R., *Learning about Politics*. New York: Random House, 1970.

Storer, N. W. *The Social System of Science*. New York: Holt, Rinehart & Winston, 1966.

Walker, J. L. "A Critique of the Elitist Theory of Democracy." In *Apolitical Politics*, edited by C. A. McCoy and J. Playford, pp. 199-219. New York: Cromwell, 1967.

Watson, J. D. *The Double Helix*. New York: Atheneum, 1968.
Wilcox, P. "Education for black liberation." *New Generation* 51 (1969): 17-21.
Willhelm, S. M. *Who Needs the Negro?* Cambridge, Mass.: Schenkman, 1970.
Wittgenstein, L. *Philosophical Investigations*. New York: Macmillan, 1958.

Scientific Interests and the Nature of Educational Institutions

The Problem Behind the Problem

One of the fundamental theses of this paper is that the basis of many of the oppressive qualities of schooling lies in the set of assumptions that educators bring to their work. That is, a fundamental difficulty rests on the models and language systems that are applied in designing educative environments and engaging in a large portion of educational research. These language systems have certain constitutive features that cause their users to approach problems in specific and identifiable ways. The modes of discourse that curriculum workers and other schoolmen employ often seem to be manipulative and deterministic—in the dominance of a vulgar behaviorism, for instance, in much of our thinking about life in classrooms. They are aimed at bringing student action into line with previously sedimented patterns of behavior extant in a collectivity.[1] The problem is not "merely" the lack of success in the many attempts at fostering creativity in schools; indeed, educators have noted this issue for years. Rather the problem lies behind this—in a fundamental ethic that all important modes of human action can be known in advance by educators and social scientists; that certainty in interaction among people is of primary import; and, underlying all of these, that the primary aspects of thought and sentiment of students should be brought under institutionalized control. The use of such modes of thought also mirrors the remarkable lack of self-reflectiveness among members of the curriculum field. That is, our "habits of thought" are exactly that: habits that have become part of our taken-for-granted reality, a reality that has become so commonsensical that we have ceased even to question it. These habitual ways of perceiving educational problems set the boundaries of curriculists' imaginations and provide a fundamental framework for a large portion of the problematic activities of schooling. In Hampshire's terms, "The limits of a man's habits of thought are limits also of what he can be expected to try to do."[2] Or as he says elsewhere:

> The more self conscious [a person] is in his criticism of his own intentions and activities, the more he is aware of the limits of his habits of classification, limits that determine the possibilities open to him. He becomes aware also of the limits set by the conventions of communication and classification into which he was born. He can begin endlessly to question and to criticize the vocabulary and the forms of language which he has learnt always to use in considering alternate ends of action.[3]

In this paper I would like briefly to sketch an area that may help curriculists to become more aware of the possible latent dilemmas involved in the modes of discourse they employ, dilemmas that contribute to the curriculum field's inability to cope with some of the repressive characteristics of institutionalized education. In essence, three major points will be argued here:

1. Educators, and especially members of the curriculum field, have taken an outmoded positivistic stance that disavows significant critical self-reflection[4] and have given it the name and prestige of *the* scientific method.

2. Because of our lack of reflectiveness we have perceived our dominant style of scientific rationality as being interest free, when this may not be the case, thereby contributing to an already strongly manipulative ethos of schooling.

3. Educators may find it necessary to seek out forms of rationality that are less restrictive than those on which they have drawn so heavily in the past if they are in fact to design more humane educational environments.

Much of the discussion that follows has been stimulated by the work of the German social philosopher, Jürgen Habermas, whose writing could provide the intellectual foundations for the argumentation among educators that is so essential for the rejuvenation of our modes of perception on the enterprise of curricular design. Habermas's studies are concerned with the increasing propensity in modern industrialized societies to rationalize and simplify interpersonal interaction, political and ethical modes of argumentation and decision making, and human conduct in general. In his terms, "instrumental action" or "purposive-rational action"—that is, the *technical* control of all means or choices between alternatives—tends to generalize itself into all aspects of man's social world so that we see no other basic alternatives to positivistic and reductive models and "rational" planning with specifiable ends in view. In this way man becomes progressively alienated from the other symbolic ways by which he relates to his world.[5] In some ways **Habermas's** analysis is similar to that of Jacques Ellul and Herbert Marcuse[6] but it goes far beyond them in analytic cogency and philosophical and historical sophistication. Of considerable importance is his work on the interest structure of science, work that may at least partially account for the dominance of certain institutionalized forms of control in schooling.

Educational Beliefs and Quasi-Scientific Consciousness

One of the things I would like to suggest here is that the dominant structures of meaning, perhaps we might call them paradigms, that educators use to ask their questions, engage in their research, and design environments for students are themselves inherently problematic. They are what Huebner might call basically technological.[7] That is, most educators have been and still are primarily interested in efficiency and smoothness of operation,[8] rather than intellectual and valuative conflict, and therefore seek out certain types of paradigms that fit into this set of interests. This fact is made even more important by the concomitant fact that the perspective on scientific rationality educators employ is also based on a rather deterministic and manipulative outlook. Perhaps the best example of how this is the case can be seen in a quote from a proponent of systems management procedures in education in which he states that in order for education to be effective, one must explicitly determine "whatever the learner is expected to be able to *do, know,* and *feel* as an outcome of his learning experience."[9] In essence, thought, action, and feeling are reduced to separate and identifiable components, each of which can and must be known before an individual engages in activity.[10] The environment is then controlled (as is the student) scientifically so that neither the individual's behavior nor his thought will deviate from the prescribed goal. In this way education supposedly becomes more like a science.

(The fact that "technique" is not the same as science is obviously ignored.)

Historically, education in general, and the curriculum field in particular, has sought to become more like a science. That is, it has sought to pattern its activity on models drawn from modes of endeavor based on objectivity, replicability, the ideal of "hard" rather than "soft" data, and so forth. The fields on which it has relied are usually the behavioral sciences, such as psychology and sociology, which seem to accept the basic paradigms of activity of the physical sciences as their own ideal, even though there is a significant amount of argumentation within the social sciences over whether they should in fact adopt a positivistic model.[11] Examples of curriculum's continuing quest to become more like a science range from the early work of Bobbitt and Charters, and the massive borrowing from sociology by Snedden, to the attempted use of systems analysis to manage educational outcomes and processes today.[12] Behind it all is a tacit structure of beliefs supporting the position that the complex problem of designing educational environments that are responsive to both institutional and personal meanings will be solved only if we become more certain of our actions and their observable outcomes. This can best be accomplished through a process of basing our forms of conception on those of the established behavioral sciences.

A crucial fact that is often neglected in the debate over procedure is that "scientific" outlooks have become so ingrained in our consciousness that they have become *values*, not merely ways of gaining knowledge. Accepted ways of operating on and perceiving their fields in the scientific disciplines generally tend to act as normative commitments once they are accepted and have existed for a length of time. This phenomenon makes it very difficult for new ideas to gain acceptance.[13] Hence, there is nothing really odd about our own intellectual outlooks becoming value stances (although it does raise some intriguing questions about our artificial separation in education between cognitive and affective functioning). What is noteworthy is the extent to which this transposition of objective outlook into strongly held norm has moved. In essence, we tend to place a rather high value on "scientific" modes of operation and take the position that other forms of knowing lean toward the metaphysical, if you will. As we shall see, this problem is compounded by our basic misperception of what science itself is like. Now I do not wish in any way to debunk scientific enterprise. It is and undoubtedly will continue to be one of the primary and richest ways man effectively deals with the complex reality in which he dwells. What I do wish to make clear is that the commonsense thought we use to legitimate a good deal of our day-to-day activity has become more and more organized around a generally empirical and factual—what for now we might call "scientific"—attitude.

This has important implications for dealing with schools as institutions and for curriculum work for at least two reasons.

1. Educators are even more deeply enamored of "scientific" procedures than the public at large. Arguments against what happens in schools are expected to be couched in scientific language. When they are not so couched, they can be ignored, since "objective" facts and data are lacking and one is arguing "merely" subjectively. The reaction by established schoolmen to these arguments when the disputations are not ignored will be rather strong since the questioners are not only challenging the concrete activity of schooling but also the fundamental valuative underpinning—that is, the "objective scientific outlook" itself—which provides the orientation on which the bulk of the huge institutional edifice rests.

2. As was mentioned, there has been an extraordinarily long history in education of borrowing the reconstructed logic and language of science while neglecting the aspects of science that make it science rather than technique. In plain terms, we have borrowed the technology of science and have consistently ignored the constitutive aspects of scientific rationality that keep it human. This is quite important. The form of science that educators have appropriated is one that gives intellectual legitimacy to the way we have thought about schooling since at least the early part of this century—that is, the model of school as factory, with the child treated metaphorically and quite often literally as an industrial product.[14] It may very well be that the manipulative ethos that surrounds many of the things curriculists are involved in (behavioral objectives is a primary example) will not be significantly altered until the basic perspectives we employ are brought to a level of awareness and challenged.

For instance, educators have adopted a view of science that regularly disregards the close relationship between science and art, between, for example, the remarkably similar symbolic experimentation of the poet and the theoretical physicist.[15] The senses of ambiguity and subtlety, of play and aesthetic awareness common to both are missing. What is found instead is a continuing quest for absolute surety and a gross operationalism that even the founder of operationalism would no doubt find a bit too conceptually simple.[16] Scientists have not necessarily proceeded through the objectively rigorous stating of operational goals. Rather, they often dwell in ambiguity and uncertainty; then clarity and a conceptual gestalt are apt to emerge. But it cannot emerge if the search for immediate operational goals and specifications—as in our own use of a naive and deterministic behaviorism in behavioral objectives—is pushed at the outset. Yet educators are apt to continue being unconsciously repressive if they are not aware of this.

This is not totally the fault of the educators though. There are constitutive aspects *within* the strict sciences that tend toward these manipulative qualities. However, it must be stressed that there are other characteristics of science—such as the tacit modes of knowing Polanyi points to[17]—which tend to mitigate against their becoming dominant. Unfortunately, as has been pointed out, in our quest for surety we have borrowed only a naive reductionism, thereby leaving these other qualities behind.

The aspects of science that we do look to are the center of a large portion of our difficulty in envisioning less repressive educational activities and institutions. And it is here that Habermas's examination of the dominant social and intellectual interests in varying forms of science is very perceptive.

Forms of Science and Their Interests

Habermas's taxonomic analysis of the logical structure of what he identifies as the three basic forms of science is quite informative. He differentiates those types of scientific activity according to their underlying structures of *interest*. That is, the three types of science are not neutral, as we usually suppose. Each presupposes a distinct "cognitive" orientation to the world and aims at different goals, and each pictures the world in its own unique fashion because of this fundamental interest. Habermas distinguishes between *strict science, hermeneutic science,* and *critical science.*[18] Let us examine these ideal types a bit more closely.

1. Strict Science. The practice of this form yields information that is based on and presupposes the interests of certainty and technical control. Examples would be physics and the social sciences that model themselves after it, such as the behavioral psychology on which curriculum work has often patterned itself so completely.

2. Hermeneutic Science. These are historical-interpretive modes of scientific activity that yield, not "information" in the sense implied in the strict sciences, but an understanding of the "social

cultural life-world." The practice presupposes an underlying interest in extending intersubjective understanding rather than control. Here we find the sciences with a "verstehen" orientation such as phenomenological psychology and ethnomethodology and symbolic interactionism in sociology.

3. Critical Science. This is more difficult to specify because it is in the process of being created now. In fact, Habermas's analysis is an excellent example of this form of action. It is an activity that seeks to illuminate the supposed and actual "necessity" of the historical modes of authority extant in industrialized and overly rationalized societies. Based on a humanized and reconstructed Marxism and also rooted in a rigorous form of the sociology of knowledge and phenomenological philosophy, critical science has as its fundamental interest the *emancipation* of individuals from lawlike rules and patterns of action in "nature" and history so that they can reflect and act on the dialectical process of creating and recreating themselves and their institutions.

If it is correct that the logics and assumptions that educators continually base their outlooks, research, and educational designs on are those of the strict sciences, then they are nearly "compelled," essentially by merely following out the logical progression of the form of thought they use, to have their primary interest in bringing human activity under technical and rational control, and to build and support institutions which seek to guarantee certainty in this regard. Hence, they often have little choice but to be oppressive. What does this imply for the future of self-reflective educational praxis?

Implications

If Habermas is accurate in his analysis, as I believe he is, then it may be essential that we—curriculists and other educators—devote a major portion of our efforts to developing a "critical science," one that will have an emancipatory interest and will persistently raise questions concerning the dominant demands in education and in other institutions for bringing all aspects of behavior under purposive-rational rubrics of technical control so that certainty will be enhanced. We must, then, look to other modes of analysis that will act as counterbalance to the perspectives usually employed in our work. The intellectual labors of the critically oriented social theorists of the Frankfurt School, of which Habermas is a part, can provide a beginning. It will mean, however, that we will have to overcome our unwarranted aversion to employing categories and forms of thought that have their historical roots in Marx and the Marxist intellectual tradition. This is a difficult task, at best. It requires a painful process of radically examining our current positions and asking pointed questions about the relationship that exists between these positions and the social structure from which they arise. It also necessitates a serious and in-depth search for alternatives to these almost unconscious lenses we employ and an ability to cope with an ambiguous situation for which answers can now be only dimly seen and will not be easy to come by. In fact, two major problems in education historically have been our inability to deal with ambiguity, to see it as a positive characteristic, and our continual pursuit of naive and simplistic answers to complex human dilemmas. The critical analysis of forms of scientific interest by Habermas further seems to imply that we must *consciously* bracket (that is, put out of operation as much as is possible) our basic ways of confronting educational problems. In this we need to act like the phenomenologist who seeks to cast aside his previous perceptions of familiar objects and attempts to constitute them anew,[19] to recreate and renew the basic aspects of an object without the limiting conceptual dominance of a previously accepted commonsense or scientific orientation.

This problem of rebuilding basic perceptions can be clarified further in looking at the field of ethnomethodology, a branch of sociology that has been profoundly influenced by phenomenology. The distinction made by ethnomethodologists between *constitutive* or *basic rules* and *preference rules*[20] is illuminating in discussing the points I have been making about the interest structure and our use of the "strict sciences." Constitutive rules are like the rules of a game; they provide basic ways of defining situations. Preference rules denote choices within this basic framework. Take courtship, for example. There are constitutive rules that define something as courtship in some parts of our society and distinguish it from other social activities, such as other forms of "stalking," if you will. Within courtship, however, there are a number of choices a courter has. He can bring flowers or candy (or perhaps pizza) and so on. These are often conscious options. Normally we do not even focus on the broader constitutive rules, though this is changing today given the important process of consciousness raising among women (and, of course, men). In fact, it usually takes a crisis of some sort to bring these basic rules to a level of consciousness. This is rather important, for it should be clear that a crisis *has* arisen in education, one which raises significant questions about the very base on which schoolmen operate. For example, the student revolt against aspects of schooling is often not so much a complaint against specific content as it is an expression of alienation from the imposition of obligatory meaning structures. The students are often challenging constitutive rules, not preferences within them.

It is possible to see that in many respects the dominant search for and "cognitive" interest in technical control and certainty acts as a constitutive framework—what elsewhere has been called a "technocratic ideology"[21]—for a large portion of educators' decisions. Within this framework of rules of meaning and within this unquestioned definition of their situations, choices can be made but usually only insofar as they conform to the basic rules that were imposed at the outset. Yet this conforms to but one set of possible constitutive interests.

We constitute our forms of knowledge and build our institutions and the activity within them on three distinct and specific interests. These fundamental interests serve to orient us in three ways: toward rationalization and technical control, toward mutual understanding in the conduct of life, and toward emancipation from seemingly "natural" constraint.[22] Each of these can serve as a possible model for comprehending and changing educational structures. The interest in understanding based on hermeneutic sciences may be helpful, but ultimately it does little to change the institutional and societal framework for educational practice, which exercises a decisive influence on the processing of our theories and data.[23] It is the last, the emancipatory interests of a critical science, that may hold the greatest promise.

Thus, the search for a process of schooling that is less economically, racially, and personally oppressive requires a concomitant effort to bring to the surface our basic rules and interests so that they may be reconstructed. It may very well be the case that the constitutive elements of the strict sciences must be subsumed under those sciences with an emancipatory image. The radical reconstruction of our modes of education can go only so far as our informed imagination and social and political sophistication will take us. To borrow an insight from Wittgenstein, the language game of the strict sciences is but one language among many. It is one form of life among others.[24] Our schools are places where humans confront each other and dwell in the complex situation of being human with others. If we legitimate our own actions as educators based on only one form of life and one primary interest, are we enabling this complexity to emerge or are we merely flattening reality?

It should be made clear here that this is not "just" a question of structured versus unstructured schooling. Not only do these terms lead to an increasing oversimplification of education, but they ignore the very real fact that the choice of "nonstructure" is as much a form of influence as other choices. Rather, the crucial point to be made is that beneath our usual patterns of decision making about educational institutions there are perspectives that may commit us to certain ways of confronting other human beings—in this case, students—that tend to ignore basic ethical issues about the proper modes by which one human being may seek to influence another or do not enable us to grapple significantly with the political and economic reasons that our educational institutions are often repressive.

This leads us into a topic I have purposely not dealt with till now, a subject that may be the most critical issue once the necessary dialectic of self-reflection has begun. One political insight is potent: that is, the interests I have discussed that are embodied in our dominant forms of social and educational thought may be related to the dominant political and economic institutions that serve as a substructure for advanced industrialized societies.[25] To raise radical questions about one may mean raising equally radical questions about the other. I ask you to ponder this last point a while.

Notes

1. Thomas F. Green, "Teaching, Acting, Behaving," in *Philosophy and Education*, ed. Israel Scheffler (Boston: Allyn & Bacon, 1966), p. 135.
2. Stuart Hampshire, *Thought and Action* (New York: Viking Press, 1959), p. 207.
3. Ibid., pp. 267-68.
4. Jurgen Habermas, *Knowledge and Human Interests* (Boston: Beacon Press, 1971), p. vii.
5. Cf. Jurgen Habermas, "Toward a Theory of Communicative Competence," in *Recent Sociology*, no. 2, ed. Hans Peter Drietzel (New York: Macmillan, 1970), pp. 115-48.
6. Jacques Ellul, *The Technological Society* (New York: Vintage, 1964); Herbert Marcuse, *One Dimensional Man* (Boston: Beacon Press, 1964).
7. Dwayne Huebner, "Curricular Language and Classroom Meaning," in *Language and Meaning*, ed. James B. Macdonald and Robert R. Leeper (Washington, D.C.: 1966).
8. Herbert M. Kliebard, "Bureaucracy and Curriculum Theory," in *Freedom, Bureaucracy, and Schooling*, ed. Vernon Haubrich (Washington, D.C.: ASCD, 1971).
9. Bela H. Banathy, *Instructional Systems* (Palo Alto, Calif.: Fearon, 1968), p. 22.

10. This separation itself is both psychologically and philosophically naive. See Hampshire, *Thought and Action*, and Maurice Merleau-Ponty, *The Phenomenology of Perception* (London: Routledge & Kegan Paul, 1962).
11. Some of the more provocative examples of arguments against patterning the social sciences after the physical sciences can be found in the work of the late Alfred Schutz. See, for example, his section "On the Methodology of the Social Sciences," in *Collected Papers I: The Problem of Social Reality* (The Hague: Martinus Nijhoff: 1967), pp. 3-96. See also Floyd W. Matson, *The Broken Image* (New York: Doubleday, 1964).
12. Cf. Banathy, *Instructional Systems*.
13. Thomas S. Kuhn, *The Structure of Scientific Revolutions* (Chicago: University of Chicago Press, 1970).
14. Kliebard, "Bureaucracy."
15. Jacob Bronowski, *The Identity of Man* (New York: Natural History Press, 1965), pp. 52-80.
16. P. W. Bridgman, *The Way Things Are* (New York: Viking Press, 1959).
17. In a paper of this nature it is difficult to argue extensively about the limited view of science on which we base a good deal of our work in education and curriculum design. The reader interested in pursuing this important question further can find insightful treatments of the logic-in-use of science in (especially) Michael Polanyi, *Personal Knowledge* (New York: Harper, Torchbooks, 1964), James Watson, *The Double Helix* (New York: Signet, 1968), Bridgman, *The Way Things Are*, and Kuhn, *Structure of Scientific Revolutions*.
18. Much of the following draws on the lucid presentation of the main thrusts of Habermas's position in Trent Schroyer, "Toward a Critical Theory for **Advanced Industrial Society**," in *Recent Sociology*, no. 2, ed. Hans Peter Dreitzel (New York: Macmillan, 1970), pp. 210-34.
19. Cf. Gaston Bachelard, *The Poetics of Space* (New York: Orion Press, 1964), p. xxviii.
20. Helen M. McClure and George Fischer, "Ideology and Opinion Making: General Problems of Analysis," mimeographed (New York: Bureau of Applied Social Research, Columbia University, July 1969).
21. Schroyer, "Toward a Critical Theory," p. 210.
22. Habermas, *Knowledge*, p. 311.
23. Schroyer, "Toward a Critical Theory," p. 211.
24. Albrecht Wellmer, *Critical Theory of Society* (New York: Herder & Herder, 1971), p. 27.
25. Ibid.

John Steven Mann

At sixteen, I decided to become a teacher. I went to a progressive school that had some of those terrific teachers who combine competence, kindness, and social vision, and I wanted to do that.

At sixteen, also, far away from school, I was given my first training in Marxism—both theoretical and practical work. I have known since then that the content of Marxism, the analysis of classes and the class struggle, was an absolutely necessary tool for any person with serious social commitment. I also learned that Marxism entailed a theory of knowledge that asserted the unity of theory and practice in a manner that was more powerful and more incisive than what my progressive teachers had mastered.

In the twenty-two years since that time I have been struggling to unite the content of these two early experiences and make a profession of this unity. I was clumsy at this. And going to college and beginning to teach in the wake of "McCarthyism," I found little help. In my eight postdoctoral years as a "professor" I have kept on sneaking up on the problem, both in my teaching and in my writing. But it has only been in the days since the era of "campus unrest" that, with the growth of a serious new working-class-based Marxist movement, I have begun to deal with the fact I had long known: that my liberal visionary progressive teachers and my Marxist revolutionary teachers taught me things that in basic ways are contradictory to each other.

The most basic contradiction is this. The progressive teachers taught me that liberal educators like themselves can lead in the building of a new social order through profound understanding and mastery of "our democratic system." The Marxists taught me that only the working class guided by a revolutionary party can end exploitation, through class struggle.

Almost all the contemporary "radical" educators of this decade
share the faith of my progressive teachers. But they are wrong.
The only way a teacher can work against exploitation and
oppression is to attack the root cause of it, which is capitalism.
And the only way teachers can attack capitalism is to apply Marxist
analysis to their own immediate democratic struggles—to put their
own struggles for justice for themselves and the children they teach
into the context of the broader class struggle.

The papers of mine that have been selected for inclusion in this
book don't reflect what I've just said; they reflect a process of
struggling to bring together two things which I'm finally able to
acknowledge don't go together. In my own mind, the process has
led to a clear-cut choice: either abandon the notion that curriculum
work can have progressive social significance, or unequivocally
embrace the Marxist analysis, with all it entails about class struggle,
and apply it to the work of curriculum. I've chosen the latter course,
and tried to write to the point in papers that don't appear in this
volume. The best I can hope for from the papers in this book is that
the reader will see the contradictions I didn't face between liberal
and revolutionary analysis and practice.

John S. Mann
University of New Mexico

9

Curriculum Criticism

The mind is like a bat. Precisely. Save
That in the very happiest intellection
A graceful error may correct the cave.
in *Mind* by Richard Wilbur

This paper takes as its premise the assertion that the language we use to talk about educational situations is inadequate. I share with many people the view most cogently and most insistently developed by Dwayne Huebner that our current mode of discourse is an instrumental language structured around assumed means-ends, cause-effect relations, and is thus convenient primarily for regarding a curriculum in its technological aspect.[1] Just as most educators would agree that this is an important aspect, so too I am sure they would agree that it is not the *only* important aspect. In this paper I want to look at a different way of talking about curricula—a way that combines elements of aesthetics and science. I shall call it curriculum criticism.[2] When I talk about what one might consider curriculum to be, I shall be stressing the aesthetic elements. Specifically, I will ask what is involved in talking about curriculum as if it were a literary object. When I ask how one may proceed to talk about curriculum so regarded, certain elements of scientific thought enter in. It is surprising only at first glance to find how well scientific and aesthetic talk get along together.

Curriculum and Fiction

For the purposes of discovering what may be involved in talking about a curriculum as a literary object, I will use as an exemplum—to be guided but not bound by—Mark Schorer's lucid treatment of the story.[3] And the first point to note is that in his criticism Schorer focuses neither on the biography of the author nor on the effect of the work on the reader, but firmly on the literary object itself. The function of his critique is to disclose meanings in the object. It seeks to help the beholder come close to, or even touch or enter into, the object, to know its meanings well.

Schorer says, "Fiction is, or can be, an art, and art, if it is about anything, is about life. But exactly because it is about it, it is a different thing from it."[4] In fiction, a boy, let us say, who has a real name and "looks" like a real boy, runs around the corner in pursuit of a balloon. There may or may not "really" have been such a boy, and for fiction this is not important. What matters, for this paper, is that this particular boy in this particular circumstance was selected for representation from a universe of possibilities. This selection is fixed in a complex set of other choices, both about what to tell and about how to tell it. The selection made, considered against the infinite background of selections passed over, constitutes an assertion of meaning.

I would like to propose that a curriculum can be regarded in the same manner. Like fiction, a curriculum can have a story, a set of facts which on the surface purport to represent life. In a curriculum, a scientist precipitates a salt or notes the effect of X rays on a photographic plate. It matters here, more than in fiction, whether there "really" was such a scientist. But putting this fact aside for a while, it matters very much in a curriculum as well as in a story that this scientist was selected for representation from a universe of possibilities. And note that the scientist is not *presented* but *represented*. It is not a chunk of raw life a curriculum contains, but a film maker's or a text writer's representation of life or selections from life. And this particular selection, like that of the boy and the balloon, is fixed in a complex set of other choices about what to represent, how to represent it, and in what context to represent it. In both cases, the curriculum no less than the story, the network of selections constitutes an assertion of meaning—a symbolic commentary upon life.

Limit and Possibility

To regard a curriculum as a literary object, then, means first of all to think of it as a set of selections from a universe of possibilities. The statement embodies some complex conceptions which may best be approached through Goethe's succinct observation that "Art exists in limitation."[5] The point has been made by many others that raw life is formless, chaotic, and without meaning until man-the-artist creates meaning by bounding it. Thus the artist whose raw material is the undifferentiated totality of life, actual as well as imaginable, possible as well as fantastic, by choosing this rather than that instant to tell and this rather than that feature to leave unstated, creates a shape and a meaning for life. I read somewhere that Stephen Mallarmé stood in terror before the blank page; while it was blank it was infinite possibility, but to write a word upon it was to limit the possible meanings of the page. The blank page was, in a sense, his perfect poem. By the same token, however, the blank page is precisely nonart, for by selecting nothing it bounds nothing and affirms no meaning. To listen to a chaotic infinite universe and then to answer with form, finitely, is to order chaos and assert meaning. Such answering is the hallmark of man-the-artist: his answers are his works of art.

If you turn this proposition around and look at it from the other side, it discloses something important—the unconditionedness of the curriculum as art. His answers are his works of art but, in addition, his works of art answer to the conjunction of his human gift of seeking forms truthfully with his human habitation of chaos. This is the artist's commitment, and his work of art is art only in so far as it unconditionally fulfills this commitment. To whatever extent a work of art answers to something else—say the desire to sway or influence or even to teach—to that **extent does it** fall short of art-fullness. It is something-else-and-art; perhaps propoganda-and-art. And this explains why technological talk cannot comprehend a curriculum-as-art. For technological talk is precisely talk about conditions, conditioning, and the conditioned. It is talk locked in a means-end cause-effect structure which cannot be bent to describe curriculum as unconditioned immediacy.

One might well ask whether there is any such thing, really, as an "unconditioned" curriculum. Clearly there is not. Nor can it be said of any other work of art that "this is unconditioned." A work of art—a curriculum, story, painting, or song—is not art but a work of hands by man-the-artist. It aspires to art-fullness, to unconditionedness. The primary assertion of any work of art is the exuberance over partaking of unconditionedness—the discovery or creation or achievement of a piece of freedom. But it is a partaking of freedom and not a being free. Art is unconditioned, but the art-object, like man-the-artist, is both conditioned and unconditioned. Thus to regard an object-of-art, or a curriculum-as-art, as unconditioned is not to forget that it is also conditioned, but merely to look at it and talk about it in its art-fullness. And surely a curriculum, which cannot be art, can be artful in some degree, and can be considered not only in terms of how it conditions and is conditioned by man, but also in terms of how it answers man's listening and seeking.

The Forms of Meaning

As with literary critique, the function of the curricular critique is to disclose its meanings, to illuminate its answers. If meaning is expressed as unconditioned selection from a universe of possibilities, then the form of the meanings asserted is the design, or patterns of relatedness, of the selections. A single selected item is not meaningful by itself, but only in its relations to other items. As E. E. Cummings points out, nouns create no movement. It is, as he put it, the poet's "ineluctable preoccupation with the verb"[6] that gives him power. Or, as someone else once noted, only an unsubtle mind sees no difference between an elephant in the White House and an elephant in the zoo.

Meaning, then, abides in the design of selections. A later section of this paper will consider tools the critic might use to get at meaning through design. For the moment I would like to propose a very general formulation: the critic discloses meaning by explaining design. To explain something is to account for it, to point to something at a higher level of abstraction in terms of which the thing to be explained can be seen to "make sense." In just this sense, D. H. Lawrence's concern with the ramifications of sexual power "explains" the emphasis he gives to physical descriptions of the men and women in many of his stories. And in this same sense Boyle's Law "explains" the cork coming out of a heated bottle and Snell's Law "explains" the oar's foreshortening. To find an explanation, then, is to find what accounts for things being as they are. Yet there are differences between the kind of statement that accounts for the behavior of a gas and the kind that accounts for the behavior of a story or a curriculum-as-art, and these differences are instructive. The expansion of gas is not (save from an unorthodox theological point of view) chosen in the sense that intense and prolonged physical description is chosen in a Lawrence story. What is explained in the comment about Lawrence, it must be remembered, is a set of choices. And if the choices are to be regarded in their artfulness, they must be regarded as chosen not for an extrinsic purpose but simply for what they themselves mean. To say what they mean, therefore, is to account for their being chosen. Their meaning *is* their reason for being chosen. Thus to account for the choices in a work of art is precisely to discover what the choices mean. Explanation of the design of choices and disclosure of meaning are logically identical, a single thing come at from opposite sides. When the relations among selections that constitute the designs of a curriculum have been explained, the meanings of the curriculum have thereby been disclosed.

Since a single curriculum, like a single story, has many designs to be explained and thus many meanings to be disclosed, no single critique is exhaustive. The critic, therefore, must be selective.

Against Dichotomy

The problem of selection among styles may be approached by noting at a somewhat superficial level the argument over "objective" and "subjective" knowing and the common tendency to associate the former with science and the latter with art. Long before the point was formalized in "creativity research" literature, artists and scientists alike recognized that the objective-science, subjective-art scheme was inadequate if not wrong. The various selections in Gheselin's collection of essays on the creative process,[7] for example, almost without exception call attention more to the similarities than to the differences between artistic and scientific work. Albert Einstein asserted that at the heart of theoretical physics was the free play of the imagination,[8] just as convincingly as the classical and classically inclined poets have asserted that the foundation of art is the objective imitation of nature.[9] More thorough and sophisticated treatments of the problem, such as Michael Polanyi's,[10] have shown that the dichotomy between objective and subjective, while possessing some logical validity, is not really a very adequate device for describing man's creative activities in science or in art.[11] Instead Polanyi suggests that science and art alike, both of which have aspects that are formal and rule-bound and independent therefore of individual perceptions, are nevertheless directed by an all-pervasive and dominant "personal" component. The "personal" component, however, while neither rule-bound nor convention-bound nor tied to formal logical operations, is not "subjective." The one necessary and sufficient constraint that separates it decisively from subjectivity is what Polanyi calls its "universal intent." The scientist's commitment, like the artist's, is to universality of statement; and this commitment assures, within the limits of human fallibility, that his intellectual freedom from other constraints is not self-serving. At every point of his inquiry, from the selection of problems to the drawing of conclusions, the scientist's work is a combination of formal rule-governed procedures and "heuristic leaps" beyond the constraints of such procedures. These leaps are what make science go into the unknown from the known; they are guided by the scientist's intuitively held "personal knowledge."

Personal Knowledge

The purpose of this parenthesis is to introduce an approach to the critic's problem of selecting from an inexhaustible realm of designs and meanings those he will study; and in introducing this approach, it seeks to forestall the objection that this first step or any other step of the critical technique proposed is merely "subjective" as compared to the "objective" accounts of curricula given by the more customary tools of research. Indeed, just as the paper has suggested that science and art are less dissimilar than is often assumed, it will now suggest that the "esthetically" oriented critique and the scientifically conceived research program are less different than may be imagined. In the first place, after all, the research project like the less customary forms of criticism[12] must begin with a decision about what to select for study. And what one selects in either case is a matter of what one's personal (not subjective) knowledge leads him to see as valuable and fruitful. The ground of these judgments is different in different cases, however. The personal knowledge that figures in the physicist's choice of a problem or a range or set of phenomena to study is knowledge about physical reality. The personal knowledge of the educational psychologist that figures in his selection is probably knowledge about psychological reality. The personal knowledge in which the curriculum critique is grounded is principally knowledge about ethical reality.[13]

This means that personally held and universally intended knowledge about good and evil or right and wrong stands as a valuable guide to the processes of the curriculum critique, including the initial process of selecting a focus of attention. In the absence of a thorough analysis of this proposition, it may be helpful to think of it as suggesting that one approaches the phenomena to be examined not with the wholly impossible "open mind of the scientist" but with a set of predispositions which are forms of designs that it would be of value to discover. The content of these models is knowledge of ethical reality and the form of the models is the form of that ethical knowledge. It is crucial to understand what this does *not* mean. It does not mean that the *content* of what one will disclose in a critique is fixed in advance by prior personal knowledge. It does mean that the dimensions in terms of which content will be sought are so fixed. The ethics-based models do not determine what meanings will be disclosed in a curriculum but they suggest the ethical dimensions which, if found in a design, will incline one to regard such a design as worth examining.

Returning, then, to the critic's problem of deciding which designs he will study, the following summary statement may be made. The critic's choices have their origin in his personal knowledge of ethical reality. The form and content of this knowledge serve together as a heuristic model; they direct the critic's attention to those designs which may be expected to have meaning within the context of his ethical knowledge.[14]

The grounding of the critique in personal ethical knowledge gives it a range of deployment that in principle is very broad compared to the range of research grounded in empirical methodology. Whether it can have the precision of the latter is another question, and whether it ought to is still another. The point I should like to make, however, is that a critique thus conceived, particularly when it can take the form of conversation among interested persons, presents the possibility of continuous discovery of new meanings in educational situations.

The Critic's Stock in Trade

To Einstein's assertion that the theoretical base of physics is founded not in experience in the laboratory but in the free play of the imagination, Toulmin adds a cautionary note. "We must not go too far," he argues. "This is not work for the untutored imagination. It may be an art, but it is one whose exercise requires stiff training. . . . Theoretical physicists have to be taught their trade and cannot afford to proceed by genius alone."[15] The same point has been made innumerable times about the artist. Without argument, and recognizing the apparent fact that untutored geniuses sometimes do accomplish great things, it seems likely that Toulmin's caution would be well taken by the curricular critic.

Thus we come to the problem of delineating the curriculum critic's trade. And the first question to be faced is whether he has one. What is there, for example, in the jargon of scope and sequence, learning experience and grade placement, objectives and articulation, that can serve as stock in the trade of discovering meaning? The answer I shall pursue here is that these and other concepts can be a part, but not all, of the critic's stock in trade provided they first undergo a transformation in logical status. The nature of the transformation may be demonstrated through a few important examples. As one might gather from earlier remarks, the basic direction of the transformation is from a technological to an esthetic mode; from a framework in which the curriculum is input in a production system to one in which it is regarded as an environing work of art that conveys meaning.

The term *learning* is a suitable first example. It is given a variety of uses, but most of them have certain properties in common. Thus it is almost always used in reference to a process that has knowledge of some kind as an end and a purpose. Almost always, too, the process is regarded as a means to be controlled in order to achieve a given end. Thus the term directs attention to aspects of schooling construed as "learning situations," and its subsumed concepts serve heuristically in the pursuit of data bearing upon the technological progress (progress by controlled means toward prespecified criterion ends) of "learners."

As data for the critic, however, the emphasis is not upon the phenomena subsumed by the concept "learning" but upon the role in the school of the concept itself. The critic's task is not the same as that of the curriculum developer's. His work, for example, does not involve calculating what arrangement of curriculum variables will, according to a given learning theory, bring about certain learning results. Rather he is interested in the fact that a given learning theory making certain assumptions is employed by teachers as a criterion for their behavior. And he is interested, to carry the example further, in the limiting conditions under which learning theory as a criterion is discarded in favor of other criteria. He may be interested in the extent to which an aspect of school activity can be said to be entailed by a conception of learning, and the relations between such activity and other activity that may be entailed by other conceptions. Or he may be interested in the different language uses of the concepts of learning theory, focusing upon its use for legitimation, explanation, prediction, or control.[16] The critic, in short, uses learning theory not to explain or control learning, but to explain patterns of events that may be regarded as resulting from convictions about learning theory. Or, to restate this in terms more nearly parallel to the discussion in section III, certain designs or patterns of choice in a school situation may be explained by regarding them as entailing assumptions and principles of a given theory of learning. Or, to state it still another way, the critic may express the meaning, say, of certain patterns of teacher behavior in terms of the premises about human nature required to explain those patterns.[17]

A second, related, example involves "knowing." The school practitioner seeks answers to such questions as what is known and what should be known. These questions concern the critic not because he seeks answers to them but because the fact that they are asked, as well as the processes the practitioner employs in seeking answers to them and the character of answers accepted, all constitute data for him. These fall into designs which it is the critic's task to analyze. Thus he will seek, for example, to discover what ideas about (1) the nature of knowledge, (2) the processes by which knowledge is acquired, (3) the values associated with knowledge, and (4) the status of knowledge in relation to other intellectual attributes, are entailed in the designs he observes. For instance, whereas the science teacher may be interested in discovering whether a pupil knows Boyle's Law or in how to get a pupil to know it, the critic is interested in discovering what meanings of "knowledge" may account for both the teacher's analysis of the problem and his teaching behavior with respect to the problem. The critic may discover, for example, that teachers vary considerably from each other and from established epistemologies in their understanding of the meaning of the scientific assertion that something is known. They vary, that is, in their understanding of the logical status of something regarded as known. And these observations in turn may account for or explain similarities and contrasts between different science instruction situations.

The point of these examples is to demonstrate the kind of transformation required to turn the material of the practitioner into material for the critic. Whereas the practitioner employs his material in the context of discovering means and ends, the critic may employ the same material as data for his analysis of the designs of educational events. Where the practitioner seeks solutions to problems, the critic seeks meaning in the manner in which problems are posed and solved. Where the practitioner may customarily evaluate his practices by examining their consequences, the critic construes practice as falling in designs that may be accounted for as expressions of meaning.

Choice and Transformation

This transformation is applicable to the bulk of the practitioner's stock. "Scope," "sequence," and "continuity" may be readily transformed from techniques employed to achieve certain ends to patterns of choice expressing beliefs about the function of schools, the nature of knowledge, or the ethical relation between teacher and student. Likewise, where the practitioner attempts to be rational about the selection of "objectives," the critic seeks to discover meaning in the fact that the need for statements of objectives is often a controlling feature in the emergence of designs in school phenomena.

The conclusion to be drawn here is that the critic's stock in trade includes knowledge of the practitioner's, as well as the ability to transform it into appropriate data for his task. But these constitute only the simpler part of the critic's stock. Even transformed in the manner described here, the familiar language of the schools is insufficient for the critic's task. And so too is the erroneous understanding of the relation between explanation and data which is sometimes associated with this language. Toulmin's examination of the explanatory statements of physics elucidates this point, and in so doing shows the way toward the more complex aspects of the critic's trade. He writes: "It is not that our theoretical statements ought to be entailed by the data, but fail to be, and so assert things the data do not warrant: they neither could nor need to be entailed by them, being neither generalizations from them nor other logical constructs out of them, but rather principles in accordance with which we can make inferences about phenomena."[18] Then again he asserts that: "There can be no question of (a given physical principle) being deductively related to these data, nor any point in looking for, or bewailing the absence of such a connection. The transition from the everyday to the physicist's view ... involves not so much the deduction of new corollaries or the discovery of new facts as the adoption of a new approach."[19]

The explanatory statements of the critic, like those of the physicist, are not formally derived by deduction or any other logical process from the data themselves, but rather are the result of adopting a "new approach." And by "new approach," Toulmin makes it clear that he means new techniques for representing phenomena. Thus he shows that the enormous explanatory power of geometric optics is a result of the discovery that light could be represented as traveling in straight lines from a source to an illuminated object. And this discovery, which was initially used to explain not new data but data that had been puzzled over literally for centuries, clearly was not produced by the performance of operations upon the data.

So too, critical discovery requires proper and inventive techniques for representing phenomena. This concept of representing, however, has difficulties.

In what sense, for example, does a straight line in the models of geometric optics "represent" a light "ray"? Is it in the same sense that an equation "represents" the motion of a particle, or in the same sense that "child-centered" "represents" a particular type of classroom or a given score "represents" achievement? What about Rutherford's billiard ball atom, and what about Wordsworth's description of woods near Tintern Abbey or E. E. Cummings' statement that "spring is a perhaps hand (which comes carefully out of Nowhere)"?

It is beyond this paper to examine these various instances of representation and to answer questions about them. An assumption is that fruitful representation in science as in art conforms more or less to the characteristics which Ramsey ascribes to what he conveniently calls "disclosure models," in contrast to the characteristics he ascribes to "picturing models."[20]

Disclosure Models

To be very brief about a complex distinction, a picturing model is one thought of as being as much like the phenomena as possible. The disclosure model is thought of only as bearing certain key structural similarities to the phenomena. The picturing model is thought of as derived from detailed observation of phenomena, much as the artist bases a portrait on careful study of a face. The disclosure model is studied for its own intrinsic qualities and this study gives rise to propositions, originally about the model, which are then superimposed upon phenomena and tested for goodness of fit. When the fit is good, then the model has potential for disclosure. Where the picturing model is judged for its static accuracy, the disclosure model is judged for its capacity to continue generating new propositions that reveal the phenomena. Thus disclosure models lead without end to the unfolding of a world. Where the picturing model closes the world, the disclosure model discloses, opens, the world. The building of disclosure models as new modes of representation, then is to be part of the critic's trade.

Of the many unanswered problems about the use of disclosure models in criticism, three in particular require attention. The first problem concerns the source of disclosure models. If they are not constructed out of observed curriculum events, what are they constructed out of? The second problem concerns the content of the models, and the third concerns the relationship between models and data. If models are not built out of data, are they then data-free?

The answers I will propose to all of these are related to points discussed earlier in the paper. It will be useful first of all, then, to recall the approach taken to the problem of choosing designs to study. It was suggested that what a critic finds worth attending to depends upon "highly abstract models" grounded in "personal knowledge of ethical reality." In the light of the subsequent discussion it should be clear that this earlier problem was a subproblem in the one now being considered, and that the "highly abstract models" of that section are the "disclosure models" of this. Here, as there, the problem originates in the observation that the data themselves do not logically entail the constructs we place upon them. And here, as there, the models are to be regarded as grounded and entailed in personal knowledge of ethical reality. That is to say that the models employed to disclose meanings in phenomena are not the result of operations upon data, but are rather the result of extensions, transformations, and deployments of intuitively held personal knowledge.

The relation of such models to data is very simple, and should allay fears that the sort of criticism being described here is "data-free." For if the function of the models is to disclose meaning in the world (and data are selected representatives of the world), then a model is useful if it does disclose meaning and useless if it does not. The Greek model of light as an antenna from the eye did not reveal or explain light phenomena; the modern model of light as "rays traveling in straight lines" does. The point is that disclosure models originating in "personal knowledge" must reveal a world and in so doing explain it, or be modified to do so, or abandoned. In observation of phenomena, then, lie the object and the proof of the model but not its source.

Finally, something must be said about the content of the curriculum critic's disclosure models. The key to this problem lies in the so far unexplained assertion that the curriculum critic's relevant personal knowledge is personal knowledge of *ethical* reality.

Ethical Reality

Curriculum, to select one of the most important views, is a form of influence over persons,[21] and disclosures of meanings in a curriculum are disclosures about the character of an influence. What one sees as important about the influence of a magnet on iron filings depends upon one's personal knowledge of magnets and filings and the structures used by physics to describe what is formally known about these. Thus it was said above that a physicist's heuristic leaps are grounded in his personal knowledge of physical reality. But what one sees as important about the influence of a curriculum over persons does not in the same sense depend upon one's personal knowledge of persons. It is a different sort of matter entirely. The curriculum critic, unlike the physicist, must regard himself as responsible to that influence, and must consider that influence from the perspective of his responsibility. This perspective certainly must be grounded in what the critic knows about right and wrong or good and bad—that is, what he knows about ethical reality—because only if it is so grounded can it, in fact, provide appropriate content for his models; that is, content that will enable him to answer his responsibility. His commitment is to disclosing those meanings that impinge upon his ethical knowledge, and he fulfills this commitment by deriving disclosure models from this knowledge.

The meanings the curriculum critic discloses, then, are meanings about which he believes ethical judgments are to be made. An appropriate final problem to be considered here, then, is whether or not his critique should include these judgments. The point could be argued well either way. If the judgments are included, there is a danger that the critic's commitment to disclosing may become a commitment to persuading, and his criticism become advocacy. Certainly this has characterized much of the curriculum literature of the past that has started out with the intent to be "theoretical."

The danger if the critic does not make ethical judgments of the meanings he has disclosed is that the judgments may never be made, or may be made improperly. Still, considering the extent to which curriculum literature is dominated by advocacy and the frequent failure of the most enlightened advocacy to bring about enlightened reform, this second danger seems small next to the first. My tentative conviction is that the critic would do well to write his critique in dimensions that to him are of ethical import, thereby giving tools to the practitioner, and allow the latter the freedom to employ the critique, or the many critiques, as he and his colleagues who design curricula see fit.

Toward a New Language

In this paper, I have tried to outline some assumptions and techniques which I believe would be helpful to people who want to talk about curriculum but who find the common forms of curriculum talk inadequate. I think that there have been two unorthodox propositions underlying all the arguments in this paper, and these I would now like to state. One proposition concerns technique. It states that the educator, in a laudable quest for a scientific approach to his problems, has allowed himself a somewhat naive view of what a scientific approach entails. In particular, he has succumbed to the myth of "objectivity" which suggests that his problems can be solved through the refinement and application of formal procedures of measurement, analysis, and interpretation, without any messy turning inward. I have proposed here that critical discoveries in education, as in the physical sciences, depend, along with good formal procedure, upon the critic's ability to draw upon knowledge that is uniquely his and is not part of any formal discipline, and to use that knowledge in a disciplined and imaginative way. While the phrase "turning inward" may be guilty, by association, of confusion, the sort of use suggested here of intuitively held unformalized knowledge is not messy, nor can formal knowledge progress unless it is considered. New understanding of what is involved in curriculum will come from those scholars who can make the heuristic leap from the data they must know well to the ethical roots of their concern.

The second proposition concerns an assumption some educators tend to make—the assumption that the measure of education is solely its products. That the product is a measure of education I cannot deny, but for two reasons the matter does not end there. The first reason is best expressed in terms of what I should like to call the premise of ethical continuity. This premise asserts that education is properly concerned with the ethical aspects of its product; that exceedingly little is known and is likely to be known (people being as complex as they are) about controlling this aspect of education's product; that the very best the educator can do, therefore, is to rely on the general tendency for good to produce good and pay very careful attention to the ethical qualities of the process of education.

Secondly, concern over the product of education seems somehow to obscure the fact that the world the educator creates through the curriculum is a world inhabited by actual children as well as by potential adults.

Why then are educators often so willing to judge educational institutions by the characteristics of their pupil-products, and so unwilling to judge or even note the qualities of the situation itself? The philosophical problem of rendering an ethical judgment of a future entity is at least as complex as the problem posed by a present entity. Is it possible that the educator's preoccupation with products involves an escape, by removal in time, from the responsibility to see and value education in ethical terms altogether? The world we create through the curriculum is a real present world, a lived-in world, and a meaning world. Ought not the educator to know and respond to its meanings?

My second proposition, then, is that curriculum is to be thought of not only as producing but also as meaning and as lived in. It is a mortal thing, and Gerard Manley Hopkins writes of mortal things:

> Each mortal thing does one thing and the same:
> Deals out that being indoors each one dwells;
> Selves—goes itself; *myself* it speaks and spells;
> Crying *What I do is me: for that I came.*[22]

Notes

1. See, for example, Professor Huebner's "Curriculum Language and Classroom Meaning," in *Language and Meaning*, ed. Macdonald and Leeper (Washington: ASCD, 1966).
2. Professor Dwayne Huebner has spoken about "critiquing" the curriculum; it is from his remarks that this idea developed. His thinking has helped me in this paper in ways that cannot be acknowledged by footnotes alone.
3. Mark Schorer, *The Story* (Englewood Cliffs, N.J.: Prentice-Hall, 1950).
4. Ibid., p. 3.
5. Cited by Schorer, ibid., p. 4.
6. Foreword to "IS 5," in E. E. Cummings, *Poems, 1923-1954* (New York: Harcourt, Brace, 1954).
7. Brewster Gheselin, ed., *The Creative Process* (Berkeley: University of California Press, 1952).
8. Albert Einstein, *Relativity*, trans. Robert W. Lawson (New York: Crown Publishers, 1961).
9. See Abrams' discussion of the transition from the classical to the romantic attitude in poetry, in M. H. Abrams, *The Mirror and the Lamp* (New York: W. W. Norton, 1958).
10. Michael Polanyi, *Personal Knowledge* (Chicago: University of Chicago Press, 1958).
11. Writing from a psychoanalytic point of view, Lawrence Kubie arrives at a very similar conclusion. He too sees the creative process as ubiquitous in its general characteristics; creative work in science and art is subtended by the

same psychological operations. See Lawrence S. Kubie, *Neurotic Distortion of the Creative Process* (New York: Noonday Press, 1961).

12. Huebner has (quite correctly I think) referred to research as "a vehicle of empirical criticism." Dwayne Huebner, "The Tasks of the Curricular Theorist," mimeographed.

13. The reason for "ethical" reality is developed in the next section. Briefly, it has to do with the fact that curriculum is an environment for persons (Dewey, Macdonald), and the curriculum critic is responsible to these persons.

14. More will be said to this point in the next section.

15. Stephen Toulmin, *The Philosophy of Science: An Introduction* (New York: Harper & Row, 1960).

16. The different purposes served by school talk are analyzed by Dwayne Huebner in "The Tasks of the Curricular Theorist," mimeographed.

17. This should not be taken to imply that the teachers "intend" these meanings. The question of intent is complicated, and beyond the scope of this paper. For arguments on the question in the context of literary criticism, see the following: Rene Welleck and Austin Warren, *Theory of Literature* (New York: Harcourt, Brace & World, 1963); William K. Wimsatt, "The Intentional Fallacy," in *The Verbal Icon* (Lexington: University of Kentucky Press, 1967), pp. 3-21.

18. Toulmin, *Philosophy of Science*, p. 42.

19. Ibid., p. 64.

20. Ian Ramsey, *Models and Mystery* (London: Oxford University Press, 1964).

21. "Influence" need not be understood technologically, that is, as a means to an end. Rather it is to be taken here in the sense of "under the influence of," to describe a present relationship. The example below in the text of a magnet and filings illustrates the usage intended.

22. Gerard Manley Hopkins, "As kingfishers catch fire . . ." in *Poems by Gerard Manley Hopkins* (New York: Oxford University Press, 1948).

10

A Discipline of Curriculum Theory

Both scholarly and professional interests would be served, I believe, by careful, self-conscious attention on the part of the curriculum theorist to the problem of the relations between his particular work and the work of other theorists, and between his work and the immanent discipline of curriculum theory. I say immanent because I believe that there is not yet a discipline of curriculum theory, but that most of the ingredients for one are present in solution, ready to be precipitated out under an appropriate catalyst. I would like this paper to suggest the form such a catalyst might take. It aims to do so by superimposing a structure upon diverse efforts in the field, thereby illuminating a set of possible relations among such efforts. The structure employed is borrowed from Joseph Schwab's well-known discussion of the basic structures of disciplines in general.[1]

Schwab contends that all disciplines manifest three kinds of structure. He calls these three kinds of structure "organizational," "substantive," and "syntactical."

Organizational Structure

In general the organizational structures of a discipline are the principles of its relation to other disciplines, or, looked at from a slightly different perspective, its position in a taxonomy of the disciplines which constitute man's organized knowledge. Of the several difficult problems related to the ordering of disciplines, the one that concerns us most directly here is the problem of defining borders and interactions between curriculum theory and other disciplines. Misunderstanding of borders and interactions impedes the orderly growth of a discipline as well as the legitimate incorporation into that discipline of insights from another. Let us consider an example. Freud's discovery that repression is instrumental in the formation of neuroses is obviously of interest to educators. But though a school and a psychiatrist may share an interest in mental health, it does not *necessarily* follow that a school should seek ways to incorporate psychiatric techniques, such as those used by the psychiatrist for digging up repressed material, into its regular curriculum. The relationship between psychiatry and schooling is complex, and proper use in the schools of the findings of psychiatry requires careful analysis of these complexities. In general, those people who have advocated the use of psychiatric knowledge in curriculum building have not made such analyses.[2] The same might be said of those who have advocated a sociological or economic solution to the problem of racial segregation in education. Careful attention to the relationship between education and the economics and sociology of racial prejudice would have revealed that the educational problem begins rather than ends with the physical presence of previously excluded ethnic groups.

Another example of an organizational problem has to do with the current wave of interest in the "structure of the disciplines." The problem of elucidating the structure of a discipline such as mathematics is not in itself an organizational problem for curriculum theory. The problem of elucidating the relation between such a structure and the practice of curriculum *is* a problem for curriculum theory. As in the above examples, the tendency has been to assume too simple a relationship, namely, that the discovery of the structure of mathematics in itself provides a solution to the problem of organizing the mathematics curriculum. While this *may* be the case, the analyses necessary to demonstrate that conclusion have not been undertaken by the advocates of the "structure of the disciplines" movement in curriculum. Bruner, Phenix,[3] and a few other scholars have suggested possible approaches to such analysis, but thorough work is still needed.

A final example of the organizational problem deals with several disciplines within the field of education itself. Considerable confusion exists over the relations between the several spheres of activity within a school system. While this confusion is an honest reflection of the enormous complexity of the interactions among these spheres, it is nevertheless damaging to the process of sorting out variables and systems of variables for study and analysis, which alone in turn can produce some systematic insight into the interactions. Thus, while in practice, for example, administration of a school system cannot occur by itself without continuous interaction with a sociopolitical system on the one hand and a teaching system on the other hand, for the purposes of study it is necessary to establish systematic boundaries to "administration," "school politics," and "teaching."

While numerous attempts have been made to delimit "curriculum," most of these efforts have not proven heuristic to the study of school phenomena because the approach taken has been semantic and definitional. A major exception to this is Macdonald's application of the principles of systems analysis to the "action spheres" of school phenomena.[4] Macdonald's identification of the system properties, boundaries, and spheres of interaction is a substantial contribution to the founding of an organizational structure for curriculum theory.

Substantive Structures

Substantive structures are sets of assumptions about the variables of interest to a discipline which control the questions asked and inquiries undertaken. There are many levels of substantive structure apparent in most disciplines. Some of them are so basic to a discipline's postulational structure that their removal or alteration would require a total revision of that structure. An instance would be the drastic alterations in geometry that result from altering assumptions about the properties of a plane.

At the other extreme are substantive structures of a highly transient nature. These are trial assumptions of all sorts, including the hypotheses that guide particular experiments and "working assumptions" employed frequently in narrative attempts at tentative explanation. Between the two extremes of the basic foundational structures of a discipline and tentative devices used in trial explanations lies the bulk of substantive structures—those that are of central concern here. These are sets of assumptions which have withstood to some extent the test of time and experiment and have achieved a degree of stability within a discipline. Typically, these structures are modified in minor ways from time to time but remain intact in basic character. The set of assumptions implicit in the basic stimulus-response (S-R) equation is such a substantive structure.

Clearly, the *S-R* idea has undergone modification over the years but remains, in essence, the basic notion that shapes the questions asked by experimental psychologists. Thus, for example, the *S-R* structure does not generate inquiry into the nature of unconscious experience. Conversely, the substantive structures of depth psychology do not generate inquiry into extinction rates under varying schedules.

Under certain conditions, substantive structures themselves become the focus of inquiry within a discipline. This happens when the explanatory power of these structures ceases to be sufficient to account for new data in the discipline. Thus, R. W. White's classic work on the "competence motive" is a response to data gathered through inquiry generated by the substantive structures of motivational psychology which can no longer be explained in terms of those structures. White finds that a new set of assumptions is needed which in part displaces and in part augments the earlier sets of assumptions.

The substantive structures employed in most curriculum work for the past thirty years have remained relatively stable. They are most clearly apparent in the well-known work of Ralph Tyler, especially in the four-step formula of stating objectives, selecting experiences, ordering the selection, and evaluating the results in terms of these objectives.[5] While the assumptions embodied in the "Tyler rationale," as it is commonly known, have contributed some orderliness to curriculum practice, they have not been especially fruitful in generating new areas of inquiry. In addition, there are a number of phenomena traditionally of concern to the planners of formal educational experience which this substantive structure does not seem capable of comprehending. Thus, there are presently a number of efforts to develop alternative or complementary substantive structures for curriculum theory. Eisner's excellent analysis of the uses of "objectives" is a step in this direction in that it calls attention to some of the limitations of the Tyler rationale.[6] A recent paper of mine examines an alternative to one aspect of the current substantive structure.[7] The general tenor of several recent Association for Supervision and Curriculum Development (ASCD) publications suggests an effort to develop new substantive structures. This is true especially in *New Insights and the Curriculum* and *Language and Meaning*.[8] In the latter publication, Dwayne Huebner's article entitled "Curricular Language and Classroom Meaning" is one of the most promising efforts to propose new substantive structures. Huebner proposes five different modes of regarding curriculum phenomena. While Huebner's paper is more suggestive than complete, it seems likely that the five modes could be developed into five distinct complementary substantive structures each with its own set of assumptions and each generating unique bodies of inquiry. The first mode, the "technological," is essentially a rationalization of the assumptions implicit in the Tyler approach. The second mode is called "political" and has as its key concepts "influence" and "power." It is no secret that influence and power play as important a role in the curriculum process as do educational objectives. The political mode of regarding curriculum phenomena would generate inquiry into this role.

The third mode, which Huebner calls "scientific," regards curriculum phenomena with respect to the way in which they generate new knowledge about the educational process. The fourth and fifth modes, the ethical and aesthetic, are at once the most intriguing and the most complex. I shall not discuss them here beyond saying that with careful work these modes could be developed into extremely productive substantive structures.

There are other efforts to reconceptualize the basic assumptions with which one approaches curriculum. One would include here some of the voluminous work in which efforts are made to examine curriculum from the point of view of Dewey's philosophy of education, as well as a great deal of work in which points of view developed in other philosophies of education and other disciplines altogether are brought to bear upon education. However, much of this work is imbedded in the structures of its present disciplines and is not articulated specifically with the intent of elucidating curriculum phenomena. As observed above in the discussion of organizational structures, the problem of "translation" of insights from one discipline to another is not as simple as it appears to be. A very ripe area awaits here for systematic work. One would assume that some such understanding went into the planning of such publications as ASCD's *New Insights and the Curriculum.*

The development of innovative substantive structures in curriculum is particularly desirable when viewed in the context of the past twenty years. In this period the Tyler approach, or "technological rationale," has been the dominant substantive structure in the field of curriculum. There is a very fortunate correspondence between this structure and the extensive technical apparatus that constitutes the dominant method of inquiry in the same period. This correspondence has facilitated the generation of an extensive body of knowledge about those aspects of education that are readily comprehended in terms of the technological rationale.

While one cannot but applaud this, one is also obliged to see an associated danger, namely, that we grow accustomed to thinking of that aspect of education we are beginning to understand as constituting the essence or even the whole of education, and fail therefore to pursue other areas in which our knowledge is embarrassingly scant. Put succinctly, we are on our way to thinking that sheer transmission of information and technique is *the* important part of education if not the whole of it. Since we are doing quite well at devising methods to accomplish this part, we tend to neglect the stickier, more frustrating, and less profitable sort of inquiry that might clarify for us such problems as the moral content of the transactions among fellow human beings in the classroom; the functioning of student's interests and aims (as these are defined by Dewey) in the classroom under various conditions; the various conceptions of the nature, function, source, and uses of knowledge that are implicitly conveyed to students through contrasting methods of transmitting knowledge; or the attitudes and feelings toward experience to which students are incidentally habituated during the course of the increasingly efficient instructional day.

Among the many reasons for this tendency (the "sputnik syndrome"), there are two that curriculum theorists might do something about. One is to develop alternative substantive structures, as Huebner and others have done. The second, without which the leads given by Huebner and others will not be followed, is to solve the problem of warranting assertions of a nontechnological sort. We have the apparatus for warranting technological assertions down pat. Given the enormous responsibilities educators feel, it is unlikely that they will venture too far with assumptions leading to assertions for which there exists no clear method of establishing warrantability. The problem of establishing warrantability for assertions brings us to the third of Schwab's structures, those he calls syntactical structures.

Syntactical Structures

Every discipline has some more or less stable system for gathering and evaluating data, posing and testing hypothetical assertions, and relating these assertions to broader generalizations and explanatory schemes. Such a system constitutes the syntactical structure of the discipline. These structures exhibit some very basic characteristics which are highly stable, such as goodness of fit between generalization and data, conformity of the inferential process to the general rules of logic, and the requirement to reduce internal contradictions by refinement of measurement or generalization or both. However, within this broad framework of stable structures, each discipline exhibits more specific syntactical structures which may be more or less stable at a given time in the growth of the discipline. The variability of these structures is related to a large number of factors in a complex way, which for the purposes of this paper need only be touched upon here.

One of the factors is the nature of the variables being investigated at a given time in a given group of studies. Thus, for example, a psychologist studying the effect of certain environmental conditions upon the manner in which unconscious symbol systems manifest themselves in conscious behavior uses a system differing markedly from that employed by a psychologist studying extinction rates under varying reward schedules. In the first case, the dependent variable is complex and not readily quantified or even observed. Variations in the behavior in question need to be established separately for each subject on the basis of extended observation and lengthy analysis. The analysis itself is guided by an elaborate system of inference. And, since the independent variables must be maintained in operation over long periods and replicated numerous times for each subject as well as across subjects, the problem of control is enormous. Given these considerations, it is appropriate that the syntactical structures in this sort of inquiry focus upon inferential procedures, elaborate descriptive apparatus, and criteria for validity of individual cases. This stands in sharp contrast to the syntax of the second case, which emphasizes through a probability model the reliability of an inferred relationship between dependent and independent variables across large numbers of subjects. It is true that there are many basic similarities between the two cases. The experimental psychologist needs to pay careful attention to the validity of his measurement of dependent variables just as surely as the depth psychologist ultimately has to confront the problem of the reliability of his inferences over large numbers. But given the present status of these two branches of psychology, it is clear that the syntactical structures most in need of focal attention differ and are specific to the kinds of problems under investigation. Further, I think it might fairly be said that the syntax of inquiry in experimental psychology is relatively stable at this point—most of its general features have been worked out in a way that seems adequate for handling the problems currently of interest. For depth psychology, by contrast, the syntax of inquiry is highly problematic and in a state of flux.

These two cases are special in that they represent two fields within a discipline or, as some would prefer to state it, two closely related disciplines. This observation points the way to two further comments about syntax. First, syntactical structures are closely related to substantive structures. It may be argued that behavioral and psychiatric efforts to explain phenomena differ not in realm of convenience of phenomena of concern so much as in the substantive structures—the guiding heuristic conceptions—with which the phenomena are approached. In a later section of this paper, the interdependence of substantive and syntactical structures will be discussed further.

The second comment is that in contrast to the difference in emphasis cited above, there may be much more basic differences in syntactical structure between more strikingly different fields or disciplines. Thus, the syntax of proof in mathematics differs in some quite essential ways from the syntax of proof in history.

In the field of curriculum theory, the syntactical problem is particularly acute. There are a number of reasons for this, but two stand out as especially worth mentioning:

1. Confusion exists between descriptive theory and "prescriptive theory." The syntax required to validate descriptive propositions is radically different from the syntax required to validate imperatives, "oughts," or prescriptive propositions. Yet the curriculum literature is noteworthy for an insidious and subtle blending of ises and oughts which make it difficult to come to grips with the problem of validation.

2. There is very little agreement as to the variables to be considered. Except for the area of "instruction"—that small part of the education process for which a "learning" paradigm is to some degree appropriate—curriculum scholars find it extraordinarily difficult to delimit the variables of concern. As was shown above, the nature of the variables in question is a determinant of the syntax to be employed. As long as each scholar bounds his variables uniquely, he must also choose, somewhat ad hoc, his own syntax. The stability of syntax resulting from interaction among scholars cannot come about until there is some degree of agreement about variables. Several efforts to delimit curriculum variables, both in terms of identifying sets within the field and boundaries of the field with other fields, have been made. In addition to work on boundaries cited in the section on "Organizational Structures" above, some important contributions have been made by Frymier, Faix, Johnson, Komisar and McClellen,[9] and others. These papers, while they bear

upon the problem of syntax in the manner just described, do not tackle this problem directly. To my knowledge there are no adequate direct efforts to delineate the syntactical structures of the discipline of curriculum theory. As is probably typical of the early development of a discipline, there is a fair amount of comment in passing and a fair amount of borrowing from other disciplines. However, the most common response to the syntax problem is to bypass it by directing inquiry at those variables for which there *is* a suitable syntax. The result is the tendency, discussed in the preceding section, to unduly focus attention on one set of problems to the exclusion of others. While it is not directly to the point, it is worth noting here a recent outstanding contribution to the syntax of inquiry pertaining to that particular set of problems. I refer to Travers' challenging comments on the required procedures for building an adequate theory of instruction. Also worthy of note here is Faix's work on structural-functional analysis.[10] There are implications here, in need of clarification and amplification, for the beginnings of a syntax for curriculum theory. But an orderly and systematic statement of syntactical principles to guide the process of acquiring knowledge about the broader range of curriculum phenomena has yet to be accomplished.

Correlation of the Structures

A discipline, I have asserted following Schwab, typically manifests three types of structure, each giving rise to specific types of problems for the discipline which are related to but separate from the process of acquiring knowledge about the variables with which the discipline deals. Taken together, these three structures might be considered to constitute the metatheoretical structure of the discipline. Considering the matter in this way, attention is directed to the relatedness of each structure to the other two. If the three are to cohere into a unified metatheoretical structure, they must compliment rather than contradict or simply bypass each other. That is to say, for example, that the syntactical structure employed must be appropriate for examination of the variables of interest to the substantive structures employed. Similarly, the organizational structure must define the boundaries of the field in a manner that is consistent with the realm of convenience assumed in the substantive structure employed. Such questions as the following need to be asked: What sort of syntax is appropriate to inquiry related to or built upon Huebner's identification of five modes of regarding curriculum events? Is Huebner's own syntax, which is drawn largely from philosophic discourse, the most appropriate way to continue with the work he has begun? Is there some point at which some sort of empirical methodology can be used to refine the models he suggests? Is it possible or desirable to try to identify specific behavioral variables related to each of the five modes? In what manner can insight achieved through the syntax of philosophical discourse best be brought to bear upon the procedures of designing educational programs?

Similar problems may be raised with respect to the more firmly established substantive structures implicit in the Tyler rationale.[11] Particularly (but not exclusively) because of the confusion between prescription and description in Tyler's position, it is difficult to know what sort of inquiry can be conducted in relation to it. And as one can see clearly in relation to Taba's[12] elaboration of the Tyler rationale, it is equally difficult to determine precisely what the relation is between curriculum theory and a host of other disciplines including history, political science, sociology, social work, etc. Thus, there is the need to work out relations between substantive and organizational as well as substantive and syntactical structures. A thorough treatment of any particular metatheoretical background for curriculum theory would require the integration of all three structures.

Curriculum Theory

Thus far, this paper has focused upon the metatheoretical foundation of curriculum theory. We turn now to the state of curriculum theory itself and to some suggestions for the further development of the field.

I believe it is well known that there are no comprehensive theories about curriculum phenomena. But even such rudiments of theory as a limited set of explanatory propositions about selected curriculum phenomena, or disciplined efforts to suggest an approach to conceptualizing the events to which a theory might pertain, are quite limited in number. There are a few truly theoretical propositions buried here and there in works designed for other purposes. Such propositions may be found, for example, in Saylor and Alexander, Inlow, King and Brownell, Beauchamp, Goodlad and Anderson,[13] and in various other curriculum texts.

Some of the work discussed above as contributing to the metatheoretical foundation of curriculum theory contains extensive descriptive apparatus coming as close to actual curriculum theory as anything written to date. Outstanding in this regard is Macdonald's systems analysis work.[14]

Beauchamp's text[15] has much to offer in the way of promising beginnings, especially with respect to his exploration of the problems involved in formulating a theory of curriculum. But his own attempt to formulate the foundations of a theory lapses into praxeology.

In a shorter work, Mauritz Johnson has contributed to the small body of truly theoretical propositions about curriculum.[16] Johnson's paper is noteworthy for several things. First, he has carefully examined much of the supposedly theoretical literature to demonstrate how it fails to be actually theoretical (his analysis parallels mine in some respects). Second, he has approached the problem of defining "curriculum" and certain curriculum phenomena specifically from the point of view of theory construction rather than from the more common point of view of curriculum troubleshooting.[17] Third, he has produced a logically ordered model ("schema" is his word) of the various parts of curriculum. The model is general and descriptive and thus potentially theoretical. A problem I see in his model is that it defines curriculum as the output of one system and the input into another system. It is not a system itself. It is an entity produced here and used there. Thus construed, it could not itself be theorized about. Rather its bounding systems would be the object of theory. Whether such theory would be curriculum theory is a possibly troublesome question.

Another noteworthy paper is Frymier's detailed discussion of elements and operations constituting the domain of curriculum.[18] His approach is theoretical rather then praxeological and with further development could constitute a major contribution.

Somewhat on the periphery of curriculum theory but nonetheless worth mentioning is a growing literature on the process of curriculum innovation. Some of these works, like Taba's,[19] are merely persuasive reports of comparatively successful techniques employed to bring about particular changes in particular schools. Other papers, especially those by Bhola and Guba,[20] while directed in part toward the solution of the particular problem of "speeding up innovation," still contain some useful theoretical propositions describing curriculum processes.

In considering the scarcity of actual curriculum theory, Johnson remarks that "the majority of educationists, educational practitioners, and scholars active in curriculum reform are oriented toward improvement rather than understanding."[21] While one might sympathize with the practitioner's need for solutions to particular problems, this sympathy should not lead the scholar into a misunderstanding of the nature and function of theory. Theory is explanatory, and explanation leads in many cases to control, or at least to prediction. In the long run, theory coupled with value commitment leads to a position about practice. But as Travers has pointed out, inquiry aimed at determining methods for maximizing a given effect is not likely to succeed very well in the absence of sound prior theory and is not likely to be an efficient approach to the development of the theory.[22] Conversely, inquiry designed in accordance with the requirements for the development of sound theory is not likely, in the short run, to yield answers to the practitioner's questions. Nevertheless, the practitioner, whose impatience with "pure theory" sometimes borders on blatant anti-intellectualism, should not overlook the likelihood that many of his most pressing difficulties are precisely the *result* of a shortsighted patchwork approach to past problems—an approach which, in the absence of sound general theory, tends to view as separate and isolated problems certain phenomena which in fact are intrinsic correlated characteristics of an entire system of phenomena. To use again an analogy I have used elsewhere,[23] the approach is not unlike that of a doctor who in prescribing a pill for a kidney ailment fails to determine whether the pill might destroy the liver while it cures the kidney. If the nature of theory and its relation to practice were better understood, the practitioner might regard the theorist with less suspicion, and the scholar who would be a theorist would perhaps feel less compelled to direct his "theorizing" toward the development of a "position." Thus, for example, in the absence of the compulsion to produce a "useful" document, the insight which initiated the "taxonomies" project[24] might instead have initiated a substantial contribution to curriculum theory.

There are a number of valid points of view as to how to proceed with curriculum theory construction. I think it would be generally conceded, however, that there are two aspects to the job—systematic speculation and systematic data gathering. One would agree with Travers that adequate theory cannot be "data-free." But one must also recognize that data collection which is not guided by shrewd systematic speculation about relations among phenomena is likely to result in dispersed rather than cohesive data. I would suggest that it may be fruitful to observe the following points in efforts to build curriculum theory. First, assumptions about syntactical, organizational, and substantive structures should be made explicit to whatever extent possible. Second, problems should be identified in relation to these structures rather than in relation to "practical" problems of schooling. Organizational structures will suggest boundaries to the phenomena to be studied. Syntactical structures rather than methodologies borrowed wholesale from other disciplines will suggest the approach to achieving warranted assertability. And substantive structures will generate models of interesting relationships among phenomena. It is at this stage, the generation of models, that speculation is appropriate. If one wanted to study team teaching, for example, it would be well first to consider from an organizational point of view whether this phenomenon is to be defined as an outcome variable of a curriculum process, an input variable in an instructional system, or as something else altogether. Then it would be appropriate to examine what sorts of evidence are appropriate for the study of the variable thus construed. Clearly, the appropriate evidence to study team teaching as the product of a system of social interactions is not the same as the appropriate evidence to study team teaching as a variable affecting achievement in a given subject. Finally, one's assumption about substantive structures will suggest patterns of relatedness among the phenomena, including team teaching, selected for study. Appropriate speculation would then be speculation as to the precise nature of these patterns of relatedness. To be productive, such speculation must take cognizance of the problems involved in refinement and validation. This does not mean that one should speculate only about phenomena for which methods of measurement and analysis already exist. It does mean that the speculations should be so cast that the problems of ultimate measurement and analysis are as simple as the intrinsic complexity of the conceptions will allow. Thus, for example, a good conception should not be sacrificed or reduced in importance for lack of immediately available operational definitions of variables. But the language used should be as precise as possible and as close to operationality as possible at the time without such sacrifice. Speculation should not be an excuse for sloppiness, but the need ultimately to measure should not be an excuse for avoiding exploration of some of the more complex components of educational experience.

If the gathering of data is intended to further the development of theory rather than to generate solutions to specific problems, the data must be interpreted accordingly. The main thrust of interpretation should be not toward application to school problems but toward refinement of models. The conclusion drawn from a study of team teaching should not be of the order of recommendations for practice but of the order of correcting speculations about the relations between team teaching and other variables of interest. In this context Travers' comments about the ultimate futility of "maximization" studies in the absence of sound prior theory is well taken. As observed above, curriculum studies often fail to contribute to theory because they are designed to produce prescriptions for maximizing certain allegedly desirable effects instead of being designed to produce understanding of relations among phenomena.

If this general approach to building curriculum theory were taken, the discipline would have a beginning. It is not clear how far this beginning would go, however. It seems likely to me, but by no means certain, that there exists a system of phenomena which it would be the unique business of curriculum theory to explain. Determination of this possibility can only occur on the basis of assuming it to be so and proceeding from there to test the assumption. One might discover that the "realm of convenience" of curriculum theory is composed of sets of phenomena most conveniently explained by further work in other disciplines. This seems to be the reasoning behind the current tendency toward hybrid disciplines such as "the sociology of education," the "politics of education," etc. My tentative conviction, however, is that there are interesting phenomena which are most conveniently construed as curriculum phenomena and which therefore can most conveniently be explained by curriculum theory. My conclusion is that there is not yet much in the way of curriculum theory, but that there can be and that, in the interest of acquiring knowledge of certain phenomena within the general field of education, there ought to be.

Summary

Schwab's analyses of the structures characteristic of any discipline seem useful in classifying and revealing relations among various efforts to lay the foundations for a discipline of curriculum theory. Further work on each of the three kinds of structures he identifies is needed, as is work on the problem of bringing together propositions about each type of structure into something approaching coherent metatheories for curriculum theory. This sort of work is essentially analytic, and like most analytic work requires a broad understanding of the phenomena involved and a strong and disciplined imagination.

With respect to curriculum theory itself—that is, highly general explanatory statements about relations among curriculum phenomena—there seems to be very little material. Most of what bears the name of "curriculum theory" is not theoretical at all but is more properly considered praxeological. Good praxeology of curriculum is extremely useful and important, but it is not the same thing as theory and does not accomplish what theory accomplishes. It enables people who cannot wait forever to make critical decisions in a reasonable manner. In the long run, however, theory rather than praxeology will produce understanding, and understanding, in addition to being intrinsically valuable, will probably result in decisions that better serve the interests of educational institutions. While there is no kind of inquiry that I would have the temerity to declare wrong (except for incompetent inquiry of any kind), it is important to note that inquiry which is intended to serve theory building rather than some other endeavor needs to be designed specifically for the purpose. This is as true for the "design" of speculation as it is for the design of data gathering, analysis, and interpretation.

It seems likely, but not certain, that there is a set of phenomena most conveniently explained through a discipline of curriculum theory. In a sense, this paper seeks to predict the discovery of such a set of phenomena in a manner vaguely similar to the way in which the periodic table predicted the discovery of the elements. The analogy has obviously limited validity. But my conviction is served by it—that a disciplined theoretical approach to curricular phenomena will lead to worthwhile discoveries.

Notes

1. Joseph Schwab, "Problems, Topics, and Issues," in *Education and the Structure of Knowledge*, ed. Stanley Elam (Chicago: Rand McNally, 1964).
2. See, for example, R. M. Jones, *An Application of Psychoanalysis to Education* (Springfield, Ill.: Charles C. Thomas, 1962).
3. Jerome S. Bruner, *The Process of Education* (Cambridge, Mass.: Harvard University Press, 1960); Philip H. Phenix, *Realms of Meaning* (New York: McGraw-Hill, 1964).
4. James B. Macdonald, "Researching Curriculum Output: The Use of a General Systems Theory To Identify Appropriate Curriculum Outputs and Research Hypotheses" (paper presented at American Educational Research Association meeting, February 1965).
5. Ralph Tyler, *Basic Principles of Curriculum and Instruction* (Chicago: University of Chicago Press, 1950).
6. Elliot Eisner, "Educational Objectives: Help or Hindrance?" *School Review* 75, no. 3 (Autumn 1967).
7. John S. Mann, "The Time-Premise in Two Approaches to Curriculum," mimeographed (Available from author, Spring 1967).

8. Alexander Frazier, ed., *New Insights and the Curriculum* (Washington, D.C.: ASCD, 1966); James B. Macdonald and Robert R. Leeper, eds., *Language and Meaning* (Washington, D.C.: ASCD, 1966).
9. Jack R. Frymier, "In Quest of Curriculum Theory," *Theory into Practice*, no. 6 (October 1967); Thomas L. Faix, "Structural-functional Analysis as a Conceptual System for Curriculum Theory and Research: A Theoretical Study" (Ph.D. thesis, University of Wisconsin, 1964); Mauritz Johnson, Jr., "Definitions and Models in Curriculum Theory," *Educational Theory* 17, no. 2 (April 1967); Paul Komisar and James McClellen, "Content Analysis of Curriculum Theory," mimeographed (available from the authors, Temple University); and "The Logic of Slogans," in *Language and Concepts in Education*, ed. B. Othanel Smith and Robert H. Ennis, (Chicago: Rand McNally, 1961).
10. Robert M. W. Travers, "Towards Taking the Fun Out of Building a Theory of Instruction," *Teachers College Record* 68 (October 1966); Faix, "Structural-functional Analysis."
11. Tyler, *Basic Principles*.
12. Hilda Taba, *Curriculum Development: Theory and Practice* (New York: Harcourt, Brace & World, 1962).
13. J. Galen Saylor and William M. Alexander, *Curriculum Planning for Modern Schools* (New York: Holt, Rinehart & Winston, 1966); Gail Inlow, *The Emergent in Curriculum* (New York: John Wiley & Sons, 1966); Arthur R. King, Jr., and John A. Brownell, *The Curriculum and the Discipline of Knowledge* (New York: John Wiley & Sons, 1966); George A. Beauchamp, *The Curriculum of the Elementary School* (Boston: Allyn & Bacon, 1966); John I. Goodlad and Robert H. Anderson, *The Non-graded Elementary School* (New York: Harcourt, Brace & World, 1963).
14. Macdonald, "Researching Curriculum."
15. George A. Beauchamp, *Curriculum Theory* (Wilmette, Ill.: Kagg Press, 1961).
16. Johnson, "Definitions and Models."
17. See my discussion in text for clarification of the importance of this point.
18. Frymier, "In Quest of Curriculum."
19. Hilda Taba, "One Model for Disseminating Curricular Innovations: Problems, Processes, and Possibilities," mimeographed (San Francisco State College, February 1967).
20. Harbans Singh Bhola, "The Configurational Theory of Innovation Diffusion," mimeographed (School of Education, Ohio State University, October 1965); Egon G. Guba, "Methodological Strategies for Educational Change" (a paper presented to the Conference on Strategies for Educational Change, Washington, D.C., November 1965).
21. Johnson, "Definitions and Models."
22. Travers "Towards Taking the Fun Out."
23. John S. Mann, "Functions of Curriculum Research," *Educational Leadership* 24, no. 1 (October 1966).
24. Benjamin S. Bloom, ed., *Taxonomy of Educational Objectives: The Classification of Educational Goals*, Handbook I, *Cognitive Domain*; and David R. Krathwohl et al., Handbook II, *Affective Domain* (New York: David McKay, 1956 and 1964).

John Steven Mann
Alex Molnar

Although since high school I have not seriously considered any life other than teaching, my initial motivation was my love of history and the opportunities teaching would afford me to immerse myself in its study. I never was much on names, dates, and places. To this day I want to make the Battle of Hastings 1144 instead of 1066, a lapse which returns to haunt me about once a year at parties. However, I did find it easy to get caught up in the sweep and power of human destiny as it moved across the centuries. So I became a high school social studies (that usually meant history) teacher, and for three years I taught and studied for my M.S. at night (in history—what else?). Those years of graduate study were important to me for at least two reasons: (1) I began to realize that historical inquiry and history itself was not a thing but a way of coming to know and that history, which I had always regarded as a subject, was, in essence, a convergence of method and content; and (2) I got enough involved in Chinese history to research and write a master's thesis entitled "Some Basic Philosophical Similarities Between the Thought of Mao Tse-Tung and the Classical Chinese Confucians."

My research left me with a much clearer understanding of Marxism-Leninism than I had previously (almost none) and a deep respect for the use of ideas in a people's struggle for liberation. In the Chinese Revolution, I saw the merging of method and substance in revolutionary practice. I began to understand thought and action as a unity, and as I think back, I now recognize that, for anything else it was, the Chinese Revolution was a radical pedagogy.

About the time I was finishing my master's thesis I accepted an experienced teacher fellowship in a program at Southern Illinois University-Edwardsville. The program director was Merrill Harmin, one of the coauthors of Values and Teaching *and a principal advocate of values clarification techniques in education. For a year I, along*

*with seventeen other fellows, was immersed in the study and practice
of what most would classify as humanistic education. I became
familiar with its assumptions and practiced in many of its techniques.
I must say I liked it. The experience was sufficiently profound that,
for the first time, I began to believe that the study of education could
be substantive and that pedagogy, as history, could compel my
interest.*

*After Southern Illinois, I went to the University of Wisconsin-
Milwaukee to work on my doctorate. That's where I met Jim
Macdonald who became my major professor. In Milwaukee my newfound interest in education became an interest in curriculum. Working with Jim, I learned a good deal, but I count those years significant, not for what I learned about curriculum as such, but for Jim's
help in understanding what William James meant by tough-minded
and what Whitehead was expressing when he declared that the essence
of education is that it be religious.*

*While I was working with Jim I got involved with ASCD and the
Radical Caucus. My contact with the caucus and my friendship with
Steve Mann, more than anything else, challenged the humanistic
orientation of my thought. Discussions, arguments, criticism, and
reflection helped me make connections between what I had read of
Mao, what I was learning with Jim, and my reality as an educator.
This process resulted in my rejection of the flabby humanism that
has become so characteristic in the dialogue and practice of many
educators. I still believe schools can be made better places for kids
than they are now and that the struggle to make them so is worthwhile: however, I also believe that the questions humanists ask about
education will not yield important answers, and the actions they
propose will not result in profound change.*

*"On Student Rights" is an experimental piece that, while funda-
mentally sound, is flawed in at least two aspects. First, like a good
deal of analysis referenced in Marxism-Leninism, it fails to account
for the significance of the spiritual dimension in human affairs.
Secondly, it does not clearly avoid the trap of advocating social
change through the activities of schools. I believe that the ideas we
developed are correct, but I also know they are not sufficient.
Though I believe that the reconciling synthesis of thought and action
must not reside in the domain of theory alone, I have yet to appreciate fully the meaning of that belief; and so perhaps everything I
write is an experiment, an attempt to understand better who I am
and what my commitments must be.*

Alex Molnar

11

On Student Rights

Student rights and responsibilities are meaningless if they are understood only as rights within schools and responsibilities to schools while excluding more general social rights and responsibilities. Such a narrow definition buttresses the school's refusal to allow students to engage in social action as a legitimate part of their education. It allows schools to channel the expression of rights into activities like student council and to perpetuate the myth that responsible student behavior is demonstrated by exercising such rights (e.g., voting for student body president, selecting the homecoming queen, etc.). And it allows student activities that threaten the school's absolute control over them or the rigid boundary that isolates schools from the struggle for human rights outside the classroom to be considered irresponsible. Acceptable student rights and responsibilities are thus rendered one dimensional and absurd. For example, now that the Vietnam war is "over," students may "study" it. But when organized protest against United States imperialism in Southeast Asia was a central event in our nation's social experience, the schools refused even to recognize the antiwar movement's legitimacy, much less encourage or allow students to study and participate in it.

Today schools remain steadfast in their refusal to sanction student involvement in struggles for social justice. We assert, however, that it is both the right and the responsibility of young people, as citizens and as students, to study and engage in progressive[1] social action as part of their education. This interpretation of student rights and responsibilities is based on two propositions fundamental to revolutionary dialectical materialism.[2] The first proposition is a belief in the unity of theory and practice; of knowing and doing.

> Our practice proves that what is perceived cannot at once be comprehended and that only what is comprehended can be more deeply perceived. Perception only solves the problem of phenomena; theory solves the problem of essence. The solving of both these problems is not separable in the slightest degree from practice. Whoever wants to know a thing has no way of doing so except by coming into contact with it, that is, by practicing in its environment.[3]

While educators pay lip service to the principle that learning is a result of the synthesis of knowing and doing, its rigorous application to schools is seen as a problem. The pervasive American myth that schools are ideologically neutral leads most educators to believe that if some students are allowed to learn through the practice of working with the Farmworkers Boycott Committee others must be allowed to learn by working with "The Christian Anti-Communist Crusade" or the American Nazi Party. This concern for "equal time" is a pseudo-problem that arises from the assumption that form can be separated from content or that thought can be separated from action. The same dialectical view that posits the unity of form and content, thought and action, also holds that all social resources and institutions should be used for human liberation rather than exploitation and oppression. Our second proposition is then, that resolution of these "dichotomies" necessarily entails progressive action. Therefore, as we stated earlier, students must have the right and responsibility to experience learning as the unity of thought and action through progressive social practice. Furthermore, schools must have the right and responsibility to do what they can to assure that students exercise this right and take this responsibility. It would, however, be incorrect for schools to encourage students to engage in any action that strengthens exploitative and oppressive social relationships, because there can be no right to oppress. Oppression does not serve education, because it requires that masses of people be prevented from perceiving their interests and acting in harmony with them.

Our view is a distinct departure from the attitudes prevalent among most of those who are also concerned with student rights and responsibilities. The issue is usually approached from a legal or a social reconstructionist perspective. There is, for example, a growing body of case law that supports the constitutional rights of students against oppressive administrative practices (e.g., *Tinker v. Des Moines*

Independent Community School District, Burnside v. Byars). The *In re Gault* decision of the Supreme Court held that "whatever may be their precise impact, neither the Fourteenth Amendment nor the Bill of Rights is for adults alone."

We agree that litigation in the light of such Supreme Court rulings can be a useful tactic. It may serve to restrain some school administrators and help achieve or consolidate certain important rights. However, the practical value of legal action is limited in several ways:

1. Neither the Supreme Court nor the lower courts can be relied on to interpret the constitution progressively.
2. Litigation is expensive, frequently too expensive for students and their families.
3. In their rulings the courts often assert that the particulars of each case warrant different conclusions. This effectively blocks the general acceptance of many rulings and necessitates more litigation. A single successful court case often leads only to the smallest and most specific remedy possible.
4. Most students, parents, and school officials are ignorant of the legal rights of students. Illegal violations of student rights are routinely accepted in many schools because of ignorance and because such rights fly in the face of the prevailing culture of the schools and those of the society that sustains them. Haberman states the case clearly:

> The great difficulty in dealing with students' rights is that the preponderance of rules by which schools are managed are traditions which cannot be contested legally since they exist in the school culture and not on paper. Everything from gum chewing to waiting outside in the rain before the building can be "officially" opened is more likely to be done as a result of school traditions than as an implementation of a school board policy or a written administrative regulation.[4]

5. Finally, there is no reason to believe that any court action would or could lead to the establishment of the kinds of rights and responsibilities we have proposed for students.

The social reconstructionist position would ask us to believe that it will be possible to transform society using a "new wave" of students who have been nurtured in the practice of democracy in school. The critical flaw in this position is that, while holding out the promise of social transformation, it actually returns the focus of the problem almost completely to the schools. One can almost hear the social reconstructionist arguing for the project method as the precursor of the revolution. Social reconstructionists fail to recognize that oppression and exploitation are a fundamental characteristic of class structure in the United States and cannot be altered by tinkering with the schools. The social reconstructionist position is grounded in the assumption that there is a theory called democracy, which exists separate from the practice of the social institutions that are said to embody it. "Democracy," existing outside its corrupt incarnations, is seen as the vehicle for reforming those institutions and making them more democratic. This is a commodity view of democracy, and we reject it. Democratic theory cannot be separated from democratic practice. The idea that it can be installed in any social institution the way ITA or "Career Education" or other curriculum changes have been installed in schools is incorrect.

Under capitalism a small number of people own the machinery needed to produce the goods we need and control our fiscal and production policies. While it is true that we elect our government, it is not by this act that we control its policies. Policy is controlled by corporations (I.T.T.) and trusts (the oil industry) both legally through the right of property ownership and extralegally through such practices as influence peddling.[5] The subsequent erosion of individual control over one's day-to-day existence has made increasing numbers of people subject to ever greater exploitation.

> Subjection in minor affairs breaks out every day, and is felt by the whole community indiscriminately. It does not drive men to resistance, but it crosses them at every turn, till they are led to surrender the exercise of their will. Thus their spirit is gradually broken and their character enervated. . . . It is vain to summon a people, which has been rendered so dependent on the central power, to choose from time to time the representatives of that power.[6]

A sense of individual impotence **short-circuits** collective action. However, collective action is essential because we do not have democracy in this country; we have the contradiction between certain democratic political rights and our subjection to racist, sexist, and economic exploitation. In these circumstances democracy can be extended only in the collective struggle to resolve this contradiction. Specifically this means a struggle between the classes of people whose interests are on opposite sides of the contradiction.

The same contradiction controls the condition of democracy in the schools. While teaching about the principles and practices of democratic political rights, schools routinely violate those rights in order to prepare the young to be docile functionaries in a capitalist social system: a system responsible for the perpetuation of inequality between classes, races, and sexes. Since schools serve to ratify the social structure rather than change it, social reconstructionist efforts to transform society through the schools are doomed to failure.

To us, then, the social revisionist view of student rights and responsibilities has less to offer even than the legal view. We affirm, instead, a view that emphasizes the unity of thought and action and the validity of progressive social struggle as a right and responsibility of students and teachers.

There are concrete steps that can be taken consistent with our view of the rights and responsibilities of students and educators:

1. Put aside the view of democracy as a commodity that can be installed like ITA, and with it abandon the school's traditional response to the question of student rights, which is, in essence, to find some things the kids can "safely" vote on.
2. Study the concrete contradictions of democracy in your own schools and community. What circumstances in your school and community reflect the democratic-antidemocratic contradiction?
3. Engage students in this analysis, under your guidance.
4. Devise with the students specific actions through which students, teachers, and others can combat the antidemocratic aspects of their situation.
5. Establish democratic procedures with the students through which points 3 and 4 can be carried out. These procedures include three major components:
   a. Treat investigation and action dialectically rather than serially. Investigation directs action, action produces new events to be incorporated into the investigation.
   b. Develop a collective method of discussion, analysis, and criticism, in which the purpose is to use everyone as a resource in order to get the fullest knowledge and develop what is likely to be the most successful action.
   c. Master the collective democratic method of making decisions by consensus rather than by vote.[7]

Even such small steps as these entail risks for a teacher because they threaten to resolve the contradiction in favor of a newer and fuller meaning of democracy. But the source of the risks is also a source of strength. Any antidemocratic aspect of school the teacher wishes to struggle against is necessarily offensive to others besides the teachers. The teacher has natural allies in both the school and the community. Once you have identified the issues the task becomes one of organizing your allies. To talk of student rights and responsibilities as we have is to see the teacher as an organizer who must identify allies among his fellow teachers, the students, and community members to develop a program organized around issues specific to his situation, guided by the principles of dialectical analysis.

Notes

1. As defined by leftist groups, *progressive* is used to describe those actions that directly oppose oppression and imperialism.
2. Dialectical materialism is the philosophical basis of Marxist thought. It encompasses an epistemology that differs sharply from idealist and mechanical epistemologies. Mao Tse-Tung's essay "On Practice" is a good introduction to this mode of thought.
3. Mao Tse-Tung, "On Practice," in *Collected Works of Mao Tse-Tung* (Foreign Language Press, 1968).
4. Martin Haberman, "Student Rights: A Guide to the Rights of Children, Youth and Future Teachers," *ATE Bulletin* 34 (August 1973).
5. The classic treatise on this subject is Henry Lloyd's *Wealth against Commonwealth* (1936); reprint ed., (New York: Burt Franklin). A more recent book is Galbraith's *American Capitalism* (Boston: Houghton Mifflin, 1956).
6. Alexis de Tocqueville, *Democracy in America* (New York: New American Library, 1956).
7. A useful statement of the rules of conduct of such collective discussion can be found in Mao Tse-Tung's essay "Combat Liberalism," in *Collected Works of Mao Tse-Tung* (Foreign Language Press, 1968).

Ross L. Mooney

PRELUDE

Lost-ness is reality lost;
reality lost is problem lost;
problem lost is solution lost;
solution lost is man lost;
man lost is life lost;
life lost is death.

Death sensed
is source again.

Hence the design
for what I've said,
showing first
the conceptual frame
I've learned to see
in those who,
coming to me
for a life to gain
in research they do,
come find, instead,
they have conceptual shells
of death to shed
and who, in doing so,
discover the source of life
to lie inside themselves,
concepts, then,
to have a frame
that grows
from inner stem,
as life released

from germinus
in consciousness,
attains a structured relevance,
such that research
then becomes a way
of generating life
and sharing of its nutriment,
serving, then,
the primal aim
of education
in the affairs of men,
i.e., sharing life-in-mind
as means to life in men.

No longer lost,
a new reality is gained;
the problem's set,
solutions have their relevance;
research comes to life again.

Ross L. Mooney
The Ohio State University

12

The Researcher Himself

Research has an inner and an outer drama. This chapter has to do with the inner drama—the researcher's intimate experience with himself during his research activity. This is not the usual view of research since most of us are in a position to see the general products of research and science but not the inner workings of a research producer, addressing himself to his task.

The situation in this regard may be likened to that which confronts most of us in seeing a play. As a member of the audience, we need only see an actor within the construction of the role taken. An actor who is watching another actor, however, will look behind the role taken into the role taking, i.e., into the way the man who is acting is handling himself in the doing of his job. The seasoned actor knows that a critical element in what happens is the way the man handles himself. This is the inner drama behind the scenes and the one that neither actors nor research producers have made public in any great degree.

Lack of public knowledge of the inner drama has its effect in educational research when teachers and students of education who have not done research face the prospect of doing research themselves. In the absence of immediate experience in production, they use such experience as is available to them to construe what they think research involves. This experience typically consists of considerable reading of textbook science, perhaps a few research reports, and a gleaning of impressions about science, scientists and research, taken from the general culture in which we live. Out of these, teachers and others deduce what they take to be the proper attitudes of a research producer. Unfortunately, what gets built out of these bits and pieces is inappropriate for guiding the beginner into fruitful research production and is often quite the opposite of what needs to be if a researcher is to achieve quality in his product and freedom of mind and spirit in his doing of research.

I am convinced that the greatest hindrance to the sound development of educational research is our too frequent failure to take into account the difference between a consumer's and a producer's orientation to research, leaving the beginning producer with a mental set which puts the emphasis at the wrong places and leaves the producer without thoughtful guidance on problems connected with the handling of himself in his work. As a consequence, the beginner works under strain, derives little satisfaction for himself and precious little for society. He soon becomes discouraged and joins the hundreds of his predecessors who, having tried research once, vow they will never touch it again. Many capable persons, sensing artificiality, never even start.

This is not only a loss to education and the general welfare, but a loss, as well, to individuals who would have a more stimulating life if they could. Research is a personal venture which, quite aside from its social benefits, is worth doing for its direct contribution to one's own self-realization. It can be taken as a way of meeting life with the maximum of stops open to get out of experience its most poignant significance, its most full-throated song. I would wish for beginners the personal joys I know can come to them.

What I have done here, in an effort to help the beginner, is to show, first, the kind of thinking which many beginners come to when drawing on their bits and pieces of experience to date, and, second, the kind of thinking which proves to be much more appropriate and useful to the experienced producer, as I have come to realize it. The first is labeled "a consumer's point of view," and the second, "a producer's point of view." After "a consumer's point of view" is presented, I point to its sources of support in our cultural heritage and to its effects on the producer who tries to use it. Then the shift is made to "a producer's point of view," showing what is meant in this context, why such a perspective offers hope and what it means to a researcher who enters curriculum research.

The style of writing is not typical of research papers. Since the center of the theme, content-wise, is the giving of one's self into the research undertaking, it has made sense to try a presentation which, in the very act of the reader's reading, would ask of him, too, that he give himself to this undertaking. To this end, long passages are marked by quotation to signify that they are to be taken by the reader much as he would take long passages in a play, i.e., to show the inner workings of a mind, organizing experience from its particular point of view. By identifying himself with these different points of view, the reader may be enabled, we hope, to invest himself sufficiently with "as if" possibilities to be challenged in his feeling and thought to the composition of his own point of view.

A Consumer's Point of View

The following passages are written as if on the inside of a person who, to date, has been a consumer of science and research in the popular vein and who now is trying to use what has already come into his experience to think his way toward the doing of research himself. He is trying to arrive at attitudes which he feels are important in keeping him on the right track:

"Research reports are written in the third person; personal reference to the researcher is left out. This must mean that it is taboo for a researcher to include himself in the research process. Therefore, in doing research, *I am to be quite impersonal, to leave myself out.*

"Research reports are written as though the events observed would have occurred had not the researcher been involved in making the observation, e.g., 'water runs downhill.' This phrase points to something that goes on between water and hills that is independent of the observer's experience of it. The truth science is after is something that exists regardless of man's experience of it. Therefore, *I am to look for truths which exist on their own account, independent of me.*

"If my research is to report on truths which are independent of me, then I must not participate in the events from which my judgments of truth come. If I would do so, I would influence the results and I would no longer be able to tell what relations would have been among the phenomena on their own account. This destroys the possibility of fundamental discoveries. Therefore, I am to watch what happens but I am not personally to take part in what happens. In other words, *I am to observe, but not to participate.*

"Centering on the truth, the scientist tells what happens whether he likes it or not. The researcher's personal likes and dislikes have nothing to do with science. The language of science is descriptive and expository; it is not sentimental. A person's sentiments can interfere because people tend to see what they want to see. It would be better if the researcher had no desires or sentiments at all. *Value* is the big word here; *I am not to be influenced by what I value.*

"When a scientist reports that 'water runs downhill,' he is expressing a truth; he is saying nothing at all about whether it is good or bad that water so behaves. If, after a truth is expressed, it is used to do good, then this action is all right, but it is not science any more; it is something else. *As a scientist, I am not to be concerned with what is 'good,' only with what is 'true.'*

"A research report presents the data and then the data reveal the answer to the problem. The researcher does not dictate *his* conclusion; he lets the *data* dictate the conclusion. Clearly, *I am to let the findings speak for themselves.*

"Research is written so that someone can do what the researcher did and find out for himself what happens. This requires a language of clear explanation, describing demonstrable conditions and events, with thought connections made logically. The researcher's feelings have no place in such expositions because feelings are fleeting and they are private, hidden in the unobservable inside of a person. What occurs in the researcher's imagination is also wholly irrelevant since it, too, is within the privacy of a researcher's inner regions. Only as feelings and imagined forms become concrete through transformation into observable acts may they enter into science, and when they are transformed, they are no longer feelings and imaginings; they are demonstrable and testable. *I am to depend on logic and testable demonstration, not on feelings and imagination.*

"Each research report tells, with considerable care, the procedures which were used. Scientists put a lot of weight on having the procedures right. Whether a work is scientific or not depends on whether scientific procedures are used. This is the criterion of science. So I will go to the authorities and I will find out what the approved procedures are; I will then use those procedures. My own thought processes are to be disciplined by those procedures and I am to be governed accordingly. It is plain that *I am to use procedures approved by scientists, not my own unproven ways of doing things.*

"Regardless of the particular procedures used in different scientific reports, one finds a similarity among them all. This is due to their common use of the scientific method. When one reads novels, plays, or poetry, looks at a painting, or listens to music, he is doing something quite different than when he reads a scientific report. Science stresses commonality, principles that run through everything, facts that abide whether man wants them or not, proof, security, reliability, basic truth on which man can build. The arts and humanities stress the unique, the unusual, the individual instance, the events on the inside of people, their feelings, dreams, imaginings, values. What is appropriate to the arts and humanities would be ruinous to science. The basic methods are different and should not contaminate one another. Therefore, *I would use the scientific method, not the methods of the arts and humanities.*

"Science is an accumulation of the tested experience of a lot of people, put into an orderly system. In comparison to the size of this experience, my own personal experience is small indeed; in comparison to the tested quality of this experience, my own personal experience is untested and fragile indeed. I would do well, in cases where my experience seems to run counter to that of science, to question the validity of my own experience and to trust science. In other words, I am to recognize that *my experience has little worth compared to the accumulated and tested experience of science.*

"Science makes progress by moving carefully from the known into the unknown. A research problem needs to be located on the edge between the known and the unknown, being fitted into the former and extending a short way into the latter. The thing for me to do, in selecting a problem, is to study science until I find one of these places; then my work can be a contribution. Otherwise, should I take a problem from what I personally need to know, my work might well be repetitious, irrelevant, fragmentary or just plain foolish. My personal needs have all sorts of aberrations in them and do not constitute a suitable source for research problems. *I am to select a problem in relation to what science needs to know, not in relation to what I need to know.*

"In doing research, the satisfactions must come from how things are done, not from the content of what is dealt with. A person dare not become intrigued or emotionally concerned with the content or he will, in proportion to that involvement, be biased, partial, personal and subjective. I am to remind myself, in doing research, that *I am to try to get my pleasures from the reliability of my procedures and not from the nature of the content with which I deal.*

"There cannot be truth in science if there is error. Mistakes simply cannot be allowed. To make a mistake myself would be most embarrassing. My choices must be cautious, my procedures must conform to standard, and my operations must be careful and thorough in every detail. I shall not forget; *I must avoid making mistakes.*"

Projected toward a world view, these statements give a picture of a universe in which a researcher is called upon to put himself as far out of his research as possible. His thinking continues:

"The universe is huge, far beyond man; the universe is filled with many events, far more than man can ever know; the operation of the universe depends on vast powers, against which man's power is weak. To run the universe, there are natural laws which, to handle so much power and diversity, must attain a perfection far beyond anything a man could dream, and against which man's mental fabrications are clumsy, partial and impure.

"These natural laws were in operation long before man came onto the earth and will be in operation long after he is gone. They change not one jot or tittle for me or for any man; they are truly impartial, impersonal and universal. If I am to learn of these laws, I, too, am to become impartial, impersonal and universal even as they are. Scientists, achieving this attitude, have been able to transcend their normal human limitations and to reach into that region which is usually outside man's direct experience. By revealing these basic laws of nature, scientists have helped man to see the truths to which he must adjust.

"Basically, man adjusts to nature. Nature creates and man fits to that creation. Man may think of himself as the product of nature's creation or as something separate from nature, in a different class, but in either case he is beholden to something which is beyond him and separated from him—something more powerful, truer and more real than he is. *My job, as researcher, is, therefore, to achieve that separation from nature which allows me most clearly to see nature's truth so that I and other men can fit ourselves to that which has to be outside of me and man.*"

This world view may have a seeming rightness and majesty about it, the sound of a familiar dedication. The statements lying back of it may also seem right, or just about right. There are good cultural and psychological reasons why this would be the case.

Why the Consumer's View Is Appealing

One reason the view seems sound is that it is familiar to us as a part of a very long cultural heritage. During the Middle Ages, we held a primary split between man and the supernatural. After the Renaissance and Reformation, we made a primary split between man and nature. This split prevailed in the formative days of our nation when we were struggling against nature to get a wilderness subdued and a continent fit for habitation. It made its deep impression. The same split holds today though the form nature takes is not now a wilderness but the physical and chemical structures out of which are manufactured our technological advances. We are still using a great share of our national energy in the conquest of physical things "out there" so that they can serve us. In this separation of man from the to-be-conquered "out there," it is easy for a researcher to assume that man is separate from that which he seeks to comprehend and to stop with a concept of research which leaves no place for the researcher in what he creates.

It is easy to accept this condition because *popularized conceptions of scientists* provide a psychological place for the scientist to be! Since he cannot normally be in nature, he can have access to truth which nature holds only by being able, from time to time, to break through his normal human barrier and occupy a suprahuman position. This is the position of the ancient witch doctor and the position which the scientist now holds in the psyche of the general public. Like the witch doctor, the scientist is seen as normally being a human among all the rest, but, by donning suitable ceremonial garments (typically a white coat), by uttering suitable incantations, otherwise meaningless (mysterious formulas and technical jargon), and by carefully following certain ceremonial procedures (scientific methodologies), he can invoke truth out of a mysterious beyond.

Primitive as this solution may seem to be, there is very little else millions of laymen can do when, assuming a split, they try to give a place in their psychological world to the people who penetrate nature on occasion and who do it so cleverly they can get nature to kill on a horrible scale, or, capriciously, to prolong life and add to its comforts. To these laymen, a scientist is somehow a man and yet a mysterious phenomenon, a different breed, a ceremonious, powerful, capricious creature, sometimes a devil bringing fantastic evil, sometimes a god bringing the most precious good. Needing to solve this problem, their easy solution is to give to the scientist that place in the psychic order which was created by our ancestors to make their life somehow tolerable when they, too, were caught with a yawning split in their assumptions and with no rational place to put phenomena that seem somehow to inhabit the regions between assumptive poles.

It might be possible for people to work their way more easily toward transcendence of these elementary splits if the education they received during formative years had transcended the splits rather than added to them. But our schooling has typically run another separation which has added to the habit of accepting splits and to the difficulty of recognizing any splits at all.

The split has come in separating the subject to be learned from the person of the learner, with each half of the dichotomy given a status independent of the other and the former given top billing. The "subject" is given the status of an entity in its own right, with its own laws of organization, its clear-cut "rights" and "wrongs," and authorities behind it. The psychological reasoning goes something like this:

"A subject exists before a particular child comes to it and will continue to exist after the child has gone. A child exists before he comes to a particular subject and will exist after he has left it, whether he has learned the subject or not. The two, subject and child, are in separate systems and are independent of each other. They have no necessary connections.

"The subject has its own conceptual order—geometry, for example. This order is necessary to the subject, *is* the subject, as a matter of fact. A student who learns geometry learns this order. When the student has fitted his mind with this order, then he knows the subject. He can be tested by being required to respond to the problems which occur in this conceptual order, and, if he gives responses which are 'right' within the system, then he is developing a 'disciplined' mind in the subject.

"It is the conceptual order of the subjects which makes it possible to stabilize the schools. The children are forever changing, coming by the thousands, staying awhile, and passing on through. This changing amorphous mass can be controlled by making the subjects the center of the system. Let the students come and be pitted against the stabilizing core of the subjects. Hire as teachers those who know a subject well and let them teach that subject. Group the students in convenient numbers and send them to a given teacher to 'get that subject.'

"If a student doesn't 'get a subject,' mark him down, for, of the two things, the subject and the student, it is the student who is in error and needs to be disciplined to fit the discipline. The 'subject' is the basic, elementary construction to which the student is to adjust. The subject contains the laws to which the student submits. The subject is the creator; the child the created."

The key to this conventional formula for education is "let the system of the schools be the system of the subjects and let the students fit that system." The center of value, of right, of organization, of psychological action is "out there" in the subjects. The job of the student is to learn how to behave from positions in systems outside himself. The job of the teacher is to see that the students most quickly and easily fit themselves to these outside existences and controls.

Brought up in this kind of education, a potential researcher is disposed to assume a separated "out-thereness" as one of the elementary conditions of existence and not question it or quest beyond it. The assumptions of a split between man and God, between man and nature, between the person of the student and the subject of his learning, are all one consistent construction.

As if this were not already enough, there may well be, for the potential researcher, still another potent experience to drive the split on home. This comes at the higher levels of education where he may enter on training to do research! This is the graduate level where one would expect transcendence of the split if that were necessary to research production. But we still have, as predominant, the consumer's orientation to research, the split and the self-abnegation.

Right up to time to do the doctoral dissertation, the graduate student's curriculum is likely to be heavily dominated by regular course work. In these regular courses, he is required again, as in high school days, to fit his mind to the conceptual system of subjects. He may, in addition, have seminars with major professors in which he might be able to brush elbows with an actual research producer and get some of the training for the inside drama on how a producer handles himself in order to get significant and creative production out of himself. This will not occur, however, unless the seminar teacher has consciously become aware of the difference between guiding a student through a subject and guiding a student through himself into creative engagement with a subject. The former and conventional orientation is much the more common so that the seminar is most likely to be another course, only "more chummy."

Where a student is most likely to confront himself, head on, is in his "individual problems" where tutorial relations may be possible under conditions where the lead is taken by the student. Then the student may operate as a producer and not be limited to the consumer's role. Yet these potentially precious hours may be very few and be low in both the student's and teacher's value system because they are hours sandwiched in to fill out a pattern of "full credits every semester" for the student and are added, without administrative recognition, to the professor's already full course-work load.

One might suppose that courses often offered to graduate students on "how to do research" would make the correction. Certainly these would have the producer's point of view! But, following unconsciously on past habits of consumer orientation, these courses, too, easily become "a course," a prescribed conceptual system presented as something for students to learn as they would learn any other conceptual system.

> The scientific method is (a) . . . , (b) . . . , (c) . . . , (d) . . . ; the general types of research are (a) . . . , (b) . . . , (c) . . . , (d) . . . ; a problem for research is well stated when (a) . . . , (b) . . . , (c) . . . , (d) . . . ; the collection and assembly of relevant data require (a) . . . , (b) . . . , (c) . . . , (d) . . . ; analysis of data is tricky in these respects (a) . . . , (b) . . . , (c) . . . , (d) . . . ; validity is important because (a) . . . , (b) . . . , (c) . . . , (d) . . . ; reliability is important because (a) . . . , (b) . . . , (c) . . . , (d) . . . ; statistics are advanced and complicated these days but the ideas in them are simple, (a) . . . , (b) . . . , (c) . . . , (d) . . . ; in writing up research, be sure to (a) . . . , (b) . . . , (c) . . . , (d) . . . ; etc.

The inference is made that one who knows these things knows how to do research. The logic is comparable to assuming that one who knows how to make a map knows how to make a journey. The student has done a lot of conceptual map making from maps made by others, and this course is one more in the series. But, coming to his dissertation, he finds the independent research then required is much more involved and very differently centered. The primary data come in the direct experiences of the journey; the directions for action come from inside one's self. Not even the map making turns out to be the same because making a map of meanings from one's own direct experiences is a different sort of thing than making maps from other people's maps. There is a major shift in one's psychological space.

But graduate students can often take "training in research" without making the shift. Coming finally to their dissertations, they struggle with themselves more than they struggle with "the problem" because they have not yet learned how to put themselves into their inquiry.[1] They still have the consumer's orientation, and so great is the pressure of tradition and habit that many students graduate with a doctorate and still do not realize the significance of the changes involved in creative research production.

So there are good reasons why you or I or anyone, Ph.D. or not, should feel somehow reasonably comfortable with a consumer's orientation. In summary:

1. We are broadly exposed to a consumer's orientation by a long and infiltrated cultural tradition which splits man from nature (or

God) and gives man no substantial place to put himself when he tries to join the two (or three).

2. We are able to accept the split and feel at home with it because of an ancient psychological inheritance which provides the position of witch doctor to solve just such problems.

3. Furthermore, we are trained in operating split-wise by our years of schooling where the self of the learner is separated from the subject to be learned, and the former is made subservient to the latter.

4. Graduate schools, which might be expected to make the shift to a producer's view in their training of research workers, get caught in the cultural tradition, the psychological milieu and habits of past schooling so that they, too, often do not help their students transcend the splits to realize the integrations needed for fruitful research production.

But, comfortable or not, it is deadly to research production and to the producer himself to try to do research within the consumer's orientation; it is much too cramped and much too anchored at the wrong places.

What the Consumer's View Does to the Producer

In condensed language, the consumer's view:

1. Cramps the producer's thoughts by requiring him to use an intellectual system based on arbitrary splits—truth versus value, logic versus feeling, universality versus uniqueness, science versus art, nature versus man, etc. Much of the researcher's strength is bound up in just getting things separated and kept in their proper places.

2. Introduces anxiety in the producer's thinking by making the arbitrary intellectual system also an arbitrary moral system. To one half of the splits are assigned the qualities that make for the good, the true, and the perfect; to the other half are assigned the qualities that make for the bad, the false, and the imperfect. The good half is the impersonal half; the bad half is the personal half. Every time a researcher makes an intellectual split, he is also making a judgment involving the placement of himself with respect to his being personally good or bad. A mistake in classification risks personal guilt.

3. Robs the producer of a positive motivation by denying him the chance to claim anything good for himself: nature cannot be claimed, for it is already presumed to be separate from him;

creation can't be his for it is nature's; truth can't be his for it, too, is nature's; ways of getting at truth can't be his because they are already prescribed by, and are the property of, science; his problem can't initially be his because it must first come from science; not even his conclusions can really be his because they must be shown as coming from independent facts and data which "speak for themselves."

4. Enforces on the producer a negative motivation by assigning him a negative, trouble-making role. Values may be his but they are misleading; feelings may be his but they are private and are to be ruled out of bounds; the uniqueness of his personality may be his but it is distorting. Self-participation in inquiry only deforms the data. Man is the imperfect one, the weak one, the little one, the partial one, the created-but-not-creating one, the deformed one, the guilty one in any aberrations. In contrast, nature is flawless, true, perfect, powerful, inclusive, creative. It is man, who, damned in the very act of being born a man, is also recurrently damned throughout his life because he is the maker of any mistakes.

With energy dissipated in anxious sortings, nothing good to belong to and nothing trustworthy to be or creative to become, the researcher has a heavy, tiring struggle in trying to do research. He can't give his energy because he can't give himself. He can't give himself because there is no substantial place to put himself which is good and hopeful and natural and freedom giving to his mind and spirit.

A good many sensitive, wholesome, and energetic teachers and administrators, sensing the artificiality, brittleness, and strain of research as conceived in the consumer's manner, will not submit themselves to doing research. They do not want to give up their freedom to engage themselves wholly in what they do. Sensing no substantial place to put themselves, so very large a place to make mistakes, and so very much of other people's maps to learn without a proportionate place to discover and develop maps of their own, not even the first beginnings of research are worth the trial to them. Self-respect prevents investments in research by this kind of person.

Others are frightened away because they fear their lack of ability to do the skill-tasks that are usually necessary in research. Much of this fear is unfounded because of the strength that is available to a person who is finding himself in what he does. A person who pursues problems of genuine importance to his personal growth releases a lot of energy for doing tasks which would otherwise seem heavy and hopeless.

Then there are people who, for one reason or another, *do* undertake to do research even though they have not transcended the consumer's view. Their reasons lie beyond the activity itself, e.g., others are doing it, advancement requires it, this is the way to play the game. In such cases, one of three types of degeneracy is likely to occur in the researcher as a consequence of his having no constructive place to put himself: (a) submissive conformity, brought on by identifying one's self with an important person in the field, taking on his ways and ideas and personality, thereby allowing the researcher to hide from himself in the cloak of another; (b) assertive demagoguery, brought on by taking science to be something pure and sacred so that, in taking the role of scientist, the researcher can think of himself as one of the "already saved," one whose word is already right, and who, therefore, need never be faced with himself; (c) ambivalent escapism, brought on by trying to take research as something done "on the side" as if one were not really doing any of it at all, thereby allowing the researcher the hope that he can escape any confrontation of himself as a consequence of his scientific pursuits. All three types of degeneracy have one cause in common, a world split between man and nature so that there is no natural place for the man to be who joins the two, and one effect in common, a denial of one's self so that one need not face himself.

Any system which allows and encourages a man to escape himself leads toward his psychic dissolution. As ancient wisdom points out and modern science confirms, a man's nature is such that he confronts himself if he lives at all. Man is actually unable to leave himself out of his life and, even though he may seem, in his own eyes, to be temporarily successful, what happens in cases of self-denial is that the image denied entrance at the front door of consciousness enters unobtrusively by the back door of unconsciousness, clad in another garb. The inner drama is then more erratic than before with the person less able to keep track of what he is doing and of what is going on around him. To press in this direction is to invite mental illness and to succeed is to break the circuit of psychic life altogether.

Clearly we do not want to promote the consumer's view if we want to produce research. We want a psychological set which, instead of being negative, abortive and eventually destructive, is quite the opposite. We want something which is freedom-giving, personally and scientifically rewarding, vigorous and progressively penetrating. We want a way of holding assumptions about research which makes it possible to integrate the pursuit of science and research with the acceptance and fruitful development of one's self. The two, science and self, can be one integrative action and, indeed, need to be one integrative action if either is to be productive and grow.

This requires a shift from a consumer's view to a producer's view. It is well to have in mind the broad nature of this shift before we try to talk directly from a producer's point of view.

The Nature of the Shift

What it means to shift from a consumer's view to a producer's view may be suggested by three analogies:

Picture a shopper going into a grocery to choose fruit to take home to eat. He needs to use a range of judgments which, focused through sights, smells and touch, make it possible for him to pick the particular fruit which he feels will be most satisfying to his taste. He judges the mellowness of bananas against the crispness of apples, against the juiciness of oranges, etc., and when he picks one of these, he then judges among the samples available from within the type he wants. His action, as consumer, is shaped within this context.

Now picture a producer of fruit and the context of his judgments. Fruit is the product of a long and complicated process. Involved are such different phenomena as sunshine and rain, heat and cold, bees and blossoms, soils and diseases, fertilizers and sprays, hired hands and wages, market prices and costs. Fruit growing involves judgments of these many things. A producer's mind has to be fitted with scores of these contexts. *What serves him to judge the fruit produced, as if he were a consumer, is important in its time and place, for he must see his product as if he were a consumer, too, but it is only a small part of the total range to which he has to be attentive.*

What folly it would be for a person to assume that the range of his judgments as a fruit consumer would, in itself, be sufficient for him to make decisions concerning what was important in production! Yet consumers of research often do just that in presuming that they can reason from what is characteristic of the research product to what is characteristic of the production process! One wishes the differences in product and process were as openly obvious in research as in fruit growing.

A second analogy, already introduced, is that of a play, contrasting the frame of reference of a playgoer watching the play (consumer) and the frame of reference of an actor in the play (producer). Though both may, at a given moment, be looking at the same bit of action on the stage, the playgoer's concern is differently oriented than the actor's. The playgoer takes the action as a cue to the unfolding of the play and takes the play as significant according as it fits into the personal experience of his life. The actor, on the other hand, takes the action as a cue, not only to the progression of the play, but to the way in which the person performing the action is handling himself in structuring his role. The playgoer can forget an actor is a person behind the role he takes, but an actor cannot forget the person because he knows that any role an actor takes is structured out of a person, as well as out of a play. The actor's progression, in observing a bit of action on the stage, is therefore (a) from himself, as if he were the actor, (b) to the play, (c) to the role, (d) to the bit of action seen; whereas the progression of the spectator, in observing the same action, is in the reverse order—(a) from the bit of action seen, (b) to the role, (c) to the play, (d) to himself. In research, the shift from consumer's to producer's orientation is just as marked. The dynamics, in consuming research, is from product to person, and, in producing research, from person to product. In production, the self of the producer is his basic ground for all that follows. The self is central and pervasive.

A third analogy, also already introduced, is that of map making, contrasting the frames of reference of one who makes maps from other people's maps with one who makes a map from his direct experience on a journey. The former is comparable to a consumer's orientation and the latter to a producer's orientation. To make a map from direct experience on a journey is to take stimuli which do not come in the shape of maps at all and to transform these cues into a map-like product. This is very different from taking stimuli which are in the shape of maps already and then making maps out of them. Though both the producer and consumer make decisions, the producer is much more caught in necessities for self-commitment, self-knowing, self-confidence, self-decision. *It is not that what the consumer does is arbitrarily wrong, for acquaintance with the maps of others is what allows a producer to construe a map of meaning to others when structuring his direct experience into a map form, but rather that what the consumer does leaves out the core which the producer must use to integrate and direct what he does.*

Coming through these three analogies are summary observations on what is involved in the shift from a consumer's view of research to a producer's:

1. A change in the kinds of judgments required.
2. An increase in the range of judgments required.
3. A shift in the focus of attention from the characteristics of the product to the characteristics of the production process.

4. A reverse flow in the dynamics of thought, being from product to person in consumption and from person to product in production.
5. A recognition of the fundamental and initiating status of the self in research production.

With these highlights we may now be ready to occupy the producer's viewpoint with greater freedom than our habits, otherwise, would have granted us.

A Producer's Point of View

A research producer can be more productive if (a) he feels open and friendly toward his universe, (b) he believes in himself as a legitimate and necessary center of his experiencing, (c) he has faith that what he can consciously do can have a worthwhile influence on his universe, and (d) he feels comfortable in thinking esthetically, i.e., with sensitivity to structural harmonies in his experiential formings and flowings. At the level of his musing on himself and his world, his thoughts may be pictured as follows:

"I exist in a universe. The universe is very large in space and time. It is an energy system, composed of many beings, each of which is an energy system having its particular space-time position. No other being occupies my particular space-time position. I am differentiated, individual. Whatever I realize of the universe, I realize from where I am, and no other being realizes life from where I am. This is my uniqueness, my being.

"Within the largeness of the energy system of the universe, the energy system which is differentiated as me is relatively small. I am included along with billions upon billions of other differentiated things. The system which is the universe is the system of these beings in one—one being, one existence, one system.

"Within this largest one, my differentiated being is joined into all the rest, into all other beings, into the whole universe. I am an intimate inclusion within all. This is my universality, my belonging.

"Relations which, followed in their outward reach, compose my universality and my belonging, compose, on their inward reach, my uniqueness and my being. This mutuality of relations in one immediacy makes the wonder of life, the source of paradox and resolution.

"This condition establishes the self of me, not as my possession, but as the means to mutuality through which the universe is formed and I am formed as one spontaneity, one existence, one life. So it comes about, the deeper truth I have known, that the respect I hold for myself is respect, at the same time, both for me and my universe. The universe is a self-reflexive integration.

"As an energy system, open to all other systems, I am constantly spending energy, which, as it leaves me, calls for my constant seeking of renewal by fresh inclusions, taken from the universe into me. This gives my life a forward thrust, as, leaning into oncoming time and space, I go from my emptyings to my fillings in the rhythmic reaching, grasping, including, using, losing, emptied reaching, that make up my days. In moving from things gone to comings, I achieve the coming of my being, my becoming, my unique sequential ordering, my emerging pattern of belongings, wrought, in space and time, into my being.

"In reaching out for food to feed my becoming, I find not all other beings are potent forms for me. I cannot eat all, breathe all, perceive all. I can only use what fits me at a specific time and place. So I have to turn into me to find what the structure may be of the emptiness there and to use that structured emptiness as means by which to search the horizon of possibilities. Thereby, I may be able to find a structured form that, fitting to the structure of my emptiness, grasped and taken into me, fits and fills my need. This is the order of claim.

"In the harmonizing of structures, whereby the shape of emptiness, from within, and the shape of potentiality, from without, have their fitting, lies the resonance of life, its happiness and fruition. In this esthetic intercourse and its confluent transformations lie also the means by which experience gets its ordering, the psyche gets its structuring and thinking gets its forming.

"I am not only a *being* with *belonging* in the universe, and a *becoming* out of these, but also a *fitter,* fitting the universe and me in reflexive transformation. Agent to this fitting is the self, performing as a womb to give birth to life's significance, allowing for the conception of being, the nourishment of belonging, and the progression of becoming. Life is a constant birth, and the experiencing of life is the experiencing of the birth of its significance. For this, the self is means in the development of an ever more universal, and therefore more fitting, man."

In such a frame of mind, a producer of research comes to the consumer's declarations (see the second section of this chapter) with reactions like these:

"Research reports are written in the third person but they are written by a first person; they are done by persons. Research is inescapably a personal formation.

"Research reports may be written as though the events observed would have occurred had not the researcher been involved, but this is not to hide the fact that when a man observes something his observing includes himself as observer. A man may generalize on his observations to say 'water runs downhill' and mean to point to events which occur, whether or not a man observes them, but this is not to hide the fact that when a man generalizes, his generalizing includes himself as generalizer. There is no escaping one's self in observing, generalizing, thinking, imagining, proving, testing, dreaming, sleeping—in any act of one's own experiencing. The self is central and though one may be privileged to speak of goings-on at places not present to him, he is not privileged to deny that it was he who spoke. The world a man knows is a world created within his experience and not apart from it.

"This is not to say that nothing exists unless a man knows it, but rather to say that what a man knows to exist involves him because the act of knowing is his action. Neither is this to say that nothing exists independent of man, but rather to say that when a man relates to any event which he takes to have been previously independent of him he is involved at the point of relating. The relations of his universe are centered through him and such truths as he knows are creations of relations matrixed in him. Truth is his truth and how universal it comes to be depends on how universal his connectedness becomes. It is a mistake for a man to look for 'truths which exist on their own account.'

"Since I participate when I observe, it is nonsense to try to split me and to say I can 'observe but not participate.' The point worth making here is that a man can give his attention in such a way as to encourage a state of mind needed for the careful searching of possibilities on the horizon beyond him or to encourage a state of mind needed for the aggressive grasping and shaping of what has already been named as wanted from among the possibilities. The former is akin to 'observing' and the latter to 'participating'; in neither case, however, is the actor himself removed from the action. It is a matter of a man giving his attention as is called for in the ebb and flow of his transactions with his environment.

"To be asked to 'not be influenced by my values' is to be asked not to be influenced by my bonds of belonging or my tentacles of becoming. It is to ask the impossible, for what I am is involved in these. Values signify the inescapable necessity of man that he select some things from among all things for his appropriate use at each specific time and place and that he so choose as to enhance the fulfillment of his life. 'Values' is a name for what is useful in 'fulfillment.' The more sensitive I can be in investing myself consciously in realizing my values through my research activity, the more profoundly I can penetrate universality. The road to conquest of sentiment and superficial identification is not through the denial of sentiment and identification, but through its ripening into conscious valuing.

"As a scientist, I am concerned with the 'good' as well as the 'true.' I see the 'good' and the 'true' as reciprocally fused in one rhythmic stride through life. Striding requires of me a foot on the ground to hold my weight and a foot on the move to carry me forward. Through the foot on the ground, I am sensitive to the question, Will the earth support me here? Through the foot on the move, I am sensitive to the question, Where would be good for me to go? The former is the question of 'truth' and the latter is the question of 'good.' Neither is serviceable to me apart from the other, for both are appendages of the one that is me and both are equally true and valuable for me. I can benefit at times by giving special attention to whether the earth will support me, for I may not be sure it will or I may be less sure of this than I am, just then, of where I want to go; then I emphasize my quest of truth. At other times, I may benefit by giving special attention to where would be good for me to go, for I may not be sure of my choice or I may be less sure of it than I am, just then, of the earth's supporting me; then I emphasize my quest of good. But, again, this is a matter of my giving attention according to the ebb and flow of my transactions with my environment. It leaves me squarely in the center of my life as the creature through whom the relatively true and the relatively good get their formation, relation, and inseparable function.

"In respect to 'findings that speak for themselves,' I know of no such data. It is a man who speaks; data are a man's formations. In speaking, a man may want to convey his feeling that some things come to him as if 'given,' such as the earth he walks on, and some things come to him as if 'arrived at' through a progression of steps. The former he may label 'data,' and the latter 'conclusions.' These labelings may help him to map an experiential journey which is easier for others to follow, but the 'data' or 'conclusions' are constructions within the speaker's experience and speech, not apart therefrom.

"Research reports emphasize testable demonstration and clear lines of relation in rational thought. This is as it should be since the purpose of such reports is to lay out conditions for experience so that a reader may, if he chooses, try to make 'the same journey' on which the scientist is reporting. He can then find out whether what happens to him is like what happened to the reporter. This is the basis of scientific proof, a way of allowing people to submit themselves to progressive circumstances which are highly similar so that they may share their responses, judge the similarity in patterns of experience and thereby sort out better what still further people could count on or not count on in their experience. Scientific proving honors, and is built upon, the careful sharing of patterns of experience of individuals where each individual is invited to invest himself and learn, in the private authority of his own togetherness, how his experience runs. Science has developed by holding to the authority of the self-experiencer.

"Testable demonstration and logic are efficient ways by which one researcher can provide the map lines to tell another how to guide himself into similar circumstances. Once in the circumstances, there is much more involved, however, than the activities which are tied directly to the making of map lines. In the midst of the experiencing, there is no way of knowing what the outcome will eventually be. One has to feel his way along and trust his feeling to guide him into moves that only later can be given a logical maplike form. He is caught as any man is caught who has not yet solved his problem. He has to imagine what it might be like to try 'a' or 'b' or 'c' or 'd' in a given situation. The more potentialities he can draw upon in his imagination, the more chance he has of being able to select the one route which will eventually turn out to be the best road to take and the best map line to draw for others. Rather than scorn feelings and imaginings, the productive researcher gives these aspects of himself a full and challenging place.

"When scientists recommend certain procedures, what they are saying is that people who trust these map lines will find that the roads recommended are useful for taking a direct experiencer from one given destination to another. They are not trying to say to people, 'take only these roads'; rather they are saying, 'if your journey requires you to move between these given destinations, then you will find these roads useful.' The individual experiencer still has the journey to take for himself and test for himself. The recommended map line is not the substitute for the journey—and this the scientist knows 'for sure.' When the journey requires him to enter new territory, he is not doing anything substantially different than when taking a recommended path; it is only that he can more readily share the pattern of his experience on the recommended routes than on the untrodden ones. To train oneself to trust only the approved procedures of scientists and not to trust oneself, as the consumer's view suggests, would be to make a great mistake.

"Likewise to follow the consumer's view in separating scientific methods from the methods of the arts and humanities is to err. Both the scientist and artist are direct experiencers; both have the problem of providing maps for their journeys. The painter does it with colors and lines; the scientist does it with experimental conditions, contraptions and conceptions. Both are seeking the extension of themselves into universality; both are operating as unique persons from their specific space-time locations in the universe. The scientist is a creator like the artist; he has the same problems of self-containment, self-development, self-assurance, self-awareness. He has, in the artist, a particularly good companion for the formative period that comes before hypotheses have been adequately expressed for test. This is that part of the scientist's work which is especially private, in which much has to go on at the feeling and imaginative level in order to evolve structure in an otherwise amorphous field of possibilities. Artists have a long history of experience in dealing with those phases of their activity. They have much to teach the scientist and it is too bad that the emphasis on the public product of science has hidden from so many people, even scientists and artists, the depth of their mutuality. A producer is a creator and there is more to be gained through sharing among creators than there is through separating differences in products and making hasty presumptions that the characteristic differences in products denote the same kinds of differences in production.

"In creating a problem to work on, a researcher is wise to proceed in a way which is just the opposite of the way recommended in the consumer's outlook. To the consumer it seems that an individual's need for problem solutions is a very erratic base on which to build science. His advice is to 'select a problem in relation to what science needs to know, not in relation to what I need to know.' In a world presumed split to start with, a choice of this kind is called for, but in a world where I am within nature and nature is within me and the two are extensions within the same integral system, there is no need for an arbitrary choice in these terms. Science is then seen as a pursuit by persons to clarify the extension of themselves into the universe. As the uniqueness of their personal position in the universe becomes clearer, their connectedness into universality becomes also clearer. This is one operation, made possible by investing oneself to the hilt and following out the clarifications.

"Hence the problem I create to work on is to be a problem of importance to me personally. In it, I can sense my purposes on their way toward fulfillment, my values under test, my self-conceptions and reciprocal world-conceptions under change. In the course of clarification of what is important to me, I come to some roads of knowledge which other scientists have already charted and, on such roads, I can expect to share my experience as I also go along. Other clarifications will require that I go into a frontier to make my own maps alone. Whether the direction which is personally important to me takes me into old or new territory, it is necessary that my guidance form within me. Otherwise there is no center of integration, no way of letting experience form where it has to form, i.e., through the self.

"This means that I am also deeply interested in the content of my problem and do not follow the consumer's advice to be disinterested in content and interested only in the reliability of my work in carrying out the right procedures. The consumer's fear is that an interest in the content means bias, prejudice, personal involvement. I sympathize with his concern that the researcher not freeze in his tracks, but I do not expect a researcher to be able to open himself into an expanding universality by making choices between content and method! He will be freer of mind and more open to growth by an arrangement which invites him to achieve his universality through accepting himself as central and investing himself in working out problems important to him. He will seek reliability of procedures, then, as a necessary part of wanting to be sure he is not fooling himself in matters important to him.

"He will expect to make mistakes and he will not think of himself as a sinner if he does make a mistake. Mistakes are things which are 'taken amiss.' It is only by knowing what one has taken amiss that one learns what is necessary to be solved, the nature of one's need, the potential structure of one's emptiness. This does not mean that one aims at making mistakes in order to be a good scientist, but it does mean that in one's ever-reaching for progressive inclusion, one will miss in some of his selections. The 'big thing' is *not* 'not to make mistakes' but progressively to integrate and use mistakes as means in this progression."

Whereas the consumer's world view presents splits by the score because of its rudimentary splitting of nature from man and the postulation of two universes, the producer's world view provides a frame of mind which integrates man and nature and presents one universe. Man can take himself to be *in* this universe, working out from his given center toward progressively increasing extensions of conscious connection. A man's total connections within the universe are doubtless millions of times more than he can consciously name at any given time or can learn to name in his lifetime. But, through conscious knowing, some of the vital connections being formed within life-on-the-make are possible of realization. Increased sense of the richness of life is also possible through cultivating a widening awareness of connections-taking-place.

Man's primary connections appear to run between what has already been included as inside his life and what he takes to be currently outside his life but facing him as potentiality of yet being included. Life evolves in the effecting of connections between what is structuring on the inside as emptiness or need and what is structuring on the outside as suitably matching potentiality for fulfilling need. The greater the range of realized connections while this in-and-out-and-in-and-out transacting is going on, the larger can be the fittings of needs to potentialities and the more can be the resulting resonance of being, belonging and becoming. This also means a greater realization of self.

Splittings which are so prominent in the consumer's view are less prominent in the producer's view, not because the producer does not use dichotomies in his thought, but because he uses dichotomies in a different way. The consumer uses dichotomies for division-into-two, whereas the producer uses dichotomies for differentiation-within-one. Psychologically, dichotomous polarities seem to be necessary in order to provide the means by which tensioned relations can be set up for the grasping of forms in experience. The situation is like that in the physiological and physical context where a man is provided with two arms so that he can have a tensioned grasp of an object from both sides when he wants to include it in some useful action. An object cannot be picked up with just "one"; it takes at least "two" in suitably opposed yet unified tension to grasp "one." This seems to be the condition psychologically as well as physically.

Psychological polarities are therefore to be accepted and used. The wrong and the danger come when a person forgets that the two arms of a man (or the two ends of a dichotomy) are useful because they are protrusions of *one* system. They allow a sense of differentiation out at their ends, but it is their togetherness in one that makes the difference a connection. Realized as differentiations-within-one, and therefore as connections, polarities can promote richness of integration, increased self-awareness and affirmation. Taken as divisions-in-two, polarities promote disintegration and denial of self.

Though the split between man and nature in western civilization has been strong in the past, we may now have come to a point in our cultural development where we can see this polarity as declaring a unity, rather than declaring an absolute separation. Science need not be taken as a witch doctor's bridge between two irreconcilable universes, but can be seen as a means of cultivating a consciousness of progressive extensions of self-in-the-universe. It is a way of realizing the character of man's home in his universe and, in its essential processes, is not different from what a child goes through when he awakens to consciously realize himself as a being, and tries, by extensions of his belonging, becoming and fitting to realize the home into which he has been born. The universe is the adult man's home and he seeks his being, belonging, becoming, and fitting in that context.

Why the Producer's View Offers Hope

There are cultural and psychological conditions which give strength to the hope that we can make the shift from split to integration in our view of science and ourselves. Man's trouble is great enough to cause him to rethink the place he wants to give himself. He has examples of how splittings between groups of men, when taken to be absolute, have led straight into the jaws of death. His feelers are out for a deeper unity which takes the splits and puts them under control so that instead of being causes of death they are enriching differentiations of a healthy whole.

For thousands of people, the challenge could not be plainer; for thousands more, and perhaps millions, the challenge is felt if not seen. Many people will respond with appreciation and hope to positive views of man. Many are tired of the frustration of having a thousand pummelings from different directions on the outside and no way on the inside to order their decisions into a simplified, hopeful, positive progression.

In the cultural tradition, there is a symbol around which hope centers when the going is rough. This is the symbol of creation, found in the great men who epitomize its human form at the level of conscious cultural realization. Creativeness is honored in the honor done to great men in all cultures. Though the honoring may be postponed until a great man's death or may be allowed to a living man only if he is in another field than one's own (social birth of a great person brings birthpangs in those out of whom new ways come), the fact remains that creativeness in man represents man's most pervading hope for going on.

What is needed now is not only the happenstance of a few creative men in the total population, but a direct and widespread honoring of conditions for cultivating creativity among people generally. People are threatened now, whole nations at a time, so that what is called for now is emergent greatness among people, whole nations at a time.

This calls for a big shift in the search for creative greatness so that we try to see it and cultivate it in every person, not in just a few. This is the primary job of educational institutions in every land. It is a particular call to education in our own land where we are daily challenged to take the world initiative on many critical matters having to do with the way man is to look at man. In our schools we need curricula which help children progressively to realize themselves as creative beings in a world needing them at their emergent best—open, centered, disciplined, esthetically dynamic. Research in education is the challenge to make the best use of man's mind in this pursuit. What is presented in the previous pages as the research producer's point of view is an orientation to attitudes for taking research as a creative enterprise in pursuit of creative development.

In this view, it turns out that a researcher in the curriculum is, in effect, trying to find ways of providing to children the kind of engagement with life which he wants also to have for himself. He wants a curriculum for them which is psychologically serving them as his inquiry is serving him. What he learns about conditions which are good for freeing him in *his* development are learnings as well for conditions which are good for freeing children in *their* development; what he learns concerning conditions which are good for freeing the children in *their* development are learnings as well for conditions which are freeing for him in *his* development. The interdependent reflexiveness of the researcher's inner and outer frames of reference carries him onward as a person while it carries him onward professionally. And what helps the child helps him.

Creativeness among persons who are reciprocally working for creativeness in themselves and each other brings a self-reflexive return which advances the energy level considerably beyond what it ordinarily is. The fittings of selves in reciprocal harmony turn loose energy otherwise lost in the striving for such fitting. In this release of energy lies the main hope that the producer's view may grow and eventually provide a power which is great enough to control the conditions for destruction which have been symbolized by the splitting-and-integration of the atom. That which is powerful enough to integrate split men may be more powerful than that which is powerful enough to integrate split atoms.

This is, at least, the ground for hope and the basis for action of the research producer. He reasons that sufficient self-reciprocity may obtain to prevent great catastrophe, and that, whatever the eventual social actuality, he can make his best contribution by living his own life in an invitation to the widest possible reciprocity. So he places himself squarely in the center of his universe as he knows it and he extends himself through children to people to the widest reaches of universality. In so doing he gains an increment of felt relation to creativeness in people of generations far gone and far in the yet-to-come so that his hope expands beyond the limits of prevented-catastrophe-for-now to the wider reaches of possibility in man's emergent future. This helps his strength and patience, though his main nourishment comes from the vitality of his immediate realizations of living now.

A researcher in the curriculum field, with this orientation, has much to think about in guiding himself into his most vital realizations of living now. Among the major questions uppermost in his mind are likely to be two: (a) What sorts of attitudes do I want to guide me as I do research? and (b) What sorts of problems do I want to work on? The following are suggestions in answer to these questions.

The Producer's Guiding Attitudes in Doing Research

1. In doing research, I do not have to act like somebody who isn't "me"; I can do research so that what I do is more and more clearly mine. This feels good and right.
2. Research is an operation by which I am trying to become a better self-teacher so that my experience can say more things to me, give me more to think about and feel.
3. I can do research just for myself if I want to. However, I can have more fun, if, on some things at least, I can share my experiences with others. When this happens, I am likely to be able to generalize myself faster than if I worked alone.
4. A man doesn't have to publish to do research; he can communicate the shape of his experience in a lot of ways, and often the best way is right on the job with those with whom he associates daily. Publication may help to put one in touch with a wider range of people who are interested in sharing in the way one likes to share; it is helpful to have that company, but it is not the measure of whether or not a person is doing research.

5. There is very little to differentiate a good teacher from a researcher since both are avid inquirers. The main difference is the degree to which the teacher consciously tries to follow what he is doing for the express purpose of benefiting from it. In research, more formality is necessary in the observing, reasoning, preplanning, and reporting. Good teachers can readily become good researchers in this more formal sense. The more sensitive and thoughtful they are, the better.

6. It is no disgrace not to know a particular skill; I need not apologize for that. What would embarrass me in my own eyes would be to forget that my authority has to come from my own handling of myself.

7. A good place to think about doing research is in the middle of some activity where I am trying to do something that is important to me. My research is then my attempt to improve my actions in getting the values I want out of my experience.

8. My research will require a clarification of what I want just as much as it will require a clarification of how to get what I want in the most effective ways. I am to expect to "change my mind" on what it is I "really" value.

9. Teaching is at the very heart of life's most cogent situations. Human behavior is then as complex as it ever gets. Research depends on a willingness to accept the complexity and work within it.

10. The curriculum can be thought of in a number of different ways. One can say it is what teachers do to have things ready ahead of the time they will need them. One can say the "true" curriculum is the experiencing going on in the children. The important point is not the particular definition but the complex of relations that have to go into the whole situation so that the whole is held as a dynamically differentiating togetherness. This is the "reality" faced by the teacher and the proper context for inquiry useful to the teacher.

11. Proof is not a sledge hammer which can drive things into other people's heads; it is a way by which A tries to show B how A thinks his experience goes together in certain circumstances so that A can depend on his experience taking the same pattern the next time the given circumstances prevail. What is proof for A will not be proof for B unless B accepts the pattern as fitting and true for his life as well. Proof is an "illustration," a "suggestion," an "offering"—not a bludgeon.

12. When I hit the "intangibles," as I most certainly will, I will

consider them as useful constructions of mine which I can make more useful by (a) specifying what is meant in concrete situations and (b) showing how the constructions fit into a larger system of constructions. To run from engagement with the intangibles is to run from the problem of organizing one's experience.

13. In curriculum building, I cannot stop with a naming of "activities" I feel are valuable for children to do; I have to know what the children are actually experiencing while they are acting.

14. The critical unit is the experience of an experiencer. This means I am not down to basic data until I know what's going on in an individual child's experiencing.

15. Studying behavior is not the same as studying experience. I can watch a child's behavior without relating the action I see to what I think the child is experiencing.

16. To be sensitive to the experiencing of a child, I have to be able to posit myself as if I were in the center of experiencing of the child. I can then organize postulations of the experience he is having.

17. I can never be the child, of course, nor can I ever know what the full inclusion of his experience may be, but there is no escape for me—my primary data are my "as if" projections.

18. These projections are, of course, within my experience. I do not get outside my experience. Projections are a function of myself.

19. The more "as if" selves I can differentiate in myself, the richer my humanity and the greater the resources for projecting reliable data in the next "as if" case.

20. What is important in "objectifying" is the capacity to hold a form in the center of attention while differentiating it from as many other forms as possible. This makes a form stand out for easy and reliable grasping.

21. Objectivity can be fostered by the way I give my attention to the field in which the form is taken to appear, i.e., by looking at the whole with the intention of seeing the whole while, at the same time, noting as many differentiations as possible within the whole. When this happens, I have a maximum of relations by which to structure forms in the field. My judgments are then more reliable.

22. Scientists who deal with inanimate material use the same basic methods I do; it is only that they can check their "as if" position in their ongoing experience with greater ease than I. My compensation is that I am already nearer what I value in life at

the point where I get my data. The physical scientist has a long way to go to make wisdom out of his knowledge.

23. I will know I'm off the track if, at any time, my getting of data seems to require that I treat others in ways I would not treat myself. When data can't be reflexive, they're not useful anyway.

24. I will not be a failure in research as long as I'm learning better how to make good use of me. I am my own final judge in this matter.

25. When I seek criticism of what I'm doing in research, I'm asking my critics to tell me how they organize their experience in situations similar to those I present. This is a good sharp way of challenging a sharing right at the point where communication can be most poignant. If my critic does not guide himself by these rules, our ships will pass in the night.

Curriculum Problems of Interest to a Producer

A researcher, with attitudes of this sort, is likely to be interested in curricular problems of the following kinds:

1. How can a teacher tell what a child is experiencing?
2. How can children be given an opportunity to reveal their experiencing?
3. Do children differ widely in the kinds of opportunities they can make use of in revealing their experiencing?
4. How many of these opportunities are provided in the curriculum and how well do these serve each child?
5. Do teachers differ widely in the sorts of cues they habitually use to try to get a projection on what children are experiencing?
6. Can teachers learn to use new cues, or is this a matter of temperament that training cannot touch?
7. How, if at all, are teachers to make use of out-of-class experiences of children?
8. Are there some experiences which teachers should never try to discover in the lives of children? Do these experiences belong to children alone?
9. Teachers sometimes say, "I just can't reach that youngster. I don't know what's going on in him and I can't find out." Does the same child affect all teachers the same way, or is this a matter of "matching personalities"?
10. To "reach" a child, is it more important to have a teacher who is "like" the student in ways of structuring experience, or who "contrasts" with him?

11. In what does "likeness" of structuring or "contrast" of structuring of experience consist?

12. How important is it that a teacher show what he is experiencing so students can see on the "inside" of the teacher's organization? Must the sharing be reciprocal for it to take place at all? Does the age of the student make a difference?

13. What is meant when we say a teacher is able to "put himself across" to the student? Is this the same as saying he is able to "put his subject across"? Can the teacher do the latter and not do the former, or vice versa?

14. Do children differ a great deal in what they are open to in their experiencing?

15. How can a teacher find out what experiences a child is open to?

16. What happens among children when they learn a teacher is trying to find out what they are open to? Are they happy or frightened? Under what conditions?

17. In what connections (relations) do children find their belonging?

18. By what pattern of progression (if any) do children expand the universe to which they feel they belong?

19. What is the relation between a student's finding what he wants to belong to and finding what he is or wants to become?

20. Are curriculums helping teachers to sense and follow children's belongings, beings and becomings?

21. In what situations will children feel free to invest themselves in a course of self-reliant action?

22. Under what conditions do children "lose track of themselves"? What are the consequences for learning?

23. What does a curriculum need to have in it to provide children with ample chances to "find themselves"?

24. When can a child be said to have "found himself"?

25. Is the assumption of a split between man and nature a necessary part of the development of a person, or is it something learned that need not have been taught at all?

26. What is done in school to create such splits or to transcend them?

27. Maybe teachers feel split?

28. To what do teachers take themselves to belong? Is their universe expanding? What do they take themselves to be and what do they see as their becoming? belonging?

29. Does the curriculum provide stimulation for teachers to grow?

30. When a teacher stops growing, can he teach his students to grow?

31. What would a curriculum look like that was designed to do the most to help teachers recognize and develop themselves as creative beings?

32. Perhaps the freedom of the students consists in the freedom of the teachers; if so, how so? If not, how not?
33. What success do teachers have in teaching values they don't believe in themselves?
34. Is it better to have a teacher teach values he believes in, even if they are "split and wrong," than to teach values he doesn't believe in, even if they are "integrated and right"?
35. Under what conditions will a child recognize a problem as his own?
36. How does a "problem in arithmetic" become a problem accepted by a child as his own?
37. What happens when "the teacher's problems" are not claimed by the students as their own? When the student's problems are not claimed by the teacher as his own? When are problems to be shared and when not?
38. Do children see creation at work and recognize it as such? Is it necessary that they "recognize it as such"?
39. To what kinds of creating are children sensitive in themselves and in others?
40. Is creativity "contagious" among a group of children? If so, under what conditions?
41. When are children better teachers than teachers?
42. To communicate about learning is it necessary that a teacher show himself to his students as a learner?
43. Is it necessary that the teacher also show that he is taking the students as his teacher? Is this a condition requisite to "reciprocity," or is this to oversimplify?
44. In what does "progression as a learner" consist? Is it an increasing capacity to be a self-teacher? If so, is the learner's best model another self-teacher?
45. Some children are said to be able to "operate intuitively" in some of their subjects. Is this the same as saying they trust their feelings and are willing to follow them in determining what is "fitting"? Can there be any learning that is not dependent on a "feeling of fit"?
46. If learning is dependent on sensitivity to fit, what does the curriculum offer by way of aids to teachers in increasing such sensitivity in children?
47. Is there a conflict between increasing sensitivity to fit and increasing capacity to think, use logic, test, objectify? What does the curriculum do to help children get themselves together in their various aspects of structuring experience so that they operate more easily whole than split?

48. What is there about history that makes it like science, that makes it like music, that makes it like language? If we cannot answer this question, how can we answer the student who asks, as he goes from class to class, day after day, "What am I to do to make all of these me?"

49. Do things have to be "the same" or "alike" to be "one"? Or can an integration occur with "differences"? If the latter, then what is it that unifies? This is the question of what it takes to unify a curriculum; what does it take?

50. In what is one to place the dynamic center of the curriculum? Can you or I work out curriculum problems without recourse to that center? Can a student work out his curriculum problems without recourse to that center? What is it that throws us all together in "the same pursuit"?

In Perspective

If an educational researcher has found a way by which he can use his involvement with curriculum problems to confront himself with problems central to the emergence of his own life-with-meaning, he has found a dynamic for his system and a way by which he can work with soundness and profit to himself and others.

If enough of us were familiar with the way by which "problems out there" come to be "problems in here," then the emphasis in this chapter might well have been upon the trip from "here to there" rather than from "there to here." For many years we have been formulating from "here to there" on the presumption that we knew what we wanted, but so many significant changes have come in the "out there" circumstances that we are now caught with more confusion than our old and presumed wants can encompass. There has to be a period now where we pull back from major emphasis on fixing things out there to resolving things within ourselves so that we come to a level which will allow us again to take the initiative with a conception that promises resolution.

Hence it is that the inner drama is the important story now. We are challenged to transcend what we have been. Life forms have to move in further extension of themselves or they die. Humanity is required to create itself anew and with more included than before. Humanity comes packaged in babies that grow to be persons. Persons are required to create themselves anew with more included than before. This is how it is done in humanity. Education fits at the place where babies become persons.

As Americans, we are proud of our political philosophy which centers the political world in the individual man. We are also proud of our great economic productivity. It might be that our pride in the former, with all we have had the chance to learn since 1776, would now allow us to see that the self of a man is the center of his entire experiential universe, not just his political universe, and that our pride in the latter would allow us to see that the creativity of a man is the center of his very existence, not just his means of acquiring consumer products. With such sources to tap, there might be a breakthrough in American life. Things might get rolling.

It is this bigger story of need and possibility we have been trying to tell through the contrast of what we have called "the consumer's view" and "the producer's view" of research. By picturing what it means for a researcher to split himself from his data source and what it means to have him together with it, we have tried to show what it means to accept one's self as the center of his experiential universe. By picturing what it means for a researcher to split himself from the source of creation and what it means to be in the midst of creation, we have tried to show what it means to accept one's self as a creative being.

Insofar as the individual researcher can find it in himself to move into a self-creative position, he will find not only a richer fulfillment in his own life, but, in the eloquent reciprocity of creation-among-selves, a richer fulfillment in others which redoubles back on him. There is a great "structured emptiness" in America waiting for those who are big enough and fitting enough to fill her need.

Notes

1. For case histories and discussion in more detail, see "Evaluating Graduate Education," *Harvard Education Review* 25, no. 2 (Spring 1955): 85-94.

part four

Postcritical Reconceptualists

A cursory look at the articles designated as postcritical reveals the looseness of the category. Several of the articles are critical of extant curriculum conceptualization and practice, but the writers themselves tend to move past the critical function. In fact, their most recent work marks the beginnings of a third stage in the reconceptualizing process. The heritage attacked and discredited now begins to give way to an affirmative new conceptual order.

I regard Professor Huebner as one of the two most important curricularists in this group, although he may well be the most important. His work spans fifteen years, and his voice has been original, alone, and insufficiently recognized for most of those years. It has been Professor Huebner who has brought the traditions of existentialism, phenomenology, and theology to the curriculum field, and this contribution is of serious consequence. Curricularists have talked of the significance of the individual and of the humanizing process for decades, but on the whole they have lacked both the conceptual and experiential tools required for a comprehensive and convincing account of either. I contend that the philosophic and theologic traditions Professor Huebner has introduced provide these missing conceptual tools; as a result, his work will stand as both source and impetus for the reconceptualist movement.

The press of historical events has understandably influenced Professor Huebner, and we find that his recent (1973) "Poetry and Power" is generally an attack on the established and specifically a warning to ASCD. In a sense this address completes a circle begun with the 1962 article "Politics and Curriculum", which, owing to lack of space, is not printed here. However, his brief step into stage two will probably be just that—brief—and Professor Huebner will likely return to his study of curricular language, which is, in effect, the creation of a curricular language.

Professor Macdonald is the other major figure in this postcritical group. His "Transcendental-Developmental Ideology of Education"[1] will stand as an important statement of direction for reconceptualists for years to come. His articles included in this volume are similarly noteworthy; in "Responsible Curriculum Development" Professor Macdonald argues for a shift from the social sciences to the humanities as bases for curriculum writing; in "Curriculum and Human Interests" we find surfacing the work of Jurgen Habermas, whose influence on the work of Macdonald, as well as on Huebner's and Apple's, is considerable.

Professors Greene and Phenix, distinguished in their fields of educational philosophy, have contributed two important essays in the postcritical vein. The themes of consciousness and of transcendence will continue to dominate reconceptualist writing; they hint at the kind of post-positivistic concern that will absorb the field in the future.

This last section also includes the work of younger and typically lesser-known yet important theorizers whose work functions to reconceive the field of curriculum. Professors **Murphy and Pilder** introduce the radical psychological and philosophical work of Hampden-Turner and **Marcuse, respectively, and hence** the notions of counterculture and cultural revolution. This early essay foreshadowed the 1973 University of Rochester Curriculum Theory Conference, which addressed itself to these same issues. Mr. Pilder's address to that meeting, "In the Stillness Is the Dancing,"[2] is a fine example of postcritical curriculum scholarship. He has taken the conceptual tools of existentialism and added the experiential. Both the "Stillness" paper and the one in this volume bear obvious relation to the life-experience of one alive in the 1970s.

Let me make note of the thematic progression in my papers. The starting point is a radical psychoanalytic analysis of individual experience. In the "Analysis of Educational Experience" I summarize the psychoanalytic argument in the preceding paper, and then use this summary as a context out of which one might formulate an educational method by which we may work toward psychic integration. In "Currere" I extend this idea of method, and show its relation to the work of three curricularists who have been influential. Finally, in "Search for a Method" the idea of method is extended further, and placed in the context of present-day educational research.

Professor Willis introduces another major reconceptualist theme: experience. Mr. Willis rightly observes that the field has focused on behavior and, like American psychology, has failed to adequately address itself to the reality of internal experience.

Francine Shuchat Shaw introduces what I expect will become a major reconceptualist focus: the idea of congruence. The correspondence among what is taught, how it is taught, and who teaches it will be explored much in the way Professor Shaw explores.

As I have suggested, this attempt to write out of one's immediate, existential experience will characterize the curriculum field reconceived. The precise form this writing will take is still unknown, but my guess is that it will be much like the writing in this section, at least in function. It will be consciously exploratory and experimental, in the tradition of science, but its intellectual heritage lies in the humanities. To what extent the two can be wed successfully is a question for the future.

Notes

1. James B. Macdonald, "Transcendental-Developmental Ideology of Education," in *Heightened Consciousness, Cultural Revolution, and Curriculum Theory*, ed. William Pinar (Berkeley, Calif.: McCutchan, 1974).
2. William F. Pilder, "In the Stillness Is the Dancing," in *Heightened Consciousness*, ed. Pinar.

Dwayne Huebner

I am a child of working class parents and of the depression who found, at first, educational success and potential career in the physical sciences in high school. Having met a great high school chemistry and physics teacher, I started by majoring in chemistry and served as a lab assistant in the local junior college. From there the armed services took over and I ended up in a program in electrical engineering at Texas A & M. It seemed natural to put my two interests together and to go into nuclear physics.

That idea lost its hold as I became more and more disillusioned with my own education and the education of some of the people around me. I was also becoming less excited by the intellectual challenges of the physical sciences.

To better understand my own poor education and to see if I could improve the education of others, I chose to study teaching. It seemed logical to start where formal education begins so I decided to major in elementary education. The University of Chicago and Teachers College, Columbia University seemed likely places because of the well-known educators associated with both places and the early influences of the two institutions. Chicago accepted my application and I entered an elementary education program in the division of the social sciences. With my background in the physical sciences and mathematics, and the corresponding lack of background in the humanities, history, and the social and behavioral sciences, I struggled with the demands to use language rather than numbers and to be with people rather than with apparatus. I did it with reasonable, if unglowing, success. I taught elementary school for two years, long enough to know that I knew very little about teaching and education.

While at Chicago, besides coming under the influence of some of their notables, I had the good fortune to come to know Paul Eberman and Virgil Herrick. Herrick and Tyler had had their conference on

213

curriculum theory while I was there, and Eberman was completing his doctorate at Chicago and was an instructor in the elementary education program. Herrick left Chicago to begin a new program in elementary education at Wisconsin, and Eberman was invited to join the new program (where he stayed until accepting the deanship at Temple). With the sensitivity of a fine human being and an excellent educator, Eberman invited me to continue graduate studies at Wisconsin with the promise of research assistantships. I stopped teaching elementary school to undertake three full years of doctoral work in education and sociology to overcome my ignorance. The work was primarily positivistic—empirical and statistical and good. Wisconsin required a minor for the Ph.D. and we got to know students and staff in other departments throughout the university. In my third year I participated in an experimental program for a dozen doctoral students from diverse departments of the university who lived in an old mansion and held weekly seminars on their various disciplines—my first face-to-face contact with interdisciplinary work. My research assistantships involved the study of handwriting and classroom interaction using a Q-sort technique. With the completion of my course work and the beginning of the dissertation, I began to sense that my statistical and empirical competencies far outweighed my conceptual competencies. My last year in the university was spent in the library and in a seminar with Hans Gerth in advanced social psychology. My philosophical interests were starting to develop. Of major formative value at that time were Talcott Parsons, Donald Hebb, Susanne Langer, Ernst Cassirer and Bertrand Russell. From that point on the intellectual development was strange, rather subconsciously self-directing, and increasingly alienating from my colleagues in education. As I began my college teaching career in a preservice program I found myself turning to the mystics of the East and West including Meister Eckhart and other Rhineland mystics and some Buddhists. The religious dimension of this took me into Tillich's three volumes of his systematic theology and gradually into the writing of other theologians. By the time I left undergraduate teaching to join the staff of Teachers College, I had stopped reading in the positivistic sciences, whether sociology or psychology, and was into existentialism by way of Marcel, Merleau-Ponty, Jaspers, Sartre and others. My interest in theology led to advising in the joint program between Teachers College and Union Theological Seminary and the very rewarding contacts with diverse theologians, including a short time as a visiting scholar with the Episcopal Theological Seminary of the Southwest.

Throughout this contact with the diverse philosophical and theological traditions, the basic operating assumptions of curriculum thought bothered me. How could one plan educational futures via behavior objectives when the mystical literature emphasized the present moment and the need to let the future care for itself? The thread that ran through my questions and my searching was an intuition that an understanding of the nature of time was essential for understanding the nature of education. This intuition turned me to the literature on time and the criticism of learning theory as only one way of conceptualizing man's temporality. Heidegger's basic work Being and Time *kept coming before me, and when the MacQuarrie translation of it became available I bought it, to remain on the shelf for a year until I had the time to get into his language. Reading Heidegger was as freeing as reading Parsons and Shils in my early sociological days, or Hebb in my early psychological days, or Langer in philosophy or Tillich in theology. New ways of thinking became available—new questions, new modes of speech. With the cracking of my native scientific bent by Heidegger, and the preparation for that crack by Langer, Tillich, and others, I found it possible to reconceptualize the educational process and to begin intentionally to weed out the work of others which would fill in bits and pieces. And so the progress to hermeneutics via Ricouer and Palmer, and to critical theory via Marcuse and Habermas. The journey has been lonely at times, but the direction feels right even though the destination seems veiled in a "Cloud of Unknowing." I am convinced that the curriculum person's dependency on scientific thought patterns, even though these have not yet found their way into practice as they should, has broken his linkage with other very great and important intellectual traditions of East and West which have profound bearing on the talking about the practice of education.*

Dwayne Huebner
Teachers College, Columbia University

13

Curricular Language
and Classroom Meanings

The educator participates in the paradoxical structure of the universe. He wishes to talk about language, but must use language for his talk. He infers that meanings exist, but has only language, or other symbol systems, as a vehicle for his inference. Hemmed in by his language, he nevertheless has audacity to tackle problems on the edge of his awareness. The educator would talk of the language of children? With what language would he do this? Would he identify the meanings significant for young people? What meanings, shaped by what language, give him the power to do so? It is as if he detected a speck in his student's eye, but failed to notice the log in his own.

Release from the confinement of existing language, or more appropriately, transcendence of existing patterns of speech is available through several channels. The theologian would argue that the vicious circle is broken or transcended only by grace, mediated through the openness and receptivity available through prayer. The esthetician would argue that literature, specifically poetry, enables lowly man to break out of his verbal prison and to achieve "a victory over language."[1] The scientist would point to his success with observation, classification, hypothesis formation, and experimentation as a way of breaking through language barriers. The critic of social ideologies would argue that "conventional wisdom" is destroyed and reformed only by the "massive onslaught of circumstance with which they cannot contend."[2]

Unfortunately, the language which shapes the thought of the

curricular specialist is not usually part of prayerful acts, nor can the educator depend upon revelation or prophecy to refresh and recondition his language. If grace operates in the educational realm, it does so through other channels. Likewise, curricular language is, again unfortunately, not within the realm of literature. The formulator and writer of curricular language is seldom an artist. The penetrating image or significant metaphor is infrequently found in pedagogical materials. This misfortune is intensified by the nearsightedness of the educator who tries to be scientific by throwing out subjective formulations, yet who never quite produces a language system which can be made, shattered and reconstituted through the creative methodologies of science.

The curricular worker is stuck, so to speak, with conventional wisdom, which yields only to the "onslaught of circumstance." The onslaught of educational circumstances is felt differently by various educators. The individual educator's professional sensory and cognitive system is a delicate instrument for detecting shifts in his educational world. His responsiveness takes the form of new actions and new speech. Fortunately, all educators have not been shaped by the same conditioning agents, their sensory and cognitive systems detect different shifts, and their responsiveness takes different forms. Who knows, from such chaos a science might emerge! Given sufficient grace, the educator might even be blessed with the highest possible form of human creation—poetic wisdom.

Today's curricular language seems filled with dangerous, nonrecognized myths; dangerous not because they are myths, but because they remain nonrecognized and unchallenged. The educator accepts as given the language which has been passed down to him by his historical colleagues. He forgets that language was formed by man, for his purposes, out of his experiences—not by God with ultimate truth value. As a product of the educator's past and as a tool for his present, current curricular language must be put to the test of explaining existing phenomena and predicting or controlling future phenomena. Such curricular language must be continually questioned, its effectiveness challenged, its inconsistencies pointed out, its flaws exposed, and its presumed beauty denied. It must be doubted constantly, yet used humbly, with the recognition that that is all he has today. Perhaps tomorrow the educator will have better language, if he stays open to the world which speaks to him, and responds with the leap of the scientist, or the vision of the poet.

Myths in Curricular Language

Two tyrannical myths are embedded deeply in curricular language. One is that of learning—the other that of purpose. These have become almost magical elements within curricular language. The curricular worker is afraid to ignore them, let alone question them, for fear of the wrath of the gods. Fortunately, curricular language is not basically a ritualistic form, although incantations are frequently offered in the educational temples identified as college classrooms and in sacramental gatherings called faculty meetings. The roof will not fall in if these elements are deprecated and partially ignored. A talisman need not be rubbed if one acknowledges that learning is merely a postulated concept, not a reality; and that goals and objectives are not always needed for educational planning.

Indeed, curricular language seems rather ludicrous when the compexity and the mystery of a fellow human being is encompassed in that technical term of control—the "learner." Think of it—there standing before the educator is a being partially hidden in the cloud of unknowing. For centuries the poet has sung of his near infinitudes; the theologian has preached of his depravity and hinted of his participation in the divine; the philosopher has struggled to encompass him in his systems, only to have him repeatedly escape; the novelist and dramatist have captured his fleeting moments of pain and purity in never-to-be-forgotten esthetic forms; and the man engaged in curriculum has the temerity to reduce this being to a single term—"learner." E. E. Cummings speaks with greater force to the same point.[3]

> O sweet spontaneous
> earth how often have
> the
> doting
>
>   fingers of
> prurient philosophers pinched
> and
> poked
>
> thee
> , has the naughty thumb
> of science prodded
> thy
>   beauty   how
> often have religions taken
> thee upon their scraggy knees
> squeezing and

buffeting thee that thou mightest conceive
gods
          (but
true

to the incomparable
couch of death thy
rhythmic
lover
          thou answerest

them only with

          spring)

   The educator confronts the human being and no language will ever
do him in or do him justice. Yet the curricular worker seems
unwilling to deal with mystery or doubt or unknowables. Mysteries
are reduced to problems, doubts to error, and unknowables to
yet-to-be-discoverables. The curriculum worker cannot deal with
these because his language is selected from the symbol systems of the
social scientists and psychologists—whereas mysteries, doubts, and
unknowns are better handled by poetry, philosophy, and religion.
His language, his pedaguese, hides the mysteries, doubts, and
unknowns from him. Likewise, he assumes that all human behavior is
caused or has purpose, and that consequently his educational
activities must be goal oriented. This leads, at times, to ignoring the
fullness of the eternal present for the sterility of the known future.
This has also led to the continual discussion of educational purpose
as if such discussion is the only valid entrance into the curricular
domain.
   As with any myth, there is sufficient truth or value in these
concepts of learning and goals or purpose, and the language which
supports them, to warrant their continual use in curriculum.
However, to the extent that these notions are tyrannical and prevent
the development of other forms of curricular thought, they serve
demonic forces. No language system is so good or significant that
other language systems cannot eventually take its place—unless it is
an esthetic form. But an esthetic form has no instrumental value.
Other conceptual models are possible for curricular problems and
phenomena, and concepts which inhibit their development must
sometimes be violently uprooted in order that the phenomena of
concern can be more clearly seen.

Traditional Curricular Tasks

More or less traditional curricular thought, at least since Tyler,[4] has operated with four basic problems or tasks: the formulation of educational "objectives," the selection of "learning" experiences, the organization of those learning experiences, and their evaluation. Other curricular writers expand or add to these four, but the basic framework does not change. Here tyrannical mythology is freely displayed. The title is "The Organization of Learning Experiences." Why not the organization of educational experiences? The formulation of objectives is the first step; necessary, incidentally, because evaluation is the final step. With these objectives, experiences can be selected, organized, and evaluated. By framing curricular tasks in this language, the curricular worker is immediately locked into a language system which determines his questions as well as his answers.

To break from this framework, the language of learning and purpose must be cast aside and new questions asked. To do this the curricular worker must confront his reality directly, not through the cognitive spectacles of a particular language system. As he does this, he is then forced to ask, "What language or language system can be used to talk about these phenomena?" His reality must be accepted, not his language; for many language systems may be used for a given reality.

The two major realities which confront the curricular worker are the activities within a classroom, or activities designated in other ways as educational, and the existential situation of choice among differing classroom activities. This is an oversimplification, of course, for the educator's primary dimension of existence is time, rather than space, and the temporal nature of these realities is ignored for this analysis.

Educational Realities

The first reality is that of educational activity. What is and what is not educational activity becomes, at the extremes, a category problem, but generally educators can walk from one classroom or school to another and point out to a noneducator what they consider to be educational activity. Furthermore, they can dream about the future and envisage educational activity in certain places or among certain people. The language problem which emerges when the educator confronts this educational activity, his first reality, is how to talk about it or how to describe it. How does the teacher talk about his instruction as he plans it or as he describes it to another? How does the supervisor describe the classroom situation as he seeks to help the teacher? How does the curriculum planner talk about events which he wants to happen in classrooms? How does the teacher educator discuss classroom phenomena with his students? How does the researcher describe the classroom events that he studies?

The power of curricular mythologies becomes visible when the problem is posed this way, for the educator is apt to describe the student as a learner, and the teacher becomes a goal setter, or a reinforcing agent. Classroom activity is seen as a learning process in action, and indeed teaching is often seen as the mirror image of learning. This problem of description of educational activity has been solved in many ways. Most methods books have some kind of solution. The studies of teaching by Hughes, Smith, Aschner, Bellack, and many others are all efforts to develop a language which can be used to describe classroom action.[5] Teachers have their own way of talking and thinking about what they are doing in the classroom. Many of the studies of newer curricula are descriptions of what teachers can do in the classroom with students. This descriptive problem is both a scientific problem and an esthetic one,[6] for it is at the level of description that science and poetry can merge.

The first reality is also related to a second problem—that of choice among viable alternatives. Selection among alternatives requires some form of valuing, or at least some hierarchy of values. The second language problem becomes that of making conscious or explicit the value framework. When values are explicated a rationality is produced which enables the maximizing of that value. In turn, this rationality contains descriptive terminology which may be used to solve the first problem. The valuing problem and the description problem are consequently intertwined, thus complicating curricular language.

The key curricular questions, rather neutral from most descriptive and value points of view, are "What can go on in the classroom?" and "How can this activity be valued?" The central notion of curricular thought can be that of "valued activity." All curricular workers attempt to identify and/or develop "valued educational activity." The most effective move from this central notion is the clarification of the value frameworks or systems which may be used to value educational activity.

Value Systems

Five value frameworks or systems may be identified. The terms which identify them are not as precise as they might be, but discussion and criticism should aid in sharpening them. For purposes of discussion, and eventually criticism, they may be labeled *technical, political, scientific, esthetic* and *ethical* values.

Technical

Current curricular ideology reflects, almost completely, a technical value system. It has a means-ends rationality that approaches an economic model. End states, end products, or objectives are specified as carefully and as accurately as possible, hopefully in behavioral terms. Activities are then designed which become the means to these ends or objectives. The primary language systems of legitimation and control are psychological and sociological languages. Ends or objectives are identified by a sociological analysis of the individual in the present or future social order, and these ends or objectives are then translated into psychological language—usually in terms of concepts, skills, attitudes or other behavioral terms. With these ends clearly in mind the language of psychology, primarily of learning, is used to generate, or at least sanction, certain activities which can produce these defined ends.

Major concerns of the curricular worker are the mobilization of material and human resources to produce these ends. Books and audiovisual or other sensory aids are brought to the students, or students are taken to actual phenomena. Teachers are trained, hired, or placed to produce the right mixture of human and material resources. Organization and, to an extent not readily recognized in curricular thought, costs are carefully scrutinized, and some effort at efficiency is made. The control of the input of materials and human resources is a major source of control of this means-ends system. Evaluation, from the point of view of the technical value system, may be considered a type of quality control. The end product is scrutinized to see if it can go on the market with the stamp of approval; or if not yet at the end of the production line, the inadequate products-in-process are shunted aside to be reworked by remedial efforts until they can return to the normal production line. Evaluation, or inspection, also serves to check the quality of activities in the producing sequence. These activities may be improved or altered if the end states are not what they should be.

Technical valuing and economic rationality are valid and necessary modes of thought in curriculum. The school does serve a technical function in society by conserving, developing, and increasing human resources which are essential for the maintenance and improvement of the society. This technical function is obvious during wartime, when schools and universities are taken over to serve national purposes. During peacetime, the same social needs exist, but the technical values and economic rationality are apt to be hidden behind the verbal cloaks which a democratic society wraps around itself. So the educator talks of the need for individuals to read, to write, to compute, to think in certain ways, and to make a living in order to exist productively in his society. Technical valuing and economic rationality are necessary in curricular thought, for problems of scarcity and of institutional purpose do exist. However, this is but one value system among five, and to reduce all curricular thought to this one is to weaken the educator's power and to pull him out of the mysteriously complex phenomena of human life.

Political

The second category, political valuing, also exists in curricular thought; more often covertly than overtly. This value category exists because the teacher, or other educator, has a position of power and control. He influences others directly or through the manipulation of resources. To remain in a position of effective power, he must seek the support of those in positions to reward him or influence his behavior in some way. His work, his teaching or educational leadership, becomes the vehicle by which people judge the worth of his influence and hence decide whether he is worthy of their support, respect, or positive sanctions. Educational activity is consequently valued by the teacher, or other curricular leader, for the support or respect that it brings him.

The teacher acts in ways that bring positive support from the principal, superintendent, parents, colleagues, or college professors. Merit ratings, promotions, positions of responsibility, respect in the community, informal leadership among staff members are all fruits of acceptable and enviable efforts. The teacher may produce classroom activity which pleases the custodian, thus assuring him of a quick response when the room needs special attention or when supplies are needed. The superintendent may act to create classroom activity which brings forth rave notices from critical reporters, or accolades from university professors, thus gaining him more prestige in the community. He may need to act in certain ways, to influence classroom activities, in order to gain maximum support for the next bond issue.

The search for increased recognition or power is not inherently bad. A teacher or educational leader must have minimal power to influence others. His efforts are apt to be more successful if he has this power, or at least the trust and respect of those who count. The rationality that accompanies this form of valuing is a political rationality, in which the curricular worker seeks to maximize his power or prestige in order that he may accomplish his work as effectively as possible.

All educational activity is valued politically. The teacher who claims to be immune is so only because he is in equilibrium with his educational community. But given a change of situation, administrators, lay attitudes, or colleagues, that one-time nonpolitically oriented teacher must again rethink how his educational activity reflects upon his standing in the local educational community. There is nothing evil or immoral about political rationality and valuing. Indeed it is necessary if personal influence and responsibility are to be maximized. Of course, if power and prestige are sought as ends, rather than as means for responsible and creative influence, evil and immorality may be produced. Yet dreams and visions are not realized without personal or professional power. Hannah Arendt, in her *Human Condition*, identifies politics as one of the great arts of man, a fact too often forgotten in this day of self-aggrandizement and materialism.

Scientific

Scientific activity may be broadly designated as that activity which produces new knowledge with an empirical basis. Hence educational activity may be valued for the knowledge that it produces about that activity. The teacher, the curricular worker, the educational researcher are always in need of more and better warranted assertions about educational activity. They can construct and manipulate teaching situations to test new hypotheses, or to produce new facts as new technologies and techniques are introduced. Whereas technical valuing seeks to maximize change in students, scientific valuing seeks to maximize the attainment of information or knowledge for the teacher or educator.

The rationality by which scientific values are heightened is some form of scientific methodology. This methodology may take the form of action research or of controlled experimental design. It may be nothing more than exposing students to new situations and ordering the forthcoming responses. Teachers may seek to create unique classroom situations which will give them more information about individual students. Researchers may expose children to new teaching strategies in order to discover necessary conditions for the use of given materials or the accomplishment of certain ends. A total packaged curriculum may be tested to produce information about how teachers and students respond to a given curriculum.

Scientific valuing is a necessary form of curricular valuing. Only as new facts are produced and as new assertions are warranted can the educational enterprise keep pace with the world of which it is a part. Only as individual teachers seek more precise knowledge about their students and about their teaching procedures can they stay abreast of the "onslaught of circumstance." Educational activity valued only for the change produced in students or for the support it brings to teachers is narrowly conceived, for it may also produce significant changes in the educator if he undertakes it with the sensitivities of the scientist.

Esthetic

The esthetic valuing of educational activity is often completely ignored, perhaps because the educator is not sufficiently concerned with or knowledgeable about esthetic values or perhaps because esthetic activities are not highly prized today in society. Scientific and technical values are more highly prized consciously, and political values are more highly prized unconsciously or covertly. Valued esthetically, educational activity would be viewed as having symbolic and esthetic meanings. At least three dimensions of this value category may be identified.

First is what Bullough calls the element of psychical distance.[7] The esthetic object, in this case educational activity, is removed from the world of use. It is a conditioned object which does not partake of the conditioned world; that is, it has no use, no functional or instrumental significance, and consequently may partake of or be symbolic of the unconditional. It is possibility realized, ordinarily impossible in the functional world. It is spontaneity captured, normally lost in the ongoing world. Because of esthetic distance, the art object, in this case educational activity, is the possibility of life, captured and heightened and standing apart from the world of production, consumption and intent. The art object has beauty. Educational activity can have beauty.

The second dimension of the esthetic category is that of wholeness and design. Because the esthetic object stands outside of the functional world it has a totality and unity which can be judged or criticized. The art critic speaks of balance, of harmony, of composition, of design, of integration and of closure. The art object may be a source of contentment and peace, of a unity to be found only in the realm of perfection, the land of dreaming innocence. Educational activity may thus be valued in terms of its sense of wholeness, of balance, of design and of integrity, and its sense of peace or contentment.

The third dimension of esthetic value is that of symbolic meaning. Any esthetic object is symbolic of man's meanings. It reflects the meanings of the artist as an individual; it also reflects the meaning existing in and emerging from man as a life form. The esthetic object, indeed educational activity, may be valued for the meanings that it reveals, and may be valued for its truth. Educational activity is symbolic of the meanings of the educator, as an individual and as a spokesman for man. The teaching of educators who are spiteful, unrealized human beings reflects these inner meanings. The meaninglessness and routine of much educational activity today reflects the meaninglessness and routine of a mechanistic world order. In the rare classroom is the possible vitality and significance of life symbolized by the excitement, fervor, and community of educational activity. Educational activity can symbolize the meanings felt and lived by educators.

Ethical

Finally, educational activity may be valued for its ethical values. Here the educational activity is viewed primarily as an encounter between man and man, and as ethical categories for valuing this encounter come into being, metaphysical and perhaps religious language become the primary vehicle for the legitimation and thinking through of educational activity. The concern in this value category is not on the significance of the educational act for other ends, or the realization of other values, but the value of the educational act per se.

For some, the encounter of man with man is seen as the essence of life, and the form that this encounter takes is the meaning of life. The encounter is not *used* to produce change, to enhance prestige, to identify new knowledge, or to be symbolic of something else. The encounter *is*. In it is the essence of life. In it life is revealed and lived. The student is not viewed as an object, an *it*; but as a fellow human being, another subject, a *thou*, who is to be lived with in the fullness of the present moment or the eternal present. From the ethical stance the educator meets the student, not as an embodied role, as a lesser category, but as a fellow human being who demands to be accepted on the basis of fraternity not simply on the basis of equality. No thing, no conceptual barrier, no purpose intrudes between educator and student when educational activity is valued ethically. The fullness of the educational activity, as students encounter each other, the world around them, and the teacher, is all there is. The educational activity is life—and life's meanings are witnessed and lived in the classroom.

Educational activity is seldom, if ever, valued from within only one of the value categories. Rather all five are, or may be, brought to bear in the valuing process. Today, classroom activity is viewed primarily from the technological value category, but political considerations are also brought to bear; and scientific, esthetic, and ethical values may be brought to bear. The proposition may be put forth that educational activity in classrooms will be richer and more meaningful if all five categories are brought to bear. Indeed, the insignificance and inferior quality of much teaching today may be a result of attempts to maximize only the technical and political and perhaps scientific values without adequate attention to the esthetic and ethical values. Classroom activity which is socially significant because of heightened technical efficiency might have greater personal significance for students and teacher if the esthetic and ethical categories were also used to value the activity. But these notions become possibilities for further search and eventually research.

Systems of Rationality

Curricular language is not simple. Many ways can be found or utilized to identify and choose "valued educational activity." The five value categories which have been proposed carry with them forms of rationality which may be used to talk about classroom activity. These forms of rationality are not adequately developed here, and require much more effort before they can be used to analyze, describe, or create educational activity. However, the general aspects are perhaps sufficiently developed to explore the dimensions of classroom meanings which may exist. Attention will be given to ethical and esthetic valuing and possible forms of rationality which may accompany them. The technical is well represented in current curricular literature. The scientific and political are hinted at in a few places, although specific curricular implications need to be developed.

Ethical Rationality

Ethical valuing demands that the human situation existing between student and teacher must be uppermost, and that content must be seen as an arena of that human confrontation. This human situation must be picked away at until the layers of the known are peeled back and the unknown in all of its mystery and awe strikes the educator in the face and heart, and he is left with the brute fact that he is but a man trying to influence another man. A man is being influenced, even if in the form of a child. And it is another man who is influencing, somehow daring to make judgments, to direct attention, to impose demands, and to recommend action and thoughts. How dare he so dare? Probably because he is aware that he has, as have all beings, the power to influence.

Awareness of the power to influence may lead to hubris, the demonic state of false pride in the educator's own omnipotence, or to the humbling recognition that with the power to influence comes the lifegiving possibility of being influenced. The humble acceptance of his power to influence and to be influenced makes possible his freedom to promise and forgive and his willingness to do so. An act of education is an act of influence: one man trying to influence another man. Educational activity is ethical when the educator recognizes that he participates in his human situation of mutual influence, and when he accepts his ability to promise and to forgive.

The educational activity differs from other human encounters by this emphasis on influence, for clearly the educator is seen, and accepted, as a person who legitimately attempts to influence. However, he operates within the uniquely human endeavor of conversation, the giving and receiving of the word at the frontiers of each other's being. It is in conversation that the newness of each participant can come forth and the unconditioned can be revealed in new forms of gesture and language. The receptive listener frees the speaker to let the unformed emerge into new awarenesses, and the interchange which follows has the possibility of moving both speaker and listener to new heights of being.

Educational activity is activity not only between man and man, however. It also involves activity between the student and other beings in the world. The student encounters other people and natural and man-made phenomena. To these he has the ability to respond. Indeed, education may be conceived to be the influencing of the student's response-ability. The student is introduced to the wealth and beauty of the phenomenal world, and is provided with the encouragement to test out his response-abilities until they call forth the meaning of what it is to be thrown into a world as a human being.

Here, then, are concepts which might possibly be used in an ethical rationality of educational activity: response-ability, conversation, influence, promise, and forgiveness. How can these concepts be used to explore the meanings of classroom activity?

First, the sanctity of response-ability and speech must be recognized. The human being with his finite freedom and his potential participation in the creation of the world, introduces newness and uniqueness into the world, and contributes to the unveiling of the unconditioned by the integrity of his personal, spontaneous responsiveness. His responses to the world in which he finds himself are tokens of his participation in this creative process, and must be accepted as such. Forcing responses into preconceived, conditioned patterns inhibits this participation in the world's creation. Limiting response-ability to existing forms of responsiveness denies others of their possibility of evolving new ways of existing.

Speech may be considered a basic form of man's response-in-the-world. Indeed, Heidegger[8] equates speech with man's reply as he listens to the world. New speech, poetic nonritualistic or nonconditioned speech, is part of this creative unfolding of the world, and demands from the other a response in kind. The expressions of young children may be pure poetry, in that they can reveal to the adult previously unnoticed newness and possibility. The new theories of the scientist are likewise poetic statements which partake of this joy of creation. Unfortunately, the expressive statements of young children are too frequently ignored or pushed into the venerable coin of the realm by tired adult questions or conditioned responses, and science is taught as a body of knowns and sure things rather than as an activity of man which illuminates the unknown *and* man's poetic character. To accept the nonconditioned speech and response of the student is to accept him, and in so doing to accept the emergence of the unformed and to-be-formed in the world.

Next, knowledge and other cultural forms must be seen as vehicles for responsibility, conversation, and promise. The various disciplines—mathematics, biology, physics, history, sociology, visual arts, drama, and others—are not only bodies of principles, concepts, generalizations, and syntax to be learned. They are patterned forms of response-in-the-world, which carry with them the possibilities of the emergence of novelty and newness. Introducing the child to the language or symbols and methods of geography or chemistry or music or sculpture is not to introduce him to already existing forms of human existence which he must know in order to exist. Rather these disciplines increase his ability to respond to the world, they increase his response-ability in the world and thus aid in the creation and re-creation of the world. Through them he finds new ways to partake of the world, and he becomes more aware of what he can become and what man can become.

Furthermore, the existing disciplines are language systems linking men to each other via a vocabulary, a syntax, a semantic, and a way of making new language. The botanist is not simply a man who is interested in plants; he is a man who talks botany with other men. Disciplines define language communities with their own symbolic rules, and knowledge facilitates the conversations which may emerge. Knowledge becomes a way of conversing between educator and student about some phenomenon in the world. The educator, as a more experienced member of the language community, responds to the student's speech critically yet supportively. Knowledge, used in the process of educational influence between educator and student, becomes an instrument of promise.

The educator does try to influence, but with the optimism and faith in knowledge as a vehicle to new response-abilities and to new conversational possibilities. In essence, he says to the student, "Look, with this knowledge I can promise you that you can find new wonders in the world; you can find new people who can interest you; and in so finding you can discover what you are and what you can become. In so doing you can help discover what man is, has been, and can be. With this knowledge I promise you, not enslavement, not a reduction of your power, but fulfillment and possibility and response-ability." The real teacher feels this promise. He knows the tinge of excitement as the student finds new joys, new mysteries, new power, and new awareness that a full present leads to a future. Too often today, promise is replaced by demand, responsibility by expectations, and conversation by telling, asking, and answering.

Finally, ethical rationality for thinking about educational activity provides the concept of forgiveness. This comes from the educator's awareness that with the power to influence is the power to be influenced. To avoid hubris, the educator must accept the possibility of error—error as he influences and as he has been influenced. Hence forgiveness becomes necessary as a way of freeing one's self and the other from the errors of the past. Forgiveness unties man from the past that he may be free to contribute to new creation. With the power to forgive and to be forgiven, the educator dares to influence and to be influenced in the present. With the possibility of forgiveness the student dares to express himself, to leap into the unknown, and to respond with the totality of his being. As long as man is finite, promise must be accompanied by the possibility of forgiveness, otherwise only the old, the known, the tried and tested will be evoked. Because the educator dares to influence, he must have the courage to permeate classroom activity with the ever present possibility of forgiveness; for if he does not, his influence carries with it seeds of destruction through omniscience which can be only demonic.

Esthetic Rationality

When classroom activity is viewed from the point of view of an esthetic rationality, quite different categories of meaning are derived. As with the ethical, a variety of esthetic viewpoints is possible, but Paul Valery's view will be used here.[9] The general scheme is that the teacher creates an esthetic object to which the students respond. Their responses may also be considered esthetic objects to which the teacher responds as a critic. The intent throughout classroom activity is not a search for preconceived ends but a search for beauty, for integrity and form and the peace which accompanies them, and for truth as life is unveiled through the acting and speaking of the participants.

Valery defines the execution of a work of art as a "transition from disorder to order, from the formless to form, or from impurity to purity, accident to necessity, confusion to clarity."[10] André Maurois expands this by stating that esthetic

order must dominate an actual disorder . . . the violent universe of the passions, the chaos of color and sound, dominated by a human intelligence. . . . In great music, the torrent of sound seems always on the point of turning into hurricane and chaos, and always the composer, . . . soars over the tempest, reins in the chaos. But it is because the chaos has overwhelmed us that we are moved when it is checked."[11]

The teacher, then, in classroom activity can tame the incipient chaos and dominate it with human intelligence. Classroom activity can seem ready to disintegrate but for the esthetic order imposed by the teacher. The influence of this ordered disorder upon the student, if it is an object or event of beauty, is to make him mute. But the response is not dead silence, nor a response of admiration, but of "sustained attention." The artist's intent is "to conjure up developments that arouse perpetual desire," "to exact of his audience an effort of the same quality as his own," and "to provoke infinite developments in someone."[12]

The students, awed by the teacher's art, can be moved, then,

"to the enchanted forest of language . . . with the express purpose of getting lost; far gone in bewilderment, they seek crossroads of meaning, unexpected echoes, strange encounters; they fear neither detours, surprises, nor darkness; but the huntsman who ventures into this forest in hot pursuit of the 'truth,' who sticks to a single continuous path, from which he cannot deviate for a moment on pain of losing the scent or imperiling the progress he has already made, runs the risk of capturing nothing but his shadow."[13]

So the student seeks to dominate his newfound chaos by his own intelligence, and as a critic the teacher responds with critical concern but sympathetic intent. Classroom activity unfolds in a rhythmic series of events, which symbolizes the meanings of man's temporal existence.

Here, then, are concepts which could serve in an esthetic rationality of educational activity: the continual caging of chaos, psychical distance or **noninstrumentality,** beauty or harmony and form, truth as unveiled meaning, and criticism. How can these concepts be used to explore the meanings of classroom activity? It would be possible to use these notions to discuss the dynamics of teacher-student interaction. Yet more fruitful in this day of knowledge and intellectual concerns is to hint at the place of knowledge in educational activity from the point of view of esthetic rationality.

First, knowledge can be viewed as the ordering of particular bits of chaos. The irrational or unconditioned constantly creeps out of all forms of knowledge. As Jaspers states:

We become aware of the fact that in cognition we have moved in categories which, even in their totality, are like a fine filigree with which we grasp what at the same time we conceal with it . . . pushing ahead restlessly into the ocean of Being, we find ourselves always again and again at the beach of categorically secure, definite, particular knowledge.[14]

In science it creeps out through the continual destruction and construction of existing concepts and theories through the methodologies of science. In social ideologies it creeps out through the onslaught of circumstance. Thus in teaching, educational activity must order, but the unbridled chaos should not be hidden from the student. To do so is to deprive him of the element which calls forth the mute response, the "sustained attention" and the "perpetual desire."

The psychical distance or noninstrumentality of valued educational activity means that the playful involvement with the tools and products of knowledge need not be subjugated to the demands of social or biological necessity. The teacher and the students can be freed from the demands of utilitarianism, and the classroom can become a place where the purity and beauty of knowledge may be enjoyed for itself. The student can be freed to use knowledge to heighten his own significance, to enlarge his own sensitivities to the world, and to realize what he could be. The nearly infinite possibilities of knowledge and knowing can be hinted at, and the mysteries of the world can be pointed to without the need to reduce them to problems to be solved.

Esthetically valued, knowledge has more than power; it has beauty. As a man-made form its balance and harmony, its composition, its integrity and wholeness, point to the peaceful possibilities inherent in human existence. The scientist, the engineer, as well as the artist, are creative artists who engage in the creative evolution of new forms and who bring harmony to a discordant world. Participating in the making of his own knowledge, the student can recognize his inherent potential to add to, and conversely to subtract from, the possibility of man-made beauty. Intellectual disciplines as well as esthetic crafts are vehicles for this continuing creation.

As an esthetic form, knowledge in educational activity becomes symbolic of man's meanings and of his discovered truths. Knowledge as an esthetic form is a token of man's responsiveness to his own feelings and inner life and to his being a part of its world. Scientific forms of knowledge point to man's willingness to listen to and observe the world around him and to be conditioned by the unknown world. Technical forms of knowledge are symbolic of man's power over the world, and of his desire to shape the world into his own image. Knowledge treated as having an existence beyond the individual or separated from man may be symbolic of man's unwillingness to assume responsibility for his own condition. Knowledge being made and remade in educational activity may symbolize that the educator recognizes that his knowledge is but one of the flowers of his life, which blooms and dies, and yet is the seed of new life.

Finally, the act of criticism becomes a part of the esthetic process. All esthetic events and forms must be able to withstand the criticism of knowledgeable and responsible critics. The utterances and acts of teacher and student are proper targets of sympathetic but critical concern. Scientific criteria of empirical validity, parsimony, and logical structure are instruments for the criticism of scientific knowledge. Pragmatic considerations can be a form of criticism of social ideologies. Teacher and students, through their conversations, engage in the mutual criticism of each other's orderings, and thus contribute to the continued transcendence of form over chaos.

In conclusion, present curricular language is much too limited to come to grips with the problems, or rather the mysteries, of language and meaning of the classroom. The educator must free himself from his self-confining schemas, in order that he may listen anew to the world pounding against his intellectual barriers. The present methodologies which govern curricular thought must eventually give way.

Identifying and proposing a solution to the twofold problem of describing and valuing educational activity identified in this paper is but one attempt, among many that should be made, to reformulate aspects of curricular language. With it other meanings of classroom activity might be identified. As Conant points out, the significance of scientific theory is not its validity, but its fruitfulness. The scientific value of these roughly sketched ideas will be their fruitfulness. Their technical and political value are of no significance. Their ethical and esthetic meanings may be pondered.

Notes

1. John Middleton Murry, *The Problem of Style* (London: Oxford University Press, 1922), p. 101.
2. John Kenneth Galbraith, *The Affluent Society* (Boston: Houghton Mifflin, 1958), pp. 9, 20.
3. Copyright 1923, 1951, by e. e. cummings. Reprinted from his volume *Poems 1923-1954* by permission of Harcourt, Brace & World, Inc.
4. Ralph W. Tyler, "The Organization of Learning Experiences," in *Toward Improved Curriculum Theory*, ed. Virgil Herrick and Ralph Tyler (Chicago: University of Chicago Press, 1950), pp. 59-67.
5. Arno Bellack, *Theory and Research in Teaching* (New York: Bureau of Publications, Teachers College, Columbia University, 1963); idem, *The Language of the Classroom* (New York: Institute of Psychological Research, Teachers College, Columbia University, 1963).
6. F. S. C. Northrup, *The Logic of the Sciences and the Humanities* (New York: Macmillan, 1947), pp. 169-90.
7. Edward Bullough, "Psychical Distance as a Factor in Art and an Esthetic Principle," in *A Modern Book of Aesthetics*, ed. Melvin Rader (New York: Henry Holt, 1952).
8. Martin Heidegger, *Being and Time*, trans. John MacQuarrie and Edward Robinson (New York: Harper & Row, 1962).

9. Paul Valery, *Aesthetics*, trans. Ralph Mannheim (New York: Bollingen Foundation, 1964).
10. Ibid., p. 158.
11. Ibid., p. 163.
12. Ibid., pp. 58, 161, 193, 161, 151.
13. Ibid. pp. 48-49.
14. Karl Jaspers, *Truth and Symbol*, trans. Jean T. Wilde, William Kluback, and William Kimmel (New York: Twayne Publishers, 1959), pp. 38, 79.

14

Curriculum as Concern for Man's Temporality

If a science is to come into existence at all, it will do so as more and more powerful concepts are introduced. Their formulation is often the work of empirical investigators, but it is philosophical, nontheless, because it is concerned with meanings rather than facts, and the systematic construction of meanings is philosophy. Wherever a new way of thinking may originate, its effect is apt to be revolutionary because it transforms questions and criteria, and therewith the appearance and value of facts.

The state of having turbulent notions about things that seem to belong together, although in some unknown way, is a prescientific state, a sort of intellectual gestation period. This state the "behavioral sciences" have sought to skip, hoping to learn its lessons by the way, from their elders.

The result is that they have modeled themselves on physics, which is not a suitable model. Any science is likely to merge ultimately with physics, as chemistry has done, but only in a mature stage, its early phases have to be its own, and the earliest is that of philosophical imagination and adventure.[1]

Langer is not quoted to legitimize this essay as philosophical, but, rather to indicate that my notions are turbulent, that I am in "a prescientific state—a sort of gestation period" and want to share my sense of adventure. It might very well be a wild goose chase, but, as a long-time curriculum specialist, I am inclined to believe that my unrest is a result of unrest in this endeavor called "curriculum."

Many gathering together under this label have sought the legitimacy of the "behavioral sciences" and have moved directly to worship what Langer terms the "idols of the laboratory." They have ignored the hard and frustrating work of disciplining the imagination. I, myself, claim no special competency in this realm. My only discipline has been the frustration of trying to live with and use modes of thought presumed effective for generating educational programs. However, this has been with the increasing uneasiness that our questions and answers and the concepts which frame them are indeed inadequate.

This growing uneasiness centers upon two central categories in curricular language: learning and objectives. It seems to me that the unquestioning acceptance of these is one of the reasons that the curriculum person has failed to generate the ideas necessary to keep educational institutions and language abreast of the times. If these categories were not used as symbols of assumed educational realities, they might more readily become pointers in the search for other ways to look at and act upon educational phenomena. For me, they point to man's temporality and the concern for it as the focus of curricular action.

Goals, Purposes, and Objectives

For the purpose of this paper there is no need to make distinctions among the various uses of the words "goals," "purposes," or "objectives." These are terms that indicate the orientation of educational activity to the future. The educator looks ahead to expected outcomes, plans for tomorrow, and attempts to specify the future behavior of the student. Inherent in these terms is the notion of value, and the pseudoconflict between tradition and evolution or reconstruction. The process of arriving at these objectives, goals, or purposes (call them what you wish) involves inspection of the past (or the present as the already-past); identification of forms of existence or aspects of life considered worthy of maintenance, transmission, or necessary for evolution; and the projection of these valued forms into the future. Basically, the determination of objectives is the search for the bridge between the past and the future; it is argument over the degree of continuity necessary for change, or the amount of change that is necessary for continuity; it is concern for the balance between succession and duration. All of these categories are concerned with society's existence "in time" and refer to man's concern for the historical continuity which gives his social forms and institutions some kind of stability, yet vitality, as they emerge from yesterday into tomorrow. Unfortunately, the educator's too easy acceptance of the function of or the necessity for purposes or objectives has replaced the need for a basic awareness of his historicity.

This search for clear and unambiguous goals is a fanciful and, to a large extent, idle search. It serves almost the same function to those over twenty-six that drugs serve for the younger—tune in, turn on, drop out. To find the purpose of the schools is thought to restore the calm and enable educators to drop out of the troublesome political process of living historically. It has almost been assumed that if the educator can clearly specify his goals, then he has fulfilled his responsibilities as an historical being. But historical responsibility is much too complex to be so easily dismissed. It is too easy to forget that debate about educational objectives is part of the continuous struggle of rival political ideologies, which has its consequences in who controls the educational environment. The problem of living historically, or at least of living as an historically aware person, is not resolved by pronouncements of goals or purposes, but by engaging in political action.

History, not sociology, is the discipline which seems the most akin to the social study of education. The historian can be interpreted as looking back to where a society has been to determine how it arrived at a given point. In so doing, he identifies certain threads of continuity to unite diverse moments in time. In contrast, the educator looks forward. He, too, seeks to identify threads of continuity to unite diverse moments in time, but these are moments of yesterday and tomorrow, not of two yesterdays. It might be said that an educator is an historian in reverse. The curriculum person deserves to be chided for his ahistoricalism—not only is he ignorant of where his own field has been or is going, but he may also be missing a possibility that historical modes of thought might lead to more powerful tools for use in curriculum design.

The present does not easily find its way into the category of goals, objectives, or purposes. To identify these values requires withdrawing from the present moment and looking down upon it as if it were past. There is always a process of inspecting something which was. By their very nature, goals, objectives, and purposes become statements of a desired future—a tomorrow. The present creeps in in the teaching. It is when the educator must deal with the student that he seemingly drops the concern for the past or for the future and focuses upon the present. If he remains focused upon the past or upon the future, he loses contact with the student, and the educational process may suffer. It is by criticizing the category "learning" that the significance of the present is brought into perspective with the past and the future.

Learning

As with the categories of purposes, goals, or objectives, learning also points to the temporality of man, to the temporality of the individual man. Learning has been associated with a change in behavior of an organism. An observer concerned with the process of learning certain specified aspects of behavior at a given time, for example at t_1 and later at t_2, seeks to identify the changed status. If change is detected and it is assumed to be related to interaction with the environment, it can be said that learning occurs. It must be emphasized that "learning" is a postulated concept. There is no such "thing" as "learning." Learning theory is postulated as an explanation of how certain aspects of behavior are changed.

The category "learning" points to those aspects of a person's existence concerned with change and continuity, change and permanence, or succession and duration. That is, this postulated category points to the fact that man is a temporal being, whose existence is not given by his occupation of space, but by his participation in an emerging universe, the meaning of which is shown by the relationship between duration and succession. In the individual, this temporal existence is given by or identified with the relationship between those aspects of his being which appear to be continuous and those which appear to change. This pointing aspect of "learning" is most clearly suggested by two phenomena.

The first has led to the quaint expression "learning how to learn." Two questions emerge from this phrase. The first is whether an infant has had to "learn how to learn" and, if so, how did he do it? "Learning how to learn" is an expression usually reserved for older children or people who have gone through some beginning "learning" experiences. The other is more facetious. Will a time come when the world is so complex and changing so rapidly that we will have to "learn how to learn how to learn"? An infinite series is possible as we step further and further back to understand and resort to more regressive nonexplanatory explanations. Would it not be better if the educator would try to reconceptualize this phenomena of human change, rather than resort to such redundancies?

The second phenomena, "creativity," forces the educator, by the logic or illogic of his own language, to ask how a person learns to be creative. The very question itself demands a definition of the word "creative." I am always struck by the mythical explanation of man's creativity found in Genesis: "So God created man in his own image." Could it be that creativity is not learned, but an aspect of man's nature? Certainly, much theological thought would support this, for theology concerns itself with the transcending possibilities of man. Perhaps it would be more appropriate to ask what prevents creativity than to ask how one learns to be creative.

Is the "learning how to learn" question a real question or does it stem from inadequate explanations of human characteristics or from explanatory systems that force us to ask misleading questions? For me, these questions stem from an explanatory system which is either being misused or misinterpreted. It seems to me that the appropriate question is not how to explain behavior change but how to explain behavior patterning or fixation.

One significant characteristic of this rapidly changing age is that it forces a relook at the nature of man. When individual and social change was a gradual process and the forces of change were limited, the problem of facilitating human change seemed real. Today, however, the same problem seems poorly defined, for the world reveals man as a being having the capacity for almost infinite change. The problem is no longer one of explaining change, but of explaining nonchange. Man is a transcendent being, i.e., he has the capacity to transcend what he is to become something that he is not. In religious languages this is his nature, for he is a creator. A common theological description of man's nature is that he participates in both the conditioned and unconditioned, or in necessity and freedom. Man is conditioned to the world; he participates in the world's structures of necessity. But given this patterning, fixation, and conditioning, he also participates in the unconditioned—in freedom, or (if you wish) in the continual creation of the world. The explanatory problem is not to explain the unconditioned, or freedom, but to explain those conditions which make man a part of the world of necessity. This, I believe, is the function of the "learning" category. It attempts to explain man's conditionedness, the patterning of his behavior. By raising questions about learning how to learn or be creative, man is probing the very nature of what it means to be a human being and hence delving into metaphysics and theology.

This meaning is tied to the meaning of time. In fact, man can be defined by his temporality. The problems of change and continuity, conditioned and unconditioned, necessity and freedom, or of fixation and creativity are essentially problems of man's temporality.

He is not a fixed being. His existence is not simply given by his being in a given place, but by a present determined by a past and a future; thus offering possibilities for new ways of being in the anticipated future. A man's life cannot be described by what he is or what he does at a given time. His life is a complete something, capable of description only when the moments from beginning to end are unified by death. Retrospection about the threads of continuity and change composing an individual is the discipline of biography. These same threads projected into the future become the concern of the educator. Might it not be possible, then, that insights into curriculum planning for the individual are to be sought in the discipline of biography, as well as within the discipline of psychology? Whether or not this is true, it does seem obvious that education must be concerned with man as a temporal being. The focus upon learning (as simply the change of behavior) has detracted the educator from this larger and more complicated phenomenon of man's temporality.

Dependency upon "learning" as the major concept in curriculum thought leads to one other problem. The very nature of such "learning" suggests abstraction and generalization. In so-called cognitive learning, certain patterns, assumed to exist with the object world, are abstracted by the individual and carried into new situations. In psychomotor learning, certain patterns within the individual are abstracted and carried into new situations. The learning process implies the possibility of abstracting certain patterns of events from a specific situation or a series of like situations and transferring them to new situations. Thus, learning is assumed to be something that happens within the individual. Education is consequently conceived as doing something to an individual. This leads to the proposition that there is the individual and there is the world, and that the individual develops in such a way that he has power over the world or to act upon the world. Such thinking leads to consideration of the individual as something distinct. Obviously, this is not the case. The individual is not separated from the world, or apart from it—he is a part of it. The unit of study, as Heidegger, among others, points out, is a "being-in-the-world." Any system of thought dealing with human change as something that happens within the individual is likely to lead the educator astray. However, if a curricular language can be developed so that the educator looks at the individual and the situation together, not separately, then his powers of curricular design and educational responsibility might be increased.

"Learning" seems inadequate as the key concept for curriculum and points to what must concern the educator, viz, the fact that man is above all else a being caught in succession and duration, or change and continuity. "Learning," however, concerns itself with only a part of this total phenomena. It explains how patterning or conditioning occurs, and focuses upon abstraction and generalization. It yanks man out of his world and freezes him at a stage in his own biographical evolution. The problem for educators is to conceptualize man's temporality and to find means to express his concern for man's temporality.

Temporality

What then is time? If no one asks, I know: if I want to explain it to a questioner, I do not know. But at any rate this much I dare affirm I know: that if nothing passed there would be no past time; if nothing were approaching, there would be no future time; if nothing were, there would be no present time.

But the two times, past and future, how can they be, since the past is no more and the future is not yet? On the other hand, if the present were always present and never flowed away into the past, it would not be time at all but eternity. But if the present is only time, because it flows away into the past, how can we say that it is? For it is only because it will cease to be.[2]

Thus is the complexity, or perhaps the mystery, of time. Among the rather extensive literature, I have found Heidegger's *Being and Time*[3] the most fruitful, although his complexity almost equals the complexity of the phenomena of time. I do not intend or presume to provide either a presentation or an interpretation of this phenomonological ontology as he develops Dasein's temporality. A similar treatment of temporality may be found in an article by Friedrich Kummel.[4] For the purposes of this paper, Heidegger's crucial idea is that "Dasein's totality of being as care means: ahead-of-itself-already-being-in (a world) as being-alongside (entities encountered within-the-world). . . . The 'ahead-of-itself' is grounded in the future. In the 'Being-already-in . . . ' the character of 'having been' is made known. 'Being-alongside . . . ' becomes possible in making present."[5] Kummel's statement further clarifies this idea:

No act of man is possible with reference solely to the past or solely to the future, but is always dependent on their interaction. Thus, for example, the future may be considered as the horizon against which plans are made, the past provides the means for their realization, while the present mediates and actualizes both. Generally, the future represents the possibility, and the past the basis, of a free life in the present. Both are always found intertwined with the present: in the open circle of future and past there exists no possibility which is not made concrete by real conditions, nor any realization which does not bring with it new possibilities. This interrelation of reciprocal conditions is a historical process in which the past never assumes a final shape nor the future ever shuts its doors. Their essential interdependence also means, however, that there can be no progress without a retreat into the past in search of a deeper foundation.[6]

Time is not a dimension in which we live—a series of "nows," some past and some in the future. Man does not have so many "nows" allotted. He does not simply await a future and look back upon a past. The very notion of time arises out of man's existence, which is an emergent. The future is man facing himself in anticipation of his own potentiality for being. The past is finding himself already thrown into a world. It is the having-been which makes possible the projection of his potentiality. The present is the moment of vision when Dasein, finding himself thrown into a situation (the past), projects his own potentiality for being. Human life is not futural; nor is it past, but, rather, a present made up of a past and future brought into the moment. From his finite temporality, man has constructed his scientific view of time as something objective and beyond himself, in which he lives. The point is that man is temporal; or if you wish, historical. There is no such "thing" as a past or a future. They exist only through man's existence as a temporal being. This means that human life is never fixed but is always emergent as the past and future become horizons of a present.

Education recognizes, assumes responsibility for, and maximizes the consequences of this awareness of man's temporality. The categories of learning, goal, purpose, or objective point to this awareness. Their present inadequacy is not a consequence of their inherent limitations; but, rather, the educator's failure to recognize these limitations. He expects them to perform work for which they are not designed. The challenge to the educator, and particularly to the curriculum specialist, is to find a way to talk about man's temporality which will increase his professional power in the world.

The Individual-World Dialectic

Temporality, or historicity, is not a characteristic of isolated man, but a characteristic of being-in-the-world. A young child emerges as he encounters different aspects of the physical world. A man who has neither participated nor lived with others is ahistorical. The springs or sources of temporality do not reside in the individual, but in confrontation between the individual and other individuals, other material objects, and other ways of thinking as they are objectified in symbol and operation. Furthermore, these springs or sources, although again not residing in society, are nevertheless unveiled, maintained, and protected by society. Thus man shapes the world, but the world also shapes man.[7] This is a dialectical process in which cause is effect, and effect is cause. The world calls forth new responses from the individual, who in turn calls forth new responses from the world.

One of man's characteristics is his ability to respond. Heschel, in answering the question, "Who Is Man?" defines him as the being who answers to the world. Heidegger states that speech is man's answer as he listens to the world. Niebuhr builds a moral philosophy around the image of "man-the-listener."[8] These responses take the form of speech, or other symbolic expressions, and of action upon or in the world. One form of man's response is his understanding of himself in the moment of vision, as he projects his own possibility for being in terms of the "having been." Man's world responds by withholding or giving, yielding or resisting, punishing or criticizing, and supporting or negating. This is the dialectic, greatly oversimplified, leading to the continual creation and re-creation of man-in-the-world.

The scientific enterprise can be interpreted as an institutionalized form of the dialectic—a three-way exchange between an individual, the natural world, and a social group. The scientist questions the world via his theories and hypotheses. Through his experimental and observational procedures the world speaks back. Other scientists, however, also answer him by offering criticism—logical, aesthetic, or even political. The scientific methods are ways in which men have institutionalized their temporality and potentiality for transcendence and emergence.[9] This process is well exemplified by the interrelationships between science, technology, and politics. New scientific explanations and theories build new material conditions through various technologies. As technology changes the world and new scientific possibilities emerge, social problems arise which demand both political and scientific endeavors. Air pollution, mass transportation, mass communication, atomic power, and space exploration are all creators of such problems.

Language, particularly poetry, as pointed out by Heidegger, is also an aspect of man's temporality and his transcending possibilities.[10] Social conflict of any type becomes another form making man's historical nature manifest. Interpersonal encounter, through conversation or other modes of meeting, including the use of types of power, also carries the possibility of change within continuity.

The responsibility of the curriculum person, then, is to design and criticize specialized environments which embody the dialectical relationships valued in a given society. These are environments expressing concern for the temporality or historicity of man and society. These environments must encourage the moment of vision, when the past and future are the horizons of the individual's present so that his own potentiality for being is grasped.[11] Education is a manifestation of the historical process, meshing the unfolding biography of the individual with the unfolding history of his society. The past becomes the means by which the individual can project his own potentiality for being. The educational environment must be so constructed that the past is in the present as the basis for projection.

Curriculum as Environmental Design

An environment which would embody the dialectical forms valued by society would require three aspects or components. The first two could as easily be identified by most learning paradigms, although this analysis suggests different categories for conceptualizing them. The environments must include components which will call forth responses from the students. The individual is thrown into a world, not necessarily of his own making, but an embodiment of the past. What aspects of the past are so valued by those controlling educational environments that they should be used to call forth such responses? What aspects of the past can become a horizon of the student's present so that his future becomes his own potential for being? Next, the environment must be reactive, or else the student must question it so that it responds to him. This aspect is also part of the valued past brought into the present of the student. Valued forms of responsiveness are maintained in speech patterns and forms of dialogue, the structural forms of the various disciplines, the social customs shaping interaction patterns, and the man-made things (e.g., automobiles, talking typewriters), which make up much of man's world. This shaping component of the world channels man's transcendence into accepted patterns of social transcendence.

Finally, the environment expressing concern for man's temporality must make possible those moments of vision when the student, and/or those responsible for him, project his potentiality for being into the present, thus tying together the future and the past into the present. Somehow, the environment must provide opportunities for the student to become aware of his temporality, to participate in a history which is one horizon of his present. Only in this way can he contribute to the continual creation of the world and recognize his own active participation as an ingredient in the transcendency of the world.

This framework provides the possible reinterpretation of the significance of the categories of purpose and learning in the educational process. Given man's temporality, the future makes sense only as the horizon of his present. Heidegger's "ahead-of-itself" is not a future "now" that can be prescribed. Rather, it is Dasein coming toward himself in his own potential for being. It is the projection of a "having-been" onto a present to create the "moment-of-vision." Hence, the so-called purpose or objective is not a specification of a determined future; it is a value category used in selecting the ready-at-hand and present-at-hand in the educational environment. This is in accord with Peters' claim that the function of this purpose category is to determine the content of the educational environment.[12] Thus, the objective is a value category to select the educational environment. In effect, the function of this value category is to screen the past and the present-as-already-past to determine which components can serve man's temporality and society's evolving history. As indicated above, these components serve to call out the environmental responses from the students which are part of the being-in-the-world dialectic.

School people are concerned not only with the temporality of the individual, but also with the temporality of the society. In their concern for duration-succession, or continuity-change, they must consider the different rhythms of continuity-change between society as a whole, and the individuals who compose it. Society shapes man, but man, in turn, shapes society. However, the man who tries to shape society beyond its limits of tolerance is out of tune with his society and must be held in check. Hence, educational institutions must concern themselves with the individual's temporality within the historical rhythm of the society.

The selection of the content of the educational environment is consequently related to the forces controlling the continuity-change rhythms. Shifting educational purposes indicate shifts in society's evolution. Arguments over school purposes are not simply academic arguments, but efforts to shift the values determining the educational environment and, hence, influencing the continuity-change tempos or rhythms of individuals and society.

Today, for instance, the components making scientific dialectic possible (materials and language systems) are readily accepted as environmental conditions, for the continuity-change rhythm produced by science and technology is almost universally accepted as good. The emphasis is not simply upon abstract theoretical science, but upon the relationship between science and its uses—technology.

However, the social sciences have done less well in the schools. Part of this is, of course, because of the adolescent state of the social sciences. However, part of it is also because the technology appropriate to the social sciences takes the form of political action, and people responsible for schools aren't about to have youngsters use these tools to poke around in certain sectors of the society. The transcendences which could emerge might, indeed, increase the tempo of social change and continuity.

Of course, certain components of the world are more continuous than changing, more durable than succeeding. In these cases, it might be possible to speak of objectives as future. These components require complete submission. Their transcending possibilities lie not in the component's relationship with the individual, but in the individual's use of the component. In Heidegger's terms, they are the ready-to-hand: equipment. The typewriter is an example for, indeed, the person is conditioned to it. A future can be identified because the typewriter is fixed, and conditioning is possible and necessary. However, in such case, the individual uses the typewriter as an extension of himself, incorporates the equipment into his being, and makes it an instrument of his own temporality. The moment of vision is equally significant. Given this ready-to-hand, this along-side-of, this past, what is the individual's potentiality for being? How can he, with the typewriter a part of him, project his new potentialities in that moment?

Thus "purpose" is really a value category used to select the educational environment. However, because of its involvement in shaping the environment, therefore, participating not only in the dialectic between individuals and society but in the rhythms of continuity and change, it falls into the political domain. Conflict and argument over educational purpose is hence a part of the political ideological struggle existing in any evolving society.

"Learning" is likewise a category for building the educational environment.[13] The study of learning in psychology is a science, evolving theories or explanations of certain aspects of change. In education, learning theories serve as technological tools to help shape the sequence of educational experiences. They enable the educator to program environments and the forms and rhythms of their responsiveness. The talking typewriter is perhaps the best example of this embodiment of learning theory into environmental form. Learning theory makes possible the determination of conditions of the environment facilitating the dialectic between the individual and his world: conditions of the material components and of the human skills which are also, then, environmental conditions.

Neither of the categories—objectives nor learning—provides guidelines for the third essential ingredient of the education environment: the moment of vision. The student, either by his own understanding or that of others, must be able to envision his own projected potentiality for being as it exists in the past-present-future. This is the uniquely human quality of the environment and requires the presence of human wisdom. This is the unique function of the teacher, the human aspect of that specific educational environment, who shares the rhythms of continuity and change, of necessity and freedom, with his students.

Notes

1. Susanne K. Langer, *Mind: An Essay on Human Feeling*, vol. 1 (Baltimore: Johns Hopkins Press, 1967), p. 52.
2. *The Confessions of St. Augustine*, trans. F. J. Sheed (New York: Sheed & Ward, 1943), p. 271.
3. Martin Heidegger, *Being and Time*, trans. John Macquarrie and Edward Robinson (New York: Harper & Row, 1962).
4. Friedrich Kummel, "Time as Succession and the Problem of Duration," in *The Voices of Time*, ed. J. T. Fraser (New York: George Braziller, 1965), pp. 31-55.
5. Heidegger, *Being and Time*, p. 375.
6. Kummel, "Time as Succession," p. 50.
7. See Peter Berger and Thomas Luckmann, *The Social Construction of Reality* (Garden City, N.Y.: Doubleday, 1966).
8. Abraham Heschel, *Who Is Man?* (Stanford, Calif.: Stanford University Press, 1965); Martin Heidegger quoted in *New Frontiers in Theology*, vol. 1, *The Later Heidegger and Theology*, ed. James M. Robinson and John Cobbs, Jr. (New York: Harper & Row, 1963); H. Richard Niebuhr, *The Responsible Self* (New York: Harper & Row, 1963).
9. See John MacMurray, *Reason and Emotion* (New York: D. Appleton-Century, 1938); Michael Polanyi, *The Tacit Dimension* (Garden City, N.Y.: Doubleday, 1966); Thomas S. Kuhn, *The Structure of Scientific Revolutions* (Chicago: University of Chicago Press, 1962).
10. Martin Heidegger, "Holderlin and the Essence of Poetry," in *Existence and Being* (Chicago: Henry Regnery, 1949), pp. 293-315; Gusdorf, *Speaking*, trans. Paul Brockelman (Evanston, Ill.: Northwestern University Press, 1965).
11. This analysis has been shaped to a large degree by my understanding of Heidegger. Unfortunately, Heidegger has not attempted a developmental ontology, and attention should be focused upon those concerned with human development who have been influenced by Heidegger's ontology.
12. Richard S. Peters, *Authority, Responsibility, and Education* (New York: Paul S. Eriksson, 1960).

15

The Tasks of the
Curricular Theorist

Obtaining a perspective of the curriculum theory movement, if one exists, is somewhat difficult. It is hard to tell whether the search for something called theory is the curricularist's attempt to establish prestige in academic circles, whether he has simply been caught up in the behavioral science web and its increased concern for theory, or whether the search really indicates a maturing search for greater rationality. The quest for perspective is further complicated by the educator's failure to discriminate among the various phenomena with which he is concerned. Within the past several years, several books and writings concerned with educational theory have become available.[1] Might these efforts also be categorized as curriculum theorizing or necessary for curriculum theorizing? With the publication of the report of the Committee on the Criteria of Teacher Effectiveness in 1952 and 1953, and the subsequent *Handbook of Research on Teaching*, there has been increased concern for and systematization of research on teaching.[2] Might these also be considered curricular from any one point of view? If they are, they have not been well integrated into the curricular theory literature. This divorce probably implies nothing more than the failure of incipient curricular theorists to get control of relevant data and resources.

This is to be expected, for attempts to theorize about curricula are recent. Determination of how recent, of course, is a function of the definition of curriculum and theory. My own preference is to date the beginning of the current interest to the 1947 Conference on Curriculum Theory held at the University of Chicago.[3] However, as Herrick and Tyler describe their efforts they would evidently date the origin much earlier, for they state "that very little progress has been made in the realm of curriculum theory in the past twenty years."[4] Today, twenty years later, the same comment could be made, that little progress has been made in the last twenty years.

The current state of the curricularist's interest in theory is illustrated by three recent documents.[5] All three documents point to the lack of organization of the ideas and efforts related to theorizing about curriculum and to the problem curricularists have with their own history of theorizing. The bibliographies in each of the three documents serve as a good starting point for a beginning awareness of this history.

There are those educators who would seek clarity about the incipient field and its potential direction by attempting definitions of *theory* or of *curriculum*. I believe, however, that definition is a stage along the way, not necessarily a beginning point. In fact, if the notion of theory is taken as a starting point, the possibilities of being led astray are increased. Certainly the intellectual community that has made the most laudable theoretical progress has been the scientific community. It seems, therefore, that if curricularists wish to increase their theoretical sophistication they should model the efforts of the scientists. The appropriate literature is vast and very informative.[6] In fact, our brethren in educational administration have made good use of such theory.[7] Yet curriculum is a somewhat different phenomenon, and theorizing about it has brought out the fact that the curricularist must be concerned not only with descriptive or scientific theory, but also with prescriptive or normative theory. That is, he who would talk about curriculum must do more than describe what goes on; many people want him to issue imperatives about what should be done. This mix up between descriptive and prescriptive theory compounds our problems and leads to a continuation of the old theory-practice distinction, thus sanctioning old saws such as "that won't work, it's just theory" or "he is no good in the classroom, for he is just a theoretician." It seems more promising to start with the interrelationships among three different activities engaged in by curricularists.

There are those who engage in educational practice: teachers, curriculum consultants, and supervisors. There are those who conduct empirical research about curricular matters. These can be professional researchers, teachers, college professors, or advanced students. There are those who talk and write about curriculum. They can be creators of new ways of talking about curricular matters, or people simply using the language of others. Practice, research, and talking (or writing) are not three distinct occupations. Indeed, the same individual could engage in all three occupations. In fact, a person who is somehow involved in matters of curriculum usually talks and practices, or talks and does research, or he may simply practice and do research without talking. The truism that there is practice, research, and talk in curriculum is not the point. The point is to untangle the relationship among these three activities, which is not an easy task or at least not an obvious task. The untangling becomes more difficult and at the same time more illuminating if we recognize that these relationships are historical and cannot be disentangled once and for all. That is, it is well to make the working assumption that there are evolving dialectical relationships among practice, empirical research, and language. How can the curricularist articulate the relationship between his practice and his language, or between his empirical research and his language, or between his practical actions and responsibilities and his research?

Language

What is theory? Whatever it is, it seems to be rooted in the language that we use to talk about what we do, and it is this language web that must be our starting point. Like a spider web, it is sticky, useful, beautiful if we are not caught in it, and all of a piece, for if one corner is touched, the whole quivers. Many curricularists are flies caught in the web of someone else's language. Some are spiders, weaving webs as a consequence of their inherited ability. But the unique characteristic of the curricularist is that he is a human being: able to be caught in someone else's web, able to make his own, but more significantly, able to stand back and behold its beauty and form, to study its structure and function, and to generate new weblike patterns. Man and his language form a paradoxical relationship. He is inevitably caught in it, yet as its creator he can seek to transcend its confines, but in so doing he builds new snares which are equally confining.

The curricularist uses language. Some of us just talk, and the talk is not related to anything other than someone else's talk. Some use language in a variety of ways as they engage in their practical thing, whether it be teaching or supervision, or any number of other activities associated with curriculum. Some use language as they engage in research about curricular phenomena. It seems to me that one of the tasks of the theorist is to identify the various situations in which we use language, and to find categories that describe the various functions our language serves in those situations. Having done this, it might be possible to tease out the relationship between language, practice, and research. Then perhaps we can undertake some historical studies that will provide the kind of historical awareness necessary for men who would be free in their world building. Without historical awareness we are apt to remain caught in a language web of our own or someone else's making.

The Use of Language by Curricularists

The search to identify the various curricular situations in which language is used and the categories to describe this language is necessary because the curricularist has too frequently assumed that his language is all of a piece. The many books written about curriculum contain a wide range of language forms. Criticism has not led to cumulative refinement because the critics fail to recognize the diversity of language usage. The failure to recognize the unique contribution of a Smith, Stanley and Shores, of a Stratemeyer, or of a King and Brownell, is partially because curricular critics have not separated out the various types of language in such proposal type books.[8] Furthermore, the curricularist's search for *the* curriculum theory, or a one-dimensional way of talking and writing about curricular phenomena, hides the fact that different educators—say teachers and principals, or teachers and textbook writers, or supervisors and the mass media romantic critics—use language quite differently because their intentions and systems of relevancies differ. Unless we can begin to differentiate among the various uses and categories of curricular language, we will not be able to refine and polish any of it. What follows then is but one attempt to identify a series of categories for distinguishing among the contexts and uses of curricular language. The categories are meant to be suggestive for further inquiry; hence their values and limitations will not be pressed at this time. The categories are not new or original but are common distinctions to be found in a variety of literature.

Curricularists, whether practitioners, researchers, or simply talkers, use language to describe curricular events or phenomena. We need not at this point get involved in attempts to identify or define curricular events or phenomena, for these attempts would push us to a kind of rigor inappropriate for this stage of inquiry. Teachers, for instance, talk in a descriptive way about what they do in classrooms.

Some of the research on teaching is an attempt to build a *descriptive language* for talking about what goes on in classrooms.[9] Some of the language used by Ashton-Warner in *Spinster* is descriptive of what went on in her classroom. But there are other phenomena or events that are also considered curricular and are described in one way or another. Description, however, need not be of events and phenomena in a given place or time. Imaginary events or phenomena—those wished or those dreamed—can also be described. In other words, *descriptive language* can be a link between a reality and an image or a dream; between a present and a future, or a future and a past. The language used to describe what could be is also or can be the language used to describe what is, and vice versa. The limitations of the educational imagination could very well be a consequence of the limitations of the language used to describe present events or phenomena.

Another form of talk used by curricularists is *explanatory language*. We try to give reasons for what occurs, to establish causes. Descriptive language permits one to skate linguistically over the surface of events and phenomena, whereas *explanatory talk* digs below the surface. *Explanatory language* seeks to explain why something occurs or how it occurs. It is usually concerned with postulated concepts and inferred relationships. For instance, the term "learning" cannot be used to describe anything; it is a postulated concept to explain a presumed relationship between two events at different times: a change in behavior. Much of the language used by curricularists, particularly that coming from psychology and the behavioral sciences, is explanatory language. To describe with explanatory language is impossible, which is probably why curricularists have a rough time talking about practice with the language of learning, and why they have been preoccupied with a pseudoargument about whether to use behavioral definitions of outcomes. It would be fascinating to establish how frequently the curricularist attempts to use explanatory language to describe what goes on or what might go on.

Very close to and perhaps even similar to the use of explanatory language is the use of *controlling language*. We use language to construct and manipulate things, events, phenomena, and people; we use it to predict what might happen and thus to determine events that become part of a cause and effect chain. The *language of control, manipulation,* or *prediction* is essentially the bringing together of descriptive and explanatory language. We talk about how to get from what is to what might be. To do this language is needed to describe what is and what will be and to articulate the inferred causal linkages between the two. The language of learning is an auxiliary symbol system to serve this in-between function, and if tied to a good descriptive language it enables us to control events or phenomena in such a way that we can predict, within statistical limits, what might happen.[10] In the *controlling language* of curriculum, however, little attention is paid to the differences between descriptive language and explanatory language, much to our loss of vision and power.

If the language used by curricularists was totally language of description; explanation; or control, prediction, and manipulation, our analysis would be relatively easy, for these are forms of language common to scientific and technological endeavors. Fortunately, or unfortunately, depending on the friends you keep, the person engaged in occupations associated with curricular phenomena also uses language in other ways. He uses it to *rationalize* or *legitimize* his actions. As he acts in a certain way or creates a given situation, he frequently needs to reassure someone, perhaps himself, that he knows what he is doing and that he has a right to do it. He uses a *legitimating language*, which serves to establish his claim that he knows what he is doing or that he has the right, responsibility, authority, or legitimacy to do it. *Legitimating language*, or the language used to rationalize action, can be interpreted as an appeal to some social group for acceptance of the rightness or appropriateness of the action undertaken. Language used to legitimate is addressed to someone else who is in a position to judge professional adequacy and competency. Explanatory language can be used to legitimate action. However, explanation of the possible causes of or consequences of action might not be accepted by the judging group as sufficient or even necessary rationalizations. Language appropriate for the legitimating action ties the reasons for the action into the functional value system of the community to which the claim is addressed. Statements of educational objectives or goals are frequently uttered as claims for legitimation. The attempt to translate goals and objectives into behavioral objectives is an attempt to shift from legitimating language to descriptive language, so goals and objectives can be tied into the language of control and manipulation. However, other forms of legitimating or rationalizing language could be identified easily in educational discourse.

The curricularist not only seeks to legitimate or rationalize his actions, he also seeks to convince or influence others to undertake similar actions. That is, he uses language to prescribe a course of action or to influence others to undertake similar actions. Such *prescriptive language* is not simply descriptive of a future course of action; it carries with it an imperative, a command, or an attempt to impose a course of action. *Prescriptive language*, while often couched in the language of ethics and morality, is, nevertheless, primarily political language inasmuch as it seeks to influence and to involve others in desired or valued action.[11] Hence, prescriptive language requires attention to the rhetorical uses of language, and to the characteristics of the recipients or listeners.

Finally, language used by curricularists frequently serves as a symbol of cohesiveness or of belonging to a particular community. It becomes, in some instances, the *language of affiliation*, which serves as a vehicle and token of cohesion. Mastering the language is frequently part of the initiation into the community, and proficiency with the language indicates one's belonging to the community. For instance, the increased use of behavioral science language in curriculum can be interpreted as an attempt by curricularists to belong to the social scientific community. The use of slogans in education also symbolizes solidarity and membership in a given community. A look at the language formerly used by curricularists could produce an awareness of the communities and subcommunities that have existed in the overall field. The language centered around the slogans "the whole child," "democratic teaching," or "structure of the disciplines" points to collegial relationships that exist or that someone wishes to establish. The language associated with Bruner's *The Process of Education* might be interpreted as a significant effort to find a way of talking about education that brings the academician, the psychologist, and the educator into a single community of concern and language.

These six suggested categories of language usage in curriculum—descriptive, explanatory, controlling, legitimating, prescriptive, and affiliative—are not meant to be discrete. They are offered as pointers to various ways in which curricularists use language in a variety of situations. The categories do not necessarily depend on the structure or form of the language; rather they depend on the use of language in a particular time and place. To explore the interrelationships among these six categories would pull me away from my intention, which is to explore the tasks for the curricular theorist. My point so far is to suggest that the language used by the curricularist in his talking and writing takes many shapes or at least serves various functions. It seems to me that one of the tasks of the curricular theorist is to articulate the uses of language within the curricular domain, and to identify the various modes of language used. When this is done, the curricular theorist can more readily critique the language forms used in curricular discourse.

The Sources and History of Curricular Language

Language is never found ready-made in the world of nature. It is a man-made phenomenon, and its source is the creative efforts of people. Furthermore, it is never a complete or finished system or tool of man; it is always in the process of being recreated, which means that it is criticized and scrutinized in a variety of ways, parts of it are dropped from usage, and new usages and terminologies are introduced. It is an evolving form, and thus has a history or past that can be articulated. Individual men are the source of its vitality and its growth, and new ways of speaking by an individual can enliven a system of discourse and open up new possibilities. To recognize language as an emerging form is to accept its limitations and to be alert and receptive to new ways of talking. To be aware of the history of this emerging form and its various sources of novelty and emergence is to increase one's ability to contribute to its vitality.

Curricularists have tended to be ahistorical in the awareness of the various forms and institutions that make up their professional gear. Too frequently our tendency has been messianic. The search is often for the new and permanent vehicles of salvation, and thus we fall prey to bandwagons and the bandwagon mentality. We have a tendency to search for the final solution, and to think that we can discover the one and only best way to talk about curricular phenomena. In so doing, we fail to operate as historical beings and shirk our responsibility for the continual criticism and creation of new language forms and new ways of speaking. To be aware of our historical nature is to be on top of our past, so we can use it as a base for projection into the future. Another primary task of the curricular theorist, then, is to articulate the history of the various language uses that he has and to search for the origins or sources of his expressions and ways of talking. This is essentially a task of intellectual history, and it requires tracing the evolution of our various ways of talking and writing about curricular phenomena.

Even a cursory glance over the language referring to curricular phenomena throughout the years indicates the multiple sources of our language. At various times curricularists have drawn freely from philosophy, theology, psychology and other behavioral sciences, sometimes various humanities and technologies, and often the commonsense language of nondisciplined people. This will probably always be the case; for except for a very few words or expressions, such as *scope* and *sequence*, we do not seem to have a vocabulary or language that is primarily our own. Whether we will ever arrive at a unique symbol system that refers to curricular phenomena remains to be seen. This uniqueness is one of the fruits of scientific inquiry.

The curricularist's dependence on a variety of other disciplines and enterprises as the sources of his language creates no insurmountable problem. Indeed, it can be a strength of the field for without built-in structures of criticism and creation, as in an established scientific community, curricular language could stagnate. Our responsiveness to a variety of other fields means that we do indeed have sources of language renewal. The only danger arises from the lack of awareness of our own actions, the recurring failure to achieve historical perspective of the shifts in ways of talking, and the potential entrapment in a given way of speaking. Somehow we must become aware of the sources of our language, and the ways we have generated productive shifts in our ways of speaking. If an historical awareness can be developed, then the dangers of entrapment and obsolescence are less menacing.

At this point the distinctions among the descriptive, explanatory, controlling, legitimating, prescriptive, and affiliative language uses may be helpful. Failure to identify multiple uses of language in curriculum has clouded the relationships between curricular language and the language used in other domains. The untangling of these complex relationships could be approached in a variety of ways. A start might be to articulate the history of one language use, such as the explanatory or the prescriptive, in an attempt to identify its sources at various times. Another start might be to turn directly to the language of a particular noneducational domain, such as psychology, and identify how psychological language has been used or misused to describe, explain, legitimate, or prescribe. For instance, the language of learning is probably not very good descriptive language, but it is handy for certain kinds of explanation and perhaps for certain kinds of control and manipulation. Philosophical language has often been used for legitimating and prescription, but is probably rather ineffectual for explanation. Literary language, such as poetry, might be good for description but inadequate for explanatory or affiliative functions. Historically, dependence on a particular language use is apt to be a function of many different variables. The reason for appropriating the languages of the behavioral sciences today is not simply that these languages offer the possibility of increased power of control, but that they are also major vehicles of legitimation and affiliation; scientific-technological language has more cash value in today's economic and political spheres. Disregard for the language of theology is only in part a consequence of the circumscribed usefulness of theological language in education; it can also be explained as a subconscious attempt to deaffiliate from religious communities. The deaffiliation from theological language communities illustrates, incidentally, the need for historical awareness. The rupture between theology and curriculum was valid at one point in the history of both curriculum and theological thought. To ignore theological language today, however, is to ignore one of the more exciting and vital language communities. Of course, theological language would not carry much weight as an explanatory language in most circles, and would prove quite ineffectual as controlling language. However, it might serve as descriptive and legitimating language.

Another value of the historical search for our language sources is that language pulled from its primary domain is disengaged from established forms of self-correcting criticisms. In psychology, for example, expressions and terms are constantly scrutinized, empirically and logically, for their validity. Meanings shift and the uses of given words or expressions are altered or dropped as new experimental data accumulate and as explanatory paradigms change. However, when a term, such as *learning*, is pulled out of psychological discourse and used in another realm, such as curriculum, the scientific checks are not brought with it. A word or expression current in curricular discourse might be no longer viable in the parent discourse system. This is also true of philosophical language, and perhaps is also illustrated by the relationships between theological language and curricular language. If curricularists can become historically aware of these patterns of shifting meanings, they can more freely draw on and reject language of other domains.

It seems to me, then, that another task of the curricular theorist is to articulate the history of the languages used by curricularists. Articulating this history would require charting the changes in the various language usages and the relationship of curricular language to language of other domains. Articulation of these relationships would require attention to established relationships and relationships that were not established for a variety of social or intellectual reasons. To articulate the patterns of relationships between curricular language and the language in other domains might increase the awareness of our connections to a host of other existing and emerging language communities.

Practice

Within the so-called curriculum field there are people concerned primarily with practice rather than with the language used to think and discourse about practice. The very close relationship between language and practice (an old and significant dichotomy usually formulated as a theory-practice distinction[12]) makes it extremely difficult to conceptualize something known as "pure practice."

What is practice? Whatever it is, it is grounded in an environment constructed by man, and it is a human event occuring within that environment. Dewey provides the support for the focus on environment. In 1902 he stated that the function of the educator is "to determine the environment of the child."[13] He developed this more fully in *Democracy and Education*, in which there is a special section entitled, "The School as a Special Environment." There he states that "We never educate directly, but indirectly by means of the environment."[14] Analysis seems more generative if the practice dimensions of curriculum are viewed initially as concern for the characteristics of the educative environment. As with the analysis of language, the task is to establish categories for discriminating among the various components of the environments, to identify the actual or potential sources of these components, and to articulate the history of educational environments.

Practice as Educative Environment

Definitions are again a stage along the way, not beginning points. To attempt to define *educative environment* would immediately draw forth old solutions and arguments rather than push us to new levels of awareness. Arguments over the meaning of education have their value, but they can also serve will-o'-the-wisp functions. If the analysis begins with schooling, we need not get involved with definitions of the meaning of education or educative environments, for the schools can be looked at historically as a set of environmental components or conditions that shift and change through time.

Obviously, schools are made up of and contain things: material. "Material" consists of books, laboratory equipment, educational media, and programs stored either in print or electronically; but the buildings as well as the furniture are also part of the "thing" environment. In one sense, the curriculum consists partly of the buildup of capital investment in the educative material. For instance, development of the reading curriculum in an elementary school can be construed as the buildup of texts and other reading materials such as paperbacks, diagnostic and remedial skill materials, and films or audio resources. The development of science curricula in the elementary school can be traced by the shift from science texts to other types of science equipment, e.g., laboratories, and other materials such as film loops. The history of secondary school curricula can be identified, again in part, by the shift from woodworking, metal, and print shops to the capital investment in science laboratories, a greater diversity of library facilities and materials, and the movement from classrooms or groups for thirty students to flexible spaces. One of the significant aspects of today's curricular changes is the increase in the range, novelty, and complexity of educative material.

Another aspect of the educative environment is the language and symbols systems used for discourse among students and teachers within that environment. Discourse systems are major focal points of research and development today. Much of the concern for the structure of the disciplines can be subsumed under the topic of how a language or another symbol system is to be used within the classroom. King and Brownell use Polanyi's notion of a "community of discourse" as a way to specify the disciplined content of the classroom.[15] Phenix's *Realms of Meaning* can be interpreted as a concern for the systems of discourse used to talk about the experiences of people in the world.[16] Smith's work focuses upon the logical dimensions of the language used within the classroom. The material environment—the books, other media, and the architectural structure of the building—determine, again in part, the forms of language or symbol systems used. An arithmetic book specifies how the young person is to use certain symbols in interaction with people in action on or with the environment. Science and social studies materials also specify, in part, the way the student might use language forms to articulate aspects of the world.

A third aspect of the educative environment consists of the patterned or conditioned behaviors of the individuals who live in that environment: teachers, students, and other personnel. The intent here is to point to the stable skills and habits normally associated with roles and institutions rather than individuals. Again, the educative environment can be articulated, in part, as a capital investment in human resources, manifest in the conditioned and interchangeable behaviors of school personnel. This does not imply that the uniqueness of the individual teacher has no significant educative value in the classroom or school; it simply means that it is possible to talk about the input and maintenance of given levels and qualities of human skill and habit. The conditioned patterns consist of symbolic skills, skills of coordinating human action and speech with material, and the habits and skills necessary for social interaction. Administrators can legitimately speak of the need of their system for skilled manpower, and the possibility of building these resources through education of the staff or by bringing in personnel with new or different skills.

Material, symbolic systems, and human resources are organized into identifiable organizational structures. That is, the patterns of relationships among people, things, and discourse or symbol systems are relatively stable through given periods of time and can be identified as particular organizational forms. The various schemes of curricular content are cases in point. The subject matter curriculum can be conceptualized as one pattern of material, symbol systems, and teacher skills, whereas the core curriculum involves different patterns of symbols, things, and human skills. Grouping patterns, such as homogeneous and heterogeneous groups, team teaching, tutorial, and other organizational schema can be described by the different patterns among discourse systems, materials, and human skills.

It seems to me that one of the tasks of the curricular theorist is to focus his attention on the characteristics of the educative environment. This involves primarily the development of a descriptive language that will enable him and other curricularists to catalog and chart the environmental dimensions of practice. It might be said, as indeed Dewey in effect did say, that the curricularist's responsibility is to fabricate an environment that educates. Focusing attention on the components of the environment as distinct from the language used to explain, prescribe, or legitimize them could increase the power of the curricularist to design more effective environments and to see them in historical perspective.

The History of Educative Environments

To see these educative environments in historical perspective and to articulate this history becomes another possible task of the curricular theorist. There are two aspects of this task. The first is to trace the development of the environmental components within specific arenas of educational activity. For instance, the history of the "teaching" of reading is in part the development of resources for "teaching" reading. The shift in the kinds of books, programmed materials, and teacher skills must be traced, for the history is not simply a shift in ideology. Individualized reading programs, for example, are functional only when there is a wealth of trade books, a range of skill development materials, and teacher skills of diagnosis and remediation. The designers and distributors of reading materials are as much a part of the history of the teaching of reading as the theorists or researchers. O. K. Moore's talking typewriter is also a part of the history of the teaching of reading. The history of science teaching can also be traced, in part, by the changes in scientific equipment, and the coordination of this equipment with the development of teacher skills and new science language patterns.

Perhaps a more important historical task is to articulate the development of the environmental components within a specific educational situation. I am suggesting partial acceptance of a form of materialistic determinism. Educators have been deficient in ignoring the social theory derived from Marx's work. Environmental conditions are as important determiners of action and history as ideas. Curricularists have traditionally shown their idealistic bias by paying more attention to rhetoric than to things and environmental conditions. Curricularists responsible for given educational situations are often alienated from their own roots because of this concern for ideas to the exclusion of concern for environment. The professional language of the curricularist often pulls him away from his own feelings and his own language, thus alienating him from his own biography. On the other hand, the language used in professional circles and meetings is often not appropriate to the conditions within the local school system and consequently alienates the individual from the history of the situation in which he assumes professional responsibility. To focus on the environmental conditions within a specific political and historical situation is to help the curricular practitioner recognize his responsibility for emerging environmental form. To be aware of the possible evolution of existing conditions within a given historical situation is to be aware that curricular change, as environmental criticism and renewal, is a function of capital investments. Historical awareness brings to the fore the problems of environmental obsolescence, including the obsolescence of human skills and habits, and the problems of environmental inertia. With an eye on the evolution of environmental form, the curricularist can more readily accept that one of his responsibilities is the renewal and creation of environmental conditions, such as material, teacher habits and skills, and discourse systems, and their organizational interrelationships.

The Sources of Environmental Components

The search for the sources of the conditioned components of the educative environment points to one of the uses of curricular language. However, the relationship between language and environmental conditions is not simply a one-way street; it is sufficiently important to be pulled out for separate discussion. The concern here is with the nonlanguage sources of environmental conditions, granted that this is an arbitrary, and in part, superficial distinction. Creating an awareness of the sources of educational conditions and how they are brought into specific situations seems to me to be one of the tasks of the theorists. Not all components of the educative environment are a consequence of educational intention or rationality. The intrusion of newer instructional media into schools, such as television, computers, talking typewriters, and architectural forms, are all a consequence of creative actions outside of the educational domain and force the educator to ask how they can be used educationally. Some of the conditioned and relatively fixed patterns of behavior of teachers are also a consequence of forces operating outside educational practice or rationality but nevertheless crucial as components of the educational environment. The same can be said of the existence of various patterns of symbol usage within classrooms and schools. Again, the search to articulate the relationship between environmental components and their sources might be accomplished in two ways. The first is detailing the existence of the various components within a given situation and then searching for the source or determiners of those conditions. The second involves scanning the society within which schools exist, and asking how various materials, symbol systems, or human skills have been or can be related to conditions within the school.

Relationships between Language and Environment

The descriptive and controlling functions of language are significant vehicles for developing and introducing new conditions into the environment. The descriptive functions of language facilitate the envisioning of new possibilities by permitting description of conditions that might exist in the future. The predictive and manipulating functions of language permit the construction or fabrication of new environmental conditions by facilitating the specification of environmental variables and their interrelationships. Writers, using story, novel, or hypothetical form, can describe students and teachers in new and strange environments, in the manner of good science fiction. The language of psychology permits the construction of new environmental conditions, such as the electronic responsive environment and other computer-based devices.[17] Psychological language also enables the conditioning of teacher skills and permits teachers to increase their behavioral repertoire in new and perhaps undreamed of ways. In fact, all of the behavioral sciences increase the curricularist's ability to fabricate new environmental conditions; as do many of the technologies used in communication and other industries.

The reverse relationship also exists. The availability of new conditions can also call forth new language responses. Developing technologies create new environmental conditions that can foster the creation of new descriptive language, increase the need for new explanatory language, and suggest the necessity or possibility of new legitimating and prescriptive language.

A reciprocal relationship exists between language and environment. Language can be used to create new environmental conditions, and new environmental conditions can lead to the emergence of new language patterns. However, these are not dependent relationships, for both language and the various environmental conditions can evolve independently. It seems appropriate that the curriculum theorist should explicate this reciprocity between language and environment.

Practice as Human Event

Curricular practice is not simply concern for the construction of the educative environment; it is also concern for the human events that occur within that environment. The theoretical problem is one of finding, creating, or borrowing a language that can be used to describe and explain human events in educative situations. Within the past several decades the curricularists have been satisfied with psychological language to describe such events, and the language of learning has been the major tool. This dependence on psychological language or the language of other behavioral scientists is almost a direct consequence of the unconscious bias of curricularists for positivistic thought.[18] The problem of talking about human action and events, however, is one that is faced by most disciplined traditions. Other philosophical traditions, including phenomenology and existentialism, and certain theological traditions have been ignored by curricularists. Heideggerian thought seems particularly valuable, as does the language of recent French phenomenologically oriented philosophers such as Merleau-Ponty and Paul Ricoeur.[19]

Practice as human event suggests the essentially temporal nature of man and points to the linkage of biography to history as a major educational concern.[20] Curricularists have ignored such questions as destiny, finitude, and the meaning and morality of the influence of one human being on another. We have tended to lump these questions under the problems of learning and objectives and have been inclined to conceptualize the phenomena of interpersonal influence as a technological problem.

But the focus on practice as human event also increases awareness of the event structure of the educator's life. Practice as human event implies that the curricularist is also a human being with a biography in conflict and harmony with other emerging biographies being played out in historically evolving institutions. A concern for the history of practice as human event calls attention to the biographical structure of people involved in educational environments. The life history of the individuals involved in educative situations becomes a potential focal point of the concern and suggests the need for conceptual systems that articulate the phenomenon of human power and the dramatic shape of human events. This, it seems to me, is another task of the curricular theorist.

Practice as Design

The practitioner can be considered a designer of educational environments for human events. This is a two-fold design problem. The first is an esthetic problem of composing the environment in such a way that events flow in valued ways. The solution to this problem requires attention to the many qualities of the environment and their interrelationships, and to the durational aspects of the interaction among the individuals within the environment. The second is a political design problem. Fabrication of educational environments is essentially social policy, involving people with different values and intentions. Reaching agreement about the characteristics of a particular environment requires a potential conflict among those concerned and the use of power to shape the environment. The resolution of conflict and the organization of power is essentially a problem of political design.

Curriculum as a form of human praxis, a shaping of a world, means that the responsible individuals are engaged in art and politics. The curricularist has tried to ignore the artistic and political dimensions of his environment building by speaking as if the design problems were essentially problems of technology and authority. Hence the ready acceptance of the science and technology as educational tools and the frequent coronation of new educational authorities. The task for the theorist is to develop conceptual tools for grouping this twofold design problem. Hence the need for the curriculum theorist to be associated with the artistic and political enterprises and their literatures.

Research

Within the curriculum field there is also research, a term covering a multitude of activities. It is frequently associated with scientific activity and presumed to be related to scientific theory. However, this is not always the case. In fact the word, *research* has a legitimating function, for research is "in," and the researcher's "thing" is valued even if the research itself is not. This legitimating function has even carried to the elementary school level, where even children carry out "research" projects. The word *research* has not been adequately distinguished from the word *search* and the meaning of *re-* has been ignored.

What is research? I prefer to identify it as the use of the unformed to create form; as a focusing on the unconditioned in order to develop new conditions; as attention to human events in order that human institutions can be created or evolve; as the dialectical relationship between criticism and creation. In scientific fields it involves creating symbolic statements that point to a presumed reality, withstand empirical criticism in the sense of predicting or explaining the phenomena of that reality, and withstand the logical criticism of the scientific community. Research is not simply the gathering of "facts," but the development of a form to "fit" those facts. The data that fit the form consequently can be explained or manipulated by the use of that form. Thus the form is a man-made institution that contains, and enables one to work with, empirical data or unstructured givens. Scientists work with them to uncover new phenomena or empirical givens and to create new symbolic forms. Scientific research in curriculum can be considered, then, as the disciplined attentiveness to phenomena related to curriculum in order to create language forms. These forms enable the curricularist to contain and work with those phenomena for the purpose of uncovering new phenomena and creating new language statements.

Research is not related simply to symbolic statements. Within a much broader context, research is a vehicle by which man keeps all of his institutions viable and vital. Human institutions are intentional. They have been created to contain certain phenomena and to enable people to work with or use them for human purposes. Through research, people responsible for these institutions criticize them to determine if they reflect the givens to be held and whether they need to be revised or completely destroyed and recreated. The empirical critique determines the adequacy of the form for the facts. The social critique determines the adequacy of the form in terms of the logical, esthetic, economic, and political values of the users.

For curricular language, then, research is a vehicle by which the curricularists criticize existing language and create new language. Existing empirical research methods are appropriate forms of critique for the descriptive, explanatory and controlling language usage. Other research methods are probably necessary for the criticism and creation of prescriptive, legitimating, and affiliative language usages. At this time, I cannot specify the nature of these research methods. I have no doubt, however, that prescriptive language has no longer life or greater permanency than explanatory language. It too must be recreated to fit the givens for which it is to be used. The same is obviously true for legitimating language, for the values it seeks to align and coordinate also shift and must be reassessed.

The conditioned aspects of the environment—materials, symbolic systems, and human skills—can also be conceptualized as institutional forms that "fit" appropriate givens. As institutional forms, they too must retain their vitality and viability. Research can be interpreted as a vehicle by which these forms are criticized and recreated that they might continue to be appropriate to empirical givens and social values. Research is necessary to determine whether materials do indeed serve their intentional function; a form of empirical criticism that need not be mediated by language. Teacher skills are also conditioned forms that embody human intention, and must be amenable to empirical criticism and recreation. Symbolic forms used in curriculum are also intentional forms subject to empirical criticism and social judgment.

Research is the human activity that maintains the vitality and viability of man-made form by subjecting it to empirical and social criticism appropriate to given historical communities. According to Tillich, man must continually protest against existing form lest it become an idol, that new form might emerge.[21] Research is a vehicle of empirical criticism directed at man-made form, so new forms can emerge. In curriculum, language is not the only man-made form; educative environments and their components are also man-made forms that must be protested against that new forms can emerge.

Conclusion

What are the tasks of the curriculum theorist? As is true of all theorists his task is to lay bare the structure of his being-in-the-world and to articulate this structure through the language and the environmental forms that he creates. His responsibility is for the forms that he creates and uses, that they might be controlled by him rather than controlling him. It is necessary that he be conscious of his man-made equipment, his languages, his environmental forms. To be aware of these man-made forms is to be aware of their history, of their sources in human activity and intention, and continually to subject them to empirical and social criticism that they be not idols but evolving tools. All educators attempt to shape the world; theorists should call attention to the tools used for the shaping in order that the world being shaped can be more beautiful and just.

Notes

1. Marc Belth, *Education as a Discipline* (Boston: Allyn & Bacon, 1965); Charles Brauner, *American Educational Theory* (Englewood Cliffs, N.J.: Prentice-Hall, 1964); John Walton, *Discipline of Education* (Madison: University of Wisconsin).
2. "Report of the Committee on the Criteria of Teacher Effectiveness," *Review of Educational Research* 22, no. 3 (June 1952): 238-63; "Second Report of the Committee on Criteria of Teacher Effectiveness," *Journal of Educational Research* 46, no. 9 (May 1953): 641-58; N. L. Gage, ed., *Handbook of Research on Teaching* (New York: Rand McNally, 1963).
3. Virgil E. Herrick and Ralph W. Tyler, eds., *Toward Improved Curriculum Theory*, Supplementary Educational Monographs, No. 71 (Chicago: University of Chicago Press, 1950).
4. Ibid., p. iii.
5. *Theory Into Practice* (October 1967); Mauritz Johnson, "The Translation of Curriculum Into Instruction" (Prepared for an invitational presession on curriculum theory at AERA in February 1968); John S. Mann, "Toward a Discipline of Curriculum Theory," mimeographed (Baltimore, Md.: Johns Hopkins University, Center for the Study of Social Organization of Schools, January 1968).
6. James B. Conant, *On Understanding Science* (New Haven, Conn.: Yale University Press, 1947); Thomas S. Kuhn, *The Structure of Scientific Revolutions* (Chicago: University of Chicago Press, 1962); Ernest Nagel, *The Structure of Science: Problems in the Logic of Scientific Explanation* (New York: Harcourt, Brace & World, 1961); Michael Polanyi, *The Tacit Dimension* (Garden City, N.Y.: Doubleday, 1966); Ralph G. Siu, *The Tao of Science* (Cambridge, Mass.: MIT Press, 1957); Stephen E. Toulmin, *Foresight and Understanding* (Bloomington: Indiana University Press, 1961).
7. Arthur P. Coladarci and Jacob W. Getzels, *The Use of Theory in Education Administration* (Stanford, Calif.: Stanford University Press, 1955); Daniel

E. Griffiths, *Administrative Theory* (New York: Appleton-Century Crofts, 1959); Andrew W. Halpin, *Theory and Research in Administration* (New York: Macmillan, 1966).

8. B. Othanel Smith, William O. Stanley, and J. Harlan Shores, *Fundamentals of Curriculum Development* (New York: Harcourt, Brace & World, 1957); Florence B. Stratemeyer et al., *Developing a Curriculum for Modern Living* (New York: Teachers College Press, Columbia University, 1957); Arthur R. King and John A. Brownell, *The Curriculum and the Disciplines of Knowledge* (New York: John Wiley & Sons, 1966).

9. Arno Bellack, *The Language of the Classroom* (New York: Teachers College Press, Columbia University, 1966).

10. Ernest Nagel, "Symbolism and Science," in *Symbols and Values: An Initial Study*, ed. Lyman Bryson et al. (New York: Harper & Bros., 1954).

11. This is a moot point. Cf. Hans Reichenback, *The Rise of Scientific Philosophy* (Berkeley: University of California Press, 1951); Richard Hare, *The Language of Morals* (Oxford, England: Clarendon Press, 1952); Patrick Corbett, *Ideologies* (New York: Harcourt, Brace & World, 1965).

12. Nicholas Lobkowicz, *Theory and Practice* (Notre Dame, Ind.: University of Notre Dame Press, 1967).

13. John Dewey, *The Child and the Curriculum* (Chicago: University of Chicago Press, 1902).

14. John Dewey, *Democracy and Education* (New York: Macmillan, 1961), p. 19.

15. King and Brownell, *Curriculum and Disciplines.*

16. Philip Phenix, *Realms of Meaning* (New York: McGraw-Hill, 1964).

17. Dwayne Huebner, "The Implications of Psychological Thought for the Curriculum," in *Influences in Curriculum Change* (Washington, D.C.: ASCD, 1968).

18. Herbert Marcuse, *Reason and Revolution* (New York: Oxford University Press, 1941).

19. See chapter 14; Maurice Merleau-Ponty, *The Primacy of Perception* (Evanston, Ill.: Northwestern University Press, 1964); Paul Ricoeur, *Freedom and Nature: The Voluntary and the Involuntary*, trans. V. Kohak (Evanston, Ill.: Northwestern University Press, 1966).

20. See chapter 14.

21. Paul Tillich, *The Protestant Era* (Chicago: University of Chicago Press, 1948).

16

Poetry and Power: The Politics of Curricular Development

Fellow educators—are we not lost? Do we know where we are, remember where we have been, or foresee where we are going? We've talked about education for individuals since Rousseau, Kilpatric, and Harold Benjamin. In our lostness, are we not jumping on bandwagons—yesterday core, group process, team teaching; today open classrooms and alternative schools—and assuming that at least these bandwagon experts know where they are? In our lostness are we not imbibing the snake oils and patent medicines—programmed individual computers, T.U., structure and disciplines, sensitivity training—hoping that we can cure our maladies? But we find that our pain has been relieved only temporarily and that we may indeed have been taken in by a new breed of pusher. In our lostness, we recite the familiar litanies of humanism and individuality, hoping that the gods of our past will recognize our goodwill, forgive us our sins of omission and commission, and restore our sight and vitality.

Why do we move around so frantically—tugging at the coattails of our also lost neighbor and sampling his diverse wares? Why do we not comport ourselves in such a manner that our center—our sense of who we are and what we are about—can be restored and reformed? Why do we not pause to feel the painful tensions and pulls in us, which are reflections of the tensions and pulls of our society? Why do we not notice more carefully the direction of technical changes, social changes, and political changes? Why do we not listen more thoughtfully to the songs of the young, the anger of the oppressed, the labored breathing of those dying of overdoses of heroin or methadone, the painful cry of those bombed at Christmas time, the prideful platitudes of those in power? Why do we not act with courage—with the awareness that creation requires risk taking as well as statistical evidence? Why do we not reflect more critically on what we and others do—to discover in our institutions our bondage to others, and the bondages we impose?

Is it because we are afraid to acknowledge that power makes up our center—a power that necessarily comes up against the power of others: principals, parents, kids, board members, text writers. We are afraid, maybe even ashamed, to acknowledge that that which we are about as educators is politics: a struggle to maintain, maybe even change through destruction and reconstruction, the world we make with others. If we acknowledge that we are political we necessarily risk defeat, or maybe the awareness that we are indeed doing someone else's thing and are alienated from ourselves. If we acknowledge that we are political we risk recognizing our importance and hearing ourselves as braying asses or clanking symbols. It is far easier or safer to proclaim the individual and to then fit ourselves into a prepared slot: buy someone else's package of objectives, materials, and bets; or put on someone else's alternative school. Then if we fail, it is their fault, not ours.

Why are we lost? I think it is because we have let the school become our center and we have become an appendage, nothing but a role or functionary in someone else's institution. Institutions do not have memories, they cannot recall their past; who established them, under what circumstances, for what purposes. The people who started them disappear in the mindless routines. Only men and women have memories, an historical consciousness, and can recall how things got started, why and by whom. If we forget or never knew that schools are a product of men and women who used their power to build or maintain a certain kind of public world, then we easily become bondsmen of those who live only in the routines. We do their things, maintain their world, distribute their awards. And they reward us by a humdrum comfortable life style, perhaps with tenure and retirement, access to the more common goods of our production lines, and permit us the privacy of sex and family life, but deprive us of public vitality and joy, clean air and water, safe, comfortable, exciting urban areas that support our well-being and sociality.

If we remember that education is a political activity in which some people influence others, and that the school is one way to organize that power and influence, then perhaps we can try to share the control of the school and use it for our political purposes. Instead of our being an extension of the school, of someone else's will and power, the school can be, in part, an extension of our will and power—a vehicle for our political concerns. If we remember this, then we can recognize that the struggle to remake the school is a struggle to make a more just public world. If the school is a vehicle of political activity, then our lack of clarity, our lack of vision about the school is a function of our lack of clarity and vision about our public world—a breakdown in our talk, our poetry, about the world we make.

We do not talk about a more just public world; we talk about school, we think about school, and we see the world through the windows and doors of the school. The school has become our place. We have become school people, our language of learning, discipline, motivation, stimulus, individualization, is school language. Our images for generating new educational possibilities are school images. So we seek more diversified and smaller packages of instructional materials, not greater public access to information without federal control, or better development of cable television for neighborhood use. We seek open classrooms, not open societies. We seek alternative schools, not alternative public worlds. And because we are school people our public statements affirm the school, defend the present public school, and hide social injustice. Our propaganda of individualism is liberal cant that hides the basic conservatism of school people and permits those who control our public world to continue to control it. Our public statements are not socially or personally liberating. They do not excite us to imagine more just public worlds. They do not harness the power of people in the political struggle to reform our present inequitable institutions. They do not enable men or women to recognize and grasp their political right to share in the maintenance and reforming of our public world.

For instance, how much individuality can school people tolerate in an institution that is compulsory? The expression "curriculum for individuals" hides from our awareness that the school is a place of control; of socialization if you prefer this pseudoscientific term that hides political domination. We maintain that control by our power. Of course, with our goodwill and out of our good graces we grant reasonable power to students to be individuals, providing they are not too individualistic in their speech, their actions, their commitments. Do we prefer the individualism of Thomas Paine, the Berrigan brothers, Ellsberg, Cleaver, Angela Davis, and the young men who went to Canada or Scandanavia rather than die in a tragic imperialistic war or the individualism of the Watergate caper boys, the .I.T.T. executives, and perhaps those in the executive offices of the federal government?

Why have the court cases for racial equality, to permit long hair and dress options in schools, freedom of high school people to print politically oriented papers sometimes critical of the schools, the rights of pregnant girls to be in school, and the rights of Amish kids to stay out of public school been pushed by a few parents and civil libertarians rather than ASCDers? Can we honestly read those three words, *curriculum for individuality*, as other than propaganda to hide from our awareness our commitments as school people, and to put a verbal gloss on our intentions, which do not coincide with our practices. If we really believed those three words, we would not only be waiting for better materials, we would also be looking for court cases to restrain the power of school people and extend the constitutional rights of children and young people in the school. We would be training educators in workshops here at ASCD to attend to the legal implications of their control of and talk to the young, as Thomas is doing for kids in Dayton. We would be building up a body of civil law about the rights of children that would be as much a part of our curricular knowledge as is child development. If we really believed those words, should not ASCD initiate movement among professional educators to modify or revoke compulsory attendance laws, to urge the U.S. postal service to stop subsidizing junk mail and advertisements and subsidize the publication of journals of opinion and fact which are dwindling in number? If we really believed these words, would we not be working with nonschool people who are trying to increase the educational possibilities that exist outside the school?

By saying these things, I do not intend to come down on the side of Reimer or Illich who tell us that school is dead and urge us to deschool society (although I grant the value of contemplating death as a way of identifying the choices we have and have not made). Those proposals are also nonhistorical for us in the United States. It is necessary, rather, to see our schools, the materials and resources within them, and the social organizational patterns that result in historical perspective. The ways that we have thought about these during the first half of this century are not the ways we should think about them during the last quarter. Since the Second World War we have assumed that more of the same with better research for better living would do it, but Jencks, among others, warns us that this is not so. Because we lack an educational poetry which stirs the imagination and harnesses our power we are forced to push our school images, our present school materials and organization to the breaking point, without conviction or results, but with a naive faith in our past ways. But the past must be rethought, not reused.

What then are we about as educators? We are not about maintaining schools, for that is the self-serving concern of school people who see their livelihood in the maintenance of that institution. We are about the conscious shaping of the future by helping the young work out, work through, or work into their futures and into our future. We have the utter gall to be concerned with the mundane destiny of individuals, ours and our students. Ours is not a power over individuals, but a power for individuals. And a power for the future of our public world. But which individuals, and what kind of future?

Oh yes, we are for the urban black, if he is not angry and will speak in moderate tones, accept our middle-class behaviors, and affirm our future, thus perhaps giving up his. Oh yes, we are for the American Indian if he will give up his past and accept our future and our last forty-five years of public policy. Oh yes, we are for the homosexual if he will stay in the closet and not let his peculiarities stain our image of the future. Oh yes, we are for women, if they will accept their female role in our male future. Oh yes, we are for the Asian Marxist or Maoist if they will recognize that the way to the future is by maintaining present power balances. We are for those individuals who will protect and maintain our image of the future, but what of their imagined futures? If their tomorrow requires that we give up some of our privileges, will we still be for those individuals?

Those are the tensions we live in, are they not? The ambivalences of our commitments become obvious, do they not? For if we use our power for the future of all young we may indeed be in political conflict with our own self-interests. We are in that conflict, which is one reason that school people, although speaking a liberal political rhetoric, are essentially conservative in the political spectrum. Our individualism is a nineteenth-century individualism, aimed at the freedom of those who partake of the prevalent means of production and consumption. But with the 1972 election, it seems that liberalism is dead. We must now acknowledge that we are rightist or leftist and that there is no middle. But the school, make no mistake about it, is in the hands of the silent majority or conservative right, which might be an explanation of why the young radical leftist teacher either becomes socialized to the school and gives up his images of the future, or finds other ways to educate the young.

So our center of power as educators, a power for the future of the individual, comes in conflict with our own future, which is frequently an extension of the present. In this conflict we shift from power for to power over and thus to the conservative inertia of school people. Let us keep looking for other reasons, but if we turn to our center of power we easily recognize that a dedicated educator risks his imaged future as he works with the young. The educator working in schools can use the rules and rewards of the school to reduce or even remove that risk. He is thus tempted to control, not to liberate, and to justify the control by the political ideology of the free individual, which was rampant when some of us in this country had slaves and when many of us were in bondage to those in political and economic control.

Don't talk psychological individualism to me. Don't preach Kant's moral imperatives tinged with a religious doctrine of salvation. That is put-down language. Given the history of American education, the talk of school people about individuals is to be taken at face value—the clean face of middle-class America, the faces of blacks and orientals and Spanish and Indians and the poor and the handicapped.

Talk, rather, about the political tasks of making a more just public world. Talk about it in such a way that the political and economic nature of education can be clearly seen. Then talk about schools as our small share in the making of a more just public world.

What are the ingredients of this talk? There are three, three rights, if you wish, to which we must attend and which must govern our talk about the public world and then the school.

First, the unconditional respect for the political, civil, and legal rights of the young as free people participating in a public world. This is what Frymier is urging. But for thousands of years we have been talking this way, and only within the past hundred—nay the past ten or fifteen have we grounded this right in law. Discrimination by race, sex, or religion has only recently come under legal attack, and gradually the rights of individuals are being publicly recognized. Now we are about to struggle to end discrimination by age—and the power over the young by adults must be brought into question. Thus Thomas, in his Student Rights Center in Dayton, is teaching kids to sit back when teachers verbally accost them or manhandle them and then to say quietly: "You know, ma'am, I can sue you for that—and I will with the support of adults who really believe in the individuality—the civil rights of kids."

The second right is the right of access to the wealth in the public domain—I mean primarily the knowledge, traditions, skills that shape and increase a person's power in the public world.

This is what we are about today, although we are not consciously aware of it. The exciting development of the past ten to fifteen years has indeed been the increase in scope, quality, and quantity of instructional materials. But expressing these developments as developments in instructional materials hides more important considerations. Instructional materials are a way—almost *the* way—that adult society makes the public wealth available to the young. The skills of teachers are the other major way. We tend to talk of these resources as means to learning, and indeed this is an appropriate way to speak—but no longer a powerful way. For instance, reading is not just a skill that must be learned, it is a tradition of using printed materials. Now children of two and three and four have access to that tradition in trade books, in *The Electric Company*, in story reading in preschools. It is an expensive business, but publishing paperback and hardcover books is now a money-making activity, so our commercial world now seeks to make this tradition available to young children. If the tradition, the wealth of print, is nòt being brought to certain kids, the question is not how can they learn to read, but how can the tradition be reworked, embodied in new materials and skills. This is a technical problem—of print technology, of the art of book writing and making, of teacher education. It is an economic problem, for it costs money to design materials for new populations. It costs money to give teachers the skills to bring the wealth of print to children who have not shared in that wealth for the first four or five years of their life. It is also a political problem, for two reasons. If private industry cannot make money distributing the public wealth, then will public funds be used to design new delivery systems for our print wealth; or will we use public monies to design delivery systems for our new traditions of death, killing innocent populations of Third World children? In addition, not all of our collective wealth in print is seen as valuable by all people. Those who want to maintain a certain kind of public world will see that some traditions are available to the young and others are not. Thus for years the language of sexual development and sexual relations was distributed via the peer group; only within recent years has it been deemed valuable enough to distribute it in print for children. Community fights over library books, books assigned to certain courses in high school, and the censorship and bias of text materials demonstrate lucidly the political control over the distribution of our print traditions. This reinterpretation of instructional materials has other explanatory power, best illustrated by the changes in the teaching of reading over the past fifteen years which now makes possible today the open primary classroom.

Remember that twenty years ago Olson at Michigan was talking about individualized reading. Then we had reading textbooks, reading workbooks, and a few elementary school libraries. We had no paperback books, few language games, and no talking typewriters. Even ten years ago Alice Miel and Leland Jacobs of Columbia were talking about individualized reading—but the practice demanded that teachers spend hours of their time cutting apart workbooks, gathering reading materials, making language games. Today the picture is different. Reading text and workbooks are becoming passé. Almost every publisher is now working on self-diagnostic and self-prescriptive materials keyed to collections of paperback books. The group reading instruction is almost over, and the day of the bluebirds, the cardinals, and the chickadees is over or can be over. As Frymier pointed out, an increased variety of materials can change the organization of the school.

What Frymier did not point out is that we have here an example of an old Marxian insight. The means of production and consumption determine (or at least influence) the relationship of one person with another. The quality of the relationship of kids to kids and kids to teacher depends on the goods in the school. Authoritarianism and dictatorships are frequently necessary when we have scarce goods. Furthermore, human skills are developed to be compatible with the goods. Teachers who develop authoritarian skills to match textbooks can easily transform diverse reading goods into textual type materials. Thus, we have an inherent tension between the rights of an individual as an individual, and the demands placed on him by the inequitable distribution of public wealth.

How do we make the public wealth of this world—the traditions, knowledge, information—accessible to children? We do so through our economy and through the political process of allocating scarce funds. We do it by training artists and technicians to redesign this wealth for children of a variety of ages. We are doing it with print—it remains to be done for the traditions of math, knowledge of man and society, the knowledge of the natural or physical world, the traditions of music, art, dance. But the problem is not a school problem. It is a problem about the shape of our public world. It is related to the debates over xerography and copyrights, the use of cable television, the rights of reporters to the privacy of their sources, the censorship of the Pentagon Papers and *Deep Throat*, the pressures of this administration on the press and the national television networks, and presidential control of information.

What we should keep in focus is the right of access to public wealth; the traditions, knowledge, and information that should be in the public realm. This is a problem of technology, of economics, and of politics. As educators we cannot simply await the development of new technologies, we must be politically active to create a public world where this access is increased. As this public world becomes more accessible to the young in a variety of materials, media, and skills, then the shape of the school will change. We should not concern ourselves primarily with the shape of the school—but with the accessibility to public wealth from which new alternatives to school will become obvious.

The last right with which we must be concerned as educators is the right of each individual, regardless of age, to participate in the shaping and reshaping of the institutions within which he lives. This right carries with it the possibility of the destruction of existing institutions and the formation of new ones. This is what community control and teacher unions and negotiation are all about. It was what teacher-pupil planning was about fifteen to twenty years ago. It is *not* what competency-based teacher education, PPBS, and performance contracting are about.

For years teachers suffered under the nearly absolute power of boards and administrators. Teacher unions corrected this. Strong community pressure groups have now come up against strong boards and teacher unions. Left unorganized is the student group, although this is being done slowly. The student rights and student advocacy movement is to this end. But the movement in education is slow because of our technical mentality of means-ends and our political conservative mentality. If we are concerned about the individual, then we must be concerned with his right to participate in governing the structures that determine his public and private life, including the school.

ASCD has backed off from this right of individuals. When first formed in the late forties, ASCD had as its major concern the development of process skills for the democratic running of schools, helping administrators and supervisors work with teachers in supportive ways to improve the schools. As the fifties and sixties unfolded and it became obvious that curricular development was a function not only of staff development, but also of planning with academicians, material specialists, laity, and kids, ASCD lost hold of its role in the development of the skills of institution building. Working with teachers and administrators was one kind of political task, working with blacks, with parents, with kids, and with interest groups was another kind of political task.

So ASCD gave up its concern for developing political competencies and leaned back in the characteristic style of liberal individualism. It said people need to know what is happening, what is new, and then in the good old spirit of American individualism they will make changes in the school.

The school is but a manifestation of public life. As educators we must be political activists who seek a more just public world. The alternative, of course, is to be school people—satisfied with the existing social order—the silent majority who embrace conservatism.

If the members of ASCD remain school people, I predict the death of ASCD as a professional organization.

Harold Shane is wrong when he said we can have a big enough umbrella to embrace all school people. To me that evokes an image of a group of people under a wind-blown umbrella, heads dry, feet in the mud, the rivers rising. We should leave the umbrella. Some of us should be building the dikes of civil rights legislation for children. Some of us should be building organizations for better governance of institutions. Some of us should be preserving and making accessible the storehouse of knowledge and traditions and information for our young and old.

Another image: this conference and those of the past few years strike me as a smorgasbord. Take your pick, please your palate, take home a memory or two—all in the spirit of free enterprise and rampant individualism. Contrast that image to the Last Supper—a few people, sharing something in common, breaking bread and drinking wine, and then changing the shape of the public world.

ASCD will surely die if the smorgasbord continues as its metaphor. It might live—smaller, more powerful—if the metaphor shifts.

James B. Macdonald

Professor Macdonald's biographical statement appears on the pages immediately preceding Chapter 1.

17

Curriculum and Human Interests

Gunnar Myrdal posed the basic problem in relation to social science that I wish to deal with today in relation to curriculum thinking. He focused on the methodological problem of how to maintain objectivity.

In the process he asked specifically how the student of social problems (and I am convinced we may read "student of curriculum" here) can liberate himself from three pervasive influences:

(1) the powerful heritage of earlier writings in his field of inquiry, ordinarily containing normative and teleological notions inherited from past generations and founded upon the metaphysical moral philosophies of natural law and utilitarianism from which all our social and economic theories have branched off; (2) the influences of the entire cultural, social, economic, and political milieu of the society where he lives, works, and earns his living and status; and (3) the influence stemming from his own personality, as molded not only by tradition and environment but also by his individual history, constitution, and inclinations.[1]

In the field of curriculum we have been fussing about with the problem of values and perspectives for some time. Ubblelohde's dissertation is an example of the recognition of the importance of this problem.[2] He has attempted to analyze curriculum theorizing from an axiological viewpoint. It is clear from this analysis that curriculum thinkers have been unaware of the different levels and kinds of value perspectives that are involved in curriculum thinking.

Recognition of value concerns in curriculum can be illustrated in terms of the designs that have arisen when priorities are established among the basic referents of curriculum. Thus, subject matter curricula are sets of value judgments that prize knowledge (cultural heritage) over social uses or personal interests. Problems of living designs prize society first; and emerging needs proposals have individual welfare primarily in mind.

At another level the justification of curriculum decisions also reflects value commitments. Different value positions result in describing curriculum variables in different patterns (or even different variables). This can be illustrated easily with the three basic psychological positions one may take. It makes a considerable difference in curriculum decisions whether one is a behaviorist, a gestaltist, a psychoanalyst, or a third force psychologist (self-realization). These are value positions that affect curriculum thinking.

Ubblelohde, for example, concludes among other things that curriculum theory is essentially an attempt to construct a theory of values, whereas curriculum designs are patterns of value judgments. The task of justifying the curriculum design is not completed simply by making the judgments.

Goodlad and Richter appear to recognize something of this sort when they examine the decision-making process in the Tyler rationale and suggest that values must be clearly identified before the specification of objectives rather than used as screens in the decision-making process.[3]

Thus, there are two levels of value that I wish to focus on as illustrations at this time; (recognizing, as Ubblelohde demonstrates, that there are still other relevant value levels) and these are problems of value at the theory and the design levels. I shall refer to these two levels as: (1) structural perspectives; and (2) rational values.

At the level of structural perspectives it appears that we approach the world or mediate reality through fundamental perceptual structures. Thus, the implication that it is possible to deal with curriculum as a purely objective descriptive phenomenon is apparently a naive wish rather than a real possibility. Instead, we are from the outset asserting a stance or an orientation even at so fundamental a level as our perceptual orientations to curriculum phenomena.

In another way, this level of structural perspectives may be at a level of meta-ethics where we discuss the character of the value judgments at the rational value level, and where we dispute the applicability of these judgments to curriculum. It is, however, already a stance that has value components.

Thus, for example, we may dispute the adequacy of a given curriculum design on the grounds that it does not meet the criteria of a good design, or we may dispute the criteria that another uses to examine a specific design. In either case we have implicit orientations involved which ground our logical activities. Perhaps these groundings are in a kind of tacit knowledge, as Polanyi talks about it;[4] but it is a personal knowledge that is more than cognitive in its content.

When we move to the level of curriculum designs the value components are even more obvious. It is clear that adherents to such supposed curriculum designs as "disciplines," or "interdisciplinary studies," or "person-centered," are basing and deriving considerable direction from value positions they hold. Thus, values appear clearly here as the source of objectives and as determinants of significant elements to account for in the curriculum design. As previously mentioned, Goodlad and Richter recognize the problem and suggest procedures to improve the "Tyler" model.[5]

It is clear that curriculum theorists or designers have not clarified the problems of value. It is probably primarily this failure that gives curriculum thinking such a diverse and circular character. We are often, for example, talking at different value levels and thus miss the whole point of each other's thinking. But it has not clearly been realized that the most fundamental level, structural perspectives, is also grounded in a value matrix of some sort. Thus, people have either assumed that we all shared the same basic perspective, or that you simply could not communicate with certain other persons.

This fundamental realization that we are all not working out of the same basic structures (or metaphors, if you wish) and that it is not sufficient simply to reason together for everything to become clarified and agreeable leaves us with the fundamental problem of objectivity noted by Myrdal. I would like to present a possible conceptual solution for clarifying and communicating among ourselves and for stimulating curriculum activity. At this point I am primarily in search of understanding for myself but optimistic that some progress is possible within the conceptual orientation I shall propose.

Knowledge and Human Interests

During the past year I have discovered a book that might have been written specifically for me at this time; that is, it spoke to me as only a few books can in a lifetime. This is probably an example of what J. McV. Hunt calls "the problem of the match." Somehow the cultural content and my personal interests and reading were "matched." At any rate, the book, by Jurgen Habermas, is called *Knowledge and Human Interests*.[6] I should like to summarize briefly the concepts proposed by Habermas and discuss these in terms of curriculum. At this point, I feel that these ideas could provide a basis for greatly improving our understanding of the problems of curriculum.

Habermas sets forth the basic proposition that knowledge cannot be divorced from human interest. He attempts to deal at length with crucial persons and ideas that demonstrate how the scientific aura of the nineteenth and twentieth centuries have resulted in a substitution of concern for a theory of knowledge by the concern for a philosophy of science. Thus, we have come to think that knowledge is derived only by empirical analytical means and that other sources of knowledge are misleading. He reminds us of Nietzsche's remark that what distinguished the nineteenth century from previous ones was not the victory of science but the victory of the scientific method *over* science.

Knowledge, in a scientific sense, has become a product of an empirical-analytic methodology. The circumstance or grounding of methodology is ignored. Where did the methodology come from, and why did it arise? Is this an example of pure random, historical trial and error learning? Habermas thinks not and I am inclined to agree with him.

On the contrary, people have historically considered knowledge to have a broad base in what are now known as the arts and sciences. It is only the positivistic methodology of science that has misled us into denying the knowledge base of the arts. Habermas distinguishes between these two as the *monologic* and *hermeneutic* understanding of meaning.

By monologic he means the abstraction of fact from value and the creation of theory explaining facts in an empirical-analytic fashion. The process of verification is a linear one called, variously, for example, education, induction, or abduction. A formalized language (e.g., calculus) is used to facilitate objectivity.

Hermeneutic understanding of meaning arises in the context of different cultural life expressions such as ordinary language, human actions, and nonverbal expressions. All of these experiences carry symbolic meanings, which, however, need a dialogic interpretation rather than monologic verification. The methodology is circular rather than linear in that the interpretation of meaning in hermeneutic understanding depends on a reciprocal relation between "parts" and a diffusely preunderstood "whole" and the correction of the preliminary concept by means of the parts. It is a method that discovers the empirical content of individuated conditions of life while investigating grammatical structures.

Habermas further argues that hermeneutic understanding has fallen prey to objectivistic tendencies, in that historians, for example, have labored under the illusion that the facts are separate from the values and ground of activity. The trouble with both modes is that they have divorced themselves from self-reflection; for objectivism deludes the knower by projecting an image of a self-subsistent world of facts structured in lawlike manner; and thus conceals the a priori constitutions of these facts. The overriding concern for methodology that follows an objectivist stance hides from our self-reflection the ground and sources of the "facts"; as Habermas notes, "representations and descriptions are never independent of standards. And the choice of these standards is based on attitudes that require critical consideration by means of arguments, because they cannot be either logically deduced or empirically demonstrated."[7]

Thus, Habermas proposes that an emergence in the nineteenth century of a self-reflective science will begin to transcend the problems of objectivism and scientism. He sees psychoanalysis as an exemplar case in illustration of a process of knowing that transcends the problem of monological and hermeneutic meaning.

Fundamental to the whole argument here is the assertion that all knowledge is grounded in human interest. This interest may be fundamental self-preservation, but even self-preservation cannot be defined independently of the cultural conditions of work, language, and power. Thus, self-preservation becomes preservation of one's fantasy of the "good life." Thus, the morality of human interest enters as a meaning structure served by knowledge and nicely caught by Bertrand Russell's comment "without civic morality communities perish, without personal morality their survival has no value." In either case knowledge is at the service of our interests.

There are, then, if Habermas' analysis is valid, three fundamental cognitive human interests that are the ground for knowledge. They are (1) a technical cognitive interest in control underlying the empirical-analytic approach; (2) a practical cognitive interest in consensus underlying the hermeneutic-historical approach; and (3) a critical cognitive interest in emancipation or liberation underlying the self-reflective approach.

I think an understanding of these three basic interests can be usefully and insightfully applied to the analysis of problems related to the knowledge of curriculum and curriculum thinking. But before examining this proposition, I should like to return to the third interest, the critical cognitive interest and its self-reflective methodology since this is the more recent conceptual emergent.

The objectivist stance toward both monological and hermeneutical knowledge tends to separate the knower from the known and facts from values. Objectivists seek theoretical cause-effect relationships or practical means-ends continuities. Neither of these serves a critical interest, since both accept the status quo as descriptively given and as separate from the knower. But the history of mankind is tied to the "good life," which is a fundamental interest related to the degree of emancipation that historically is objectively possible under given manipulable conditions. It is, in other words, an interest in *overcoming causes* and *redefining means-ends relationships* as social conventions in the service of persons.

The methodology of this approach is self-reflective. Thus, using psychoanalysis as an example, one begins with a metapsychological construct that, though not empirically verifiable, does provide a systematically generalizeable schema that accounts for the history of infantile development with typical variations.

This allows the analyst to make interpretive suggestions for a story the patient cannot tell. However, these suggestions can be verified only if the patient adopts them and tells his own story with their aid. In this methodology the object of inquiry participates in the inquiry process via self-application of general ideas. Generally, this methodology (1) provides a general scheme for many histories or particulars with alternatives; (2) must be validated by self-reflection but cannot be refuted this way; and (3) has explanatory power in overcoming "causes" (rather than explicating them).

Curriculum and Human Interests

Although there is a great deal more that could and should be said about knowledge and human interests, moving into some possible meanings for curriculum seems more provident at this time.

I hope this discussion of knowledge and human interests will provide a setting for getting at the problem of value in curriculum thinking. The applicability of concerns about knowledge to curriculum concerns should be obvious, since knowledge about curriculum is not only part of our total knowledge, but also is composed of the very knowledge, knowers, and processes of knowing that we are concerned about. Thus, the application of ideas from a theory of knowledge is a fundamental activity of curriculum thinking.

My basic proposition about curriculum is that at all levels and specifically at what I call the structural perspectives and rational values level (curriculum theory and design), the basic phenomenon that underlies all activity is the existence of human interest that precedes and channels the activity of curriculum thinking.

The second proposition, following from the same source, is that three basic cognitive interests—(1) control, (2) consensus, and (3) emancipation—may be seen as the basic sources of value differences in curriculum.

Providing the evidence necessary to test these propositions necessitates a lengthy and laborious process that has not yet been completed. At this time it seems only reasonable to touch possible areas for further exploration.

At the level of structural perspectives in curriculum where our theorists describe the elements and variables with which we are concerned and set the ground rules for designing, we are perhaps most implicitly influenced by human interests coming through the forms described by Myrdal (i.e., tradition, environment, and personality).

After careful examination of twenty-six leading theorists Ubblelohde concluded that a categorization of their work at different levels was possible.[8] His argument is reasonably compelling to me and I suggest that we may select as examples for the brief examination possible here from his categories. At what I call the structural perspectives level this would include Virgil Herrick, Dwayne Huebner, Joseph Schwab, Alice Miel, Ivan Illich, and some of my own work. (This group is, of course, only as representative as the original sample of twenty-six theorists.)

It is, I believe, possible to identify major structural perspectives shaped by dominant cognitive interest in many of these theorists. I shall try to illustrate this briefly with reference to Schwab, Illich, and Herrick. It should be noted that I am taking the liberty of inferring a general thrust and position for all three men through examination of some of their specific works.

It seems to me that Herrick illustrates as well as any theorist at this level a cognitive interest in control. That is, the social theory base of his work and the empirical thrust of his research are reflected in his two basic theoretical tasks: (1) defining the relevant elements or variables involved in curriculum; and (2) creating a system of decision making for curriculum designing.

Perhaps the best single statement of his position can be found in his chapter in *Toward Improved Curriculum Theory*, where he deals at length with both tasks.[9] It is clear that he had an overriding concern for cognitive forms that would make for more effective decision making in the development of curriculum designs.

Schwab, on the contrary, performs the interesting role of designing by theorizing that theory is useless or not possible in curriculum. At this fundamental value level Schwab would appear to be motivated by more practical means-ends cognitive interests in arriving at common consensus about the nature of education practice. Schwab's monograph dealing with the practical in curriculum goes to some lengths to propose (among other things) the above position and to urge a practical consensus by examining in detail what actually goes on in the classroom.[10]

When we move to Illich, we are in another realm of interest.[11] Illich would appear to be saying that his major thrust in the critical cognitive interest is in the emancipatory realm. He agrees that curriculum designs can be constructed from theory, but abhors the process as *control* in the service of a larger system that is oppressive. Thus, Illich would dissolve curriculum theory because of its control potential and develop a curriculum on a much less institutionalized or formalized basis.

Whether other theorists who could be identified might be so easily associated with the three major interests proposed here is difficult to say. I suspect not; the curriculum field may be likened to all growing persons, eventually the categories or the shoes pinch. However, it probably matters less whether anyone is pure in interest than whether the theorists know what interests they represent.

Moving to the level of rational values, or the curriculum design level, rather than dealing with individuals, I shall suggest that traditional types of designs reflect basic cognitive human interests. The corollary, again, will be only loosely fitted to the categories, but suggestive of the value base from which these designs arise.

Following from the idea of three basic referents for curriculum we have witnessed the development of curriculum designs that have been roughly classified as subject or discipline centered, social problems or issues centered, and person or child centered. Each of these, it is suggested, flows from a structural perspective that reflects a primacy of one of the three basic conjunctive interests.

The control interest has been mainly associated with the subject matter or disciplines approach. (For example, see Bloom, Bruner, etc.[12]) This has been most recently elaborated into a definition of structures of the disciplines, and modes of inquiry that have been defined in terms of behavioral objectives and programmed for individualized instruction. This process is a logical outcome of a fundamental interest in control of learning as an outcome of any curricula.

The problems of living or social issues design (for example, see Stratemeyer, et al.[13]) primarily reflect a fundamental interest in consensus, or resolution of conflicts between mutual social expectations. Solutions of problems are not given ahead of time, but it is expected that objective dialogue and study of these problems will lead to consensus on action. These designs reflect a practical concern for knowledge rather than the more theoretical concern of the disciplines.

The third type of design, called person or child centered, or emerging needs, can most closely be associated with the emancipatory interest. Then the rhetoric of developing individual potential or fostering self-realization is embedded in a cognitive interest in freeing people from limitations and creating new conditions and environments. This fundamental interest shapes the implied values (as is also the case of each of the others) of the selections of variables, psychologies, ethical theories, and what have you, that go into developing curriculum designs.

Thus, a cursory look at basic perspectives and design values suggests that the analysis projected by Habermas will clarify the problems of objectivity and source of values, which pervade curriculum thinking. The initial attempt to relate individual theorists and specific types of designs is promising, at least suggestive of future activity.

Illustrations of Value Orientations

As an illustration of the potential meaning of the ideas that have been presented, I should like to move to an action context in curriculum development. Thus, it appears to me that the application of values around the three kinds of human interests leads to varying designs and to varying praxes.

The concept of praxis is a valuable one, especially when used as Paulo Freire does to mean action with reflection, in distinction from either reflection without action (intellectualism) or action without reflection (activism). Thus, curriculum development is seen as praxis or action with reflection.

What I shall briefly propose is that three different prominent models for development can be seen as related to the cognitive human interests of *control, consensus,* and *emancipation.* It is these fundamental human interests I propose that explain most of the variations in approach rather than some other sorts of empirical or rational criteria.

The three curriculum development models (proposed as exemplars or as ideal types) are: (1) the linear-expert model, (2) the circular consensus, and (3) the dialogical model.

Linear-Expert Model

A basic interest in control leads to a common linear-expert dominated model. Thus, the procedures employed most advantageously by the national curriculum projects in science and mathmatics over the past fifteen years or so fit this model.

In very general terms, the projects are initiated by experts (usually in discipline areas), who begin by preparing materials to be tried out, fed back to the experts, rewritten and piloted, and then revised for broad distribution.

The central features of this procedure are expert domination of the process and the attempt to maximize control by aiming all feedback procedures at gaining the greatest possible amount of student achievement and teacher satisfaction. Thus, the whole process is controlled and monitored with specific goals in mind, and it is the experts who make the initial and final decisions about the validity of the content and process.

This approach, I may add in passing, finds its logical fruition in the behavioral objectives movement.

Circular Consensus Model

A second model might be likened to what used to be called "grass roots" curriculum development. Essentially what this approach sought to do was engage the local staff of schools in the clarification and specification of aspects of the curriculum (experts are on call).

This approach requires considerable faith in the use of group process and a conviction that unless teachers are centrally involved in the process of curriculum development, texts, documents and materials will be misused or relatively meaningless.

There is some rhetoric of control in this process, but it appears for purposes here that consensus and communication are more important outcomes in this process. Thus, the teachers, staff, and community participate and knowing appears central.

At present the community school curriculum development activities seem to be the direct outcome of this basic interest.

Dialogical Model

The third approach might best be called the dialogical model in the sense that it is out of a dialogical process that the curriculum emerges.

We in the United States do not have a great deal of experience with this model because it actively involves the student in curriculum development. Paulo Freire, on the other hand, has demonstrated this sort of model in literary programs for South American peasants.

In general, this approach would follow from the idea that leaders (staff and other adults) would identify student leaders and with their help try to find major ways of providing a "match" between the cultural resources the adults know about and the needs and interests of students.

General curriculum themes or topics would be prepared by leaders who would engage students in dialogue, and the worth and direction of this material would be validated and verified by each student in his own self-reflection. The closest available illustration of this process would, I suppose, be some of the core curricula, or interdisciplinary activities.

Conclusion

What I have offered here might be generalized to all education much as Paul Goodman talks about progressive education. Goodman says that progressive education is a political movement. I suspect that in many ways all curriculum design and development is political in nature; that is, it is an attempt to facilitate someone else's idea of the good life by creating social processes and structuring an environment for learning.

Thus, objectivity is not simply the province of the science or control element of education. This approach also has a political position. (See, for example, John S. Mann and Michael Apple for insightful analysis of this theme).

Curriculum designing is thus a form of "utopianism," a form of political and social philosophizing and theorizing. If we recognize this, it may help us sort out our own thinking and perhaps increase our ability to communicate with one another.

What has been said here is offered in the spirit of an emancipatory interest. If the general scheme has meaning for individuals, each must use it within the self-reflective area of his own experiences and validate and/or verify it on that basis.

The kind of analysis offered here will not do away with disagreements, of course. But if this analysis has validity we may at least hope that understanding, if not agreement, will be enhanced among curriculum thinkers. It might also help bring curriculum thinking and development under a more rational scrutiny; so, the ideals of Virgil Herrick will have been further enhanced.

Notes

1. Gunnar Myrdal, *Objectivity in Social Research* (New York: Random House, 1969), pp. 3-4.
2. Robert Ubblelohde, "An Axiological Analysis of Curriculum Theory" (Ph.D. diss., University of Wisconsin-Milwaukee, July 1972).
3. John Goodlad and Maurice Richter, "The Development of a Conceptual System for Dealing with Problems in Curriculum and Instruction" (USOE Contract No. SAE-8024, Project No. 454, 1966); see Ralph Tyler, *Principles of Curriculum and Instruction* (Chicago: University of Chicago Press, 1950).
4. Michael Polanyi, *Personal Knowledge* (Chicago: University of Chicago Press, 1958).
5. Goodlad and Richter, "Development of a Conceptual System."
6. Jurgen Habermas, *Knowledge and Human Interests*, trans. Jeremy J. Shapiro (Boston: Beacon Press, 1971).
7. Ibid., p. 312.
8. Ubblelohde, "Axiolgoical Analysis of Curriculum Theory."
9. Virgil Herrick, "The Concept of Curriculum Design," in *Toward Improved Curriculum Theory* (Chicago: University of Chicago Press, 1950), pp. 37-50.
10. Joseph Schwab, "The Practical: A Language for Curriculum," in *Curriculum and the Cultural Revolution* (Berkeley, Calif.: McCutchan, 1973).
11. See, for example, Ivan Illich, "The Breakdown of the Schools: A Problem or a Symptom?" *Interchange* 2, no. 4 (1971).
12. Benjamin Bloom, "Mastery Learning and Its Implications for Curriculum Development," in *Confronting Curriculum Reform*, ed. Elliot Eisner (Boston: Little, Brown, 1971), pp. 17-48; Jerome Bruner, *"The Process of Evaluation* (Boston: Harvard University Press, 1960).
13. Florence Stratemeyer et al., *Developing a Curriculum for Modern Living* (New York: Teachers College Press, Columbia University, 1957).

Maxine Greene

I grew up in a family that discouraged intellectual adventure and risk. To me, the opera and the Sunday concerts in the Brooklyn Museum Sculpture Court and the outdoor concerts in the summer were rebellions, breakthroughs, secret gardens. Since the age of seven, of course, I was writing—mostly stories in hard-covered notebooks to give to my father, because I knew no way of communicating with him. I think it was a sublimation; and I wrote so much—in journals, on the backs of old compositions, on flyleaves—I developed a kind of facility. Later, I wrote out all my pain and guilt and embarrassment and loss in journals and notebooks, while I was trying to write novels when I graduated from college. Some years later, when I entered therapy, I realized that I was using the notebooks as a way of ridding myself of my perplexities and confusions, instead of really dealing with them. Also, I let a lot of my passion find its way into that kind of private writing—and that may have caused a writing block in other domains. Anyway, I have not used journals since those first days of therapy—although I sometimes write down descriptions of things or feelings, and I sometimes write lines of poetry or metaphors or something, but it is different; and I now try to tap the subjectivity I was releasing into those notebooks when I write other things, even philosophy.

My occupational history is not interesting. I married a doctor when I was quite young, had a child, took care of the medical office, entered politics in a way, later became Legislative Director of the American Labor Party in Brooklyn, where I edited a newspaper and learned how to make speeches on price control and the United Nations and things I scarcely think about now.

I forgot to say that the roots of all that were probably in a trip I took to Europe in my late teens where I got involved with people going to fight in Spain and then worked for the Loyalists in Paris and had to be forced to come home and finish school. That got me into activity for Republican Spain, speech making, writing, stuff; and it made me very very antifascist (prematurely, as they used to say). Anyhow, while married to my doctor I wrote two and a half novels, the first two "almosts," but finally failures. And I wrote many rejected articles and things and published a little—once (to my great delight) in Mademoiselle. *And I had odd jobs, none glorious, some lowly, some hard. And then—after the big war— I was divorced, remarried, and decided to go back to school for an M.A.—after quite a few years out of Barnard, where I had majored in history and minored in philosophy.*

I went to NYU quite accidentally, because it was the only place where I could be a special student on my own time (when my daughter was in school). Most convenient class met two afternoons a week, was history and philosophy of education, taught by Adolphe Meyer, George Axtelle, and Theodore Brameld in a kind of troika. I had never thought about education before, had never heard of Dewey (partly because Marx and Freud at that time dominated my thinking, or some of my thinking). I think I stumbled on Albert Camus myself at that time, treated The Myth of Sisyphus *and* The Rebel *as new secret gardens, all mine. Anyway, I was a hard-working student in the class, was asked to assist the next time around, and suddenly I was hooked. I got an M.A. in philosophy of education. I made up one called philosophy and literature, and another on the individual while I was writing my dissertation. I wrote a dissertation on the eighteenth century, because I never really cared for the eighteenth century, and I thought I would do better with a subject I could distance. I did a whole intricate, interdisciplinary thing called "Naturalist-Humanism in 18th Century England: An Essay in the Sociology of Knowledge," partly because my sponsor, George Axtelle, wanted me to do something on humanism. I think. I made a mural, sort of; and I suppose some of it was all right, because they liked it at NYU, but I have never looked at it since. In the course of doing that, I took a seminar with Brameld—half on existentialism (mostly Kierkegaard and Sartre) and half on positivism; I remain grateful to Brameld for that. I even helped write—did write—an article for* Educational Theory *under his name and some fellow-students'. I started teaching off-campus courses, because I was only part-time, full-time—on things like perspectives on world literature, east and west, and I learned. I even taught American literature. I needed to publish, asked William Brickman, editor of* School and Society, *if I could do profiles for him, proceeded to do some on*

Robert Maynard Hutchins, the president of Harvard, the president of M.I.T., Dean Francis Keppel at the Harvard Graduate School (no, the last was for the Saturday Review *later on, along with one on John Gardner, and some others).*

A new chairman took over our department at NYU, and he was one of Rudolph Carnap's students and did not like me, and suddenly I was teaching in the English department—quite unprepared but excited enough. Having published, then, and with a Ph.D., I got a job as assistant professor of English at Montclair State College in New Jersey. I traveled there from Queens every day, had a little boy home by then, could only manage the commute for a year. But I learned a lot about world literature, from the Iliad *to Shakespeare, and I am glad I had the opportunity. Back to NYU to teach English and some educational theory, finally became an associate professor there, published more— an article on tragedy, that was a lead article in the* Saturday Review *in 1959, and that got me invited to give a public lecture at the University of Hawaii and to teach a summer session there (which I did in 1960 and 1962). Then I was asked to Brooklyn College, where I could teach philosophy of education again. And I started doing* The Public School and the Private Vision *because of a seminar I gave in Hawaii and my desire to pull my various fields (literature, history, educational theory) together.*

Also, I started getting papers accepted at the Philosophy of Education Society and actually got invited to give a main session paper in 1963, I think. I was very much into multiple ways of knowing and the problem of the "pseudo-question" and "the uses of literature" and so on. At length, I was a program chairman and, a few years later, president of the Philosophy of Education Society and the regional one (something still hard to believe). And I was lucky enough to publish in a few journals, to write prefaces to paperback novels (by Conrad and George Eliot), to review lots of books, to speak in quite a few places.

In 1965, I was asked to come to TC to edit the Teachers College Record; *and for about seven years I was based in the English department here, teaching half my courses in philosophy and the social sciences (where I have been full-time since 1973, I guess). I was editor—meaning full responsibility and an editorial eight times a year for the first four years of my tenure (four in the fifth year, when the journal became a quarterly)—until I really wanted to do other things more. I taught philosophy of literature; the arts and American education; philosophy, literature, and the visual arts; criticism and contemporary art forms, other things. Now I teach social philosophy, modern philosophies of education, the philosophy of John Dewey, a* seminar in existentialism and phenomenology, *plus the arts and American education and philosophy, literature, and the visual arts. In 1967, I wrote* Existential Encounters for Teachers *in about six weeks or so. And I did lots of chapters in people's books on esthetics, mostly, literature, etc. And then came* Teacher as Stranger. *And I am now on a book on moral education, based on my Horace Mann Lecture in 1973; and then I want to revise* The Public School and the Private Vision; *and I don't want to die before I read at least a tenth of what I want to read, before I learn something, before I really can say I understand what teaching is.*

Maxine Greene
Teachers College
Columbia University

18

Curriculum and Consciousness

Curriculum, from the learner's standpoint, ordinarily represents little more than an arrangement of subjects, a structure of socially prescribed knowledge, or a complex system of meanings which may or may not fall within his grasp. Rarely does it signify possibility for him as an existing person, mainly concerned with making sense of his own life-world. Rarely does it promise occasions for ordering the materials of that world, for imposing "configurations"[1] by means of experiences and perspectives made available for personally conducted cognitive action. Sartre says that "knowing is a moment of *praxis*," opening into "what has not yet been."[2] Preoccupied with priorities, purposes, programs of "intended learning"[3] and intended (or unintended) manipulation, we pay too little attention to the individual in quest of his own future, bent on surpassing what is merely "given," on breaking through the everyday. We are still too prone to dichotomize: to think of "disciplines" or "public traditions" or "accumulated wisdom" or "common culture" (individualization despite) as objectively existent, external to the knower—there to be discovered, mastered, learned.

Quite aware that this may evoke Dewey's argument in *The Child and the Curriculum*, aware of how times have changed since 1902, I have gone in search of contemporary analogies to shed light on what I mean. ("Solution comes," Dewey wrote, "only by getting away from the meaning of terms that is already fixed upon and coming to see the conditions from another point of view, and hence in a fresh light."[4]) My other point of view is that of literary criticism, or more properly philosophy of criticism, which attempts to explicate the modes of explanation, description, interpretation, and evaluation involved in particular critical approaches. There is presently an emerging philosophic controversy between two such approaches, one associated with England and the United States, the other with the Continent, primarily France and Switzerland; and it is in the differences in orientation that I have found some clues.

These differences are, it will be evident, closely connected to those separating what is known as analytic or language philosophy from existentialism and phenomenology. The dominant tendency in British and American literary criticism has been to conceive literary works as objects or artifacts, best understood in relative isolation from the writer's personal biography and undistorted by associations brought to the work from the reader's own daily life. The new critics on the Continent have been called "critics of consciousness."[5] They are breaking with the notion that a literary work can be dealt with objectively, divorced from experience. In fact, they treat each work as a manifestation of an individual writer's experience, a gradual growth of consciousness into expression. This is in sharp contrast to such a view as T.S. Eliot's emphasizing the autonomy and the "impersonality" of literary art. "We can only say," he wrote in an introduction to *The Sacred Wood,* "that a poem, in some sense, has its own life; that its parts form something quite different from a body of neatly ordered biographical data; that the feeling, or emotion, or vision resulting from the poem is something different from the feeling or emotion or vision in the mind of the poet."[6] Those who take this approach or an approach to a work of art as "a self-enclosed isolated structure"[7] are likely to prescribe that purely esthetic values are to be found in literature, the values associated with "significant form"[8] or, at most, with the contemplation of an "intrinsically interesting possible."[9] M.H. Abrams has called this an "austere dedication to the poem *per se,*"[10] for all the enlightening analysis and explication it has produced. "But it threatens also to commit us," he wrote, "to the concept of a poem as a language game, or as a floating Laputa, insulated from life and essential human concerns in a way that accords poorly with our experience in reading a great work of literature."

For the critic of consciousness, literature is viewed as a genesis, a conscious effort on the part of an individual artist to understand his own experience by framing it in language. The reader who encounters the work must recreate it in terms of *his* consciousness.

In order to penetrate it, to experience it existentially and empathetically, he must try to place himself within the "interior space"[11] of the writer's mind as it is slowly revealed in the course of his work. Clearly, the reader requires a variety of cues if he is to situate himself in this way; and these are ostensibly provided by the expressions and attitudes he finds in the book, devices which he must accept as orientations and indications—"norms," perhaps, to govern his recreation. *His* subjectivity is the substance of the literary object; but if he is to perceive the identity emerging through the enactments of the book, he must subordinate his own personality as he brackets out his everyday, "natural" world.[12] His objective in doing so, however, is not to analyze or explicate or evaluate; it is to extract the experience made manifest by means of the work. Sartre says this more concretely:

> Reading seems, in fact, to be the synthesis of perception and creation. . . . The object is essential because it is strictly transcendent, because it imposes its own structures, and because one must wait for it and observe it; but the subject is also essential because it is required not only to disclose the object (that is, to make *there be* an object) but also that this object might *be* (that is, to produce it). In a word, the reader is conscious of disclosing in creating, of creating by disclosing. . . . If he is inattentive, tired, stupid, or thoughtless most of the relations will escape him. He will never manage to "catch on" to the object (in the sense in which we see that fire 'catches" or "doesn't catch"). He will draw some phrases out of the shadow, but they will appear as random strokes. If he is at his best, he will project beyond the words a synthetic form, each phrase of which will be no more than a partial function: the "theme," the "subject," or the "meaning."[13]

There must be, he is suggesting, continual reconstructions if a work of literature is to become meaningful. The structures involved are generated over a period of time, depending upon the perceptiveness and attentiveness of the reader. The reader, however, does not simply regenerate what the artist intended. His imagination can move him beyond the artist's traces, "to project beyond the words a synthetic form," to constitute a new totality. The autonomy of the art object is sacrificed in this orientation; the reader, conscious of lending his own life to the book, discovers deeper and more complex levels than the level of "significant form." (Sartre says, for instance, that "Raskolnikov's waiting is *my* waiting, which I lend him. Without this impatience of the reader he would remain only a collection of signs. His hatred of the police magistrate who questions him is my hatred which has been solicited and wheedled out of me by signs, and the police magistrate himself would not exist without the hatred I have for him via Raskolnikov."[14])

Disclosure, Reconstruction, Generation

The reader, using his imagination, must move within his own subjectivity and break with the common sense world he normally takes for granted. If he could not suspend his ordinary ways of perceiving, if he could not allow for the possibility that the horizons of daily life are not inalterable, he would not be able to engage with literature at all. As Dewey put it: "There is work done on the part of the percipient as there is on the part of the artist. The one who is too lazy, idle, or indurated in convention to perform this work will not see or hear. His 'appreciation' will be a mixture of scraps of learning with conformity to norms of conventional admiration and with a confused, even if genuine, emotional excitation."[15] The "work" with which we are here concerned is one of disclosure, reconstruction, generation. It is a work which culminates in a bringing something into being by the reader—in a "going beyond" what he has been.[16]

Although I am going to claim that learning, to be meaningful, must involve such a "going beyond," I am not going to claim that it must also be in the imaginative mode. Nor am I going to assert that, in order to surpass the "given," the individual is required to move into and remain within a sealed subjectivity. What I find suggestive in the criticism of consciousness is the stress on the gradual disclosure of structures by the reader. The process is, as I have said, governed by certain cues or norms perceived in the course of reading. These demand, if they are to be perceived, what Jean Piaget has called a "continual 'decentering' without which [the individual subject] cannot become free from his intellectual egocentricity."[17]

The difference between Piaget and those interested in consciousness is, of course, considerable. For one thing, he counts himself among those who prefer not to characterize the subject in terms of its "lived experience." For another thing, he says categorically that "the 'lived' can only have a very minor role in the construction of cognitive structures, for these do not belong to the subject's *consciousness* but to his operational *behavior*, which is something quite different."[18] I am not convinced that they are as different as he conceives them to be. Moreover, I think his differentiation between the "individual subject" and what he calls "the epistemic subject, that cognitive nucleus which is common to all subjects at the same level,"[19] is useful and may well shed light on the problem of curriculum, viewed from the vantage point of consciousness. Piaget is aware that his stress on the "epistemic subject" looks as if he were subsuming the individual under some impersonal abstraction;[20] but his discussion is not far removed from those of Sartre and the critics of consciousness, particularly when they talk of the subject entering into a process of generating structures whose being (like the structures Piaget has in mind) consists in their "coming to be."

Merleau-Ponty, as concerned as Piaget with the achievement of rationality, believes that there is a primary reality which must be taken into account if the growth of "intellectual consciousness" is to be understood. This primary reality is a perceived life-world; and the structures of the "perceptual consciousness"[21] through which the child first comes in contact with his environment underlie all the higher level structures which develop later in his life. In the prereflective, infantile stage of life he is obviously incapable of generating cognitive structures. The stage is characterized by what Merleau-Ponty calls "egocentrism" because the "me" is part of an anonymous collectivity, unaware of itself, capable of living "as easily in others as it does in itself."[22] Nevertheless, even then, before meanings and configurations are imposed, there is an original world, a natural and social world in which the child is involved corporeally and affectively. Perceiving that world, he effects certain relations within his experience. He organizes and "informs" it before he is capable of logical and predicative thought. This means for Merleau-Ponty that consciousness exists primordially—the ground of all knowledge and rationality.

The growing child assimilates a language system and becomes habituated to using language as "an open system of expression" which is capable of expressing "an indeterminate number of cognitions or ideas to come."[23] His acts of naming and expression take place, however, around a core of primary meaning found in "the silence of primary consciousness." This silence may be understood as the fundamental awareness of being present in the world. It resembles what Paulo Freire calls "background awareness"[24] of an existential situation, a situation actually lived before the codifications which make new perceptions possible. Talking about the effort to help peasants perceive their own reality differently (to enable them, in other words, to learn), Freire says they must somehow make explicit their "real consciousness" of their worlds, or what they experienced while living through situations they later learn to codify.

The point is that the world is constituted for the child (by means of the behavior called perception) prior to the "construction of cognitive structures." This does not imply that he lives his life primarily in that world. He moves outward into diverse realms of experience in his search for meaning. When he confronts and engages with the apparently independent structures associated with rationality, the so-called cognitive structures, it is likely that he does so as an "epistemic subject," bracketing out for the time his subjectivity, even his presence to himself.[25] But the awareness remains in the background; the original perceptual reality continues as the ground of rationality, the base from which the leap to the theoretical is taken.

Merleau-Ponty, recognizing that psychologists treat consciousness as "an object to be studied," writes that it is simply not accessible to mere factual observation:

> The psychologist always tends to make consciousness into just such an object of observation. But all the factual truths to which psychology has access can be applied to the concrete subject only after a philosophical correction. Psychology, like physics and the other sciences of nature, uses the method of induction, which starts from facts and then assembles them. But it is very evident that this induction will remain blind if we do not know in some other way, and indeed from the inside of consciousness itself, what this induction is dealing with.[26]

Induction must be combined "with the reflective knowledge that we can obtain from ourselves as conscious objects." This is not a recommendation that the individual engage in introspection. Consciousness, being intentional, throws itself outward *toward* the world. It is always consciousness *of* something—a phenomenon, another person, an object in the world. Reflecting upon himself as a conscious object, the individual—the learner, perhaps—reflects upon his relation to the world, his manner of comporting himself with respect to it, the changing perspectives through which the world presents itself to him. Merleau-Ponty talks about the need continually to rediscover "my actual presence to myself, the fact of my consciousness which is in the last resort what the word and the concept of consciousness mean."[27] This means remaining in contact with one's own perceptions, one's own experiences, and striving to constitute their meanings. It means achieving a state of what Schutz calls "wide-awakeness . . . a plane of consciousness of highest tension originating in an attitude of full attention to life and its requirements."[28] Like Sartre, Schutz emphasizes the importance of attentiveness for arriving at new perceptions, for carrying out cognitive projects. All of this seems to me to be highly suggestive for a conception of a learner who is "open to the world,"[29] eager, indeed *condemned* to give meaning to it—and, in the process of doing so, recreating or generating the materials of a curriculum in terms of his own consciousness.

Some Alternative Views

There are, of course, alternative views of consequence for education today. R. S. Peters, agreeing with his philosophic precursors that consciousness is the hallmark of mind and always "related in its different modes to objects," asserts that the "objects of consciousness are first and foremost objects in a public world that are marked out and differentiated by a public language into which the individual is initiated."[30] (It should be said that Peters is, par excellence, the exponent of an "objective" or "analytic" approach to curriculum, closely related to the objective approach to literary criticism.) He grants that the individual "represents a unique and unrepeatable viewpoint on this public world"; but his primary stress is placed upon the way in which the learning of language is linked to the discovery of that separately existing world of "objects in space and time." Consciousness, for Peters, cannot be explained except in connection with the demarcations of the public world which meaning makes possible. It becomes contingent upon initiation into public traditions, into (it turns out) the academic disciplines. Since such an initiation is required if modes of consciousness are to be effectively differentiated, the mind must finally be understood as a "product" of such initiation. The individual must be enabled to achieve a state of mind characterized by "a mastery of and care for the worthwhile things that have been transmitted, which are viewed in some kind of cognitive perspective."[31]

Philip H. Phenix argues similarly that "the curriculum should consist entirely of knowledge which comes from the disciplines, for the reason that the disciplines reveal knowledge in its teachable forms."[32] He, however, pays more heed to what he calls "the experience of reflective self-consciousness,"[33] which he associates specifically with "concrete existence in direct personal encounter."[34] The meanings arising out of such encounter are expressed, for him, in existential philosophy, religion, psychology, and certain dimensions of imaginative literature. They are, thus, to be considered as one of the six "realms of meaning" through mastery of which man is enabled to achieve self-transcendence. Self-transcendence, for Phenix, involves a duality which enables the learner to feel himself to be agent and knower, and at once to identify with what he comes to know. Self-transcendence is the ground of meaning; but it culminates in the engendering of a range of "essential meanings," the achievement of a hierarchy in which all fundamental patterns of meaning are related and through which human existence can be fulfilled. The inner life of generic man is clearly encompassed by this scheme; but what is excluded, I believe, is what has been called the "subjectivity of the actor," the *individual* actor ineluctably present to himself. What is excluded is the feeling of separateness, of strangeness when such a person is confronted with the articulated curriculum intended to counteract meaninglessness.

Schutz writes:

> When a stranger comes to the town, he has to learn to orientate in it and to know it. Nothing is self-explanatory for him and he has to ask an expert . . . to learn how to get from one point to another. He may, of course, refer to a map of the town, but even to use the map successfully he must know the meaning of the signs on the map, the exact point within the town where he stands and its correlative on the map, and at least one more point in order correctly to relate the signs on the map to the real objects in the city.[35]

The prestructured curriculum resembles such a map; the learner, the stranger just arrived in town. For the cartographer, the town is an "object of his science," a science which has developed standards of operation and rules for the correct drawing of maps. In the case of the curriculum maker, the public tradition or the natural order of things is "the object" of his design activities. Here too there are standards of operation: the subject matter organized into disciplines must be communicable; it must be appropriate to whatever are conceived as educational aims. Phenix has written that education should be understood as "a guided recapitulation of the processes of inquiry which gave rise to the fruitful bodies of organized knowledge comprising the disciplines."[36] Using the metaphor of the map, we might say that this is like asking a newcomer in search of direction to recapitulate the complex processes by which the cartographer made his map. The map may represent a fairly complete charting of the town; and it may ultimately be extremely useful for the individual to be able to take a cartographer's perspective. When that individual first arrives, however, his peculiar plight ought not to be overlooked: his "background awareness" of being alive in an unstable world; his reasons for consulting the map; the interests he is pursuing as he attempts to orient himself when he can no longer proceed by rule of thumb. He himself may recognize that he will have to come to understand the signs on the map if he is to make use of it. Certainly he will have to decipher the relationship between those signs and "real objects in the city." But his initial concern will be conditioned by the "objects" he wants to bring into visibility, by the landmarks he needs to identify if he is to proceed on his way.

Learning—A Mode of Orientation

Turning from newcomer to learner (contemporary learner, in our particular world), I am suggesting that his focal concern is with ordering the materials of his own life-world when dislocations occur, when what was once familiar abruptly appears strange. This may come about on an occasion when "future shock" is experienced, as it so frequently is today. Anyone who has lived through a campus disruption, a teachers' strike, a guerilla theatre production, a sit-in (or a be-in, or a feel-in) knows full well what Alvin Toffler means when he writes about the acceleration of change. "We no longer 'feel' life as men did in the past," he says. "And this is the ultimate difference, the distinction that separates the truly contemporary man from all others. For this acceleration lies behind the imper-manence—the transience—that penetrates and tinctures our con-sciousness, radically affecting the way we relate to other people, to things, to the entire universe of ideas, art and values."[37] Obviously, this does not happen in everyone's life; but it is far more likely to occur than ever before in history, if it is indeed the case that change has speeded up and that forces are being released which we have not yet learned to control. My point is that the contemporary learner is more likely than his predecessors to experience moments of strangeness, moments when the recipes he has inherited for the solution of typical problems no longer seem to work. If Merleau-Ponty is right and the search for rationality is indeed grounded in a primary or perceptual consciousness, the individual may be fundamentally aware that the structures of "reality" are contingent upon the perspective taken and that most achieved orders are therefore precarious.

The stage sets are always likely to collapse.[38] Someone is always likely to ask unexpectedly, as in Pinter's *The Dumb Waiter*, "Who cleans up after we're gone?"[39] Someone is equally likely to cry out, "You seem to have no conception of where we stand! You won't find the answer written down for you in the bowl of a compass—I can tell you that."[40] Disorder, in other words, is continually breaking in; meaninglessness is recurrently overcoming landscapes which once were demarcated, meaningful. It is at moments like these that the individual reaches out to reconstitute meaning, to close the gaps, to make sense once again. It is at moments like these that he will be moved to pore over maps, to disclose or generate structures of knowledge which may provide him unifying perspectives and thus enable him to restore order once again. His learning, I am saying, is a mode of orientation—or reorientation—in a place suddenly become unfamiliar. And "place" is a metaphor, in this context, for a domain of consciousness, intending, forever thrusting outward, "open to the world." The curriculum, the structures of knowledge, must be presented to such a consciousness as possibility. Like the work of literature in Sartre's viewing, it requires a subject if it is to be disclosed; it can only be disclosed if the learner, himself engaged in generating the structures, lends the curriculum his life. If the curriculum, on the other hand, is seen as external to the search for meaning, it becomes an alien and an alienating edifice, a kind of "Crystal Palace" of ideas.[41]

There is, then, a kind of resemblance between the ways in which a learner confronts socially prescribed knowledge and the ways in which a stranger looks at a map when he is trying to determine where he is in relation to where he wants to go. In Kafka's novel, *Amerika*, I find a peculiarly suggestive description of the predicament of someone who is at once a stranger and a potential learner (although, it eventually turns out, he never succeeds in being taught). He is Karl Rossmann, who has been "packed off to America" by his parents and who likes to stand on a balcony at his Uncle Jacob's house in New York and look down on the busy street:

From morning to evening and far into the dreaming night that street was a channel for the constant stream of traffic which, seen from above, looked like an inextricable confusion, forever newly improvised, of foreshortened human figures and the roofs of all kinds of vehicles, sending into the upper air another confusion, more riotous and complicated, of noises, dusts and smells, all of it enveloped and penetrated by a flood of light which the multitudinous objects in the street scattered, carried off and again busily brought back, with an effect as palpable to the dazzled eye as if a glass roof stretched over the street were being violently smashed into fragments at every moment.[42]

Karl's uncle tells him that the indulgence of idly gazing at the busy life of the city might be permissible if Karl were traveling for pleasure; "but for one who intended to remain in the States it was sheer ruination." He is going to have to make judgments which will shape his future life; he will have, in effect, to be reborn. This being so, it is not enough for him to treat the unfamiliar landscape as something to admire and wonder at (as if it were a cubist construction or a kaleidoscope). Karl's habitual interpretations (learned far away in Prague) do not suffice to clarify what he sees. If he is to learn, he must identify what is questionable, try to break through what is obscure. Action is required of him, not mere gazing; praxis, not mere reverie.

If he is to undertake action, however, he must do so against the background of his original perceptions, with a clear sense of being present to himself. He must do so, too, against the background of his European experience, of the experience of rejection, of being "packed off" for reasons never quite understood. Only with that sort of awareness will he be capable of the attentiveness and commitment needed to engage with the world and make it meaningful. Only with the ability to be reflective about what he is doing will he be brave enough to incorporate his past into the present, to link the present to a future. All this will demand a conscious appropriation of new perspectives on his experience and a continual reordering of that experience as new horizons of the "Amerika" become visible, as new problems arise. The point is that Karl Rossmann, an immigrant in an already structured and charted world, must be conscious enough of himself to strive towards rationality; only if he achieves rationality will he avoid humiliations and survive.

As Kafka tells it, he never does attain that rationality; and so he is continually manipulated by forces without and within. He never learns, for example, that there can be no justice if there is no good will, even though he repeatedly and sometimes eloquently asks for justice from the authorities—always to no avail. The ship captains and pursers, the business men, the head waiters and porters all function according to official codes of discipline which are beyond his comprehension. He has been plunged into a public world with its own intricate prescriptions, idiosyncratic structures, and hierarchies; but he has no way of appropriating it or of constituting meanings. Throughout most of the novel, he clings to his symbolic box (with the photograph of his parents, the memorabilia of childhood and home). The box may be egocentrism; it may signify his incapacity to embark upon the "decentering" required if he is to begin generating for himself the structures of what surrounds.

In his case (and, I would say, in the case of many other people) the "decentering" that is necessary is not solely a cognitive affair, as Piaget insists it is. Merleau-Ponty speaks of a "lived decentering,"[43] exemplified by a child's learning "to relativise the notions of the youngest and the eldest" (to learn, e.g., to become the eldest in relation to the newborn child) or by his learning to think in terms of reciprocity. This happens, as it would have to happen to Karl, through actions undertaken within the "vital order," not merely through intellectual categorization. It does not exclude the possibility that a phenomenon analogous to Piaget's "epistemic subject" emerges, although there appears to be no reason (except, perhaps, from the viewpoint of empirical psychology) for separating it from the "individual subject." (In fact, the apparent difference between Piaget and those who talk of "lived experience" may turn upon a definition of "consciousness." Piaget, as has been noted,[44] distinguishes between "consciousness" and "operational behavior," as if consciousness did *not* involve a turning outward to things, a continuing reflection upon situationality, a generation of cognitive structures.) In any case, every individual who consciously seeks out meaning is involved in asking questions which demand essentially epistemic responses.[45] These responses, even if incomplete, are knowledge claims; and, as more and more questions are asked, there is an increasing "sedimentation" of meanings which result from the interpretation of past experiences looked at from the vantage point of the present. Meanings do not inhere in the experiences that emerge; they have to be constituted, and they can only be constituted through cognitive action.

Returning to Karl Rossmann and his inability to take such action, I have been suggesting that he *cannot* make his own "primary consciousness" background so long as he clings to his box; nor can he actively interpret his past experience. He cannot (to stretch Piaget's point somewhat) become or will himself to be an "epistemic subject." He is, as Freire puts it, submerged in a "dense, enveloping reality or a tormenting blind alley" and will be unless he can "perceive it as an objective-problematic situation."[46] Only then will he be able to intervene in his own reality with attentiveness, with awareness—to act upon his situation and make sense.

It would help if the looming structures which are so incomprehensible to Karl were somehow rendered cognitively available to him. Karl might then (with the help of a teacher willing to engage in dialogue with him, to help him pose his problems) reach out to question in terms of what he feels is thematically relevant or "worth questioning."[47] Because the stock of knowledge he carries with him does not suffice for a definition of situations in which porters manhandle him and women degrade him, in which he is penalized for every spontaneous action, he cannot easily refer to previous situations for clues. In order to cope with this, he needs to single out a single relevant element at first (from all the elements in what is happening) to transmute into a theme for his "knowing consciousness." There is the cruel treatment meted out to him, for example, by the head porter who feels it his duty "to attend to things that other people neglect." (He adds that, since he is in charge of all the doors of the hotel [including the "doorless exits"], he is "in a sense placed over everyone," and everyone has to obey him absolutely. If it were not for his repairing the omissions of the head waiter in the name of the hotel management, he believes, "such a great organization would be unthinkable."[48]) The porter's violence against Karl might well become the relevant element, the origin of a theme.

Making Connections

"What makes the theme," Schutz writes, "is determined by motivationally relevant interest-situations and spheres of problems. The theme which thus has become relevant has now, however, become a problem to which a solution, practical, theoretical, or emotional, must be given."[49] The problem for Karl, like relevant problems facing any individual, is connected with and a consequence of a great number of other perplexities, other dislocations in his life. If he had not been so badly exploited by authority figures in time past, if he were not so childishly given to blind trust in adults, if he were not so likely to follow impulse at inappropriate moments, he would never have been assaulted by the head porter. At this point, however, once the specific problem (the assault) has been determined to be thematically relevant for him, it can be detached from the motivational context out of which it derived. The meshwork of related perplexities remains, however, as an outer horizon, waiting to be explored or questioned when necessary. The thematically relevant element can then be made interesting in its own right and worth questioning. In the foreground, as it were, the focus of concern, it can be defined against the background of the total situation. The situation is not in any sense obliterated or forgotten. It is *there*, at the fringe of Karl's attention while the focal problem is being solved; but it is, to an extent, "bracketed out." With this bracketing out and this foreground focusing, Karl may be for the first time in a condition of wide-awakeness, ready to pay active attention to what has become so questionable and so troubling, ready to take the kind of action which will move him ahead into a future as it gives him perspective on his past.

The action he might take involves more than what is understood as problem-solving. He has, after all, had some rudimentary knowledge of the head porter's role, a knowledge conditioned by certain typifications effected in the prepredicative days of early childhood.

At that point in time, he did not articulate his experience in terms of sense data or even in terms of individual figures standing out against a background. He saw typical structures according to particular zones of relevancy. This means that he probably saw his father, or the man who was father, not only as bearded face next to his mother, not only as large figure in the doorway, but as overbearing, threatening, incomprehensible authority who was "placed over everyone" and had the right to inflict pain. Enabled, years later, to confront something thematically relevant, the boy may be solicited to recognize his present knowledge of the porter as the sediment of previous mental processes.[50] The knowledge of the porter, therefore, has a history beginning in primordial perceptions; and the boy may succeed in moving back from what is seemingly "given" through the diverse mental processes which constituted the porter over time. Doing so, he will be exploring both the inner and outer horizons of the problem, making connections within the field of his consciousness, interpreting his own past as it bears on his present, reflecting upon his own knowing.

And that is not all. Having made such connections between the relevant theme and other dimensions of his experience, he may be ready to solve his problem; he may even feel that the problem is solved. This, however, puts him into position to move out of his own inner time (in which all acts are somehow continuous and bound together) into the intersubjective world where he can function as an epistemic subject. Having engaged in a reflexive consideration of the activity of his own consciousness, he can now shift his attention back to the life-world which had been rendered so unrecognizable by the head porter's assault. Here too, meanings must be constituted; the "great organization" must be understood, so that Karl can orient himself once again in the everyday. Bracketing out his subjectivity for the time, he may find many ways of engaging as a theoretical inquirer with the problem of authority in hotels and the multiple socioeconomic problems connected with that. He will voluntarily become, when inquiring in this way, a partial self, an inquirer deliberately acting a role in a community of inquirers. I am suggesting that he could not do so as effectively or as authentically if he had not first synthesized the materials within his inner time, constituted meaning in his world.

The anaology to the curriculum question, I hope, is clear. Treating Karl as a potential learner, I have considered the hotels and the other structured organizations in his worlds as analogous to the structures of prescribed knowledge—or to the curriculum. I have suggested that the individual, in our case the student, will only be in a position to learn when he is committed to act upon his world. If he is content to admire it or simply accept it as given, if he is incapable of breaking with egocentrism, he will remain alienated from himself and his own possibilities; he will wander lost and victimized upon the road; he will be unable to learn. He may be conditioned; he may be trained. He may even have some rote memory of certain elements of the curriculum; but no matter how well devised is that curriculum, no matter how well adapted to the stages of his growth, learning (as disclosure, as generating structures, as engendering meanings, as achieving mastery) will not occur.

At once, I have tried to say that unease and disorder are increasingly endemic in contemporary life and that more and more persons are finding the recipes they habitually use inadequate for sensemaking in a changing world. This puts them, more and more frequently, in the position of strangers or immigrants trying to orient themselves in an unfamiliar town. The desire, indeed the *need*, for orientation is equivalent to the desire to constitute meanings, all sorts of meanings, in the many dimensions of existence. But this desire, I have suggested, is not satisfied by the authoritative confrontation of student with knowledge structures (no matter how "teachable" the forms in which the knowledge is revealed). It is surely not satisfied when the instructional situation is conceived to be, as G. K. Plochmann has written, one in which the teacher is endeavoring "with respect to his subject matter, to bring the understanding of the learner in equality with his own understanding."[51] Described in that fashion, with "learner" conceived generically and the "system" to be taught conceived as preexistent and objectively real, the instructional situation seems to me to be one that alienates because of the way it ignores both existential predicament and primordial consciousness. Like the approach to literary criticism Abrams describes, the view appears to commit us to a concept of curriculum "as a floating Laputa, insulated from life and essential human concerns. . . ."[52]

The cries of "irrelevance" are still too audible for us to content ourselves with this. So are the complaints about depersonalization, processing, and compulsory socialization into a corporate, inhuman world. Michael Novak, expressing some of this, writes that what our institutions "decide is real is enforced as real." He calls parents, teachers, and psychiatrists (like policemen and soldiers) "the enforcers of reality"; then he goes on to say: "When a young person is being initiated into society, existing norms determine what is to be considered real and what is to be annihilated by silence and disregard. The good, docile student accepts the norms; the recalcitrant student may lack the intelligence—or have too much; may lack maturity—or insist upon being his own man."[53] I have responses like this in mind when I consult the phenomenologists for an approach to curriculum in the present day. For one thing, they remind us of what it means for an individual to be present to himself; for another, they suggest to us the origins of significant quests for meaning, origins which ought to be held in mind by those willing to enable students to be themselves.

If the existence of a primordial consciousness is taken seriously, it will be recognized that awareness begins perspectively, that our experience is always incomplete. It is true that we have what Merleau-Ponty calls a "prejudice" in favor of a world of solid, determinate objects, quite independent of our perceptions. Consciousness does, however, have the capacity to return to the precognitive, the primordial, by "bracketing out" objects as customarily seen. The individual can release himself into his own inner time and rediscover the ways in which objects arise, the ways in which experience develops. In discussing the possibility of Karl Rossmann exploring his own past, I have tried to show what this sort of interior journey can mean. Not only may it result in the effecting of new syntheses within experience; it may result in an awareness of the process of knowing, of believing, of perceiving. It may even result in an understanding of the ways in which meanings have been sedimented in an individual's own personal history. I can think of no more potent mode of combatting those conceived to be "enforcers of the real," including the curriculum designers.

But then there opens up the possibility of presenting curriculum in such a way that it does not impose or enforce. If the student is enabled to recognize that reason and order may represent the culminating step in his constitution of a world, if he can be enabled to see that what Schutz calls the attainment of a "reciprocity of perspectives"[54] signifies the achievement of rationality, he may realize what it is to generate the structures of the disciplines on his own initiative, against his own "background awareness." Moreover, he may realize that he is projecting beyond his present horizons each time he shifts his attention and takes another perspective on his world. "To say there exists rationality," writes Merleau-Ponty, "is to say that perspectives blend, perceptions confirm each other, a meaning emerges."[55] He points out that we witness at every moment "the miracles of related experiences, and yet nobody knows better than we do how this miracle is worked, for we are ourselves this network of relationships." Curriculum can offer the possibility for students to be the makers of such networks. The problem for their teachers is to stimulate an awareness of the questionable, to aid in the identification of the thematically relevant, to beckon beyond the everyday.

I am a psychological and historical structure, and have received, with existence, a manner of existence, a style. All my actions and thoughts stand in a relationship to this structure, and even a philosopher's thought is merely a way of making explicit his hold on the world, and what he is. The fact remains that I am free, not in spite of, or on the hither side of these motivations, but by means of them. For this significant life, this certain significance of nature and history which I am, does not limit my access to the world, but on the contrary is my means of entering into communication with it. It is by being unrestrictedly and unreservedly what I am at present that I have a chance of moving forward; it is by living my time that I am able to understand other times, by plunging into the present and the world by taking on deliberately what I am fortuitously, by willing what I will and doing what I do, that I can go further.[56]

To plunge in; to choose; to disclose; to move: this is the road, it seems to me, to mastery.

Notes

1. Maurice Merleau-Ponty, *The Primacy of Perception*, ed. James M. Edie (Evanston, Ill.: Northwestern University Press, 1964), p. 99.
2. Jean-Paul Sartre, *Search for a Method* (New York: Alfred A. Knopf, 1963), p. 92.
3. Ryland W. Crary, *Humanizing the School: Curriculum Development and Theory* (New York: Alfred A. Knopf, 1969), p. 13.
4. John Dewey, "The Child and the Curriculum," in *Dewey on Education*, ed. Martin S. Dworkin (New York: Teachers College Press, Columbia University, 1959), p. 91.
5. Sarah Lawall, *Critics of Consciousness* (Cambridge, Mass.: Harvard University Press, 1968).
6. T. S. Eliot, *The Sacred Wood* (New York: Barnes & Noble University Paperbacks, 1960), p. x.
7. Dorothy Walsh, "The Cognitive Content of Art," in *Aesthetics*, ed. Francis J. Coleman (New York: McGraw-Hill, 1968), p. 297.
8. Clive Bell, *Art* (London: Chatto & Windus, 1914).
9. Walsh, "Cognitive Content."
10. M. H. Abrams, "Belief and the Suspension of Belief," in *Literature and Belief*, ed. M. H. Abrams (New York: Columbia University Press, 1957), p. 9.
11. Maurice Blanchot, *L'Espace littéraire* (Paris: Gallimard, 1955).
12. See, e.g., Alfred Schutz, "Some Leading Concepts of Phenomenology," in *Collected Papers I*, ed. Maurice Natanson (The Hague: Martinus Nijhoff, 1967), pp. 104-5.

13. Jean-Paul Sartre, *Literature and Existentialism*, 3d ed. (New York: Citadel Press, 1965), p. 43.
14. Ibid., p. 45.
15. John Dewey, *Art as Experience* (New York: Minton, Balch, 1934), p. 54.
16. Sartre, *Search for a Method*, p. 91.
17. Jean Piaget, *Structuralism* (New York: Basic Books, 1970), p. 139.
18. Ibid., p. 68.
19. Ibid., p. 139.
20. Ibid.
21. Maurice Merleau-Ponty, *Phenomenology of Perception* (London: Routledge Kegan Paul, 1962).
22. Merleau-Ponty, *The Primacy of Perception*, p. 119.
23. Ibid., p. 99.
24. Paulo Freire, *Pedagogy of the Oppressed* (New York: Herder & Herder, 1970), p. 108.
25. Schutz, "On Multiple Realities," in *Collected Papers I*, p. 248.
26. Merleau-Ponty, *The Primacy of Perception*, p. 58.
27. Merleau-Ponty, *Phenomenology of Perception*, p. xvii.
28. Schutz, "On Multiple Realities," in *Collected Papers I*.
29. Merleau-Ponty, *Phenomenology of Perception*, p. xv.
30. R. S. Peters, *Ethics and Education* (London: George Allen & Unwin, 1966), p. 50.
31. R. S. Peters, *Ethics and Education* (Glenview, Ill: Scott Foresman, 1967), p. 12.
32. Philip H. Phenix, "The Uses of the Disciplines as Curriculum Content," in *Theory of Knowledge and Problems of Education*, ed. Donald Vandenberg (Urbana, Ill.: University of Illinois Press, 1969), p. 195.
33. Philip H. Phenix, *Realms of Meaning* (New York: McGraw-Hill, 1964), p. 25.
34. Ibid.
35. Alfred Schutz, "Problem of Rationality in the Social World," in *Collected Papers II*, ed. Maurice Natanson (The Hague: Martinus Nijhoff, 1967), p. 66.
36. Phenix, "Uses of the Disciplines," p. 195.
37. Alvin Toffler, *Future Shock* (New York: Random House, 1970), p. 18.
38. Albert Camus, *The Myth of Sisyphus* (New York: Alfred A. Knopf, 1955), p. 72.
39. Harold Pinter, *The Dumb Waiter* (New York: Grove Press, 1961), p. 103.
40. Tom Stoppard, *Rosencrantz and Guildenstern Are Dead* (New York: Grove Press, 1967), pp. 58-59.
41. Cf. Fyodor Dostoevsky, *Notes from the Underground*, in *The Short Novels of Dostoevsky* (New York: Dial Press, 1945). "You believe in a palace of crystal that can never be destroyed . . . a palace at which one will not be able to put out one's tongue or make a long nose on the sly." p. 152.
42. Franz Kafka, *Amerika* (Garden City, N.Y.: Doubleday Anchor Books, 1946), p. 38.
43. Merleau-Ponty, *The Primacy of Perception*, p. 110.
44. Piaget, *Structuralism*.
45. Richard M. Zaner, *The Way of Phenomenology* (Indianapolis, Ind.: Bobbs-Merrill, Pegasus Books, 1970), p. 27.
46. Freire, *Pedagogy of the Oppressed*, p. 100.

47. Alfred Schutz, "The Life-World," in *Collected Papers III*, ed. Maurice Natanson (The Hague: Martinus Nijhoff, 1967), p. 125.
48. Kafka, *Amerika*, p. 201.
49. Schutz, "The Life-World," in *Collected Papers III*, p. 124.
50. Schutz, "Some Leading Concepts of Phenomenology," in *Collected Papers I*, p. 111.
51. G. K. Plochmann, "On the Organic Logic of Teaching and Learning," in *Theory of Knowledge and Problems of Education*, p. 244.
52. Cf. footnote 10.
53. Michael Novak, *The Experience of Nothingness* (New York: Harper & Row, 1970), p. 94.
54. Schutz, "Symbols, Reality, and Society," in *Collected Papers I*, p. 315.
55. Merleau-Ponty, *Phenomenology of Perception*, p. xix.
56. Ibid., pp. 455-56.

Philip Phenix

My earliest intellectual enthusiasms were in the field of mathematics. The elegance and clarity of that discipline fascinated me and still do. I recall at the age of fourteen inventing a beautiful new proof of the Pythagorean theorem. What a thrill! At Princeton I went on to major in mathematical physics. Princeton was a great center for such studies, and still is. Einstein had just come to Princeton and I had the joy of having my senior thesis in 1934 read by him and commented on with compliments on my mastery of the technical apparatus of relativity theory. I have a letter from him on the subject that I hold as a great personal treasure. On graduation I decided to become an actuary for the Metropolitan Life Insurance Company, putting my mathematics to practical use and trying my hand at administrative work in a large business organization.

I worked in that post for five years, becoming head of the mathematical section, supervising some twenty-five employees, and being elected to fellowship in the two societies of professional actuaries, through passing a series of rigorous examinations. During this same period I became interested in the problems of religion through participation in the meetings of the Religious Society of Friends (Quakers), and finally decided to leave business and mathematics and study philosophy and religion. This I did at Union Theological Seminary in New York, where I studied under such greats as Reinhold Niebuhr and Paul Tillich, whose thought profoundly influenced my own view of things from that time forward.

During World War II I served as an Air Force Meteorologist, and there got my first experience in teaching, as I was assigned to give instruction in the mathematical and physical theory of forecasting. In the latter part of my military career I became an army chaplain, serving both in the Pacific and the European theaters as a transport chaplain on troop ships.

After the war I taught philosophy and religion at Carleton College in Northfield, Minnesota, as well as serving as the first chaplain of the college. Later I was dean of the college for two years. At Carleton I gained my first experience in educational theory, having served as chairman of several committees of educational inquiry and curriculum revision. Eventually these interests led me to Teachers College and to professional interest in education as a field of study, with one year of work as program associate of the Hazen Foundation in New Haven, with major concern for grants to colleges and universities with interesting programs in respect to concern for students and a humanistic approach to the curriculum.

In the years 1948-50 I completed my Ph.D at Columbia in philosophy of religion. My dissertation was a study of theological dimensions in modern physics, thus combining my long-term interest in mathematical physics with my later concerns for religious thought. At Columbia I had the privilege of studying with such outstanding men as John Herman Randall and Ernest Nagel in the history and philosophy of science, as well as continuing my association with Niebuhr and Tillich at Union Seminary. All of these men were members of my dissertation committee.

In 1954 I joined the faculty at Teachers College in the Department of Foundations of Education, succeeding John Childs, eminent interpreter of the educational thought of experimentalism, especially John Dewey's. In this period I also began my major writing efforts. My first book was in the philosophy of religion. Entitled Intelligible Religion, *it was an attempt to frame a believable empirical view of religion within modern categories of understanding. I published a major general text,* Philosophy of Education, *four years later, and followed this with a book,* Religious Concerns in Contemporary Education, *the next year. In 1961 I wrote* Education and the Common Good: A Moral Philosophy of the Curriculum, *detailing my views of the relation of values to public education in a democracy. This was followed by* Realms of Meaning, *which I consider my major work, dealing with the epistemology of the various ways in which experience can be interpreted through the several groups of disciplines. My book* Man and His Becoming, *containing my Haley lectures in 1963, dealt with the disciplines as revealing facets of human nature.* Education and the Worship of God, *my Riverside lectures, developed the theme of religious dimensions in the various disciplines.*

In summary, I would say that my intellectual development has been a sustained effort to gain a comprehensive and integral outlook

on life and to find means of communicating this outlook in my teach-
ing and writing. The thinker I find most congenial is A. N. Whitehead,
whose union of the mathematical and scientific outlook with the
ethical, religious, and esthetic is a model of the human quest for
wholeness and humaneness.

Philip Phenix
Teachers College
Columbia University

19

Transcendence and the Curriculum

The purpose of this paper is to show the significance of transcendence for the interpretation and evaluation of educational theory and practice. I shall begin by stating what is meant by this concept, indicating certain allied and contrasting ideas, and analyzing several dimensions of experience to which it pertains. I shall then apply the concept, showing its relation to a number of general dispositions that are important in teaching and learning. Finally, I shall suggest somewhat more specifically the consequences for the curriculum that flow from acknowledging and celebrating transcendence.

The method used in this analysis may be characterized as both phenomenological and empirical. It is phenomenological in that I endeavor to categorize certain phases of human consciousness as immediately presented in introspection. It is empirical in that throughout an appeal is made to human experience, without recourse to supernatural interventions, or if the latter are to be acknowledged, that their meaning is to be interpreted in terms of experiential categories. Thus I am engaging in what is customarily called natural theology, as distinguished from revealed theology. I do not begin with a presumed commitment to the faith of a given historic community, but with what I presume to be universal or universalizable experiences, the analysis of which is open to the scrutiny of natural reason.

I confess that there is a faith underlying these reflections, and that it probably consists of a certain cluster of commitments and primordial persuasions that have their genesis in the life of the community of learning as I have experienced it. Accordingly, this effort may be regarded as the explication of what I consider to be certain faith presuppositions of the educative community, utilizing some of the conceptual apparatus of modern philosophical natural theology, with deductive elaborations to show what educational aims and practices are coherent with those presuppositions.

The Meaning of Transcendence

Transcendence may be regarded as the most characteristic concept for the interpretation of religious phenomena. Religious experience is the experience of transcendence. Note that I do not say "experience of the transcendent," implying an object which an experiencing subject apprehends. I prescind from the ontological question at this point in order to concentrate on the phenomenology of the immediate experience of transcending. It is not that the ontological question is unimportant or irrelevant. I prescind from it because the experience of transcendence is the necessary starting point for formulating the meaning of any ontological assertions and because I am convinced that the being of transcendence embraces and unites what are called objectivity and subjectivity.

The term *transcendence* refers to the experience of limitless going beyond any given state or realization of being. It is an inherent property of conscious being to be aware that every concrete entity is experienced within a context of wider relationships and possibilities. Conscious life is always open to a never-ending web of entailments and unfoldings. No content of experience is just what it appears to be here and now without any further prospects or associations. All experience is characterized by an intrinsic dynamism that in principle breaks every bound that rational patterning or practical convenience may establish.

The sense of this fundamental category can perhaps be made clearer by referring to some of the cognate terms that have been employed in the theological tradition to point to it. The one most akin is "infinitude," which expresses the never-finished enlargement of contexts within which every bounded entity is enmeshed. To affirm the finiteness of anything is to presuppose a participation in infinitude that makes it possible to acknowledge the finite. Finitude is thus a specification of limitation within the ambience of infinitude—a deliberate stemming of transcendence for purposes of conceptual or active control.

A second allied concept is "spirit." Spirit is the name given to the property of limitless going beyond. To have a spiritual nature is to participate in infinitude. Reason refers to the capacity for the rational ordering of experience through categories of finitude. Spirit makes one aware of the finiteness of the structures imposed by reason. To say that persons are beings with spirit is to point to their perennial discontent and dissatisfaction with any and every finite realization. Thus it is sometimes said that spirit finds its exemplification more in the yearning impulses of feeling and the innovative projects of will than in the settled conclusions of intellect.

The essential quality of transcendence is manifest also in the secular concept of idealization, which is central, for example, in the nontheistic, naturalistic thought of John Dewey. Every actuality is set within a context of ideal possibility. Every end realized becomes the means for the fulfillment of further projected ideals, and this is a process that is generic to human experience. Much the same idea is implicit in Dewey's concept of continuous growth—of that valuable growth that leads to further growth. The qualitative test of growth is whether it is consistent with a limitless enrichment of realizations through the progressive actualization of ideal possibilities. This vision of continuous, progressive reconstruction of experience as the norm of human existence is a nontheological interpretation of the fundamental religious concept of transcendence.

Dimensions of Transcendence

The general concept of transcendence may be analyzed into at least three principal dimensions: temporal, extensive, and qualitative. Temporal transcendence refers to infinitude of process. The experience of temporal passage in its essence is a consciousness of transcendence, for it manifests an ineluctable going beyond. Heroditus was the first among Western thinkers to point to the primordial character of temporal flux, within which the logos of reason was a subordinate principle of order. In modern philosophy Bergson was perhaps the foremost exponent of the basic dynamism of reality, which he called the *elan vital*, apprehended by an act of intuition that yields profounder insight than the static conceptions of discursive reason. Whitehead also made "creative advances into novelty," i.e., continuous temporal transcendence, the most fundamental presupposition of his system of categories for describing reality.

To be humanly alive is to experience each moment as a new creation, to know that this moment, though continuous with the past, is yet a distinct and fresh emergence, which will in turn yield to still further novel realizations. Every human present, retrospectively regarded, is perceived as created, and prospectively regarded, as a destiny. These two terms—*creation* and *destiny*—are the two temporal poles between which transcendence ranges. As such, they are perennially important theological categories. The experiential meaning of creation—of being created—is the consciousness of retrospective temporal transcendence of prior states of being. The experiential meaning of destiny, and of participating in creative activity, is the consciousness of prospective actualizations beyond every particular attainment. The various ideas in the religions of mankind referring to the preexistence or immortality of the soul aim to symbolize the temporal dimension of transcendence both in its retrospective and prospective modes.

A second dimension of transcendence is extension. Limitless going beyond is experienced not only with reference to time but also in respect to inclusiveness. The classic philosophical statement of this dimension of transcendence is supplied by the doctrine of internal relations, which is the central idea and the key to philosophical idealism, though not exclusively wedded to that way of thinking. According to this doctrine, any entity is constituted by the set of relationships that it has with all other entities. Thus nothing exists in isolation, but always in relation. Reality is a single interconnected whole, such that the complete description of any entity would require the comprehension of every other entity.

One influential formulation of the principle of extensive transcendence is found in Whitehead's Philosophy of Organism, in the concept of "ingredience." According to Whitehead's system, the ingredients that go into the constitution of every event include all other past events, each apprehended according to an appropriate measure of relevance. Hence every actual occasion or event is a particular mirroring of the whole universe.

Something of the same idea is implicit in modern field theories and in the ideas of contextualism and ecology. An electron, a magnet, a chunk of matter, or a person is never an isolated, separate entity, but exists in a context of electrostatic, magnetic, gravitational, or personal field relationships. In the last analysis, every being is a being-in-relation, and is what it is and behaves as it does by virtue of its participation with other beings.

The theological expression of the principle of extensive

transcendence is supplied by the doctrine of monotheism and of the divine omnipresence. There is a single ultimate ground of all being, and all beings are mutually related in that common unitary reality. Hence, every particular experience contains the possibility of evincing the limitless wealth of participations to which it is heir, thereby bearing witness to a principle of transcendence toward wholeness that is one hallmark of religious orientation.

To the temporal and extensive dimensions of transcendence a third may be added, namely the qualitative. This dimension refers to the consciousness of limitless possibility of going beyond in degrees of excellence. It is the source of the principle of criticism that levies judgments of relative worth on concrete actualizations. What this principle affirms is that no actual occasion or finite grouping of occasions constitutes a complete qualitative achievement, but that beyond all such realizations higher fulfillments are possible.

This dimension of qualitative transcendence is well exemplified in one of the central concepts in Tillich's theology, that is, in what he terms the *protestant principle*. By this term he does not refer primarily to the historic movement called Protestantism, but rather to the principle of protest that denies qualitative ultimacy to any actuality, be it institution, person, belief, or cultural norm. According to this principle, the religious consciousness is manifest in the refusal to accord supreme worth to any and every realization of nature or humanity. Implicit in such refusal is commitment to an inexhaustible ideality that renders a judgment of partiality and insufficiency on whatever exists.

The theological expression of qualitative transcendence is also contained in such concepts as divine holiness, righteousness, and perfection. That God is holy, righteous, and perfect experientially signifies the persuasion of the human consciousness that no finite reality is of supreme worth, the creative restlessness of the human spirit that never remains content with any historic attainment, and the perennial protest of the prophetic conscience against the absolutizing of limited goods.

Universality and Negation of Transcendence

It has been suggested that transcendence is a primordial category for the interpretation of human experience in the sense that it is an elemental and ineluctable aspect of the human condition. That is to say that transcendence is universal. It is phenomenologically not the case that some persons, called "religious" or "spiritual" types, experience it while others do not. I am arguing that human consciousness is rooted in transcendence, and that analysis of all human consciousness discloses the reality of transcendence as a fundamental presupposition of the human condition. To be sure, this same human consciousness also discloses aspects of finitude. Acts of demarcation, of limitation, and of closure are manifestly present in human behavior. What I maintain is that all such finite determinations are imbedded in and are specifications of an indeterminate ground of creative advance into novelty, of contextual relations, and of qualitative gradations.

The relation of finite and infinite in man has the paradoxical property that boundless creative lures, outreachings for wider relations, and strivings for ideality, all of which transcendent tensions challenge the status quo of finite realizations, cause persons to negate transcendence in order to save themselves from the threatened dissolution of actual attainments. The denial of spirituality in the name of individual self-sufficiency or various forms of absolutism, of institution, race, class, nation, tradition, or doctrine, is evidence of this flight from transcendence. This negative self-protective movement is what the Judaic and Christian traditions have called sin. As theologians in these traditions have regularly pointed out, the pervasive and persistent denial of transcendence is, in fact, prime evidence for the presence and power of transcendence. This is the meaning of the myth that portrays the devil as a fallen angel, that is, as a spiritual agent employing his creative transcendence to generate an illusion of self-sufficing autonomy.

General Dispositions

We are now in a position to proceed with a discussion of the significance of the experience of transcendence for the enterprise of education. Certain qualities of life are associated with transcendence, and at the same time play a decisive role in teaching and learning. I submit that these general human dispositions provide a set of criteria for a transcendence-oriented curriculum as contrasted with one that is predicated upon the neglect or denial of transcendence.

Hope

The first disposition engendered by the experience of transcendence is hope. Hope is the mainspring of human existence. As existentialist thinkers remind us, conscious life is a continual projection into the future. Even though the adventure may project one into the unknown, it is animated by an affirmation of the movement forward in time. Without hope, there is no incentive for learning, for the impulse to learn presupposes confidence in the possibility of improving one's existence. It can be argued that widespread loss of hope is one of the principal causes of the educational problems that beset contemporary America. When widespread social dislocations, dissolution of customary norms, dehumanization, and other malaises of social and cultural life cause people to feel impotent, no technical improvements in the content or methods of instruction will induce people to learn well. On the other hand, those who are buoyed by strong hope can overcome substantial formal deficiencies in program or technique. The explicit acknowledgment of transcendence as a ground for hope may therefore contribute significantly to the efficacy of education.

Few recent thinkers have so persuasively argued that a transcendent hope is the driving force for personal and collective achievement as Teilhard de Chardin. He saw the cultural and educational crisis of our time primarily as a faltering of hope; by presenting a cosmological vision in which man's conscious responsible striving for progress is viewed as continuous with the upward drive toward coordination that has powered the entire evolutionary ascent, he endeavored to provide intellectual warrant for an animating hope that can give mankind the heart to continue learning.

Creativity

The recognition of transcendence as inseparable from the human condition lends special emphasis to the disposition toward creativity. To be human is to create. The fashioning of new constructs is not an exceptional activity reserved for a minority of gifted persons; it is rather the normal mode of behavior for everyone. Dull repetitiveness and routinism are evidences of dehumanization. In this respect the institutions and practices of education have often inhibited, rather than fostered, humaneness, by inculcating habits of automatic conformity instead of imaginative origination.

The prime enemy of creativity is the flight from transcendence which in the theological tradition of the West has been termed sin. Insofar as educators function as agents for transmitting and confirming cultural traditions unchanged, they are ministers of sin. When they presume to act as authorities dispensing to the young knowledge and values that are to be accepted without question, they act as enemies of transcendence. On the other hand, the educator who affirms transcendence is characterized by a fundamental humility manifest in expectant openness to fresh creative possibilities. To be sure, he does not ignore or discount the funded wisdom of the past. He does not regard it as a fixed patrimony to be preserved, but as a working capital for investment in the projects of an unfolding destiny.

Creativity is fostered by having due regard both for transcendence and for immanence. By the experience of immanence I mean the sense of importance in what is actualized in existence. Immanence and transcendence are intimately related. Immanence is the treasure deposited by the creative activity of transcendence. Existential realizations lose their savor when the freshness of transcendent impulse that ushered in their birth is forgotten, and projected enterprises degenerate into quixotic gestures when the sustaining and ennobling structures of past actualizations are rejected. The educator thus fosters creativity when he loves and respects the traditional learning, conceived as immanence, to be transformed and rejuvenated in the service of transcendence.

Awareness

The dispositions of hope and creativity correspond to the temporal dimension of transcendence. Corresponding to the extensive dimension are the dispositions of awareness: sympathy, empathy, hospitality, and tolerance, that is to say, openness outwards, as well as toward the future. In acknowledging transcendence, one adopts a positive attitude toward all other persons, other cultures, and other social groups, in fact, toward all other beings, including the objects of nature. Accepting transcendence frees one from the self-protecting isolation that regards the different or the unfamiliar as a threat to be avoided. Alienation is evidence of the flight from transcendence, and separation and exclusion are manifestations of the primary sin of striving for self-sufficient autonomy.

No teaching can occur without a predisposition toward relation on the part of the teacher who seeks to shape the life of the student and to mediate to the student his (the teacher's) life of relation with the circumambient world. Nor will the student learn effectively in the absence of a hospitable openness to that world and to those who assist him in establishing satisfying relationships with it. This factor of sensitivity is the main theme in Buber's pedagogical theory. For him, the clue to significant education does not reside in the specific methods or contents of instruction, but in the presupposition of the primacy and the power of the elemental relation, which is the source of all being. He sees the primordial relation as a reality in which one may confidently dwell, and within which the particular categories and connections of reason and practice are secondarily discriminated. This assumed indwelling by the teacher in transcendence can help to release the student's powers of awareness, thus providing strong catalysis for learning. In turn, teachers who are inured to self-defensive closedness may be liberated to wider sympathies by sharing in the relatively unspoiled freshness of young people who affirm the world and celebrate the possibilities of ever-deepening relationships within it.

Doubt and Faith

Corresponding to the qualitative dimension of transcendence are the twin dispositions of constructive doubt and faith or, combining the two, faithful doubt. A central insight of Tillich's thought is this intimate linkage of doubt and faith within the context of transcendence. Tillich argues that really serious doubt—the radical questioning of any and every alleged finality—is only possible to one who is grasped by a transcendent faith, that is, who enjoys a confidence that wells up from the creative grounds of being and does not rest on any objectified security structures. This position is summarized in Tillich's reformulation of Luther's doctrine of justification by faith in the state of sin to read justification by faith in the state of doubt. The serious doubter is justified by his faith in the unconditioned ground of being manifest in the very seriousness of his activity of doubting.

The educator rooted in transcendence helps to foster a constructive disposition toward doubt, that is, a spirit of criticism. Such a spirit is to be distinguished sharply from the destructive doubt of the cynic or skeptic or from the attitude of indifference engendered by dilettante sophistication. The latter dispositions are essentially faithless, in the sense that they presuppose the futility of any sustained quest for truth or right on the grounds that the perennial struggle of mankind to achieve demonstrable securities has proven unsuccessful. Abandoning the search for ultimate certainties, the skeptic unwittingly cuts the ground from under serious inquiry itself, thus discrediting even his own activity of doubting. The Cartesian insight still holds, though in modified form: I doubt, therefore I am. The secure foundation of the human condition as a spiritual being is the faith-evidencing activity of concerned and responsible doubting.

The teacher who is spiritually aware does not seek to protect himself from the insecurity of uncertainty, perplexity, and irremediable ignorance. He does not try to hide behind a screen of academic presumption and professional expertise, embellished with mystifying jargon. Nor does he confuse the role of teacher with that of authoritative oracle. He does not expect or encourage his students supinely to accept his beliefs or directions. On the other hand, he shares with conviction and enthusiasm the light that he believes he possesses, and encourages his students to do the same, resolutely resisting in himself and in his students the paralysis and sense of futility associated with skepticism and indifference.

Wonder, Awe, and Reverence

Consummating the dispositions associated with the experience of transcendence are the attitudes of wonder, awe, and reverence. Consciousness of infinitude entails a sense of the manifold powers and possibilities of the reality in which one's existence is embedded. This sense is the root of the impulse to learn. Dewey spoke of the unsolved problem as the stimulus for thought. I believe his concept of the problem as basically the blocking of organic drives was too narrowly biological, and that a sounder, more positive, and more distinctly human formulation would be that thought grows out of wonder, which in turn is rooted in the spiritual act of projecting ideal possibilities. Thus instead of regarding human learning primarily as a means of biological adaptation, it may be thought of as a response to the lure of transcendence. Indeed, the very notion of adaptation appears to be meaningful only in terms of the process of creative invention for the purpose of realizing specific ideal harmonies.

Wonder refers to the suspenseful tension of consciousness toward the unknown future in response to the attraction of unrealized potentialities. It includes the vague adumbration of enriching relationships yet unestablished but beckoning. It is the hovering shadow of an answer resident in every question seriously asked. Awe is the sense of momentousness excited by the experience of transcendence. It is the source of persistent interest in learning and of patient efforts toward realization, born of the sense that the human career, as well as the cosmic enterprise of which it is a part, is an affair of capital importance. Reverence betokens a recognition of one's participation in transcendence as a surprising and continually renewed gift, in contrast to the view of one's existence as a secure possession and as an autonomous achievement. The reverent disposition saves one from the arrogance of self-sufficiency which interferes with openness to creative possibilities in learning, and issues in a spirit of thankfulness for the gift of life that makes study a welcome opportunity and not a chore and an obligation.

Consequences for the Curriculum

The acknowledgment of transcendence suggests a curriculum that has due regard for the uniqueness of the human personality. If a person is a creative subject, then the core of his selfhood can never be defined in terms of objective formative patterns that are common to a social group. To be sure, for practical purposes provision must be made to enable the young to participate effectively in the common life. But it makes a great difference whether the patterns of culture are regarded as essentially constitutive of the personality or as resources for use by a personality whose springs of being lie at a deeper level than any social norm, that is to say, in transcendence.

A curriculum of transcendence provides a context for engendering, gestating, expecting, and celebrating the moments of singular awareness and of inner illumination when each person comes into the consciousness of his inimitable personal being. It is not characterized so much by the objective content of studies as by the atmosphere created by those who comprise the learning community. Its opposite is the engineering outlook that regards the learner as material to be formed by means of a variety of technical procedures. In contrast, the curriculum of transcendence requires a context of essential freedom, though not of anarchy, which is the correlate of indifference and of skepticism about the structures of being. Freedom in the school of transcendence is based on openness to fresh possibilities of insight and invention and provision of ample cultural and interpersonal resources for the formation of unique structures of existence.

Concern for Wholeness

The lure of transcendence is toward wholeness. It follows that the educator in responding to that incitement creates a curriculum that fosters comprehensiveness of experience. The argument for education of the whole person in the last analysis rests on the consciousness of transcendence. In a technical, success-oriented society the payoff is found in specialized competence. From the standpoint of personal and social efficiency, the arguments for breadth of knowledge and skill are few and unconvincing. To be sure, there must be some with sufficient scope of understanding to be able to coordinate the parts of the social mechanism. Yet even their comprehensiveness can be conceived in narrow managerial terms. The case for general education for all rests finally on the nature of persons as essentially constituted by the hunger for wholeness.

A curriculum designed to respond to this hunger is obviously multidisciplinary. It affords opportunities for the enrichment of understanding in diverse areas of human experience, as, for example, in the theoretical, the practical, and the affective domains. Narrowness and exclusivity of concentration are incompatible with the demands of transcendence.

On the other hand, it is important not to be misled into the advocacy of superficial generality in the plan of studies. Since transcendence has a qualitative as well as an extensive dimension, it is just as essential to provide opportunities for intensive understanding as for extensive range of studies. That is why the curriculum of transcendence is multidisciplinary in nature. The disciplinary character insures depth of penetration—a progressive enlargement of insight within the framework of methods and categories that has proven fruitful in inquiry. It cannot be overemphasized that transcendence is not simply openness-in-general. It presupposes that being has structures. These structures are the immanent patterns of transcendence. Hence the necessity for discipline. Transcendence is not an invitation to anarchy but to glad obedience to the structures or logos of being. These patterns are the objective norms for knowledge and for conduct, and they are what the various disciplines aim to disclose. Productiveness of insight in any discipline is evidence that the categories and procedures that define it in some degree reflect the logos of being.

The criterion of wholeness, then, is not incompatible with specialized inquiry. It does, however, require that each specialized mode of investigation be understood in relation to other such modes. Each disipline is founded upon certain deliberate limitations and simplifications which make it possible to advance understanding of inexhaustibly complex realities. What consciousness of transcendence does is to make one aware of the partiality of each disciplined outlook and sensitive to the many-sidedness of the reality that one confronts. Recognition of partiality of perspective is evidence of a more comprehensive perspective from which the judgment of partiality is rendered. Transcendence leads to the acknowledgement that the truth of any discipline mode is never the whole truth, and to active interest in the relationships and complementarities among the various disciplines. In this sense, the curriculum in the light of transcendence is interdisciplinary as well as multidisciplinary.

Thus the awareness of transcendence provides justification for a broad and variegated curriculum securely grounded in the specialized disciplines. Studies are pursued in depth according to the tested methods of these disciplines, yet always with an eye to the similarities and contrasts with other disciplines and in full awareness of the need for complementation by alternative perspectives. Furthermore, though the various disciplines are conceived as channels of insight into the structures of being, it is not assumed that any standard or traditional set of disciplines provides the full and final disclosure of the nature of things. Hence consciousness of transcendence encourages an open-textured orientation toward the very enterprise of disciplinemaking, hospitality toward the emergence of fresh discipline perspectives, and willingness to replace partial outlooks that have served well in the past with more comprehensive or penetrating ones as they emerge in the successive transformations in the evolution of culture. On these grounds, the transcendence-oriented educator helps his students to be alert to the realities of intellectual mutations, revolutions, and inventions, and endeavors to create an atmosphere and an expectation in which his students may share in the construction of new and more illuminating patterns of thought.

Education for Inquiry

The recognition of transcendence suggests a characteristic perception of the central task of teaching and learning as dedication to the practice of inquiry. The transcendent perspective is opposed to all outlooks that presuppose a fixed content of knowledge, beliefs, or skills that the learner is meant to acquire. The assumption that anything is knowable with completeness and certainty arrests inquiry and closes the channels that lead on to deeper and wider insight.

On the other hand, transcendence is compatible with confident acceptance of the possibility of valid knowledge, once its partial, limited, and contingent character is acknowledged. Inquiry then includes as an essential element the charting of these contextual limitations and the careful definition of the boundaries by which particular perspectives are characterized.

Commitment to inquiry is thus opposed to two polar positions: dogmatic finality or certainty and nihilistic skepticism about the possibility of warranted knowledge. The confident practice of inquiry rests on faith in the intelligibility of reality together with an acknowledgment of the boundless depth and the interconnections of the structures of intelligibility.

The orientation toward inquiry is one of the widely recognized aspects of recent curricular theory and practice and need not be described in any detail here. My intent in the present essay is only to show how this particular curriculum emphasis is related to the consciousness of transcendence and to suggest that it has its source and sustenance in that awareness.

The Practice of Dialogue

Inherent also in education carried on according to the norms of transcendence is the practice of dialogue. The extensive dimension of transcendence presupposes a lure toward ever wider associations of complementarity and of enriching relatedness. It is incompatible with all self-sufficient isolation and exclusiveness of perspective. Hence growth in understanding is to be sought by engaging in the activity of open-ended, continuing communication. The indissoluble unity between teaching and learning is affirmed in the recognition that enlargement and refinement of insight are possible only through the mutual stimulation of conjoint inquiry. One learns effectively only as he seeks to make his perspectives intelligible to others and in turn seeks to enter into their perceptions. A practical consequence of this insight for the curriculum maker is that he organize the teaching-learning enterprise with maximum provision for dialogic activity. Such activity consists of more than mere conversation or discussion. Real dialogue is a high skill requiring sympathetic and practical leadership based upon the will to communicate, which in turn is founded on the capacity to enter sympathetically and expectantly into the minds of other persons, which capacity is evidence of transcendence.

The Cultivation of Transcendence

In the foregoing I have sought to explicate the concept "transcendence" as a fundamental category for interpreting human experience and to suggest some of the relationships of this concept to the process of education. I have indicated that some important human values have their roots in transcendence, and I have argued that transcendence is the basic presupposition of a certain set of curricular goals and styles. Insofar, then, as one is committed to these values and educational aims, it is natural, in concluding such an exposition and analysis as this to inquire how the experience of transcendence may be so cultivated as to foster the desired educational realizations.

I answer this question with four points. First, there is a sense in which the consciousness of transcendence cannot be cultivated, since according to the position set forth here it is an inescapable reality of human existence. To exist is to participate in transcendence. Infinitude is essential, not accidental, in the being of persons. One may deny transcendence, but as I have claimed, the very act of denial bears witness to it. Accordingly, transcendence simply *is*, and is not an option to be elected or rejected as a component of human experience.

Nonetheless, in the second place, cultivation of transcendence is possible in the sense that one learns to accept and welcome it and to live in the strength and illumination of it. The primary way to affirm it is by the practice of the life that stems from it. Thus, by living hopefully and creatively, with faith and reverence, by experiencing the joys of responsible freedom, by seeking for wholeness of disciplined understanding, and by engaging in continual dialogic inquiry, one tacitly acknowledges the presence and power of transcendence.

Third, an important factor in the cultivation of transcendence is the witness of those who consciously celebrate it in their own existence. When fearful and self-protecting tendencies tend to obscure the light of infinitude and doubts tend to annihilate rather than transform, one may bolster flagging faith by turning to others in strong grasp of transcendence. In this respect the teacher by his own mute witness may play a central role in the maintenance of the primordial grounds of learning morale.

Fourth, and finally, the awareness of transcendence may be clarified and fortified by articulating conceptual tools for describing and interpreting this fundamental experience. Such conceptual articulation provides a kind of rational justification for the basic presuppositions by which one lives. When the fundamental grounds of existence are made explicit in this way, they may be less subject to erosion by the forces of irrational fear and self-defensiveness than if they remain purely tacit. Thus philosophical theology of education, of which the present essay is intended to be an illustration, may contribute to the nurture of the awareness of transcendence and to the curricular consequences that are associated with it.

William J. Murphy
William F. Pilder

William Pilder and William Murphy met and worked together at Indiana University. Both have since left academe, Mr. Murphy to work and live on a farm, and Mr. Pilder to teach in a Montessori school in Connecticut.

20

Alternative Organizational Forms, Cultural Revolution, and Education

Introduction

There is a notion prevailing in much discourse on change that it is possible to talk about change without indicating the direction the change should take. The intent of this paper is to refute this notion. The intent rests on the assertion that the Western world is now experiencing a cultural revolution largely as a result of technological development. This revolution is an attempt to overthrow a technology that Marcuse describes as resulting in "intensified subjection of individuals in enormous apparatus of production and distribution, in the deprivatization of free time, in the almost indistinguishable fusion of constructive and destructive social labor."[1] Marcuse is convinced that the so-called rationalization of technology is actually a form of unknowledged political domination. Inherent in this revolution is the possibility of realizing a completely new development in man, and the vision of the new man is what must compel the efforts to change social institutions.

Western society, especially the United States, stands on the threshold of post-scarcity where it is possible to begin to create a system of social relationships based on a commitment to the absolute freedom and equality of the person, instead of on divisions of class, race, and so forth. One writer claims that,

post-scarcity means fundamentally more than a mere abundance of the means of life: it decidedly includes the *kind* of life these means support. The human relationships and psyche of the individual in a post-scarcity society must fully reflect the freedom, security and self-expression that this abundance makes possible. Post-scarcity society, in short, is the fulfillment of the social and cultural potentialities latent in a technology of abundance.[2]

Oppression can now be made to give way to liberation. Not to be for this liberation is to continue aggrandizing oppressive forms of social relationships.[3] Strategies of development that fail to come clean on their position on this issue of the direction of social change continue their relationship to a dying culture and fail to confront oppression.

Because most of the organizational forms that make up the social structure of Western society rest on a set of values that are not in concert with the new possibilities for man, these forms must be confronted squarely from a new value base. To fail to confront from this new value position is simply to tinker with present organizational forms and such tinkering in no way changes the oppression resulting from these organizational arrangements. People who talk of alternative organizations from value-free positions are playing word games.[4] Frequently political expediency is given as a rationalization for these games, but this divides the world into two planes of reality: one plane where the moral judgment functions and another where judgments are made in terms of political effectiveness. This kind of thinking provided justification for many during the Nazi's administration of death for 6 million human beings.[5]

The cultural revolution and organizational forms meet head on in the contemporary crisis of authority. We will begin by describing this crisis. Then the analysis will be applied to the school as an organization. Finally, we will present a development strategy for creating new forms of organization for education.

The Contemporary Crisis of Authority

In times of relative social stability power resides mostly in those who say yes to prevailing norms and arrangements. Today in America this power of the yes is related to injustice in economic, social, and racial relationships; it is related to forms of management that are responsible for laying waste vast amounts of material and human resources; it belongs to political power that directly violates the will of the people; it continues to pay lip service to a bankrupt culture while upholding the sanctions of that culture over individual freedom. But the yes continues to be said by a powerful few.

Unfortunately, it is impossible to identify the few who are responsible, because they are huge, impersonal, bureaucratic conglomerates. "They" control our lives, but "they" are mysterious, invisible, demonic forces. To live at all in the modern world is to live in an ambience of formal organizations where decisions are made that are no one person's responsibility.

The term *formal organization* will be used in a more or less technical sense to cover all sorts of bureaucracies, private and public. A distinctive mark of such organizations is that they make a clear-cut distinction between the acts and relationships of individuals in their official capacity within the organization and in their private capacity. Decisions of individual decision makers in an organization are attributed to the organization and not to the individual. In that sense, they are impersonal. Individual officeholders are in principle replaceable by other individuals without affecting the continuity or identity of the organization. In this sense, it has sometimes been said that an organization is immortal.[6]

So the immortal organizations keep saying yes no matter how many individual, personal no's are thrown against them. Despair in the face of such personal impotence makes the violence of some manifestations of dissent at least understandable, at best forgivable.[7]

But personal violence will not directly confront the problem of formal organizations, and unless these organizations are dealt with on that basis, the real problem goes untouched. This is not to delimit the courage or necessity of confrontation based on asserting personal rights against an oppressive organization. At times this kind of confrontation appears necessary before people are willing to deal with the organization. Attica is a case in point. But after the confrontation there is still the matter of a formal organization that must be addressed as such.

One of the basic problems of these organizations is the manner in which decisions are made.

Finally, we come to the third proposition lying behind the theory of social decisions, namely, the proposition that an action is rational if and only if it is the best means to attaining one's objectives. Whatever particular form this principle of rationality takes, subjective or objective, it is still based on the assumption that the essence of an action is its producing an end-state of affairs, an objective. In as much as every action is, or ideally should be, purposive in this sense—by definition—then it naturally follows that a rational action could only be one that is defined in terms of a "bringing about a change" or a "production of a state of affairs." Given a casual theory of action, rational behavior, or action, has to be defined in casual terms, i.e., ends and means.

Quite apart from the question-begging nature of this conception of "rationality," it has certain obviously objectionable moral consequences; for it reduces the relationship between individual human beings to the category of means to an end, a category in which they do not belong. It makes the only point of a rational action the function that it plays in "means-ends" chains. The only point of keeping a promise, for instance, is the effect that doing so will have on my own ends or the ends of others. This way of looking at rationality reflects what seems to me to be essentially an amoral position, for it reduces morality, which is a matter of the relations between human beings, to what is useful or expedient for some purpose or other.[8]

A growing number of persons are becoming aware of the extent to which formal organizations control human behavior and influence persons in deleterious directions. The need and power to say no is bringing people together, and around their no is forming a revolutionary elite that will be the vanguard of all major social change in the West. Authority for decisions is being taken back by the individual, who then begins to experience the problems of acting as a person in contexts that keep expecting nonpersons. David Cooper presents the problem well.

We can perhaps talk about "madness," which is the genocidal and suicidal irrationality of the capitalist mode of governing people, and "Madness," which is the individual tentative on the part of actual identifiable people to make themselves ungoverned and ungovernable, not by undisciplined spontaneity, but by a systematic reformation of our lives that refuses aprioristic systematization but moves through phases of destructuring, unconditioning, de-educating and defamilializing ourselves, so that we at last get on familiar but unfamilial terms with ourselves and are then ready to restructure ourselves in a manner that refuses all personal taboos and consequently revolutionizes the whole society.[9]

Here all the old sources of authority are under direct attack, leaving the individual with the problem of personal identity without the traditional aids. From the point of view of the status quo, this is indeed "Madness"; from the point of view of the individual striving to be a person who acts, the status quo is the real "madness."

Here then is the crisis of authority: Western man lives out his life in an ambience of formal organizations that exercise almost total control over his person. Decisions are made within these organizations in a manner which makes the person subservient to organizational objectives. A split then occurs on the personal level where behavior in the organization and personal action no longer relate. The condition is schizoid and produces the alienation characteristic of many bureaucratic lives. In the face of this alienation a growing consciousness of the need to say no to a social fabric made up of formal organizations is developing. The no challenges directly all the sources of authority and has profound implications for education.

Education as Countereducation

In a society based on formal organizations that negate the highest possibilities for human development, education must counter prevailing social expectations. The educational enterprise in this context becomes in every sense political.[10]

> In the society at large, the mental space for denial and reflection must first be recreated. Repulsed by the concreteness of the administered society, the effort of emancipation becomes "abstract"; it is reduced to facilitating the recognition of what is going on, to freeing language from the tyranny of the Orwellian syntax and logic, to developing the concepts that comprehend reality. More than ever, the proposition holds true that progress in freedom demands progress in the *consciousness* of freedom. Where the mind has been made into a subject-object of politics and policies, intellectual autonomy, the realm of "pure" thought has become a matter of *political education* (or rather: countereducation).[11]

The word *counter* as a negation becomes necessary because the role of education has essentially been that of socializing children for life in a network of formal organizations, a socialization that itself denies their possibilities. The melting pot of the Common School has become a pressure cooker to prepare food for the immortal bureaucracies.

The best description for how the pressure cooker functions is provided by Ivan Illich's "phenomenology" of schooling.[12] The phenomenology presents the process of schooling as age-specific, teacher related, classroom bound, and based on a graded curriculum. Each of these elements contributes to the creation of the apolitical, amoral, passionless man desired by bureaucratic societies.

An illustrative example of the effects of making schooling age-specific is the current national concern with the problem of reading. How much of the problem relates to the practice of saying to every child when he has reached the magic age of entry into school, "Now you must learn to read"? Then when significant numbers fail to respond to this *school* time, perhaps because their *personal* time for learning to read is either already past or yet to come, there exists a national reading problem. All of this is to say nothing about the destruction resulting from forcing children into time frames unrelated to their rhythmns of development and the consequent failure experiences. Much of the suffering and impotence of poor people in the ghettos of this country is not unrelated to the failures schools create by the age-specific organization.[13]

"Innovations" like the nongraded school organization or "individually prescribed instruction" do not begin to touch the problem of age-specific organization. They are simply more fancy means to the same end.[14] Similarly, to return to the "national reading problem," all the techniques in the reading world will not help a problem that rests on a school organization with destructive commitments.

Schools likewise rest on an organizational commitment that learning is inextricably related to teaching.[15] Instruction is only behind defense on the list of national expenses. The student-teacher dichotomy is established where everyone "learns" to defer to authority, even if it does not correspond to personal experience. Personal judgments give way to teacher's opinion about what it is important to know. All of this is, of course, the perfect preparation for bureaucratic life where the organization's objectives may not relate in any way to personal goals. Learning to relate to teacher is much like relating to general or boss. Lieutenant Calley is a rather graphic symbol of where the myth about teaching and learning ends.

A good deal of rhetoric has been developed recently around the idea of "humanizing" the schools, which attempts to get at the teaching problem. The teacher role is modified to that of facilitator who is supposed to be much more concerned with the self-actualization of the student than the teacher was. But this still fails to get at the root of the problem: the organizational objective of a school to emphasize teaching rather than learning. The self-actualization kick is just another more subtle form of teacher (social) control. Marcuse's analysis is apt.

It [self-actualization] isolates the individual from the one dimension where he could find himself: from his political existence, which is at the core of his entire existence. Instead, it encourages nonconformity and letting go in ways which leave the real engines of repression in the society entirely intact, which even strengthen these engines by substituting the satisfactions of private and personal rebellion for a more than private and personal, and therefore more authentic, opposition. The desublimation involved is itself expressive in as much as it weakens the necessity and the power of the intellect, the catalytic force of that unhappy consciousness which does not revel in the archetypal personal release of frustration—hopeless resurgence of the Id which will sooner or later succumb to the omnipresent rationality of the administered world—but which recognizes the horror of the whole in the most private frustration and actualizes itself in this recognition.[16]

The third element of Illich's phenomenology of schooling is the classroom bound nature of learning to which a school is committed. The artificiality and unreality of this commitment is obvious; witness the history of innovations like field trips, community experience, and so on. Lately there are schools without walls and internships of all kinds. Again these changes attempt solution to a problem by getting new ways to do the same thing. The walls of the classroom keep expanding as the school desparately fights to retain its control over learning. The most "ingenious" innovations make the classroom omnipresent—on the streets of the city, in the museum, etc.

The last element of the phenomenology is the graded curriculum. Here we divide knowledge into tidy compartments, translate the comparments into competencies, behavioral objectives, units, modules, and tests. And all of these elegant divisions have direct relation to a **person's** ability to have passage rights in society, even though exposure to the hurdles of an infinite number of curricula has little relation to what a person might do in that society.[17]

As an organization the school makes learning age-specific, teacher related, classroom bound, and based on a graded curriculum. These organizational commitments of the school have nothing to do with learning but are excellent preparation for life in a bureaucratic society. They deny the highest possibilities for human development by colluding with a society based on the same denial. The school must be confronted as an organization that denies development, and in that confrontation the society is likewise engaged. Such confrontation is therefore a political action whose goal is a new society, a new man.

The simplest solution to the problem of schooling would be to abolish schools. Such solutions provide little help for immediate action. The final section of this paper suggests a strategy for developing real educational alternatives that deal directly with schools as **they now exist but at the same time** honor the political commitments to the cultural revolution already described.

Organization Development as Political Action

Organization development is an approach to modifying organizations that rests fundamentally on the use of the T-group or its theory of learning. The T-group originated in 1947 at Bethel Maine and has since been variously named depending on how it is being employed: T-group, Laboratory Training, Sensitivity Training, Basic Encounter Group, Group Development, Personal Growth Laboratory, Executive Development, Managerial Grid Seminar, etc. Proponents and developers of the T-group have consistently stressed its behavioral science base; the same is true of the field of organization development, which is an outgrowth of the T-group. In this emphasis on the scientific use of the intensive group experience, little has been said about the value base on which the technique rests and the consequent political implications. Perhaps this silence has been deliberate in order to avoid opposition from prevailing powers. The silence would also be consistent with a philosophy of science that divorces "scientific inquiry" from its political implications: the divorce that enables the Pentagon to use the "pure" research of the universities for its own value commitments. Rather than being pregnant, the silence is vacuous, and power abhors a vacuum. Once again: It is empty to talk about change without indicating the direction of change. The present demands explicit commitment to a value base that counters current trends, or current trends will continue toward global destruction.

In this final section, we will explain the political implications of organization development, by describing what occurs in the climate of the T-group and relating these developments to current organizational patterns, specifically bureaucratic patterns. We will try to show how the personal developments that take place in the T-group provide a basis for creating truly alternative organizations. Further, these alternatives become consistent with the aspirations of the cultural revolution imperative to the future of man.

Charles Hampden-Turner identifies five characteristics of T-groups that contribute to the psycho-social development of participants:

1. Existential nothingness—an encounter with the absurd
2. The small group climate
3. The enforced confrontation
4. The moratorium
5. The rebellion against authority[18]

These characteristics are helpful in describing what happens in the T-group experience and can be related to current organizational, bureaucratic expectations.

Existential Nothingness

The T-group begins in a social vacuum, literally nothingness. Members are not able to relate on the basis of their roles or status outside the group. Competence is deprived of formal status as each one is thrown on his unadorned self as he faces the others.

As the horror of nothingness is forced rudely upon the T-group participants, its corollary becomes evident also. If nothing external to the group gives it meaning, then the members can choose to become anything they desire and will mutually confirm. Their sweating palms and thumping hearts testify to the "dizziness of freedom." With no existing definitions or meanings in the environment, *every meaningful statement is perforce creative and a denial of nothingness.*[19]

Here there is a radical questioning of all the ways of relating that constitute life outside the group. Who can practice elitism without recognized status or bureaucratic **structure**? What is up and what is down? Then if the new meanings created by the group are more compelling than the old meanings, the power of the old meanings is seriously eroded. This is at the heart of the common reentry problems suffered by group participants. Of course, if organizational patterns are not simultaneously altered with the personal changes, the new learnings soon disappear and business goes on as usual.[20] But if specific structural changes in organizations could be made that develop out of the new meanings and modes of relationship that result from the group, alternatives to bureaucratic forms begin to emerge.

What changes specifically here is the mode of decision making characteristic of the bureaucracy. Decision-making power depends on the role one has and its place in the vertical organization. In highly complex and fluid environmental conditions, this type of decision making becomes exceedingly inefficient and ineffective. From the point of view of information alone, bureaucratic decisions are poorly made because too few participate as information sources. In the T-group, everyone participates in the decisions made and this process would greatly enhance organizational decisions for a society as fluid and complex as ours.[21]

Another aspect of this concensus mode of decision making is the need to return power to people now oppressed by bureaucratic structures. If bureaucrats can learn to behave as persons rather than as outmoded roles, perhaps some of the present oppression can be eradicated.

The question might be asked at this point: "What right do you have to subject everyone in an organization to the T-group's encounter with nothingness? Isn't such subjection another kind of oppression and manipulation? Our response would be that if the purposes of the counter are made explicit, there is no manipulation. The present oppression demands an overt counter, and the counter must (perhaps the tragic necessity of the time) employ all the techniques at its disposal being always transparent about its commitments. Both My Lai and Attica seem related to prevailing modes of perception that present issues of conscience for everyone. Choices must be made.

Another way of looking at the T-group social vacuum is through Kohlberg's research on stages of moral development.[22] The six stages, from least development to highest, are (1) obedience, (2) egocentric instrumental relativism, (3) personal concordance, (4) law and order, (5) social contract, and (6) conscience orientation. In the T-group vacuum one is deprived of stages 1, 3, 4, or 5, and therefore must choose between 2 and 6.

Small Group Climate

The small group climate provides one-dimensional, individualistic, lonely, bureaucratic man with a taste of community. For persons whose lives are characterized by the absence of community—and that is the case for most in bureaucratically dominated societies—the idea of the group frequently has negative connotations. The self is usually seen as in tension or competition with the group rather than as being able to find fulfillment and freedom there. In the small group climate, when the group develops effectively, the person is able to experience the meaning of *community as prior to the* individual. This experience cuts at the heart of the individualism which is so basic to a society where many summarize their ethical stance as, "doing my thing, but not hurting anybody."

Against this extreme individualism two things may be said. First, the relation between social practices and institutions and the self is not simply one of support or encouragement. To put it that way is to imply that there could be selves without society, that society is at most a device for helping the self do what it could do alone but only very laboriously, and that eventually the self can outgrow society and be realised in splendid isolation. The plain truth is that without a society there are no selves, that, as Aristotle said, the community is prior to the individual, that the selves to be realized are given their essential qualities by their societies, and that the process of self-realization is a process of continuous involvement with society, as society not only shapes but employs everyone's inner riches. The upshot is that thought about possible styles of life or about the nature of man is necessary to give sense to the idea of individuality.[23]

Kateb's second point has to do with the fact that the fully realised self includes a common spiritual or philosophical insight or understanding.

Since community in this sense is absent from the life of bureaucratic man, the bureaucracy is filled with truncated selves that are easily engineered for its own purposes. Theory x operates most bureaucracies and there is little opposition.[24] A strategy for undercutting this oppressive atmosphere is to employ the small group as an effective project team within present bureaucratic structures. These groups or teams function as temporary systems or "adhocracies" within the organization able to address immediate problems or needs as they arise.

The temporary system or adhocracy can only be understood in the context of the preceding remarks on community, if it is to be anything more than a superficial technique for rearranging isolated individuals to perform new kinds of errands for the boss. The adhocracy is an alternative to present bureaucratic waste of human potential to the extent that it begins to allow for the integration of individual and organizational needs. This will happen only if the adhocracy is established as an authentic community involved in a task that it helps define as well as accomplish. To employ the adhocracy as an organization development strategy thus entails a total systems change; a temporary system cannot survive if it is placed in competition with a "permanent" system in a win-lose relationship. One cannot build a new ship with the planks of the old and still keep the old ship afloat. The adhocracy is a post-bureaucratic form of organization based on a set of values anti-thetical to those prevailing in the bureaucracy; it is not simply a technical device for carrying on the same old business.

As a first step toward a post-bureaucratic mode of organization, the adhocracy is an effective device. Large cumbersome institutions that are now failing to address the crucial issues for which they are responsible could begin to create a plurality of small, tightly knit groups that would relate to these issues. A school of education organized under hopelessly irrelevant departmental headings that isolate individuals from each other and come from a mentality that belongs at best to the early fifties could be transformed into a set of project teams. Such teams would be immeasurably more effective in relating to schools as they now oppress the young and would be much more satisfying to the university personnel who staff them. This assumes, of course, that university personnel are concerned with something more than self-aggrandizement. The professor would have to give up a lot of his comfortable illusions. Again, unless such value issues are confronted, the adhocracy will be little more than a technique for rearranging the professors. The adhocracy is first a *way of thinking* about organizing people and then a technique for doing so. There cannot effectively be the one without the other.

Enforced Confrontation

The enforced confrontation between participants in the T-group is vital to any kind of group process and structure.

This means essentially that to paraphrase the opening pages of Simmel's essay, no group can be entirely harmonious, for it would then be devoid of process and structure. [Aristotle leveled somewhat the same criticism against Plato.] Groups require disharmony as well as harmony, disassociation as well as association; and conflicts within them are by no means altogether disruptive factors. Group formation is the result of both types of processes. . . . Conflict as well as cooperation has social functions.[25]

This characteristic runs counter to the superficial harmony typical of bureaucratic environments. Here the conflict is never brought into the open, but instead goes underground to become a hidden agenda, under-the-table dealings, secret meetings, suspicion, mistrust, the endless list of bureaucratic qualities that lay waste human potential.[26]

The absence of open conflict likewise prevents the development of any really cohesive groups in bureaucracies except those that happen by chance. If adhocracies are to be established on any systematic basis, conflict issues would have to be faced squarely, which necessitates learning a number of new behaviors for persons involved. Dealing with confrontation and conflict on the personal level demands that the effects of one's behavior on others be examined closely. Likewise the effect of others' behavior on oneself becomes an issue requiring a good deal of personal investment in a situation, if one is not to be simply controlled by others. Neither of these aspects of behavior are part of the bureaucrat's repertoire. Women and children would not burn in Vietnam if they had to be faced by those responsible for delivering the napalm. The impersonal bureaucratic decision makes such destruction possible. Making decisions more personal may help to decrease the consumption of napalm. At the very least, institutions responsible for education ought to devise decision-making structures more in concert with being a human being in a technocracy.

If the institutional culture of a school of education in no way transcends the culture that can destroy a country in order to save it, what can be honestly expected of the public school "served" by that school of education?

Moratorium

The moratorium provides the individual an opportunity to step back from the press of daily responsibility in order to get a fresh perspective on his life and create more satisfying directions if he wishes. Such periodic stepping back is an inherent part of personal development and necessary if a person wishes to avoid stagnation. The pulling back is frequently perceived as a regression, but is a necessary prelude to subsequent advancement.

In bureaucratic settings, task orientation is usually so strong that there is adamant resistance to any pulling back to question the meaning of the tasks being performed. For instance, try suggesting a semester moratorium on business as usual to a university faculty in order to ask the fundamental question about what's going on, "Is this worth doing?" This is the very question and kind of moratorium that would ideally precede the movement into post-bureaucratic modes of organization.

Rebellion against Authority

Within the T-group experience, individuals learn to discover authority within themselves rather than allowing themselves to be extremely defined. The significance of such a discovery should be obvious in the context of what has already been said about the present crisis of authority in Western society. Subsequent to the discovery of the self as an efficacious agent is the discovery of the importance of community; this too has already been mentioned.

Thus there are three moments in the developmental strategy outlined here: (1) a negation of prevailing norms and expectations (implied in the negation is a new value base, a new vision of man in a post-scarcity environment); (2) a discovery of self as a source of power and authority, as a moral being both capable of and responsible for shaping the world; and (3) a discovery of community as prior to the individual demanding political action and commitment.

The T-group has been described as one technique that relates to the three moments of this developmental strategy and is basic to the field of organization development. Post-bureaucratic modes of organization, including the adhocracy, are possible products of organization development strategies. The basic directions of these strategies are similar to the directions encouraged by the T-group, though the T-group may not be a specific part of the strategy. *The use of the T-group here is meant to be illustrative and not to mean that this specific technique is necessary or sufficient in any overall strategy.*

Rather than view these strategies as value-free, purely technical approaches to change, this discussion has attempted to view them as political action, asserting that the present demands explicit positions on the crucial issues facing the world. For education, basically concerned with human development, neutrality in a context that threatens development on all sides is criminal. Silence is a scandal.

The organizations related to education in a society bent on the destruction of human potential must transcend that society in every sense. The transcendence begins with a no, loud and clear. What follows is to create the yes implied by that no, and this is the long, tedious work of building post-bureaucratic, educational alternatives.

Notes

1. Herbert Marcuse, "Industrialization and Capitalism in the Work of Max Weber," in *Negations: Essays in Critical Theory* (Boston: Beacon Press, 1968), p. 223.
2. Murray Bookchin, *Post Scarcity Anarchism* (Berkeley, Calif.: Ramparts Press, 1971), p. 11.
3. Although there are a number of movements against the oppression of adults, there are few against the oppression of childhood. Paul Goodman might be considered a one-man movement; see his "What Rights Should Children Have?" *The New York Review of Books,* 23 September 1971.
4. An approach that might discourage the proposing of alternative forms from a value-free base is political-economic analysis. This type of analysis has not been applied to many social organizations in the nonprofit sector. Notable exceptions are the empirical works of Victor Fuchs, *The Service Economy* (New York: National Bureaucracy of Economic Research, 1968); Martin Zald, *Organizational Change: The Political Economy of the YMCA* (Chicago: University of Chicago Press, 1970); and Martin Katzman, *The Political Economy of Urban Schools* (Cambridge, Mass.: Harvard University Press, 1971).
5. A. V. Sampson, *The Psychology of Power* (New York: Pantheon Books, 1966), pp. 3-4.
6. John Ladd, "Morality and the Ideal of Rationality in Formal Organizations," *Monist* 54 (October 1970): 488-516.
7. This personal violence is often called such by those in no position to do so; for example, Lieutenant Calley calling the acts of the Vietcong violent. Along with this problem of psychological projection has been the need to stereotype those who hold a radical ideology seriously as violent bombthrowers who could not possibly have a rewarding theory of human conduct. William Appleman Williams writes of the American failure to take Marxism seriously in *The Great Evasion* (Chicago: Quadrangle Books, 1964). For readings on another stereotyped ideologue—the anarchist—see Leonard F. Krimerman, *Patterns of Anarchy* (New York: Anchor Books, 1966), and Robert Wolff, *In Defense of Anarchism* (New York: Harper & Row, 1970).
8. Ladd, "Morality," p. 515.
9. David Cooper, *The Death of the Family* (New York: Vintage Books, 1971), p. 97.
10. For a review of the literature on the subject of politics and education, see William J. Murphy, "Politics and Education: A Definitional Study of the Literature" (Unpublished manuscript, Indiana University, 1971).
11. Herbert Marcuse, "Repressive Tolerance," in *A Critique of Pure Tolerance,* by Robert P. Wolff, Barrington Moore, Jr., and Herbert Marcuse (Boston: Beacon Press, 1964), p. 112.
12. Ivan Illich, *Deschooling Society* (New York: Harper & Row, 1970).
13. The age-specificness of schooling is only one of many rules that make up the bureaucracy of education. The rules and formalities of the educational bureaucracy are not given as much study as the dimension of hierarchy in the bureaucracy. For empirical studies on the effect of hierarchy, see James

Anderson, *Bureaucracy in Education* (Baltimore: Johns Hopkins Press, 1968); Fred Carver and Thomas Sergiovanni, *Organizations and Human Behavior* (New York: McGraw-Hill, 1969); Robert Owens, *Organizational Behavior in Schools* (Englewood Cliffs, N.J.: Prentice-Hall, 1970); Simon Wittes, *People and Power: A Study of Crisis in the Schools* (Ann Arbor: Institute for Social Research, University of Michigan, 1970).

14. Some writers dealing with organizational change propose that change will occur when there are structural changes in the organization. See Jerald Hage and Michael Aiken, *Social Change in Complex Organizations* (New York: Random House, 1970); and Victor Thompson, *Bureaucracy and Innovation* (University of Alabama Press, 1969).

15. For an argument against this notion, see Calet Gattegno, *What We Owe Children: The Subordination of Teaching to Learning* (New York: Outerbridge & Dienstfrey, 1970).

16. Marcuse, "Repressive Tolerance," pp. 114-15.

17. Ivar Berg, *Education and Jobs: The Great Training Robbery* (New York: Frederick A. Praeger, 1970).

18. Charles Hampden-Turner, *Radical Man* (Cambridge, Mass.: Schenkman, 1970), p. 157.

19. Ibid., p. 159.

20. For a review of the research on this problem, see John P. Campbell and Marvin Dunnette, "Effectiveness of T-Group Experiences in Managerial Training and Development," *Psychological Bulletin* 70 (August 1968): 73-104.

21. See Warren G. Bennis and Philip Slater, *The Temporary Society* (New York: Harper & Row, 1969), especially the chapter entitled "Democracy Is Inevitable."

22. Hampden-Turner, *Radical Man*, p. 160. For a review of Kohlberg's research, see Kenneth Keniston, "Moral Development, Youthful Activism, and Modern Society," *The Critic* (September-October 1969).

23. George Kateb, "Utopia and the Good Life," in *Utopias and Utopian Thought* (Boston: Beacon Press, 1967), p. 241.

24. "Theory x" refers to a set of assumptions regarding a mechanistic concept of authority. See Douglas McGregor, *The Human Side of Enterprise* (New York: McGraw-Hill, 1960), for his description of "theory x" as well as "theory y," which is a vivid utopia of more authentic human relationships.

25. Lewis Coser, *The Functions of Social Conflict* (New York: Free Press, 1969), p. 31.

26. For an interesting account of the informal operations in an organization, see Melville Dalton, *Men Who Manage* (New York: John Wiley & Sons, 1960).

William Pinar

In 1967 I was a sophomore at Ohio State, attending meetings of the Committee to End the War (which soon became the local chapter of S.D.S.), reading and discussing Marx, Sartre, Camus, Kafka, Nietzsche, and Kierkegaard. These people had an ineffably important influence on my thinking and life, although today it is only Sartre of the group that I read with any regularity. Those years—1967, 1968, 1969—were, as they were for millions, times of pain, confusion, and anger. The continuance of the war, the riots on campuses, in the cities and the accompanying awareness of racism, classism, sexism, as well as personal events involving my parents and my peers all contributed to an extraordinary period. The only constant I can recall during those years, besides the war, was school. By the time the committee had become S.D.S. I had left it, and hours not spent in class and in the library were spent living through difficult personal times. Regardless how difficult these times became, or how unnerving public events became, I was always able to study. My major had changed from music to history to English, but my ambition and earnestness about each had remained the same. By the end of my junior year, I had settled on English, with minors in psychology and education. In winter 1969 in a seminar on urban education, I met Donald Bateman. His politics, which were then "new left" and soon became Maoist, his pedagogy, which was like Freire's, and his humanness, which was pervading, affected me deeply.

Summer 1969 found me in school in Columbus, and one of the courses I was taking was Education 860, an introductory course in curriculum taught by Paul Klohr. Paul's importance to me I cannot state simply. Let it suffice to say that he and Don Bateman have been the major teachers in my intellectual life.

Learning of my impending move to Long Island (I had taken a job teaching English in Port Washington) and of my interest in the

*curriculum field (which began in his course), Klohr introduced me to
Dwayne Huebner at Columbia. I enrolled in a course that fall;
Huebner made a striking impression, as he continues to make, each
time I listen to him read a paper. Only Maxine Greene affects me
similarly.*

*Teaching at Schreiber High School was more influential than I
can say here. I think the collection of my students' writing (which
I published as* Shadowgraphs: Sketches from a Suburb) *indicates
something of the nature of those two years. While on Long Island
I met Willa Bernhard, who then taught at Bank Street and at
Sarah Lawrence. Her friendship and conversation were valuable.*

*I returned to Columbus those summers and full time in 1971,
when I was reading Freud, Jung, Reich, Hampden-Turner, and Freire,
and I wrote a rather rambling dissertation that tried to be a
psychoanalytically-based humanities curriculum design. Paul Klohr
and Don Bateman were friends as well as teachers. Alexander
Frazier and L. Jane Stewart helped me then, as did the friendship
of Francine Shuchat Shaw.*

*Summer 1972 I came to Rochester, read Doris Lessing and
Virginia Woolf, did Hatha Yoga postures, and began meditating.
At Rochester many have assisted, but to mention everyone and
mention them properly risks awkwardness. Nonetheless, I must
acknowledge the support and encouragement of Bill Lowe, Bob
Osborn, Sheila Molnar, and James Doi. Ira Weingarten, Madeleine
Grumet, and Russell Coward have been friends and colleagues as
well as graduate students. Jeannine Korman, a friend as well as a
secretary, has been more than helpful.*

*As far as the curriculum field is concerned, the individuals whose
papers fill this book have been the most important. Outside the
field, Virginia Woolf has become nearly a fascination, I still read
Sartre and Jung, and have taken up Husserl, Merleau-Ponty, and
Zen Buddhism. What all this means, and where it is leading are,
as my papers indicate, questions that absorb me now.*

*William Pinar
The University of Rochester*

21

Sanity, Madness, and the School

Introduction

During the last twenty-five years criticism of the school has been especially incisive, at times virulent. Social critics like Goodman, Friedenberg, and Henry and school critics like Holt, Herndon, Kozol, and Kohl have been persistent and persuasive in their attacks. Perhaps such writing culminated two years ago with the publication of a report of the Carnegie Commission, the comprehensive *Crisis in the Classroom*.

One theme common to almost all criticism is the contention that the schooling experience is a dehumanizing one. Whatever native intelligence, resourcefulness, indeed, whatever goodness is inherent in man deteriorates under the impact of the school. The result is the one-dimensional man, the anomic man, dehumanized and, for some critics, maddened.

The latter charge has been made repeatedly and cogently by what might be termed a new school of British psychoanalytic thought, the most well-known spokesman of which is R. D. Laing. Two other analysts who seem to share Laing's fundamental belief that what is generally considered normal is actually dehumanized and mad are D. Cooper and A. Esterson.

This investigation is an exploration of this charge that socialization is roughly equivalent to going mad; specifically it explores how the schooling experience contributes to this psychic deterioration. The theoretical base of this study is the science of persons: psychology, or to employ a term used by Laing and Cooper, the science of persons in relation to persons: social phenomenology. Cooper's (1971a) definition is pertinent here.

By "phenomenology," I mean the direct experience of a person or object without the intervention of preconceptions about that person or object. It is a matter of apprehending the person or object in its pristine reality rather than through the obscuring panes of glass that represent our preconcepts.

Thus, we will examine the *lebenswelt* (to use Heidegger's term), the world of lived experience of persons in school, including various modalities of experience, such as thoughts, images, feelings, reveries, and so on. We will focus the inquiry on the impact of teachers on students, the impact of the oppressors on the oppressed. By such a focus heretofore unexamined effects of the process of schooling can be elucidated.

Before explicating effects, it is essential to clarify what is meant by schooling. As many have pointed out, the informing image of young people implicit in American schooling is that children are basically wild, unpredictable beasts who must be tamed and domesticated. Hence they cannot be trusted until they have internalized the values of socially controlled and emotionless adults. One American psychologist, in a recent essay, summarizes this image thus (Bugental 1971):

In sum, the view of the child as a wild animal to be tamed seems to be like an empty vessel to be filled. There is relatively little respect for the child's own resources and relatively great emphasis on control and doing things—albeit benignly conceived things—to the child.

Hence to speak about American schooling is to speak about the "banking" or "digestive" concept of education, the latter term being the one Sartre employed to describe the process in which information is "fed" to pupils by teachers in order to "fill them out." (Sartre as quoted in Freire 1970.) The former term is explained by Paulo Freire in his *Pedagogy of the Oppressed*.

Education becomes an act of depositing, in which the students are the depositories and the teacher is the depositer. Instead of communicating, the teacher issues commiques and makes deposits which the students patiently receive, memorize, and repeat. This is the "banking" concept of education, in which the scope of action allowed to the students extends only as far as receiving, filing, and storing the deposits. They do, it is true, have the opportunity to become collectors or cataloguers of the things they store. But in the last analysis, it is men themselves who are filed away through the lack of creativity, transformation, and knowledge in this (at best) misguided system. (Freire 1970)

Freire elaborates on the concept, noting that teachers are primarily narrators, bestowing knowledge as a gift upon those whom they consider to know nothing. Teachers project onto their students an ignorance which necessarily negates the possibility of education and knowledge as processes of inquiry. The effects are decidedly injurious. As he writes, "For apart from inquiry, apart from praxis, *men cannot be truly human.* Knowledge emerges only through invention and re-invention, through the restless, impatient, continuing, hopeful inquiry men pursue in the world, with the world, and with each other."

Teacher-bankers, however, deposit rather than inquire. Freire lays out, in outline fashion, their attitudes and practices:

(a) the teacher teaches and the students are taught;
(b) the teacher knows everything and students know nothing;
(c) the teacher thinks and the students are thought about;
(d) the teacher talks and the students listen—meekly;
(e) the teacher disciplines and the students are disciplined;
(f) the teacher chooses and enforces his choice, and the students comply;
(g) the teacher acts and the students have the illusion of acting through the action of the teacher;
(h) the teacher confuses the authority of knowledge with his own professional authority, which he sets in opposition to the freedom of the students;
(i) the teacher is the subject of the learning process, while the pupils are mere objects. (Freire 1970)

What is the psychological, or more precisely, the phenomenological (in David Cooper's sense) impact of such attitudes and practices? The cumulative effect is madness, as we shall see.

Serious study of schooling and of the writings of Laing and Cooper enable one to identify and explicate twelve effects of schooling. In actuality, these effects cannot be clearly distinguishable. They overflow, if you will, into each other, and manifest themselves in the idiosyncratic manner of each individual. For purposes of elucidation and generalization, however, such analysis is useful.

Let us examine each effect in some detail in hope of giving us some sense of etiology which can aid us, at some later point, in formulating a rationale for an ambience which is confirming and affirming, i.e., schooling for sanity.

Hypertrophy or Atrophy of Fantasy Life

Fantasy is an integral aspect of our experience. Schooling, however, often has two distortive effects upon fantasy life. To illustrate these distortions, let us examine briefly two fictional children, Dorothy and Paul.

Dorothy comes to school well-rested and nourished. During the first lessons of the morning she remains alert, listening carefully to the teacher and to the questions and comments of her peers. Perhaps she herself participates verbally. Soon, however, due to the narrative character of the experience and its alienation from her existential reality (Freire 1970), Dorothy catches herself looking out the window, staring at the swing, wondering what recess will be like today, wondering if she will play with Paul, whom she likes more and more. "Dorothy, Dorothy!" prods the teacher. "Pay attention; you're daydreaming again." Dorothy's gaze returns to the teacher and again she listens to the lesson, but the sheer drone of the teacher's voice as he discusses the major rivers of Brazil lulls her into daydreaming about recess again. She continues to gaze at the teacher; she appears alert; however, she is not there; she is on the playground, at home, at some imaginary place, but she is not in the classroom. As Dorothy moves through the grades, teachers and guidance counselors may remark: "Oh, yes, Dorothy. A fine girl. Somewhat withdrawn, a tendency to daydream, a bit dull, but a fine girl." Such people might well take the advice Melanie Klein once gave to a child psychoanalyst:

One of the many interesting and surprising experiences of the beginner in psychotherapy. . . is to find in even very young children a capacity for insight which is often far greater than that of adults. To some extent this is explained by the fact that the connections between conscious and unconscious are closer in young children than in adults, and that infantile repressions are less powerful. I also believe that the infant's intellectual capacities are often underrated and that, in fact, he understands more than he is credited with. (Holbrook 1967)

If Dorothy seems withdrawn and dull to school people, perhaps they should look to themselves in constructing an etiology. As well as Klein's observation, one is reminded of a statement by another psychoanalyst: "suffice it to say . . . that every child, before family indoctrination passes a certain point and primary school indoctrination begins, is, germinally at least, an artist, a visionary, and a revolutionary."

In contrast to Dorothy, Paul, for numerous reasons (few of which are his own probably), forces himself to pay attention all of the time.

Of course he catches himself daydreaming on occasion, perhaps he even wonders if he'll see Dorothy during recess, but he reprimands himself for inattention, and once again forcefully concentrates on the lesson. As the years pass, the task becomes simpler; his mind wanders infrequently; it is wedded to the lesson. Of him his teachers may remark: "Paul? A bright boy. I always have his attention. A bit unimaginative, however, and it's difficult to get him to take the initiative, but a bright boy."

In both cases, recognizably prototypical to a frightening extent, what began as harmless responses to the schooling process took on an autonomy of its own. When one is "absent" for much of a six-hour period, day after day, year after year, one becomes "absent" most of the day, day after day. One is not in the "real world." In fact, one may be designated, at some point, as psychotic. On the other hand, when one is "present" most of the time, and that "presence" is achieved by violence—e.g., Paul forced his daydreams from his head, rendering his fantasy life lifeless—one loses an integral part of oneself. One is impoverished and made one-dimensional. Paul, long before he is graduated, has lost something of himself; he is no longer fully human. By the time he becomes middle-aged, Paul may be like the mother H. S. Sullivan (1953) has described:

The mother had become a sort of zombi—unutterably crushed by the burdens that had been imposed on her. She was simply a sort of weary phonograph offering cultural platitudes, without any thought of what they did to anybody or what they meant. Though she was still showing signs of life, everything had died within.

Division or Loss of Self to Others via Modeling

Regularly during the schooling process children are urged, implicitly and explicitly, to model themselves after others. In some cases, these models are political heroes such as George Washington or Abraham Lincoln or Martin Luther King, Jr.; sometimes they are "outstanding" (as designated by the teachers) peers, "straight-A" students, athletic stars, student government officials, or people who are combinations of these. Whom the child is to model himself after is of limited importance; it is the process of modeling, of being like someone else, that must be examined.

To get them to desire to be like someone else, children must learn to be dissatisfied with themselves. Dissatisfaction with oneself is almost always the introjected nonacceptance by a significant other. One psychoanalyst terms this phenomenon learning to see oneself with the eyes of the other (Cooper 1971a). Such introjection is necessarily violent; internalization of external condemnation necessarily represents a violation of self. Such introjection means that "existent" alongside the self is a nonacceptance of that self; the merging becomes a self turned against itself, a divided self, or, in extreme cases, a self lost to others. The phenomenon is commonly termed self-hatred, but the degree of nonacceptance need not be that extreme to cripple and even paralyze the self.

Freire (1970) discusses the phenomenon in more political terms. "The oppressed suffer from the duality which has established itself in their innermost being.... They are at one and the same time themselves and the oppressor whose consciousness they have internalized."

Contrasting the consciousness of the oppressor with the consciousness of the oppressed, Hegel (quoted in Freire 1970) writes: "The one is independent, and its essential nature is to be for itself; the other is dependent and its essence is life or existence for another. The former is the Master, or Lord, the latter the Bondsman."

The self turned against itself seeks to be like someone else. The seeking is dangerous; one's identity is constantly in question, since it resides outside oneself. One feels ontologically insecure (Laing 1969), and such insecurity prevents and arrests man's ontological vocation of becoming more human, more himself (Freire 1970). Such insecurity also increases the likelihood of being designated schizophrenic.

Sartre, in *Being and Nothingness* (quoted in Laing 1969), gives an example of modeling, which he terms "bad faith":

Let us consider this waiter in the cafe. His movement is quick and forward, a little too precise, a little too rapid. He comes toward the patrons with a step a little too quick. He bends forward a little too eagerly; his voice, his eyes express an interest a little too solicitous for the order of the customer. Finally there he returns, trying to imitate in his walk the inflexible stiffness of some kind of automaton while carrying his tray with the recklessness of a tight-rope walker by putting it in a perpetually unstable, perpetually broken equilibrium which he perpetually re-establishes by a light movement of the arm and hand. All his behavior seems to us a game. He applies himself to chaining his movements as if they were mechanisms, the one regulating the other; his gestures and even his voice seem to be mechanisms; he gives himself the quickness and pitiless rapidity of things. He is playing, he is amusing himself. But what is he playing? We need not watch long before we can explain it: he is playing at *being* a waiter in a cafe.

In schools, particularly in secondary ones and those for "higher learning," one notes countless "persons" playing at being a student, a professor, an intellectual, a bohemian, a "freak," a "politico," and so on, playing at being some *thing* other than themselves. They are not themselves; quite literally, they are out of their minds; they are mad.

Appropriate here is Freire's posing of a central pedagogical problem, one which we must deal with:

The central problem is this: How can the oppressed, as divided, unauthentic beings, participate in developing the pedagogy of their liberation? Only as they discover themselves to be "hosts" of the oppressor can they contribute to the midwifery of their liberating pedagogy. As long as they live in the duality in which *to be is to be like,* and *to be like is to be like the oppressor,* this contribution is impossible. (1970)

Dependence and Arrested Development of Autonomy

One educator has written of the "risk that the children will be influenced by what-they-feel-they-ought-to-feel, or by what-they-feel-the-teacher-thinks-they-ought-to-feel" (Creber 1965). That risk is usually reality.

Students, "good" students that is, more than comply with the instructions of teachers. They come to depend upon them; they come to need them, just as they came to need the instructions of their parents. "One of the first lessons," David Cooper writes, "one is taught in the course of one's family conditioning is that one is not enough to exist in the world on one's own" (Cooper 1971a).

Mere compliance lays bare the political nature of the teacher-student relaitonship. To prevent students from seeing this reality, the school must make the student desire to be instructed, and eventually, need to be instructed. For the need to be deeply rooted, the student must forget that he has this need; finally, the student will forget that he has forgotten he has the need. He will consider the necessity of instruction "natural" and he will look askance at any one who suggests otherwise.

This repressive process requires that the dependency the young child has upon his parents be transferred to the teacher in some form and to some extent. Such a transference is not difficult to achieve. Generally speaking, the difference between a transference relationship and a "real" relationship is never clear (Cooper 1971a). Specifically, many parents predispose their children to respect and like their teachers, by stressing the "importance of education" or the "wisdom of teachers." And the warm, "outgoing" teacher makes transference easier and more complete. The collusion of parents and teachers in transferring the child's dependence and deepening it becomes evident, and so do the nature and outcome of the cooperation. A passage from Erich Fromm's *The Heart of Man* (1968) is clarifying:

The pleasure in complete domination over another person (or other animal creature) is the very essence of the sadistic drive. Another way of formulating the same thought is to say that the aim of sadism is to transform a man into a thing, something animate into something inanimate, since by complete and absolute control the living loses one essential quality of life—freedom.

With domination, concomitant dependence, loss of freedom, the development of autonomy is arrested. Autonomy means making one's own rules (Cooper 1967), being one's own instructor in a sense, and making "external laws conform to the internal laws of the soul, to deny all that is and create a new world according to the laws of one's own heart" (quoted in Hampden-Turner 1970). The kind of obedience to authority, what Piaget termed the morality of the heteronomous personality, that schooling engenders is inherently maddening. It requires loss of self to the control of others, atrophying the possibility of morality as well as autonomy. For it is only to the extent that people have freedom to make choices that they can live as moral beings (Bugental 1967).

A quite different yet somewhat useful way to discuss this issue is to contrast the characteristics of children termed "field-dependent" with those termed "field-independent." Those who are "field-dependent" seem unable to free themselves from the constraints of the situation in which they find themselves. They tend to be dependent on environmental supports, i.e., other- rather than self-validating; they seem unable to initiate activities. In fact, such children have been found to be passive in many respects, readily submissive to authority. They evidently lack insight regarding their "inner life" (which is a charitable way of saying they have lost themselves); they usually fear their aggressive and sexual feelings; and, finally, they tend to have low self-esteem and low self-acceptance. In contrast, "field-independent" children do not seem to require environmental supports; they tend to be self-validating; they take initiative; they are active; they are aware of their "inner life" and unafraid of their impulses, sexual or otherwise. They tend to like themselves (Allport 1961). Revealingly, parents of "field-dependent" children, on the whole, punished their offspring severely and often. They consistently forbade them to be assertive or independent and generally imposed their own standards. In contrast, parents of "field-independent" children encouraged them to make decisions, punished them little and then for being dependent. These children, in sum, were free to become autonomous to a much greater extent than their "field-dependent" peers (Allport 1961). What is wrong with this research is what is wrong with much research, the pretense at objectivity and detachment. As Charles Hampden-Turner has written, "To detach oneself and treat others like so many objects is not to be value-free but to choose to devalue others" (Hampden-Turner 1970). Those children who were incapable of validating themselves were not merely "field-dependent" (a "neutral" term); they were objectified, inanimated shells of the human possibility. Their parents, as the Fromm passage would imply, were not merely more "strict"; they were sadists, engendering dependence, arresting the development of autonomy, and therefore, turning their children into things, beings-for-others. Such "people" are dehumanized and dehumanizing; they have lost themselves to others; they are mad.

Criticism by Others and the Loss of Self-Love

The importance of self-love is almost impossible to overstate. Carl Rogers has argued that the lack of it represents man's basic disease (Rogers, in Bugental 1967).

Self-love is a prerequisite for love of others (Fromm 1968). "One can no longer think of loving another person until one can love oneself enough" (Cooper 1971). It is also a prerequisite to agency, as we saw in the preceding section.

Whether self-love is initially intrinsic to the person or whether it is largely a function of the attitudes of significant others is an issue beside the point here. The point here is that the attitude toward self can be altered, and often it is mutilated, by significant others. Some of the ways families perform this feat have been well documented (Laing and Esterson 1970); some of the ways schools perform it have not.

One important way involves the attitudes and behavior of fellow students. However, this particular locus of damage has an etiology, crucial to an adequate understanding of the process, too lengthy to be properly discussed at this point. It will be examined in the context of affiliative needs in the following section.

Let us focus upon the effect of criticism by teachers, the implicit criticism of marks or grades, and the often resulting criticism of parents.

As we have seen, the student's relationship to the teacher is often a transference one, continuing and usually strengthening the initial dependence upon the parents. Thus the child comes to depend upon validation from these significant others, and his identity resides outside himself, in some way related to those who have taken him from himself. The child often attempts to model himself after prototypical "persons," approved by the authorities. These developments effectively prevent him from developing autonomy. In such a position, he cannot help but introject the self-hating attitudes that his teacher-bankers hold of him.

Even "liberal" teachers who hold "discussions" and employ the so-called inquiry method make children feel inadequate. Regardless of the method, as long as the "banking" concept is operative, the teacher pretends knowledge and projects ignorance onto the students. All questions have more or less correct answers, according to this view. Another expression of it is found in William Glasser's *Schools Without Failure*:

almost all schools and colleges are dominated by the *certainty* principle. According to it, there is a right and a wrong answer to every question; the function of education is then to ensure that each student knows the right answers to a series of questions that educators have decided are important. (Glasser 1969)

The student grapples for the answer to the question, but simple statistical probability makes it unlikely he will come up with it. Even if the teacher "respects" diverse answers, one is still made to feel a bit remiss if one's answer does not coincide with the teacher's.

As well, one cannot possibly get "A" in all one's subjects; inevitably one is made to feel deficient in one area or another. The world "deficient" is important. If the child merely discovered that he disliked, say, arithmetic, the effect would be quite different. However, arithmetic is one of the "fundamentals"; the stress given it must mean it is very important; to earn less than "A" means, baldly stated, that one is less than what one should be.

Parents collude with teachers, criticizing their children if their marks fail to meet their standards, which, of course, they often fail to meet. Again, at home, the child is made to feel deficient; he cannot possibly get "A" in everything; he must be only "above average" or "average," and since his attitude toward himself is contingent upon the attitudes of others, he necessarily comes to experience himself as "average" or perhaps even "below average"; he comes to share the view he is "not living up to his potential." One's sense of worth, one's love for oneself, contingent as it has become upon performance and resulting attitudes of others, is bound to be diminished. Michael Novak says it well:

Success is perceived as luck, a grace, a gift; failure as the lot of the damned. The myth of success renders useless the concept of internal worth, and countless Americans seem to feel insecure, helpless, and worthless when the lottery of success has not selected them. Even the notion that one must work hard in order to be worthy of success is commonly absorbed into the syntax of success: one works hard, not with the sense of dignity that comes from inner growth, risk, and expansion, but with a hope of vindication from beyond. The myth of competitive work is seldom oriented toward an internal sense of dignity; it is other-regarding, outwardly expectant, full of foreboding.

In the context of such dynamics, what is education? "Education . . . is leading a person out of himself and away from himself" (Cooper 1971a).

Thwarting of Affiliative Needs

People generally, not just children, need to feel affiliated with each other (Sullivan 1953). The word is derived from the Latin: *ad* meaning to, and *filius* meaning son. The point is that affiliation is not to be understood in the modern connotation of membership in a club or similarly formed group, but as a feeling of association as strong as familial connections once were.

Several writers indicate that the affiliative needs are stronger and the consequences more deleterious if they go unmet during adolescence. For example, H. S. Sullivan characterizes the expression of such needs as one of those most important stages in the development of what he terms "the mature personality" (1953). He employs the term *intimacy*, defining it as "collaboration with at least one other, preferably more others, and in this collaboration there is the very striking feature of a very lively sensitivity to the needs of the other and to the interpersonal security or absence of anxiety in the other." He writes that "intimacy is that type of situation involving two people that permits validation of all components of personal worth." Its importance, in terms of human growth and development, cannot be overstated. Alfred Adler, in *The Education of Children* (1930), emphasizes the desirability of the cultivation of friendship during the preadolescent and adolescent years. "Children should be good friends and comrades with one another," he writes. Regarding parents and teachers, he insists that "in the period of adolescence only that type of parent and teacher can continue in this capacity of guide to the child who has hitherto been a comrade and sympathetic fellowman to his charge."

Even the most superficial observation of life-in-school reveals that affiliative needs not merely go unmet, they are actively thwarted, and in several ways. One way, which was examined with a different focus earlier, involves the fostering of a dependency relationship on the teacher. If the child comes to rely on the teacher for instruction (broadly defined), he cannot feel close to his peers. The tie is vertical, not horizontal, and because the relationship is a "transferred" one, the child competes for the "love" of the teacher just as he would for the "love" of the parent. As a result, his peers become his competitors, and ultimately, his enemies. As Freire writes, "the dominated consciousnesses is dual, ambiguous, full of fear and mistrust" (1970).

Competition for the affection and attention of the teacher is not the only kind of competition operative in the school. The methodology of teaching is founded upon competition. One attempts to guess the answer first, complete the assignment first or best, and, of course, get the highest marks. Jules Henry comments:

In a society where competition for the basic cultural good is a pivot of action, people cannot be taught to love one another. It thus becomes necessary for the school to teach children how to hate, and without appearing to do so, for our culture cannot tolerate the idea that babes should hate each other. (Henry 1968)

Yet, "without the experience of trust, the child will never become a trusting member of a society, who is able to love and care for others" (Mead 1970). "Love one another" teachers and others mouth regularly; the real message, and the one many if not most children learn is "hate one another." If we ever become serious about our ideals, then we must begin living them, especially in the school. Teachers must come to love their students. What is love?

Love lets the other be, but with affection and concern. Violence attempts to constrain the other's freedom, to force him to act in the way we desire, but with ultimate lack of concern, with indifference to the other's own existence or destiny. (Laing 1967)

Rather than love, teachers continually intervene, instruct, and criticize. Such behavior from teachers cannot be absorbed, at least for long. One must defend oneself, and if possible, strike back. Anger is always reactive. However, because the teacher is in a politically inaccessible position and because the teacher has formed a dependency relationship against the child, the child cannot risk very easily the teacher's rejection, for to do so would be tantamount to self-rejection, since in a parasitic relationship one's sense of self is usually contingent upon the other's sense of oneself. Since the child cannot react to the violence of the teacher, i.e., vertical violence, he "displaces" his anger and aggression and expresses it horizontally. Quoting Candido Mendes, Freire (1970) explains this phenomenon:

Chafing under the restriction of this order, they often manifest a type of horizontal violence, striking out at their own comrades for the pettiest reasons.

"The colonized man will first manifest this aggressiveness which has been deposited in his bones against his own people. This is the period when the niggers beat each other up, and the police and magistrates do not know which way to turn when faced with the astonishing waves of crime in North Africa. . . . While the settler or the policeman has the right the livelong day to strike the native, to insult him and to make him crawl to them, you will see the native reaching for his knife at the slightest hostile or aggressive glance cast on him by another native; for the last resort of the native is to defend his personality vis-à-vis his brother."

It is possible that in this behavior they are once more manifesting their duality. Because the oppressor exists within their oppressed comrades, when they attack those comrades they are indirectly attacking the oppressor as well.

In the context of the school, this phenomenon is manifested in disagreement, arguments, and fights among children. The general ill will one finds in schools is a direct function of teacher- (and parent-) initiated violence. The damage done to the affiliative need is incalculable. Children grow up as if among enemies. When one considers the rather strong possibility that "the individual human's personality is determined by the quality of his relationships with other people" (Pearce and Newton 1963), is it any surprise that so many chronological adults are the way they are? As Hampden-Turner observed, "where injustice reigns *between* men it will reign also *within* them" (1970). Considering the horror that is the interpersonal reality of the school, one winces at these words of psychiatrist William Glasser (1969):

In the context of school, love can best be thought of as social responsibility. When children do not learn to be responsible for each other, and to help each other, not only for the sake of others but for their own sake, love becomes a weak and limited concept. Teachers and children need not love each other in a narrow family way or even narrower romantic sense, but they must learn to care enough to help one another with the many social and educational problems of school.

This writer is reminded of a brief passage in F. Scott Fitzgerald's *The Crack-up* (1956): "The test of a first-rate intelligence is the ability to hold two opposing ideas in the mind at the same time and still retain the ability to function. One should, for example, be able to see that things are hopeless yet be determined to make them otherwise."

Estrangement from Self and Its Effect upon the Process of Individuation

One aspect of self-estrangement is physical. The discomfort of school furniture results in a diminution of physical feeling. One simply cannot tolerate physical discomfort hours after hour, day after day, year after year, without suppressing such discomfort. One necessarily loses much of one's ability to experience tactile sensations. One becomes numbed.

What are the effects of the psychic discomfort caused by competition, criticism, and aggression? One effect is a continual, usually subliminal anxiety, the consequence of which is a "useless disturbance of the factors of sentience which immediately preceded its onset" (Sullivan 1953). In some cases, "the effects of severe anxiety remind one in some ways of a blow on the head" (Sullivan 1953).

How is the process of individuation—the "slow imperceptible process of psychic growth" (Jung 1969)—affected? The answer becomes clear as we examine in some detail the nature of the process. The extent to which it develops appears to be contingent upon the extent to which the ego is willing to listen to the messages of the self (Jung 1969). It can be real only if the person is aware of the process and consciously making a connection with it. The person must participate in his development (Jung 1969).

We have examined already some of the ways schooling numbs children to their own experience, and we will examine ways in the upcoming sections. One way, appropriate here as an illustration, is the disconfirmation of self one observes in school. It is easy to imagine the following exchange. "I don't feel like doing this assignment," complains Mary to her teacher. "I don't care what you feel," the pedagogue replies, "do it." To a teacher, or to her parent: "I don't like school." "Mary, you just feel that way. You don't really. You like school." Of course, the disconfirmation is rarely that crude, but even subtler expressions of the same attitude have the same effect. The voices inside are systematically ignored, dismissed, or refuted by others. Almost inevitably, the child learns to ignore, dismiss, or refute the messages from within. The effect on the process of individuation is shocking and obvious.

The cognitive stress of schooling tends to make children think rather than feel. Often the child becomes more and more cerebral at the expense of his feeling, numbing him to the messages of his unconscious. The school, when especially effective, produces master "thinkers" whose computations are as offensive as they are logical. Considerations of feeling are beside the point, evidently. The controversial psychotherapist Arthur Janov makes an important point about this matter. He writes: "Lack of feeling is what destroys the self, and it is lack of feeling which permits destruction of other selves" (1971). Placed in a Jungian context, Janov's point is clear.

Von Franz, a Jungian, writes (in Jung, 1969):

in order to bring the individuation process into reality, one must surrender consciously to the power of the unconscious, instead of thinking in terms of what one should do, or what is generally thought right, or what usually happens. One must simply listen, in order to learn what the inner totality—the Self—wants one to do here and now in a particular situation.

Inattention to internal messages, especially perusal of philosophies external to and, in all likelihood, incongruent with oneself, represents denial of self and atrophy of feeling and of self.

Adherence to externals is evidenced by social conformity. By the time children reach junior high school, they have lost touch with themselves and with each other to the point that they must mimic each other's speech, dress, and habits in order to feel human and close. All such attempts fail, of course. One cannot simulate genuine humanity and interpersonal intimacy. Von Franz writes (Jung 1969): "It is . . . useless to cast furtive glances at the way someone else is developing, because each of us has a unique task of self-realization. . . . The fact is that each person has to do something that is uniquely his own."

Moreover, it is only by an unconditional devotion to one's own process of individuation that one can experience genuine intimacy. A corollary follows: self-estrangement means other-estrangement. I cannot get in touch with you if I cannot get in touch with me.

Self-direction Becomes Other-direction

"The fundamental fact in human development," writes Alfred Adler in *The Education of Children,* "is that dynamic and purposive striving of the psyche" (1930). In fact, he writes a few pages earlier, "From a psychological point of view, the problem of education reduces itself . . . to the problem of self-knowledge and rational self-direction." Under the influence of schooling, however, self-direction gives way to other-direction. The child, when forced to do an assignment he does not wish to complete or any order or instruction with which he does not wish to comply, must shift the origin of action from inside to outside. After several years of such shifting, activity is rarely initiated from the self, but by the other. Of course, a warm teacher and/or a highly competitive classroom effectively destroy the capacity to direct oneself. This phenomenon is pervasive enough that before a young person can ask himself "Who am I?" he must ask himself "Whose am I?" The political implications, as well as the psychic ones, are frightening.

Janov (1971) poses the problem as one of pathology.

> The neurotic is often indecisive because he is split between repressed needs and doing the should. The normal can decide for himself because he feels that self and what is right for it.
>
> The neurotic relies on others to supply the shoulds . . . . In this way, he maneuvers his life so that people go on providing shoulds for him and he never allows himself to function according to his feelings.

Such an analysis is overly simple to be sure, but the point is there nonetheless.

One phenomenon that accompanies this shift from intrinsic to extrinsic motivation is the muddling of motives. It occurs when the child reads a story or works an arithmetical problem to please the teacher or his parent, and it leads to writing essays to obtain a high mark rather than to communicate. The process is particularly prevalent in chronological adults, especially in those who have been schooled for many years. Such people often marry for financial or social reasons rather than for love, obtain Ph.D.'s for status rather than to inquire and to learn, and they often have children to live their emptied-out lives over vicariously rather than to propagate the species.

As David Cooper writes: "Any meaning derived from a source outside our acts murders us" (1971b).

Loss of Self and Internalization of Externalized Self

Another dimension of this process of losing oneself to others is the possibility of filling the loss by internalizing the externalized, e.g., the other-directed self, resulting in objectification.

One loses one's self-centeredness (Cooper 1967, 1971), the crucial capacity to live from the "inside out," or, to put it another way, the ability to live from the subjective center of one's being. One hemorrhages (Sartre 1943), loses one's life-blood, is filled with embalming fluid, which is the alien that is the estranged self, the self fabricated by unaware compliance and collusion with significant others.

This "self" is a thing, an image such as "good student," "intellectual," "hard worker," in any case, a *role*, but not a subjective being. The internalization of this role, this thing, objectifies the self, rendering it more or less stable but quite dead. As objects, as "things," the oppressed "have no purposes except those their oppressors prescribe for them" (Freire 1970).

Thus, schooling produces hollow men, obedient automatons programmed to make the correct computations, strangers to themselves and to others, but madmen to the few who escape, half-crazed, to search for what has been stolen from them. The radical test for one of the latter "lies in his decision to be stronger than his condition and if his condition is unjust, has only one way to overcome it, which is to be just himself" (Camus 1956).

Internalization of the Oppressor:
Development of a False-Self System

If the externalized "self" is not internalized, then the alienated "self" that is his teacher will be internalized (Cooper 1967), or the child will develop a false self-system (Laing 1969), a facade, a mask to prevent friction with the instructor or to protect (or so he might think) the real self. Both these possibilities are dehumanizing and hence, to some extent, maddening.

The teacher—he who plays at being a teacher—has, as we have noted in the case of the child in the preceding section, externalized himself into the world, e.g., he has emptied his subjective reality into a role or object form of being-in-the-world, and he has internalized this objectification (Cooper 1967).

Because his own subjective, inchoate sense of identity has been arrested or eroded, the child needs to identify with another. If the transference has been achieved to an adequate extent, then the child will identify with the dehumanized object that is his teacher. The concomitant interiorization is mutilating, often deadly, to the developing being-for-itself. It is interesting to note that this madness has "official" sanction.

I would like to suggest that what the teacher must be, to be an effective competence *model*, is a day-to-day working *model* with whom to interact. It's not so much that the teacher provides a model to *imitate*. Rather it is that the teacher can become a part of the student's internal dialogue—somebody whose respect he wants, *someone whose standards he wishes to make his own*. It is like becoming a speaker of a language one shares with somebody. The language of that interaction *becomes a part of oneself*, and the standards of style and clarity that one adopts for the interaction become a part of one's own standards. (Bruner 1966)

Freire puts it another way: "the oppressed do not see the 'new man' as the man to be born from the resolution of this contradiction, as oppression gives way to liberation. For them, the new man is themselves become oppressors" (Freire 1970).

Perhaps the child has failed to transfer his dependence to the teacher; assume he has little need to identify himself via another. Assume he still wants to succeed. He must be obedient, but he need not believe in what he does. He comes to view the schooling process as a game, with a myriad of rules to follow in order to win, and himself as a player. Such a schizoid state and concomitant development of a false self-system is probably characteristic of many students.

One cannot, however, "play the game" hour after hour, day after day, year after year, without coming to view one's life as a game, with the self split into observer-player. Such a "person" is incapable of authentic participation in anything: love relationships (any relationship for that matter), employment, child rearing, etc. It is all a game, not for real, and the mask he brings to the "board" is as unreal as his perception. Such a *weltan-schauung* almost inevitably results in cynicism and possibly nihilism. When one is empty, one is completely vulnerable to the metaphysical emptiness outside, and too threatened by a real person to be accessible to what might help mend the split, what might fill or nourish the atrophied self. For, as several writers have pointed out (Laing 1969), rather than protecting the self, the false self-system isolates it from genuine and intense contact with others, rendering the self crippled, violated, withered. It may die, leaving a walking, talking automaton who works, sexes, sleeps, but who never lives. Or, if the self fights for life, the conflict, if manifested in socially unacceptable behavior, may earn the person the designation of "schizophrenic."

In any event, the child is maddened. Schooling, as currently conceived, leaves him few options.

Alienation from Personal Reality Due to Impersonality of Schooling Groups

Membership in a group whose members number more than twelve to fifteen is depersonalizing. (Aside from considerations that will become obvious in the discussion to follow, the numbers chosen are not entirely arbitrary. See *Radical Man* for a brief but illuminating discussion of the historical significance of the number twelve (Hampden-Turner 1960). Although these numbers are no guarantee of course, especially when one considers that even in a family of four the members can be quite ignorant of the personal reality of each other (Cooper 1967), larger numbers absolutely preclude the possibility of sharing, even to a minor extent, the personal realities of the members. Larger groups almost always have a mystique, an impersonality which facilitates one's forgetting of oneself, what Kierkegaard termed the "herd instinct" (1971). One tends to become one's surface, one's body, a being-in-itself. This tendency remains, even after leaving the school. H. S. Sullivan comments that "there are a remarkable number of people who have ways of being social as the devil without having anything with the other people concerned. They live very sharply restricted rules" (1953).

People who live hours, days, and years in groups whose reality is established by the teacher or by a curriculum guide often forget what one's personal reality is, if others have personal realities, or if everyone is "emptied-out" in exteriorized existence. People, especially some school children, must wonder what it would be like for someone, even the teacher, actually to *do* something, to express one's insides, something of one's personal reality. (Hence the at-first-blush bizarre behavior of some "Yippies," painting their bodies, sexing in public, etc. Some authentic action to jar those asleep?) Certainly some so-called discipline problems are merely similar attempts at jarring the collective unreality of the school. Michael Novak (1970) views the matter this way:

> our society puts great stress on intimacy, the personal touch, communication, and unity, but it also teaches persons to be silent about their deepest feelings, fears, terrors, longings, even with those dearest to them.

Often it is only in solitude that one's personal reality can be preserved, and its preservation is nothing less than the preservation of sanity. Kierkegaard considered solitude, as enriching inwardness, a sine qua non for individual development. In fact, he viewed the ability to be with oneself the supreme test of the individual, for those who cannot tolerate solitude are reduced to mere "social animals" (1956). A contemporary writer, the psychoanalyst Hannah Segal, also emphasizes the importance of solitude, contending that the basis of thought and communication is communication with oneself (Holbrook 1967). The sheer impossibility of seclusion, of quiet in the school, forces us to ignore ourselves and eventually to empty ourselves out. On this matter David Cooper writes (1967):

> In our age we are totally conditioned to interference from others, we gravely lack the conditions for the full development of the capacity to be alone. For most of us the root of interference commences in the cradle and does not end before the grave. It requires considerable artifice to escape the process even momentarily. And yet I believe that it is only on the basis of an adequate capacity to be alone that we can find a true way of being with others. We have to rediscover the lost meaning of the Taoist principle of *wu vei*, the principle of nonaction, but a positive nonaction that requires an effort of self-containment,

an effort to cease interference, to "lay off" other people and give them and oneself a chance.

One must be able to be with oneself before one can be with others. One must be able to reflect on oneself, feel oneself, and develop a loving, caring, intimate relationship with oneself (Cooper 1971b). Love, in this and any context, means letting oneself, or another, alone with affection and concern (Laing and Esterson 1970). Only then can people genuinely be with each other and not interfere with each other (Cooper 1967).

Desiccation via Disconfirmation

In human society, at all its levels, persons confirm one another in a practical way, to some extent or other, in their personal qualities and capacities, and a society may be termed human in the measure to which its members confirm one another.

The basis of man's life with man is twofold, and it is one—the wish of every man to be confirmed as what he is, even as what he can become, by men; and the innate capacity in man to confirm his fellow-men in this way. That this capacity lies so immeasurably fallow constitutes the real weakness and questionableness of the human race: actual humanity exists only where this capacity unfolds. On the other hand, of course, an empty claim for confirmation, without devotion for being and becoming, again and again mars the truth of the life between man and man.

Men need, and it is granted to them, to confirm one another in their individual being by means of genuine meetings: but beyond this they need, and it is granted to them, to see the truth, which the soul gains by its struggle, light up to the others, the brothers, in a different way, and even so be confirmed. (Buber, as quoted in Laing 1969)

Confirmation (not collusion of automatons to perpetuate the mystification of reality) does not characterize the school. One waits for response, for genuine reply to one's being, but all one seems to get is questions, instructions, ignorance.

Let us briefly examine how the process of schooling works to disconfirm the child. Of course, any school whose operative principle is the banking concept of education necessarily ignores the child. However, even in a so-called child-centered school, a teacher cannot possibly adequately attend to the question that is the child's being. Often even the slightest recognition from another, which at least confirms one's presence in another's world, is absent. "No more fiendish punishment could be devised," William James once wrote, "even were such a thing physically possible, than that one should be turned loose in society and remain absolutely unnoticed by all the members thereof." Yet for how many in our huge, impersonal schools does this "fiendish punishment" come close to being the interpersonal reality? When one considers recognition in its deepest sense, in sensitive, caring reply to another's existential insides, have we not indeed constructed such a hell?

As a consequence, children learn to participate in symbolic forms of gratifying this need. However, all such symbolic attempts are bound to fail. Moreover, "the result of any symbolic behavior is to shut off feeling" (Janov 1970), which, as we have seen, atrophies the emergent self. What are examples of such attempts? Some children frequently attempt to answer questions. This behavior elicits recognition, not genuine reply of course, but even so, it is acknowledgment. Unfortunately it is disconfirming. Often the answer is incorrect, or only partially correct, and in any case, with twenty to thirty students in a classroom, how often can each child expect such recognition, superficial and disconfirmatory as it is?

Another basic substitutive behavior is termed deviant or disruptive behavior. Teachers and administrators often explain such behaviors (from talking "out of turn" to throwing wads of paper) as "he merely wants attention" and *dismissed* as that. Often punishing these children is unsuccessful in that the disruptive is repeated. However, from one point of view, the behavior is successful. The child is at least acknowledged and his existence confirmed, even if negatively.

An illustration of this phenomenon follows:

Then one day as Lyndon sat watching Miss Schatzman, something about her reminded him of the ladies in the summer school back in Catherine County. Thinking back to that time he began to feel as he had often felt then. He wanted the teacher to pay *attention* to him. He wanted to let him do something interesting, or better yet to *show* him something new and help him do it. He felt more and more fidgety and nervous. Then he stood up, walked quickly to an empty seat, and sat down again. All the moon lady did was to grasp Lyndon by the shoulder and guide him back to his assigned seat, without a break in whatever she was saying. At least she had noticed him, and so had most of the kids in the room. (Valentine)

As R. D. Laing notes (1969):

The need to be perceived is not, of course, purely a visual affair. It extends to the general need to have one's presence endorsed, or confirmed by the other, the need for one's total existence to be recognized; the need, in fact, to be loved.

Yet, in American schools, one goes unnoticed, unloved, and if one is not to feel *de trop*, one must interfere with the lives of others. In our death throes, we mangle each other, leaving scarred fragments of what we might have been.

Atrophy of Capacity to Perceive
Esthetically and Sensuously

One obvious cause of the atrophy of the child's ability to perceive sensuously and esthetically is the sheer dreariness of school architecture. School is invariably an ugly place, unimaginatively designed, its classrooms often an uninviting green or brown, the seats hard and overly straight: all has been built with one criterion—efficiency (Callahan 1962). One must learn not to see while living several hours daily for years in such places. One hardens, and begins to block out sensitive perceptions of the outside.

In two other ways the schooling experience disables us to perceive esthetically. The impulse behind this disabling is made quite clear by Eric Fromm (1968):

While life is characterized by growth in a structured, functional manner, the necrophilous person loves all that does not grow, all that is mechanical. The necrophilous person is driven by the desire to transform the organic into the inorganic, to approach life mechanically, as if all living persons were things. . . . Memory, rather than experience; having, rather than being, is what counts. The necrophilous person can relate to an object—a flower or a person—only if he possesses it; hence a threat to his possession is a threat to himself; if he loses possession he loses contact with the world. . . . He loves control, and in the act of controlling he kills life.

One way the necrophilous drive is manifested in school involves the relentless inspection and explication of the alive and the beautiful. In the sciences, for example, one learns to see phyla, phenomena, losing the child's astonishment at the beauty of the natural world. No longer does one see a tree, one sees a sycamore or an oak, one observes photosynthesis; in brief, one learns to see everything but the tree. Laing and Cooper put it this way (1964): "The analytic-instrumental approach to the world and to oneself entails a language which expresses the result of the analytic process, but the language then expresses an analytically *reduced* reality."

In the humanities one learns to understand "how a poem means" (Ciardi 1960), a novel means, and one learns to interpret, for there is latent as well as manifest content. Works of art come to have little or no impact upon the perceiver, unless it be a narrowly cognitive one. One learns to deflect the impact onto a critique, so that when one leaves a showing of, say Frank Gilroy's film "Desperate Characters," one comments on the acting of Shirley MacLaine, or on the direction, on anything rather than *feel* the desperation in the characters. We see but do not see. We respond but do not feel. One English educator observes "Emphasis on abstract verbalization, on intellectual concepts cut off from their roots in concrete sensuous experience, is destructive of literary sensitivity and enjoyment" (Rosenblatt 1968). Inspection renders the object lifeless, analysis murders, and the intellectual's gaze turns all to stone. Ours is an age petrified by cognition, moribund by scholarship. David Holbrook says it well (1967):

> The mind, trained in "rigorous disciplines," ceases to be "open" and "relaxed." The student ceases to be able to allow doubts, uncertainties, disturbance in his own inner world, and so ceases to respond to literature in a creative way. He is defended against it by an intellectual approach—he no longer feels, no longer knows what he feels, and is no longer capable of being moved, or opened to fresh experience. He "appreciates" rather than speaks his true responses. To be stirred, puzzled, moved, upset is to experience a range of reactions—trivial to fantastic—which, if he experiences them in the examination room, will lead to hesitancies and callownesses that will penalize him.

The context is limited but the point is not.

Esthetic experience does involve feeling; it involves the shattering of the "existent" inner order, permitting a new synthesis. People who are fixed or frozen inside, whose order is inviolate, are only half alive. Nothing less than psychic rebirth into an order in flux, sensitive and alive to the fluidity outside, permits an identity capable of the sensuous and the esthetic. David Cooper writes that some people achieve this (1967)

> by momentary craziness, catching themselves up again before invalidation supervenes, or by lysergic acid diethylamide or mescaline or marijuana, or simply by getting drunk, or by listening to some music or seeing a picture which shatters their pre-established inner order and provokes an autonomous effort to piece themselves together again. All esthetic experience consists in this sort of adventure.

The schooling process obviously precludes such experience. The focus is study, development of the intellect, and in a culture whose classic dilemma is the hypertrophy of the intellect, such foci preclude the development of an esthetic and sensuous sensibility.

Conclusion

The cumulative effect of the schooling experience is devastating. We graduate, credentialed but crazed, erudite but fragmented shells of the human possibility.

What course of action can be recommended to correct this state? Laing and Cooper are less explicit about the outlines of reformations.

One surmises, however, that an intensive adherence to one's "within" forms the basis of renewal strategies. What configurations this loyalty to one's subjectivity must take and what such configurations mean for theorists of the process of education are not yet clear. To these questions we must proceed next.

References

Adler, Alfred. *The Education of Children*. New York: Greenburg, 1930.

Allport, Gordon W. *Becoming: Basic Considerations for a Psychology of Personality*. New Haven, Conn.: Yale University Press, 1955.

_____. *Pattern and Growth in Personality*. New York: Macmillan, 1961.

Bradford, L. P., Gibb, Jack R., and Benne, K. D., eds. *T-Group Theory and Laboratory Method*. New York: John Wiley & Sons, 1964.

Bruner, Jerome. *The Process of Education*. Cambridge, Mass.: Harvard University Press, 1960.

_____. *Toward a Theory of Instruction*. Cambridge, Mass.: Harvard University Press, 1966.

Bugental, James F. *Challenges of Humanistic Psychology*. New York: McGraw-Hill, 1967.

_____. *The Human Possibility*. EPRC, 1971.

Callahan, Raymond. *Education and the Cult of Efficiency*. Chicago: University of Chicago Press, 1962.

Camus, Albert. *The Rebel*. Trans. Anthony Bower. New York: Vintage, 1956.

_____. *Resistance, Rebellion, and Death*. Trans. Justin O'Brien. New York: Alfred A. Knopf, 1961.

Ciardi, John. *How Does A Poem Mean*. Boston: Houghton Mifflin, 1960.

Cooper, David. *The Death of the Family*. New York: Pantheon, 1971a.

_____. *Psychiatry and Anti-Psychiatry*. New York: Ballantine, 1971b.

_____. *Self and Others*. New York: Pantheon, 1967.

Creber, J. W. Patrick. *Sense and Sensitivity*. London: University of London Press, 1965.

Ellis, Albert. *Reason and Emotion in Psychotherapy*. New York: Lyle Stuart, 1962.

Fitzgerald, F. Scott. *The Crack-Up*. New York: New Directions, 1956.

Freire, Paulo. *Pedagogy of the Oppressed*. New York: Herder & Herder, 1970.

Fromm, Erich. *The Art of Loving*. New York: Harper & Row, 1956.

_____. *The Heart of Man*. New York: Harper & Row, 1968.

Glasser, William. *Schools Without Failure*. New York: Harper & Row, 1969.

Hampden-Turner, Charles. *Radical Man: The Process of Psycho-Social Development*. Cambridge, Mass.: Schenkman, 1970.

Henry, Jules. *Culture Against Man*. New York: Random House, 1968.

Holbrook, David. *The Exploring Word*. London: Cambridge University Press, 1967.

Holt, John. *How Children Fail*. New York: Pitman, 1964.

_____. *How Children Learn*. New York: Pitman, 1969.

_____. *The Underachieving School*. New York: Pitman, 1969.

Janov, Arthur. *The Primal Scream*. New York: Dell, 1971.

Jung, Carl. *Man and His Symbols*. Garden City, N.Y.: Doubleday, 1969.

Katz, Joseph. *No Time for Youth*. San Francisco: Jossey-Bass, 1968.

Kierkegaard, Soren. *Diary*. Trans. Peter Rohde. Secaucus, N.J.: Citadel Press, 1971.

Laing, R. D. *The Divided Self*. New York: Pantheon, 1969.

———. *The Politics of Experience*. New York: Ballantine, 1967.

———, and Cooper, David. *Reason and Violence*. New York: Humanities Press, 1964.

———, and Esterson, A. *Sanity, Madness and the Family*. New York: Penguin, 1970.

Maslow, Abraham. *Toward a Psychology of Being*. New York: Van Nostrand Reinhold, 1968.

Mead, G. H. *Mind, Self and Society*. Chicago: University of Chicago Press, 1934.

Mead, Margaret. *Culture and Commitment*. New York: Natural History Press, 1970.

Moffett, James. *Teaching the Universe of Discourse*. Boston: Houghton Mifflin, 1968.

Muller, Herbert J. *The Uses of English*. New York: Holt, Rinehart, & Winston, 1967.

Pearce, Jane, and Newton, Saul. *The Conditions of Human Growth*. New York: Citadel, 1963.

Rogers, Carl. *On Becoming a Person*. Boston: Houghton Mifflin, 1961.

———. *Carl Rogers on Encounter Groups*. New York: Harper & Row, 1970.

Rosenblatt, Louise. *Literature as Exploration*. New York: Noble & Noble, 1968.

Roszak, Theodore. *The Making of a Counter-Culture*. Garden City, N.Y.: Doubleday, 1969.

Sontag, Susan. *Against Interpretation*. New York: Farrar, Straus, & Giroux, 1961.

Sullivan, H. S. *The Interpersonal Theory of Psychiatry*. Ed. Perry, Helen S., and Gawel, Mary L. New York: W. W. Norton, 1953.

Valentine, Charles A., and Valentine, Betty. Unpublished manuscript.

Weil, Simone. *The Need for Roots*. New York: G. P. Putnam's Sons, 1952.

White, Robert, ed. *The Study of Lives*. New York: Atherton, 1963.

Whitehead, Robert. *The Disappearing Dais*. London: Chatto & Windus, 1966.

Yankelovich, Daniel, and Barrett, William. *Ego and Instinct*. New York: Random House, 1970.

The Analysis of
Educational Experience

We knowers are unknown to ourselves, and for a good reason: How can we ever hope to find what we have never looked for? Our treasure lies in the beehives of our knowledge. As for the rest of life—so-called experience—who is serious enough for that? Or has time enough?

Nietzsche

The law for the development of the self with respect to knowledge is this, that the increasing degree of knowledge corresponds with the degree of self-knowledge, that the more the self knows, the more it knows itself. If this does not occur, then the more knowledge increases, the more it becomes a kind of inhuman knowing for the production of which man's self is squandered, pretty much as men were squandered for the building of the pyramids, or as men were squandered in the Russian horn-bands to produce one note, neither more nor less.

Kierkegaard

This paper is divided into three parts. In the first I will attempt to assess some aspects of the psychic condition of many of us in the West in such a way as to make more intelligible calls for "value reassessment in education."

In the second section I will sketch the outline of a method of inquiry that may permit us to understand more profoundly the nature of educational experience in the humanities. In the final section I will discuss some difficulties with the method.

Assessment

I recognize the potential pretentiousness of attempting an evaluation like this. Permit me to qualify my statements by confessing, at the outset, the limitations. I am describing psychic life at a broad conceptual level, which necessarily involves some projection, in the conventional psychoanalytic sense of that term. Such an admission does not seriously undercut the legitimacy of the perception, although given the presence of certain factors in the perceiver, that is obviously a strong possibility. The cogency and clarity of the assessment is contingent on the "cleanness," if you will, of the perceptual mechanism. "Cleanness" is largely a function of self-knowledge. If I know, for example, that I suffer from periodic melancholia, then presumably I am more sensitive to the projective nature of any sociocultural analysis that includes melancholia or related states. One might then check empirically with additional caution to attempt to ensure some empirical basis for one's analysis. Yet, ultimately, as I hope to show later, one can never totally rid oneself of such psychic and hence projective bases for one's formulations. (This is a point, of course, that has been made before. Michael Polanyi is often cited for his recognition of the "personal" nature of knowledge; more recently Alvin Gouldner has cited the presence of "domain assumptions" that necessarily and revealingly color the research hypotheses of sociologists. Then again, philosophers like Soren Kierkegaard and Friedrich Nietzsche have, in different traditions, made essentially similar observations.)

In fact, I will argue that the development of a sophisticated understanding of one's psychic state will probably result in more accurate and eventually more comprehensive social or educational observations, as well as having psychically and educationally beneficial consequences for the researcher himself.

What then can be said of our condition? It seems to me two words more powerfully characterize our state than any others. They are *disintegrated* and *unaware*.

Disintegration refers to phenomena associated with personality, which is, more or less, a public construct. Lack of awareness refers to our absorption at the levels of personality (and then only at superficial levels) and to our estrangement from a certain level of experience that is crucial to the possibility of certain forms of education.

One somewhat obvious symptom of our disintegrated state is our tendency to manifest different selves when we are in the company of different people. It is not so much that some of us *choose* to modify our behavior given certain objectives and certain circumstances, as that *it happens*.

A utilitarian approach demonstrates a certain willfulness, a certain integration of selves. Rather, one observes that certain individuals elicit certain responses, and these responses happen without a self-willed "intervening variable," that is to say one has become a person observably different than the person one has known on other occasions.

This self is in a sense lost to others. One is not free to be as one wishes, or as one is (the question of the possibility of genuine identity will be discussed in another place); one is caught, at least in some situations, in what many psychoanalysts have called a "transference" relationship. To oversimplify somewhat, this means that the nature of one's present relationships is primarily determined by the nature of one's earlier relationships to "significant others," typically one's parents. It has become a psychoanalytic truism to say that if one's relations with one's parents were colored by, say, shame and doubt, then one's relations with others who somehow "remind" one (and this usually occurs "unconsciously") of those parents are also characterized by shame and doubt. Recently, with our fascination with behaviorist theory and concomitant therapies, like desensitization therapy, we tend to remain unaware of these historical roots of current behavior.

Related to this phenomenon we have termed "self lost to others" is the matter of self lost to role. Due to several factors, many of us experience nothingness (or a state akin to that) when and where we probably should experience being. Of course some existentialists like Sartre assume this hollowness or lack as somehow central to our condition. I agree, but consider the state abnormal, rather than a final statement about our condition. At any rate, this nothingness, and its attendant anxiety, prompts if not compels most to search for stability and being outside themselves. One form this search takes is what has been characterized as interpersonal collusion; another involves absorption in what Sartre termed one's project; yet another is the identification of self with role.

It is somewhat remarkable the extent to which people use this notion of role to discuss their behavior. (I understand one can take courses in "role theory" in departments of psychology and sociology.) When the identification with role is so strong that one's behavior is defined by one's role, then we observe another form of disintegration and unawareness: the self lost to role. Kierkegaard described a similar phenomenon when he discussed the "ethical man." As you recall, this prototypical individual determines his behavior by referring to rules. If, for example, I am a professor and you are a student and we meet in my office, then I can presumably refer to the pertinent rule and apply it to the situation. The equation that results determines my action. Perhaps you see how this process occurs in reference to roles. I have an idea of what a professor is and how a professor properly behaves, and when in doubt I apply that idea (or role) and behave accordingly.

There certainly is stability in this arrangement, except to the extent that one's suppressed and repressed interior demands expression, i.e., to the extent one's unconscious discloses itself. It is also contingent on how loyally one's fellows participate in role-defined behavior and how closely people's conceptions of role resemble each others'. The point here is that one can escape to a degree from one's anxiety, but it is at the expense of one's freedom and of the possibility of genuine identity. That is, if one becomes one's role, then one cannot be oneself. One achieves "thingness," but not genuine being. (This analysis does not suggest that one cannot be oneself and also be, say, a professor. The distinction is that one's professorship is an expression of oneself, not vice versa.)

Underlying both states—self lost to others and self lost to roles—is the lack of psychic integration they indicate, and our lack of awareness of this disintegration. The fact that we are multiple "selves" raises the question: If I am this in that situation with these people and that in this situation with these people, and so on, then which "self" or "selves" is legitimate? (Of course, they are all legitimate in a sense, but to whom does one go for so-called important decisions like marriage, career? Which self will persist; which will fade; how should one live in order to please which self? And so on.) Or, as Michael Novak has observed, probably prior to the general question "Who am I?" is "Whose am I?" Who, under what circumstances and in what ways, influences my behavior, my thoughts, my moods? Why do these particular causal relationships exist? If much or all of this personality is in fact conditioned and, while "mine," not me, how might I begin to discover who, in fact, I am? How might one conceptualize this process of discovery, this coming to self-awareness, and communicate to others such a conceptualization?

If it is a matter of bringing out what is there already, and hence one form of what might legitimately be termed education, what is the nature of educational experience? It is this last question to which I shall address myself in the remainder of this paper.

Outline of a Method

I acknowledge the gravity of this assessment; I have described it in more detail in other places and obviously so have others. Further, I want to focus our attention today more on this method I propose than on the factors that account for its present pertinence.

I argue that we are not integrated, and further that many of us have forgotten that we are not integrated. In *The Integration of Personality* Jung notes that in so-called modern times we fill our minds with diversions: newspapers, radios, television all occupy our attention, and divert it from ourselves, so that "consciousness of the inner world becomes darkened and may eventually disappear altogether. But 'forgetting' is not identical with 'getting rid of.' On the contrary, the situation has become worse: instead of facing the enemy, we risk being attacked from the rear, where we are unaware and defenseless."

How is one to remember? How is one to begin to focus one's attention on oneself, in a noncritical, even nonevaluative way, so that one can illuminate this inner world? How is such illumination related to integration?

One is reminded of certain meditative disciplines that currently attract considerable interest in the West. One thinks of transcendental meditation, Zazen, the Zen Buddhist practice, various forms of Yoga, and the work of the Russian mystic Georges Gurdjieff. Each of these disciplines, I understand, can perform important functions in the process of turning inward. Yet none of them attempts to direct this focus in the context of educational experience. To explicate the nature of educational experience and at the same time work to integrate and hence become aware of oneself requires a different method, employing some assumptions of most meditative work, as well as some assumptions of psychoanalysis and phenomenology.

Alvin Gouldner in his *The Coming Crisis of Western Sociology* discusses the importance of what he terms "domain assumptions" in the theoretical formulations of social theorists. As you may recall, these are typically unexamined assumptions of a global sort: man is rational, progress is inevitable, etc. These tacit notions influence in often subtle but always decisive ways research hypotheses, methods, partial theories, and so on.

Martin Duberman the historian has made essentially the same point in a different context. In a book in progress I underline the importance of that hypothesis. I argue further that in the work of Gouldner and Duberman one finds the inchoate stage of a research method that would not only examine the nature of one's "domain assumptions," but also illuminate the larger inner world of which domain assumptions are a part.

This notion of "inner world" recalls Edmund Husserl's and Martin Heidegger's use of the term *lebenswelt*. Simply stated, *lebenswelt* refers to the world of lived experience, the preconceptual experiential realm that, given our current condition, is usually beyond our perceptual field. In fact, it becomes severed and inaccessible to our conscious selves rather early in our lives. Given the generally rigid outer forms or outer perceptual rootedness of North American culture, and the sometimes brutal quality of that culture, one begins early to ignore messages from within, then forget that one is ignoring, so that one becomes one's "image" or role or whatever. The educational problem partially involves the question of returning that gaze inward, without immediately disrupting our public, exterior lives.

The medium of movement in this method is to be primarily cognitive, or intellectual. That is not to say emotional dimensions are to be excluded; they, along with other dimensions of educational experience, will be rendered verbally, edited through the intellect.

Jung noted two fundamental forms of thinking: the associative and the directed. Dewey of course viewed the educational task as one of reconstructing experience to identify the operative factors in a situation so that one can make more useful and growth-enhancing choices in the future. We agree that the task involves the reconstruction of experience, but to a different end than Dewey conceived.

The objective is first to render one's own educational experience (these terms include what Dewey calls educative and miseducative experience) into words, using the associative form of minding. The second is to use one's critical faculties to understand what principles and patterns have been operative in one's educational life, hence achieving a more profound understanding of one's own educational experience, as well as illuminating parts of the inner world and deepening one's self-understanding generally. The third task is to analyze others' experience to reveal what I call basic educational structures or processes that cross biographical lines.

There is a second order of consequences to be expected. One necessarily focuses one's attentiveness on oneself nonevaluatively free-associating (at least within the context of educational experience) and brings to the surface latent emotions and intellections, hence making more accessible the *lebenswelt*, the preconceptual. Further, this development of what some transpersonal psychologists term "psychic openings" enables one to gain greater access to one's current experience. This movement toward greater awareness of the present should make the researcher more existential in his lifetime, more detached from current roles and emotions, and more able to recognize the origin of those roles and selves and to form those public expressions, i.e., his personality, according to his (the genuine self) wishes.

Kierkegaard said it simply: "The more consciousness, the more self, the more consciousness, the more will, and the more will, the more self." What is this genuine self? It is not just the ego, superego, or id in traditional Freudian psychoanalytic theory. It involves roughly what Husserl referred to as the "transcendental ego" and what some Eastern spiritualists refer to as the "third eye." It remains continuous over time and permits observation of lower-level psychic workings: the superego, the emotions, the behavioral patterns, etc. It permits the possibility of volition, hence of intentionality, hence of will. Its "existence" is determinable empirically, but that is for another place.

The method, as I conceive it now, would render two orders of consequences. It would yield information regarding the nature of educational experiences and their fundamental existential structures, and it would yield the researcher biographic information that would enhance "insight" and cultivate the inner-centeredness and focus that are essential to psychic integration.

The method is like a Rorschach ink blot test in that it elicits material from the unconscious, drawing on the associative faculty. However, the analyst of educational experience is not especially interested in such material as the analysand's sexual life. We are interested in the nature of educational experience, and while that adjective can be defined broadly to include the general developmental process, it is more manageable and useful to narrow our investigations to experience associated with educational institutions as they are currently conceived.

So questions of a not wholly rhetorical nature would be asked the analysand-analyst in the initial stages of that individual's investigation. Serving a similar eliciting function as the blots of ink in the Rorschach test, they would ask such questions as: What has been the nature of your educational experience? How do you use that term; that is, how do you distinguish between educational and noneducational experience? What areas of study have interested you, at what times in your life, and what psychological factors were operative that might account for that interest? What teachers influenced you, and which ones did not, and how do you account for differential effects? Consider not only your memory of the teaching style and learnedness of the instructor but also your own developmental and educational status at the time. Are you able to generalize about those teachers you found important and those you did not? Are you able to generalize about your states when you were more receptive to the teaching of another or another area of study? What factors influenced your decision to attend college or university? To attend graduate school? What "place" in your psychic life does your academic career play? What is the nature of your interest in the field of education, in the subfield of curriculum? What are your motives for advanced study?

Other questions are of course possible. An exhaustive list is not necessary, however; their function is to initiate free associative thinking within these rather broad boundaries. A semester or several years later, the researcher may begin a systematic scrutiny of his or her descriptions, attempting to answer more precisely these questions or other questions he himself considers pertinent and hermeneutical. (Although it is difficult to write free-associatively knowing one is to examine this writing later critically, this difficulty should not be so intense as to be a problem.)

Ideally at least, the researcher will want to share this material with fellow researchers. Such an arrangement obviously demands professional discretion on everyone's part. While basic existential structures of educational experience will emerge, the idiosyncratic details of individual biography, given the culture's developmental status, are best kept absolutely private. It may become necessary to establish a code of ethics with legal concomitants, as in the psychoanalytic profession.

This is obviously a long-term effort. Consider, however, the possibilities. Part of the criticism of much theoretical work in education is that it is divorced from the actual experience of teachers and students. Conceptualizing theory, as does R. D. Laing, as the articulation of existential experience helps effect the synthesis. Theory, at least in part, becomes the rendering of experience into words, the translation of the private *lebenswelt* into public language. It is, so to speak, the translation of practice into theory. Another part of the criticism of the field of curriculum is that it lacks its own research method; those who work in the field of curriculum are forced to rely on techniques developed by sociological theorists and psychologists. Here, admittedly in inchoate form, is the outline of a method that clearly and originally is an educational research method employable for the elucidation and analysis of educational experience. Moreover, it offers the possibility of humanizing the researcher.

What is meant by the phrase "basic existential structures of educational experience"? Of course some theorists of human experience have denied that human existence has structure or even that it can be elucidated to any extent. Kierkegaard and Nietzsche were such theorists, as was Kafka, although, of course, it is inaccurate to characterize him as a theorist in any formal sense. Yet there have been theorists who have elucidated basic structures of human life; Husserl is one, so is Heidegger, One recalls Heidegger's positing of "care" as one such existential structure.

The analyst of educational experience or the educational experientialist attempts to discover what factors are operative in educational experience, what relations among what factors under what circumstances, and finally, what fundamental structures describe or explain the educative process. In a sense, these structures would represent the "last stop" in the realm of the conceptual, the most fundamental level of analysis possible before entering the preconceptual, the *lebenswelt*, the ineffable.

Such structures would be somewhat analogous to Jung's notions of archetypes and the collective unconscious. Jung writes that "a more-or-less superficial layer of the unconscious is undoubtedly personal. Yet this personal unconscious appears to rest upon a deeper layer that does not derive from personal experience and achievement but is inborn. This layer is the collective unconscious." So, while it is true that each's person's intellectual biography will be unique, it will eventually become possible to uncover the world of transpersonal educational experience and to disclose the most profound understanding of the educational process possible. Since this conceptual level will lie below the details of individual experience, the structures identified may also transcend historical circumstance and cultural milieu.

Difficulties

The first probable objection is that I have merely raised, albeit in different form, the ugly head of "introspectionism." As you may recall, the line of reasoning in that philosophy of psychology went like this: Each of us learns from our own experience what pain, hunger, intention, etc. are, and each identifies one's inner experiences and then infers that others experience similarly. However, some critics, like Norman Malcom of Cornell University, have objected that such a line of thinking tends to lead to the conclusion that one typically does not and perhaps cannot understand the psychological language of another, which, of course, is a variant of psychological solipsism. Further, it also leads to the conclusion that one's own identification of one's inner experience might be inaccurate, and one might not even know it to be inaccurate. For example, what I take to be "resolve" or "determination" may not correspond to what others identify as "resolve"; it also may be that what I take to be resolve differs each time I make the identification, although I take it to be the same. And if it were indeed different each time, I could not be said to be identifying anything. Thus introspectionism assumes that each one of us makes accurate identifications of our mental states. Or if it is nonsensical to determine whether or not one's identification is accurate, then it is neither accurate nor inaccurate, and therefore not an identification of anything. Introspectionism, Malcolm concludes, is a self-refuting doctrine, which proves that our concepts of mental states and events must not be divorced from human behavior.

We reply as follows. It is true that one cannot infer that others have precisely or even roughly similar experiences of anger, fear, purpose, and so on. It is precisely this difficulty that makes the understanding of human experience so staggeringly problematic. However, this is not to endorse or adopt a form of psychological solipsism. It is possible to break through one's transferences and projections to some extent. That extent depends on such factors as the personality of the other, the expectations and fantasies operative in the situation, one's calmness, and so on. Yet, trustable knowledge of the other's experience must wait for trustable knowledge of one's own experience, the transcendence of one's natural ego, and the development of the transcendental ego. This perspective gives access to a layer of experience that allows clear perception of lower levels of one's own and others' experience, the world of personality.

It seems obvious that many make inaccurate identification of inner experience. In an earlier work, for instance, I alluded to a process I termed "the muddling of motives." One motive or "drive" given certain psychosocial conditions, can easily become another motive. For example, the literature of abnormal psychology includes the finding that certain boys steal cars due to certain sexual conflicts.

My guess is that these young men were at least not fully aware of this "cause" of their behavior. For another example, it is difficult not to observe a certain defensiveness among certain of one's colleagues when certain of their ideas are discussed. It is as if their investigations were prompted by "needs" for achievement, affiliation, or identification with another scholar or an institution, that is, for basic confirmation, rather than by curiosity and interest in the pursuit of what the ancients called Truth. Of course scholarly activity would necessarily involve these needs, but in many cases these motives become submerged, and thus is created the ambitious young researcher whose research interests seem curiously related to what is fashionable at the time and who evidences little awareness of the "domain" motives that account for his behavior.

If one reflects in a historical way on the evolution of one's views, not only about one's work, but also about the course of one's life, one cannot help but note a number of instances in which one seems to have been mistaken regarding the nature of a situation, a person, or oneself. This state is what Freire's term "submersion in reality" hints at, although he uses it in a more explicit political sense. One comes to understand that one is perpetually unaware of much that is pertinent to a complete understanding of the present (of the past and future also). The fact that one can reflect and understand a matter that was misunderstood does not imply that one is understanding nothing, rather it suggests a certain evolution of one's powers of understanding. This evolution can be conceptualized as a slow, continued emergence from reality, a transcendence of self from circumstances. This process is tantamount to what is called humanization, and it is precisely that, a becoming of what we are, a bringing out of what is there but obscured if not buried by conditioning. That sense of bringing out of course recalls another term: *education*.

So, experientialist analysis does not assume correct identification of mental states. Such an assumption is unwarranted, but it is also unwarranted to conclude it is not possible to make a correct identification. It may be likely that we can achieve only a more-or-less correct identification, but identification must be attempted. By focusing one's attentiveness inward, the long, slow process of access to the *lebenswelt* begins, offering the hope of finally transcending it.

So the outline is sketched. There are several next steps. Briefly, they involve the development of procedural specifics regarding use of the method; explication of the method's roots in psychoanalysis and phenomenology; examination of theoretical difficulties like those hinted at above; further conceptualization of essential educational structures. All of this involves an experientialist reassessment of the notions of value and education.

Bibliography

Duberman, Martin. "The Historian as Ghost." *New York Times,* 13 July 1973.

Gouldner, Alvin. *The Coming Crisis of Western Sociology.* New York: Basic Books, 1970.

Jung, Carl. *The Integration of Personality.* New York: Farrar & Rinehart, 1939.

Kierkegaard, Soren. *The Sickness Unto Death.* Translated by Walter Lowrie. Doubleday, Anchor Books, 1954.

Laing, R. D. *The Divided Self.* New York: Pantheon Books, 1969.

Malcolm, Norman. "Behaviorism as a Philosophy of Psychology." In *Behaviorism and Phenomenology,* edited by T. W. Wann. Chicago: University of Chicago Press, 1964.

Novak, Michael. *The Experience of Nothingness.* New York: Harper & Row, 1967.

Polanyi, Michael. *Personal Knowledge.* New York: Harper Torchbooks, 1964.

Currere: *Toward Reconceptualization*

I state as fact—absolutely no one, either in the East or in the West, writes or speaks a sentence that is not a gross error.

Jean-Paul Sartre

Our time has been distinguished more than by anything else, by a drive to control the external world, ... and by an almost total forgetfulness of the internal world. If one estimates human evolution from the point of view of knowledge of the external world, then we are in many respects progressing.

If our estimate is from the point of view of the internal world and of oneness of internal and external, then the judgment must be very different.

R. D. Laing

We spend most of our time and energy in a kind of horizontal thinking. We move along the surface of things going from one quick base to another, often with a frenzy that wears us out. We collect data, things, people, ideas, "profound experiences," never penetrating any of them .... But there are other times. There are times when we stop. We sit still. We lose ourselves in a pile of leaves or its memory. We listen and breezes from a whole other world begin to whisper. Then we begin our "going down."

James Carroll

> ... for the ego is a dream
> Till a neighbor's need by name
> Creates it.
>
> W. H. Auden

1

The curriculum theory field has forgotten what existence is. It will remain moribund until it remembers.

2

Much if not most of the work in the field derives from the work of Tyler. Kliebard, Huebner, and Macdonald, as well as others, have explained why Tyler's rationale and hence that tradition are not viable.

The conceptual-empiricists work to achieve conceptual consensus in order to use the empirical methods of the behavioral sciences to control and predict curriculum phenomena. Huebner, Apple, and others have pointed to some of the difficulties of borrowing conceptual and research tools from other traditions and transplanting them to the field of curriculum.

A third group's work can be characterized as revisionist or reconceptualist in function. I wish to suggest a context in which the work of three revisionists—Huebner, Greene, and Macdonald—might be placed, and then examine the nature of this context, which I call *currere*.

3

Are Tyler's questions and those asked in 1926, 1950, 1957[1] no longer pertinent or possible? Are they simply cul-de-sacs? Who asks them in 1973?

Greene does not; nor does Huebner. Examine Huebner's titles: "Curricular Language and Classroom Meaning," "Curriculum as Concern for Man's Temporality"; "Toward a Remaking of Curricular Language."[2] Where among these essays does one find Tyler's questions? Is it because questions of design, development, instruction, and evaluation—the perennial foci of the curriculum field—are no longer useful or interesting?

Greene of course works more in educational philosophy than in curriculum, but when she writes in curriculum it is significant. Let us note two of her titles and return to this work later; "Curriculum and Consciousness" and "Cognition, Consciousness, and Curriculum."[3]

Macdonald seems to continue to write about development and objectives. Consider, for example, a "Transcendental Developmental Ideology of Education."[4] The correspondence with earlier more traditional work, however, is superficial. Both in theme and in function Macdonald's work is of a different order than, say, Tyler's, Taba's, Beauchamp's, or Short's.[5]

4

If the curriculum theory field is not about design, development, instruction, and evaluation, then what is it about? What should it be about?

Huebner insists, as would most, that the curriculum field is not a knowledge-producing discipline in the sense that history or psychology is. Rather, curriculum is an environment-producing field (hence the notion of design, one supposes).

Mann would seem to assent to this view, although his conception of the field is more political and practitioner-orientated than is (or was) Huebner's.

As does Mann, as do most in the field, including Greene and Macdonald, Huebner brings to bear on the notion of curriculum the work of others in other disciplines. Huebner calls on Heidegger, Tillich, in fact, on much of the existentialist tradition, both religious and secular. This application of others' work to problems and aspects of curriculum is consistent with Huebner's contention that curriculum inquiry is not a knowledge-producing process. Necessarily a field so conceived must take from others; it is a field of translation and application.

While translation and application are important, they are finally flawed functions for the curriculum theory field. Huebner himself has indicated, in part, why.

The curriculum theorist as designer, says Huebner, is like a travel guide who plans (if she or he is a "progressive" planner, with the student's "input") the educational journey. Objectives are formulated. Destinations include, let us say, London, Paris, and so on. Let us also say that this curriculum theorist is also a practitioner and will accompany me on this trip, calling my attention to points of interest and instructing me in the history, sociology, psychology, etc. of say, London and Londoners.

The conditions are ideal. The traveler-students knows where she or he wishes to go, what she or he wishes to learn. The guide-theorist-practitioner has designed the trip, taking care of travel, housing, and so on, so that these aspects of the journey are handled esthetically and ethically, as well as efficiently. The guide is learned, interesting, even stimulating. The trip goes pretty much according to plan, but not rigidly so; time is left open enough to pursue momentary interests; the guide and student-traveler develop an amicable, dialogical, perhaps even genuinely exploratory relationship. Afterward, both participants acclaim the trip as successful.

6

This is an oversimplification to be sure, but an important kernel of truth remains. This is where, ideally, the curriculum theory field is or will be, if it is a field preoccupied with design, development, instruction, and evaluation.

7

What is important about this journey, or any journey? Is it that I saw London and Paris, that I answered my questions, that I learned much about the history, psychology, and so forth of where I visited? Does it even have to do with my relationship with the guide?

Its importance has to do with all of this, of course. But it lies elsewhere, too. It has to do with the implications of the following questions.

How does it feel to be uprooted from the geographical, social, and psychological ambiance in which I live my day-to-day life? How do I experience the guide? What is my experience of London, of the Abbey, the tourists, the city's bustling sedateness? What is it like, if one is Anglo-Saxon in heritage, to find oneself among one's ancestors? What psychological and cultural connections exist between me and them? How do I experience their self-assuredness, their haste, their courtesy? What is the experience of being a tourist, a stranger, in a land not one's own? What is my emotional life on this trip? Is it intimidating, exhilarating, revealing, obfuscating? What goes on? Perhaps the physical and social setting is sufficiently contrasting to the one I know in the United States that I can discern more clearly the nature of the relation between objective conditions, that is the public world, and inner conditions. How do I respond? What is the nature of the "I" who responds? What place in my psychic life does this trip take? What are my motives? What is the nature of my interest in a journey, in this particular journey? What is it about London, Paris, etc., that draws me here; why not Moscow, Constantinople? What do I make of this guide? What can I learn from her or him; what can she or he learn from me? What are this guide's motives? What is the nature of the guide's interest in me? In her or his work?

These questions regarding the nature of one's inner experience, point to that level of existence known as the *lebenswelt*. Let us study this *lebenswelt*, the experience of the educational journey; it is the study of curriculum reconceived, that is, *currere*.

8

The word *curriculum*, as any curriculum specialist will acknowledge, carries many meanings. Laymen seem to use it to indicate a course of study, specifically the materials or artifacts used in a course of study. Theorizers like Mauritz Johnson and William T. Lowe[6] restrict its use to "intended learning outcomes." For others, like Lewis and Miel,[7] the focus is on process, and "curriculum" is roughly synonymous with "education." For various other theorists it seems to mean primarily design and planning, or development of materials, instructional strategies and packages, and for some it is nearly indistinguishable from instruction and evaluation.

Scholarship like that of Huebner, Macdonald, and Greene seems to stretch the word further; curriculum theorizing is apparently criticism; the introduction and application of other traditions (like existentialism) to a professional educational audience. Some of my own work is in this vein.

I propose yet another meaning of the word, one stemming from its Latin root, *currere*. The distinction is this: current usages of the term appear to me to focus on the observable, the external, the public. The study of *currere*, as the Latin infinitive suggests, involves the investigation of the nature of the individual experience of the public: of artifacts, actors, operations, of the educational journey or pilgrimage.[8]

So understood, the field is not only an environment-producing discipline, involving the formulation of objectives, design, even criticism, as it is understood presently. It is a knowledge-producing discipline, with its own method of inquiry and its own area of investigation. *Currere*, historically rooted in the field of curriculum, in existentialism, phenomenology, and psychoanalysis, is the study of educational experience.

9

Curriculum as design suggests a blueprint or sign, and to have veracity and utility, signs must be rooted in experience. What relation do designs bear to the *lebenswelt*? In "Sanity, Madness, and the School" I indicated the nature of the relation for many: estrangement, an emptying out into hollowness, madness.

Yet we study these signs, make new ones, and how are they related to the existence of those in school, those who study? They are not truly related, and continued interest in them without study of the *lebenswelt*, indicates that we have forgotten what existence is.

10

Not all have forgotten. Huebner has not. He writes of conversation, language, meaning, temporality. His work, because it is rooted in existence, or at least its memory, is important, perhaps the most important in the field. But is there not a flaw?

In one essay he writes, as we noted earlier, of the danger of borrowing concepts and methods from other traditions, uprooting them from their historical and intellectual contexts, and placing them in alien ambiences. He makes this important point in regard to the use by many educators of concepts like "learning."

But what does he himself do? He carries the existentialist tradition to the curriculum field. If curriculum is not objectives, design, development, instruction, and evaluation, then what is it? (In fairness to Huebner, as late as May 1973 he indicated that he planned eventually to become "programmatic."[9] But I suspect he understands that that would undercut his previous efforts, which have worked by implication to dismiss the importance of program development.) The production of an environment? No, to the extent that is possible and desirable we must leave that to the teacher.

11

What are temporality, language, meaning rooted in? Blueprints? So-called instructional packages designed to manipulate motivation? Although concepts of different orders, they can all be characterized as aspects of existence and, in the educational context, of *currere*. They point to the experience of the journey or the pilgrimage, to the nature of my existence within the context of education. (For convenience's sake, I argue in "The Analysis of Educational Experience" that we restrict our use of this term *education* to experience associated with educational institutions.) These aspects point to *depassement*, to totalization, to that relation between self and other (including artifact) that constitutes knowledge and knowing.

12

The questions of *currere* are not Tyler's; they are ones like these: Why do I identify with Mrs. Dalloway and not with Mrs. Brown?[10] What psychic dark spots does the one light, and what is the nature of "dark spots," and "light spots"? Why do I read Lessing and not Murdoch?[11] Why do I read such works at all? Why not biology or ecology? Why are some drawn to the study of literature, some to physics, and some to law? Are phrases like "structures of the mind" usable and useful? If so, are these varying structures, and in what sense do they account for the form intellectual interests take or for their complete absence? What constitute "structures," and what are their sources?

Why am I fascinated with Sartre for several years, then with Marxism, and then with Zen Buddhism? What psychic or environmental conditions, or interface of the two, prevailed that might indicate something like a "cause" or an explanation for the timing of such interests?

Which teachers drew me to them, and what was it about me or them that accounts for this "drawing"? What is its nature: intellectual, emotional, sexual? Why have I become a teacher; what are my motives, the nature of my interest in teaching, in studying; and what relation to my psychic life do they bear?

Such questions suggest the study of *currere*. The information our investigations bring us is the knowledge of *currere*. It is its own knowledge, and while its roots are elsewhere, its plant and flower are its own; it is another species, a discipline of its own.

13

Macdonald also hints at this in much of his work. He continually calls for the focus of curriculum to be on the individual, in process, in an "actions curriculum." He calls for "esthetic and moral criteria that focus on the quality of living experiences in the process of encountering the curriculum."[12] The word *curriculum* here appears to connote materials, something external, to be encountered. What interests Macdonald here is not the curriculum (so defined) but the "living experiences . . . encountering the curriculum." This living and encountering suggests *currere*.

14

An emphasis on the individual and his experiencing is significantly evident in Greene's "Curriculum and Consciousness."[13] She writes that the "reader," using his imagination, must move within his own subjectivity and break with the common sense world he normally takes for granted." The reader "must 'go beyond' what he has been." In the student's search for meaning, "he moves outward into diverse realms of experience." He must recreate and regenerate in terms of his own consciousness the materials of a curriculum.

Yes. But what is the nature of "movement within one's own subjectivity, the dynamics of breaking with the commonsense, taken-for-granted,[14] world? What is involved? What is one's experience of this? What does it mean to go beyond oneself, how does one articulate it, understand it, experience it? What is a search for meaning? What does it mean to reconstruct curriculum materials in terms of one's consciousness?

Clearly, language analysis is no help here. Nor would be the so-called empirical methods of the behavioral sciences. Those tools are designed to answer a different order of question. What is required is a self-hermeneutical, phenomenological method that will help the investigator gain access to the *lebenswelt*, or that realm of *lebenswelt* associated with *currere*.

Later in the essay, Greene likens the "learner" to a newcomer just arrived in town. Partly due to objective conditions of so-called modern times, partly due to the unfamiliarity of "unlearned" codified knowledge, the student requires a map, which Greene compares to the "prestructured curriculum." She develops the analogy:

> For the cartographer, the town is an "object of his science," a science which has developed standards of operation and rules for the correct drawing of maps. In the case of the curriculum maker, the public tradition or the natural order of things is "the object" of his design activities . . . [education] is like asking a newcomer in search of direction to recapitulate the complex processes by which the cartographer made his map. The map may represent a fairly complete charting of the town and it may ultimately be extremely useful for the individual to be able to take a cartographer's perspective. When that individual first arrives, however, his peculiar plight ought not to be overlooked: his "background awareness" of being alive in an unstable world; his reasons for consulting the map; the interests he is pursuing as he attempts to orient himself when he can no longer proceed by rule of thumb. He himself may recognize that he will have to come to understand the signs on the map if he is to make use of it. Certainly he will have to decipher the relationship between those signs and "real objects in the city": But his initial concern will be conditioned by the "objects" he wants to bring into visibility, by the landmarks he needs to identify if he is to proceed on his way.[15]

15

First, the matter of map making. The cartographer must be one learned in the area he will map, and in the codification of that area, in the craft of map making. It is true there is room here for a technician whose specialty is artful maps, easily deciphered maps, but the important work is to be done of course by the scholar-cartographer. While there is room for the specialist, and granted his speciality has a relative importance, his work is a craft, a specialty, hardly a science (as Eisner[16] would evidently have it). Even if we could agree conceptually on various aspects or elements involved in making maps more intelligible—given varying developmental levels of potential readers—and more artful, it is unclear how useful information gained by so-called empirical methods would be, except to regiment and standardize procedures and principles of map altering. (The map is drawn; the specialist alters, makes other maps, based on "original" work for mass consumption.) Certainly different individuals decide who will work with which aspects of the making, but (recalling some of Goodlad's work) how much can we make of this until we fall into political science?

16

Secondly, what is the objective value of asking the newcomer to imitate the cartographer in his calling? Unless, of course, the newcomer wishes it. But most newcomers come to town for other reasons; their use of maps is incidental, casual; they resort to them, as Greene notes, when they can no longer proceed by "rule of thumb." Surely it is an inflated view of one's craft to ask all to learn it, if only to discard it later. The recent so-called curriculum reform movement was predicated on an analogous notion.

How often, one wonders, is the newcomer-student asked his reasons for coming to town. His reasons are rarely his own.

17

So one's reasons for traveling are often not one's own. So one is coerced into acquiring skills and information that one failed to request. What sense lies in this arrangement?

The possibility of sense lies is one's experience: of oneself, of others, of artifacts, of journey and pilgrimage. To realize this possibility of sense involves the study of *currere*.

18

Since, however, the journey does occur frequently for reasons not one's own, one important context of *currere* is political. Thus the importance of Mann's work and presence and of Huebner's, Bateman's,[17] and Apple's, among others. The analysis of *currere* in "Sanity, Madness, and the School" is partly political.

Elucidation of one's journey and probable concomitant cultivation and awareness of one's existential freedom—the possibility of psychological freedom—all lie, in a sense, in a broader social or anthropological context. One's existential freedom is necessarily and importantly colored by one's practical and political freedom. It goes without saying that as long as wealth is distributed unreasonably unevenly and, more importantly, along class, race, and sex lines, then objective conditions are such that groups of people are unable to manifest practically and politically their existential and psychological freedom.

This is true given our general developmental state, which in part is to say, given our profound and often unconscious addiction to consumption. This is of course pervasive, dominating the intellectual life, as well as the emotional. This compulsive acquisitiveness is ultimately self-destructive, both cause and consequence of one-dimensionality, madness, etc. (This analysis is for another place. Suffice to say that the mere transferral to the underclasses of the consumptive drives and capabilities of the middle and upper classes would be disastrous, psychically as well as ecologically. Much more desirable is Illich's notion of income ceilings.)

A further reservation. Political life is inevitably a lower order of existence than one need settle for. While it is work necessarily done, given the fact of political and economic injustice, it must be done detachedly, with ultimate concern for one's so-called enemies. Surely our objective is an end to war, on whatever level, not its perpetuation.

19

Analysis of this sort is appropriate to the study of *currere* only as it provides a context for *currere*, only as it widens our understanding of the nature of the pilgrimage. It is similar to discussing the distant that may well influence and is influenced by the close-at-hand.

The close-at-hand is of course our internal experience of, for example, literature. Our method of inquiry thus recalls phenomenology in that our study focuses on that which presents itself in our consciousness. My relation to the collectivity, vice versa, is more abstract, hence more removed and distant.

If political analyses, anthropological analyses, and so forth are not directly related to *currere*, then we have fallen away from our task, from ourselves, into other disciplines, attempting to translate for another audience and another tradition, the knowledge of yet another tradition. Given the traditional conception of a curriculum theorist, such a tendency is understandable, even expected, but to be resisted. We cannot understand profoundly the nature of a discipline in which we are not scholars, in which we do not write and live. For example, to summarize aspects of Marxist thought for teachers is to be a popularizer, a sort of intellectual "middle man" in whose care the cognate groceries decay a little and the prices increase a little. It is a necessary trade, but it is essentially derivative and contingent. It is easily made too much of.

20

How to begin to investigate the realm of *currere*? What method is employable? In "The Analysis of Educational Experience" I discussed the barest outlines of a method that presented itself to me then.

We require a strategy that will allow us to "bracket" the educational aspects of our taken-for-granted world. That is, we must attend to the contents of consciousness as they appear. One loosens one's usual holds on thinking that reflect cultural conditioning and result in vaguely instrumental and sharply other-directed thinking. Further, such cognitive, in fact, ontological modes tend simply to reflect the acquisitive, compulsively consumptive marketplace modes of the larger culture. The self, the psyche, becomes "unemployed" (to use Gouldner's word), unnecessary, hence ignored often forgotten. The mind still works associatively (in, as we noted, a vaguely instrumental way—what must I do? How can I best do this?) but unconsciously; in such ontological conditions "we" are identified with our public selves, our roles, and so we are what Heidegger termed the natural ego. Of course to perform the "eidetic reduction," to bracket specific contents of consciousness, requires loosened identification with the contents, hence a perspective not equivalent to them. Husserl rightly terms this point of view the transcendental ego, continuous over time and place and person. If one experiences any continuity in one's educational experience, in fact in one's life, such a sense (and in most of us it is only a sense, a feeling, a shadow behind us of which we are only vaguely aware) hints at the possibility of such a perspective. Most of us of course experience discontinuity, disjuncture, continual transformation which indicates the continued evolution of self (selves), which are the so-called natural egos. (There are those of course who impose continuity and permanence on their lives by force, by adherence to rules, by complete submersion in their conditioning. Such people are rightly viewed as one-dimensional automatons.)

So, the problem initially is to get under one's exteriorized horizontal thinking, to begin to sink toward the transcendental place, where the lower-level psychic workings, those psychic realms determined by conditioning and genetic code, are visible.

By oneself or with another to focus on a question and allow the mind to free associate, making note of intellections and emotions, is not free association in the sense that most classical psychoanalysts use the term, although the connection is clear. Free association in the experientialist analysis is more pointed, more focused, less fruitfully allowed to roam. (Yet this need not be compulsively avoided. One may gain unexpected and valuable information by seemingly unrelated associations.) For example, say one is now reading Sartre's *Search for a Method*,[18] the first section regarding the relation between existentialism and Marxism. One might find oneself asking: What sort of man would write like this? As I read I try to attend as closely and uncritically as I can to the print, to merge my attention with that which is codified on the page. The degree of abstractedness in Sartre, of hugeness or globalness, can be experienced as expanding and loosening what then feel like constraints in my mind's structure, what Freire might in part mean by "limit situation." (Such sentences might constitute a very preliminary phenomenological or experientialist account of one aspect of cognitive development, of what Piaget in part might mean by "decentering").

But why do I find *Search for a Method* pertinent? As I begin to free associate, using the question like a Rorschach ink blot, intellections are bracketed: it is one of my dilemmas: what is the relation between the individual and the collective, between self and other, between internal and external? How does context influence self and vice versa? What are my political obligations, if any, and what is the status, ontologically[19] speaking, of politics? Sartre writes of the anthropological context in which *existenz* dwells. That one finds oneself, finds self-consciousness, already constituted, but existentially free to constitute the constituted, is to be able to remake what is already made. But such existential freedom is prevented practical manifestation in politically and economically oppressive cultural contexts. And so on.

These reflect my internal questions, and to reconstruct, as Greene calls for in "Curriculum and Consciousness," the artifact in terms of my own consciousness is to allow it presence within me, uncritically, to observe if and how it "fits," if it is the next "piece" in the developing intellectual gestalt, to "test it" against memories of past experience, that is *Erlebnisse* or the *Erfuhrung* (accumulation of past *Erlebnisse*), again against the *Erlebnisse* or present experience. Of course my questions will persist, but partial answers present themselves, and I begin to understand the nature of my interest in the *Search for a Method*.

This briefest of examples can only hint at the total process; a more complete explication awaits the accumulation of necessary information. Another brief example, however, may further indicate the kind of free association that is appropriate for this method of inquiry.

This, simply enough, involves remembering one's first experience associated with school, and free associating about those early experiences. The task this strategy involves is recording a chronology of associations, beginning with earliest events and continuing to the present.

In both free-associative techniques, the aim is to free associate as much as one can, allowing oneself to fall into past experience, to record this experience with as little editing as possible. That is to say, one holds one's critical or instrumental form of minding in abeyance. In practice, this is not as problematic as one might imagine. The degree to which one can cultivate the free-associative process and permit oneself to relive early and present experiences is the degree to which the data gathered are phenomenologically accurate. If one's critical faculty intrudes, combatting it is of no avail; it must simply hold itself in abeyance while the other minding form is operative.

21

When sufficient data have accumulated (and the question of when may well be left to the investigator) the analysis begins. I am less sure about the proceedings of the next series of steps, simply because in my own analysis I have not yet reached this point. But here is the expectation.

A sort of model (it's not completely applicable) is the textual analysis practiced by students of imaginative literature. In this work the focus turns more on theme than style, imagery, etc., although all aspects of the writing are pieces of the puzzle.

Depending on the nature of the data examined (it might be a series of associations in regard to a book one is reading or it might be historical material from, say, one's first years in school), the questions that guide the analytic process may be the same as or similar to the questions that prompted the free-associative process initially. Or they may be broad questions like: What correspondences do I find between conditions in my private life and those in my academic life? That is to say, what do I read and what intellectual or thematic relation exists between the reading and the living? What seem to be characteristic responses to various teachers, to various forms of work (writing, reading, library work), to various types of work (philosophy, history, etc.), and what motives can be inferred? And so on.

The appropriate questions to ask probably cannot be determined sensically until the material is ready for analysis, although it is true, particularly if the investigator works alone, that one can become sufficiently close to this sort of information that a detached, objective, critical analysis is made problematic. In such a case another versed in this method and approach may help the student of *currere* formulate the questions and even participate in the analysis.

22

This is slow and arduous work. The possibilities, however, are interesting enough to warrant the intellectual expenditure.

First, let us note the potential rewards that may accrue for the investigator. I discuss these first because I believe this aspect of educational research (and of research in allied areas of study, like the humanities and the social sciences) has received too little attention.

As well as providing one's colleagues with hopefully new, interesting, and useful information, one's research work, as much as it is possible (and this obviously varies according to the field) ought to benefit the researcher personally.

While self-analysis and introspection can be unfruitful and even self-destructive, with proper guidance and strict adherence to the spirit and rules of "experientialist" analysis, one can reverse one's outer-directedness, one's enslavement to the stimulus-response reality of the present public world. (Which is not to say, of course, that one is totally self-absorbed and ineffective publicly. The converse is the case.) In other terms, one is able to think vertically as well as horizontally.

This process of turning inward to examine one's *currere* will lead to a generalized inner-centeredness and hopefully initiate or further the process of individuation, leading to the gradual formation of the transcendental ego. These are heady claims, indeed, and while they seem probable to me, they are conjecture at this point. Evidence awaits further analysis.

More in the tradition of psychotherapy, one's investigations are certainly intended to gain insight, specifically about the nature of one's educational experience, but, since such a development can be kept fragmented from the other realms of one's life, only with great effort, this will lead to "insight" generally; regarding, say, patterns operative in one's affiliative being, which may sometimes be self-destructive. Many psychotherapists agree that such insight is a necessary although not a sufficient condition for psychic amelioration. While the method's primary intent is informational and analytic rather than curative, it can be so done as possibly to aid the latter process.

A second possibility, perhaps of more interest to present readers, is the potential for benefit to the academic community, and specifically the curriculum field.

Obviously we will begin to obtain information regarding the experience of *currere*, the experience of the maps (artifacts), the guides (cartographers or actors), and the journey (more than operations in Duncan's essay[20] in fact, the experience of all three elements). This information will be in several forms and of varying accessibility. One form may be historical, another more free associative, perhaps in some cases akin to the interior monologue in the fiction of Virginia Woolf, or in a quasi-analytic contemplation of a particular work of literature, of philosophy, or whatever. A sense, both intuitive and more narrowly cognitive, will begin to emerge of the nature of *currere*.

This sense leads us to a third and probably less obvious consequence. Using the metaphoric language of a depth psychology, one can hypothesize that the material rendered into print, not present ordinarily in one's consciousness, comes from a preconcious or unconscious. Jung tells us that, broadly speaking, there exist two layers of unconscious.[21] "A more or less superficial layer of the unconscious is undoubtedly personal. Yet this personal unconscious appears to rest on a deeper layer that does not derive from personal experience and achievement but is inborn. This layer is the collective unconscious." Of course contained in this collective unconscious, he explains, are archetypes, fundamental structures, so to speak, of the human personality.

Arguing analogously, it seems plausible that initial information generated by this method will be in fact idiosyncratic. However, later information derived by free association and information derived by critical analysis of the associative kind of information, will reveal aspects of a collective or transpersonal realm of educational experience. That is to say, once we get past the individualized details of an individual's biography, we may gain access to a transbiographic realm of *currere*.

If this indeed is possible, we might gain information that is very important indeed. There may exist fundamental structures or processes that are observably quite different when manifested in individual personality but are the same when studied at the level of their roots. These might be basic structures or processes of the educative process in the humanities.

When I reach this point, I am always reminded of Heidegger's postulation of fundamental structures of human existence. He argued that as seemingly unrelated and hopelessly complicated as a human being in the world is on the surface, underneath one discerns fundamental structures. One of these is care. I don't take Heidegger to mean what most of us mean when we use the word *care*. (As you may recall, Heidegger observes that most of our talk is chatter, gossip, no more significant or related to our centers than are baseball statistics. So Heidegger does not use the word in its ordinary sense.) I construe the word to mean, loosely, what I think Zen Buddhists mean by the word *attachment*. That is, usually without awareness, we respond to stimuli (people, artifacts, emotions, thoughts) evaluatively, as if with an opinion. We are drawn to certain sets of stimuli, repelled by others, and while many stimuli do not elicit responses strong enough to warrant words like *drawn* and *repel*, they nonetheless elicit, and usually contiguously, some assessment. This is to say we do not live without attachment, we are attached, negatively or positively, to that which enters our "perceptual field." In Heidegger's view, this is care. We might reach a similar conceptual level in this work.

23

What's the use of it? someone will ask. Such an inevitable, necessary, and complicated question deserves more attention than I am willing to give it at this writing.

At a more global level, we Americans have been and are impulsive instrumentalists. We use ourselves, our families, our work; in a word we *use*, rather than appreciate, contemplate, speculate, and so on, although we occasionally do these also. Gouldner has a fine section in *Crisis* regarding this matter, and he characterizes those parts of ourselves we don't use (given certain objective or external conditions) as the "unemployed self." It is an amusing as well as explanatory phrase.

So understandably one would ask, what good is a method, or less baldly, what is its utility?

More narrowly, we can observe that those of us in the curriculum field have been instrumental in a specific way that I think Kliebard rightly characterizes as ameliorative. So I understand the importance and staggering difficulty involved when I propose that the fundamental function of our field shift from prescription and guidance to understanding. How is understanding useful?

It is a necessary question because actions have consequences. Freire reminds us that the Greeks called this *praxis*. The sort of work I envisage is *praxis* but perhaps not in a popularized sense of the word.

Let us say we discover, as I have suggested most briefly in "The Analysis of Educational Experience," that one such basic process is *depasser*, or exceeding one's biographic situation, and this exceeding is a complicated function of one's encounter with certain forms of scholarly work. Assume we reach this understanding via the route of various individuals' expressions of the process. We then understand the process, and we also understand to some extent how this process or structure is manifested in various varying personalities, under varying conditions, and so on. If this were so, then one would be able more accurately to assist the novice traveler to read signs and interpret events more fruitfully: in a word, to travel (to study) with wise companionship.

This is very far away indeed. Before we learn to teach in such a way, we must learn how to learn in such a way. And this means that we teachers, and this has been implicit throughout, must become students, students of *currere*, which is to say students of ourselves, before we can truthfully say we understand teaching in this sense.

The analysis of *currere*, if it proceeds in the way I suspect it can, involves a shift in perspective, involving not simply cognitive insight (and of course such insight is not simple), but so-called affective insight as well. It beckons organismic change. While this sounds exorbitant, in practice it is not.

If the analysis proceeds correctly, then it proceeds in all conscious realms of the investigator's experience, although this method understandably focuses itself on *currere*. This turning inward, the process of individuation, is change of consciousness. A shift in the source of behavior signals a shift in the behavior itself. Thus *praxis* is effected.

24

Currere is thus experience in educational contexts (probably most fruitfully pursued in the humanities, at least initially); it is the kernel of a reconceived and revitalized curriculum theory field.

Truth is neither in the words nor in the theories that they spin out; truth is in the experiences that each of us has, and the value of words and theories is not that they communicate truth, but that if all is aright they may help us grasp and comprehend the truths of our experience.... Such is the praxis of *Geisteswissenschaften*, the sciences of the spirit.

Robert McClintock

Notes

1. See *The Foundations and Technique of Curriculum Construction,* The Twenty-Sixth Yearbook of the National Society for the Study of Education, vol. 26, pt. 2 (Chicago: NSSE, 1926), p. 9; Virgil E. Herrick, "The Concept of Curriculum Design," in *Toward Improved Curriculum Theory* (Chicago: University of Chicago Press, 1950), pp. 37-38; and Florence Stratemeyer et al., *Developing Criteria for Modern Living* (New York: Teachers College Press, Columbia University, 1957), pp. 7-21.
2. Chapters 13, 14; in William Pinar, ed., *Heightened Consciousness, Cultural Revolution, and Curriculum Theory* (Berkeley, Calif.: McCutchan, 1974).
3. See chapter 18; Pinar, ed., *Heightened Consciousness.*
4. Pinar, ed., *Heightened Consciousness.*
5. Hilda Taba, *Curriculum Development: Theory and Practice* (New York: Harcourt, Brace, & World, 1962); George Beauchamp, *Curriculum Theory* (Wilmette, Ill.: Kagg Press, 1968); Edmund Short, "Knowledge Production and Utilization in Curriculum," *Review of Educational Research* 43, no. 3 (Summer 1973).
6. Mauritz Johnson, Jr., "Definitions and Models in Curriculum Theory," in Edmund Short, ed., *Contemporary Thought on Public School Curriculum* (Dubuque, Iowa: William C. Brown, 1968); William T. Lowe, *Structure and the Social Studies* (Ithaca, N.Y., and London: Cornell University Press, 1968).
7. Arthur J. Lewis and Alice Miel, *Supervision for Improved Instruction* (Belmont, Calif.: Wadsworth Publishing, 1972).
8. Huebner used the word pilgrimage most recently at the 1973 University of Rochester Curriculum Theory Conference. See his "The Remaking of Curricular Language," in *Heightened Consciousness,* ed. Pinar.
9. At the Rochester Conference.
10. Virginia Woolf, *Mrs. Dalloway* (London: Hogarth Press, 1925); see Doris Lessing, *The Summer Before Dark* (New York: Knopf, 1973).

11. Iris Murdoch, for example, *The Time of the Angels* (New York: Viking, 1966), or *A Severed Head* (New York: Viking, 1961).
12. See chapter 17.
13. See chapter 18.
14. Huebner uses this term.
15. Chapter 18.
16. Elliot W. Eisner, *Confronting Curriculum Reform* (Boston: Little, Brown, 1971).
17. "Politics and the Curriculum," in *Curriculum Crossroads*, ed. A. Harry Parson (New York: Teachers College Press, Columbia University, 1962).
18. Jean-Paul Sartre, *Search for a Method* (New York: Knopf, 1963).
19. Despite the word's specific philosophical denotations, I use it here as the best adjectival form of the word *being*.
20. James K. Duncan and Jack P. Frymier, "Explorations in the Systematic Study of Curriculum," in "Curriculum Theory Development," ed. Paul R. Klohr, *Theory into Practice* (October 1967).
21. Carl Jung, *The Integration of Personality* (New York: Farrar & Rinehart, 1939).

Search for a Method

Introduction

As we know, discipline inquiry requires both a subject and a method for inquiry. That this book is subtitled *The Reconceptualists* suggests dissatisfaction with established research methods and, by implication, with that area that is traditionally researched in the field of curriculum. In the preceding chapter I briefly outlined in a way that differs markedly from, say, Schwab,[1] why the traditional questions we ask in curriculum, the methods we have employed to answer the questions, and the answers themselves, have stalled and stumped us to the point where the adjective *moribund* is commonly used to described the state of the field. Resurrection of this Lazarus requires two parts: identification of the area we wish to investigate that can be investigated and a systematic procedure by which to investigate it.

First, a note about these traditional areas of concern. It appears to me, as it evidently does to Schwab and others, that the areas of curriculum development and design have not proved amenable to systematic study. Furthermore, the attempts to borrow con-ceptualizations of theory development from the social sciences have never surpassed the borrowing stage, and this is no accident.[2] Meanwhile criticism of current research conceptualization grows louder both inside and ouside the social sciences.[3] Ours is a time of transition.

The reconception of the field that I will propose is not a break with the past. There are definite precedents for it in the field,[4] although I have not noticed much awareness of them; that is understandable given our nearly compulsive adherence to conventional and now almost useless ideas of what our work is. In the preceding chapter I impressionistically outlined some of these precedents in the work of three important curriculum theorizers. Now I wish to discuss my view of the nature of the reconceptualization and to propose a research method that is appropriate to this redefined area of inquiry.

The paper is usefully divided into the following parts. First, brief speculation regarding our dissatisfaction with current research methods, which I see as intimately related to a similar discontent in the social sciences. Secondly, description of four structural elements of educational experience, and in the present case, the educational experience of literature. After concluding a sketch of this one area to be researched in a reconceived curriculum field, I will allude to its parent disciplines. Finally, I will describe the present state of a method that will encourage disciplined inquiry into the area.

Dissatisfaction

It is clear we are in a critical stage in our work. I suppose it is a crisis, as Gouldner suggests, but the dimension of the dilemma interests me less than an understanding of what will or can come of it. I acknowledge that I am outside my field of expertise when I discuss this matter, but I offer my impressions—however naive a historian or philosopher of science may find them—because they are importantly related to what I previously characterized as a "phenomenological" research method. (Why I now place phenomenological in quotation marks will become evident later.)

Positivistic, so-called empirical research methodologies now unmistakably occupy center stage. Clearly they represent an advancement over the research methods used in the first decades of educational research. Even so, many scholars are dissatisfied, and this dissatisfaction has been adequately expressed by writers in disparate traditions like Polanyi in philosophy and Gouldner in sociology and by recent critics in the curriculum field. One way the dilemma poses itself is: for the sake of precision, clarity, and utility, we have taken to studying that which is observable and, at times it seems, quantifiable. Not surprisingly this approach necessarily omits something, whether we call this something the tacit dimension after

Polanyi, synnoetics after Phenix, or domain assumptions after Gouldner. What is noteworthy is that most of us agree that quantitative research answers many questions well, other questions not as well, and some questions not at all. Not interested in berating a concept of research for not doing what it cannot do, I have been attempting to formulate a method that would allow those interested to study the latter category of questions, which is roughly equivalent to the something we know is missing and is the source of our dissatisfaction.

I continue to refer to what it is I think many of us wish to study as "something" not to be vague, but to convey the yet unknown nature of the "object" of investigation. It is, in a sense, a tacit dimension, and it also encompasses domain assumptions, but finally we are vague about what it is. Needless to say, I have not found it. But I am working, and I have found some tracks, if you will, and I am ready to suggest a tentative outline of a method of looking.

Tracks

In a word, the manifestation of this unknown in the field of curriculum involves the concept of experience. It is experience in a special sense, as I tried to indicate with the use of the word *currere* in the previous chapter. Briefly, experience is not thought or feeling, or sensation, although these three notions are embedded in it. They typically serve as both media for and partial content of experience, but they do not exhaust it. This use of the concept recalls the work of Husserl, and the idea of the *lebenswelt*, or life-world. With these words I introduce the scholarly tradition known as phenomenology, which I cannot, in the space of this chapter, satisfactorily explain to those unfamiliar with it. I can only provide a tenuous bridge to where I want to go with it. As Merleau-Ponty explains in the preface to *Phenomenology of Perception*, all codified knowledge, including that which comprises science, is derived from and contingent on a prior level or realm that is preconceptual or pre-ideational in nature. This is the fundamental substratum of knowledge, and gaining access to and describing this layer, is the proper objective of "pure science." However, we have become so severed from this layer that we have forgotten its existence. Thus our intellectual systems, uprooted from their proper basis, take on an autonomy and abstractedness that make intellectual life Kafkaesque. As in *The Trial*, these systems make a certain sense, although finally we know they are false and their claims unwarranted. Yet without proper theoretical grounding our minds work mechanistically, asking the wrong questions, forced to accept a logic that oppresses us. Until we recognize, as Joseph K. did not, that our dilemma is metaphysical, not just technical and logical, we are nearly certain to be arrested. Rather than constantly asking "how many," "what," and "how" questions, we must force ourselves to ask "why" and not be satisfied until we get to the source. The source and the *lebenswelt* are related; they may be equivalents.

From my present state of understanding, this layer is not "out there" in the world, although it becomes a transparent yet disfiguring veil over the world. It lies inside us, and to search for it, I am convinced, involves heightened awareness of our immediate experience. As vague and viscous as experience often is, I am persuaded that it constitutes our only link to this now lost preconceptual layer, which is the basis, as Merleau-Ponty explains, of all codified knowledge.

This search is not at all equivalent to what is called the introspectionist movement in American psychology, which was discredited during the years just before and after the turn of the century. For example, it is clear to me that internal experience has its external and observable behavioral manifestations, although it is also clear that to the untrained eye and given the current developmental stage of technology, internal experience often might as well be buried, unobservable, inside. At this point we are not ready for a study that transcends the internal-external and subject-object splits or apparent splits. What is appropriate now is a research project that aspires to the *lebenswelt* and is confined to an identifiable and limited area of experience. For several reasons I have chosen literary experience as this area to be explored in this certain way, a way that I know I have yet to explain.

Curriculum as Educational Experience

In the field of English curriculum there is a nascent subfield characterizable as the study of the psychosocial consequences of studying and teaching literature. (For those scholars of literature who read this, I hasten to add the assurance that such a study in no way challenges or diminishes the value of literature or art on its own terms. Any attempt to reduce a work of art to its psychic effects on the reader would be tantamount to a variant of the genetic fallacy.) Louise Rosenblatt has done interesting work in this area, which she discusses in the following way.[5] The experience of literature permits exploration of self and others in an intimate, individualistic way. It allows study of individuals in a variety of contexts: psychological, cultural, historical. Vicarious experience itself encourages a breadth and depth of view that so-called ordinary or life experience rarely includes. And so the argument goes.

Other writers have dwelt on these aspects of literary experience, and some have underscored what they see as the unique contribution that literature can make to self-study. Yet, aside from asserting such potentialities, no one has systematically studied this relation between literary experience and psychosocial and cognitive development. Similarly, apologists for the humanities in general have, in varying ways, argued that study in the humanities "humanizes" the student. Yet to my knowledge, no in-depth description and analysis of this phenomenon called "humanization" has ever been done.

I do not intend to berate my colleagues' work by such an appraisal. It is at this point that investigation becomes extremely complicated, and I become more and more convinced that this seemingly insurmountable complication has to do with our estrangement from the preconceptual and from our interior experience of literature. To surpass this point requires both a heuristic conceptualization of the dilemma and a research method that permits us to work fruitfully.

This psychosocial study of literary experience suggests aspects of a larger study: the educational experience of literature. The two are of course not the same; I see the former subsumed in the latter. It is this concept—educational experience, and in the present case, the educational experience of literature—that most broadly and simply summarizes the area to be researched. Understandably, the idea is too complex to study in this form, so for purposes of analysis its fragmentation is necessary. (The last steps of the explicative process must be synthetic, to return us to where we conceptually began, although granted on an ontologically different level. This matter of procedure or method must wait a little longer.) At this point let me lay out four of the structural elements that comprise this notion of the educational experience of literature. These categories are not discrete but overlapping; however, each one calls for a unique focus.

1. The first element is the literary text itself, in literary terms. There is little need to explain this first element. The text must be taken on its own terms and understood independently of its determinants and consequences. Of course textual analysis is the focus of literary criticism, as is the study of determinants, whether authorial or societal. Psychoanalytic and Marxian criticism have made interesting contributions to studies of the text.

2. The second element is the text's place in literary and intellectual history, and it is much related to the first. Rather than attending to the text exclusively, attention here is given to its place in the history of the novel and in the intellectual history of the particular culture in which the text appeared and, most broadly, to the relation between art and culture: between art and the sociopolitical forces in the midst of which it was created. This area is also a traditional focus of literary study.

3. The third element is the response or reply of the reader. With this element or step (I do not wish to be rigid about procedure, but I do suggest that these elements can be viewed as developmental steps that, as you will see, coincide with the method) we enter the relatively unknown territory of the educational significance of the text. This element involves the response of the student, a sort of phenomenology of reading. The subject records what occurs while he or she reads, what intellections and emotions surface and at what time and place in the text. Description of the immediate physical and interpersonal environment is appropriate.

I must emphasize that this stage involves description of the contents of consciousness, not analysis, which is appropriate at times for the fourth element and step.

4. The fourth element is the context of the reader, which I currently understand to have the following parts:

a. The first of these is biography. Perhaps an illustration will help explain what is involved here. A student, now in her mid-twenties, recalls an earlier time. "It was my nineteenth year, and I was commencing my second year of study at the university. I had grown up unusually dependent on my parents, as I was then beginning to understand, and now that I was away from them and their nearly complete domination of me, I was left alone and profoundly uncertain. Without their loud presence to direct me, I was aimless, and my consciousness, so long focused on them, fell back, as it were, on myself. Literally it was as if I had spent my life gazing at those in front of me, and now in their absence, my gaze slips down, first to the wall across from me, then to the floor, to my feet, then to my body and finally to my internal thoughts and feelings. These I had had to keep hidden much of the time, given the external demands of my home environment. Now, without external distraction, my attention slips inside.

"At this same time I found myself engrossed, not merely studying but absorbed, in the fiction of Sartre and Camus. Formal philosophy interested me in the abstract, but when I encountered it concretely in a class I was bored, my need somehow unmet. The physical and social sciences seemed distant; what drew me intellectually was literature, and literature of a certain sort."

I interrupt here to ask the questions that must be asked here: why is this student drawn to existentialist literature at that point in her life? Is there always a correspondence between biographic situation and intellectual interests? If so, what is the nature of the correspondence? Is it dialectical; does each inform the other; and if so, in what ways, to what ends? These questions suggest areas for study in this biographic aspect of educational experience.

b. The second component of the context of the subject involves the notion of intellectual gestalt. This is the ideational configuration which is one's image (although that word does not convey the complexity of it) of the so-called community of scholars, the intellectual world, and the history of thought. However dormant our awareness of it may be, we, at least many of us, carry with us a picture of the boundaries and content of the disciplines and how various groups of scholars tend to regard themselves and others. This takes concrete form of course when we chat with our colleagues in physics or medicine or in other fields of education. We gain partial and distant understanding of what they are about and what relation our work bears to theirs. These understandings and impressions are actually quite complex; they form a gestalt that not only helps to determine but also partially becomes one's theoretic point of view. Its role in research and scholarship is similar to domain assumptions; it shapes research conceptualization in ways we are usually unaware of. To understand its precise role in these matters is one aim of study in this realm. Other questions come to mind: To what extent is this gestalt formed by formal study and by informal conversations? To what extent is the individual's unique organization of this information a consequence of information received (environment) and to what extent is it a function of genetically determined cognitive structures?

c. The third aspect of the reader's context is his or her conceptual lens. Like the intellectual gestalt the lens is also a configuration of impressions and information, of what experience is. So it can be thought of as the individual's language system, which is used to describe and explain what he perceives, both in himself and in others. While one's language almost invariably lies in the public semantic domain, connotative meanings usually differ sufficiently to make necessary individualistic study. Where does this language, which in the Heideggerian sense forms a lens through which we view the

world, come from? Surely from our parents, but also from our
teachers, friends, and, especially for those of us who have spent
much if not most of our lives in educational institutions, it derives
from educational experience. For the student of literature, one's lens
or conceptualization of self and experience derives in varying degrees
from the novels and poems she reads. Often such a person borrows
the language characters use, and in her identification with them,
applies it to herself and her situation. So it is that the life-force that
comprises the *lebenswelt* comes to us and is thus transformed by our
cognitive lens. This translation of preconceptual into conceptual
works to determine the content and meaning of our experience, and
it usually does so unconsciously. What is the formative process of
this lens, and what relation exists between it and the books we read,
the teachers with whom we study—in short, to our educational
experience? With which literary characters do I empathize, which do
I scorn or ignore, and to what extent is this process of identification
explainable by an understanding of my lens? Which script or which
parts of it do I take as my own, and to what extent does it shape my
reception of information? How does it conform to apparently deeper
psychic structures? Such questions suggest the study of the cognitive
lens.

d. Finally, the fourth element I have identified thus far as part of
an understanding of the context of the subject is the psychological.
Questions like these present themselves: If a novel is assigned in a
course, then why or why not, in a psychological sense, am I able to
read it, to immerse myself in it? Or, in a "free" situation, why am I
reading this poem now? What drives, needs, impulses seek expression
now, why, and what symbolic, in this case literary, form do they
take? What is the nature of my identification with this character?
Why do I read Virginia Woolf urgently and cannot abide James
Joyce?

This concludes a brief mapping of aspects of one's educational
experience of literature.

Roots

This is not the time to explain the relation between this incipient
area of study and those fields from which it grew. I hope the
following short sentences will suffice. First, this developing point of
view has embedded within it a depth or dynamic psychological
model of human being; nonetheless, there are important divergences.
Such a model portrays the individual as partially unaware of what

occurs in him or her at present, and that heightened awareness of the present is at least partly contingent on dredging up one's remembered past, to gain what psychoanalysts typically call insight into the nature of one's early experience and its relation to present behavior. One presently edits information and that which is presented but not recognized enters and is stored in preconscious and unconscious layers. The technique of free association permits access to the contents of the unconscious. It is stretching the concept, but one can regard literary texts as a kind of Rorschach test onto which the self projects itself. You can begin to divine how certain psychoanalytic concepts and techniques may be employed in an analysis of educational experience.

Further, the present is created also by what is not the case, that is, the future. Some existentialists, Heidegger notably, have contributed to our understanding of the importance of what one imagines or wishes to be the case in the future in determining what is the case in the present. Of course both the past and the future in all their complexity converge on the present to mingle with one's immediate environment and with one's functioning self to create what Sartre has termed a situation. After Tillich and Marcel, one is continually being called, or lured, and a proper path lies ahead, which is partly explicable by understanding the components of the present, by reclaiming the movement and direction of the past, and by assessing the meaning of one's imagined, aspired to, and feared future. This is possible because objective knowledge is possible, as phenomenologists like Husserl and Merleau-Ponty explain. Part of what we must do is reestablish contact with the preconceptual and describe the essences of both substances and situations as they disclose themselves to us. Such an absolute perspective or transcendental ego (to be distinguished from the natural ego, which is the predictable *persona* or public self that the behaviorists attempt to explain) is not a given, but a developmental possibility indicated by transpersonal psychology and Zen Buddhist psychology. It is hoped that this method carries with it beneficial developmental consequences.

This approach, then, is grounded in existentialism, phenomenology, Jungian psychoanalysis, the radical psychiatry of Cooper and Laing, and aspects of literary and educational theory.[6] The ambition is that it surpass these roots and become an area in its own right, with its own boundaries, content, and research method.

The Present State of the Method

One responds to educational situations—whether they be artifacts like poems, or actors like teachers or peers, or combinations of these— in certain understandable ways. We can decipher the educational meaning of the present by studying this response, by (a) recalling and describing phenomenologically the past and then analyzing its psychic relation to the present; (b) describing one's imagined future and analyzing its relation to the present; and (c) placing this phenomenological-psychoanalytic understanding of one's educational present in its cultural and political context, which I must add is the least-developed step at this time.

So finally we can characterize the method. It is (a) regressive, because it involves description and analysis of one's intellectual biography or, if you prefer, educational past; (b) progressive, because it involves a description of one's imagined future; (c) analytic, because it calls for a psychoanalysis of one's phenomenologically described educational present, past, and future; and (d) synthetic, because it totalizes the fragments of educational experience (that is to say the response and context of the subject) and places this integrated understanding of individual experience into the larger political and cultural web, explaining the dialectical relation between the two.

Notes

1. Joseph Schwab, "The Practical: A Language for Curriculum," in *Curriculum and the Cultural Revolution*, ed. David E. Purpel and Maurice Belanger (Berkeley, Calif.: McCutchan Publishing, 1972).
2. For example, George Beauchamp, *Curriculum Theory* (Wilmette, Ill.: Kagg Press, 1968).
3. Alvin Gouldner, *The Coming Crisis of Western Sociology* (New York: Basic Books, 1972). Also, Isidor Chein, *The Science of Behavior and the Image of Man* (New York: Basic Books, 1972).
4. In the work of Maxine Greene, Dwayne Huebner, and James B. Macdonald. See chapter 23.
5. *Literature as Exploration* (New York: Appleton-Century, 1938).
6. The Jungian and Laingian aspects are more evident in earlier chapters. See chapters 21 and 22.

George Willis

In imaginative literature the voyage has long been a symbol of the development of insight. But like Odysseus's or the Ancient Mariner's, most fictional voyages end in a homecoming, in the recognition of an old world seen in new ways and in the discovery of tasks yet to be done. Perhaps, then, William Pinar has classified as reconceptualists those people in curriculum who have unfinished business in common with the voyagers of fiction.

If this is true, then I suppose my own intellectual voyage began at Hamilton College, where I had the opportunity to study philosophy and English language and literature within a liberal arts tradition, among men who had a healthy regard for the adequacy and consistency of ideas and who taught as if they had advised Joseph Schwab on the early drafts of his papers on curriculum. A year's study at Harvard provided a close-up look at currents in pedagogy and in educational policy-making. There followed three years of practice as a secondary school English teacher.

But dissatisfied with my grasp of educational theory, of the external demands made by institutions on individual students, and of the internal demands made by individuals on themselves to render experience meaningful, I returned for doctoral work to Johns Hopkins University, where, I hoped, I would have the opportunity to increase my knowledge of education generally and to synthesize ideas drawn from such areas as analytic philosophy, existentialism and phenomenology, esthetics, and linguistic and literary theory. I was not disappointed, for I studied education as an autonomous, intellectual discipline and curriculum as its multifaceted, integrating center.

As have others, I have discovered that the usual modes of conceiving curriculum are incomplete, and the work of reconceptualizing is complex and arduous. Nonetheless, the task is not without its intrinsic satisfactions; curriculum theorizing is something which both merits and demands, in the words of Melville's Ishmael, another voyager and kindred spirit, "all deep, earnest thinking."

George Willis
University of Rhode Island

25

Curriculum Theory and the Context of Curriculum

If the finally significant business of philosophy is the disclosure of the context of beliefs, then we cannot escape the conclusion that experience is the name for the last inclusive context.

John Dewey

Perhaps the most perplexing problem that has troubled curriculum theorists is how to account for quality in human experience, for experience is an extraordinarily difficult thing to pin down and to theorize about. Experience seems to have both reflective and nonreflective dimensions and to consist of an ever-fluctuating mixture of inseparable reactions sometimes roughly classified as cognitive, affective, and psychomotor. In short, *experience* seems to be a somewhat vague but all-embracing term that designates an amazingly wide and complex set of human phenomena comprising the most basic material of all education. Thus, we might expect to find curriculum theory attempting to develop some comprehensive conceptions about the nature of experience. Yet, I contend, curriculum theorists have been notably deficient in this regard.[1] In fact, one can philosophize about values or study the needs of society to determine what subjects in what combinations ought to be taught; one can study the structures of subject matter and the way learning takes place to determine how subjects can be learned efficiently; one can create techniques for evaluating the degree of this efficiency or for developing specific curricula; or one can attempt to formulate a metatheory of curriculum: one can do any or all of these things and still not necessarily come to grips with the underlying problem of how to conceptualize and deal with experience.[2] Surely one of the greatest weaknesses in the traditional approaches to curriculum has been that theorists of almost every stripe have failed to account fully for the complex nature of this problem, persistently confounding outward activity with inward experience. The practical result has often been that activities recommended to or prescribed for teachers have failed to meet the interior, experiential needs of students, puzzling and embarrassing teachers perceptive enough to recognize the cleavage and embittering those conscientious enough to regard themselves as unappreciated technicians. Three examples drawn from recent writings on curriculum may suffice to illustrate the problem.

Basic Principles of Curriculum and Instruction by Ralph Tyler is still the best known and most influential book on curriculum.[3] In it, however, Tyler gives scant attention to the problem of experience, and what attention he does give is marred pervasively by a subtle contradiction. He begins the section devoted to the learner with this statement: "Education is a process of changing the behavior patterns of people. This is using behavior to include thinking and feeling as well as overt action."[4] Although the behavior patterns of people undoubtedly include both thinking and feeling, as well as many other things, the operational definition of education that Tyler falls into throughout the book is entirely behavioristic; that is, it identifies behavior with overt action only. In other words, Tyler publicly acknowledges all such things as curriculum, instruction, and learning to include wide and expansive ranges of sometimes nebulously identified behaviors, whereas operationally and covertly he assumes them to be identical with discretely discernible and quantifiable actions.

His approach first assumes that predetermined educational purposes are desirable, and he next claims that identifying the activities of contemporary life is the best way to determine educational objectives. While acknowledging that identifying adult activities indicates neither that they are desirable, nor that they will be the activities of the future, nor that they necessarily account for children's needs and interests, Tyler points out that these difficulties can most satisfactorily be resolved by "screening" them through subject specialists, philosophers, and psychologists. It is difficult to disagree with a point as circumspect as this; if the experts cannot agree on what the needs are, who can? But Tyler states further:

> It is well to keep . . . two meanings of the term "needs" distinct so that they will not be confused in our discussion. The first use of the term represents a gap

between some conception of a desirable norm, that is, some standard of philosophic value and the actual status. Need in this sense is the gap between what is and what should be. The other use of the term by some psychologists represents tensions in the organism which must be brought into equilibrium for a normal healthy condition of the organism to be maintained.[5]

Obviously, not only can these two kinds of needs be confused, but also the philosophers and psychologists can actually be in outright disagreement about what kind of need deserves what kind of practical attention and when. (Pity, then, the poor curriculum specialists and teachers.) So appeal to the experts is no solution in itself, unless the experts are willing to submit their potential differences to arbitration.

Tyler, however, skirts this problem. Since the former needs are easily operationalized and expressed in behavioristic terms, a part of the curriculum can be designed to meet each of them. In other words, if a child needs to know how to read, he can be taught to do so by having him replicate (although perhaps in successive stages, each appropriate to his own stage of development) the reading activities of a skillful adult. In fact, the bulk of Tyler's book is an explication of how to do just this sort of thing: fractionalize, replicate, and evaluate outward activity. Yet, having mentioned the latter kinds of needs, those far more closely connected with the quality of the inward experiences of people engaged in outward operations, he simply drops all recognition of them. This, in itself, may not be necessarily bad, particularly if Tyler leaves his readers with the idea that a delicate balance must be struck between the two kinds of needs throughout all portions of the curriculum; however, he strongly implies (disastrously, I think, and with almost no insight into the nature of thinking, feeling, or psychic processes in general) that the latter needs, the "tensions in the organism which must be brought into equilibrium," are preponderantly physical and can thus be treated in the same way as the former: by designing a discrete portion of the curriculum to satisfy each. He further suggests that this is just what the curriculum builder should do, although at the same time taking care to see that the school does not attempt what can better be accomplished informally or by other social agencies.

Tyler is not so foolish as to deny that a good deal of overlap exists between various needs and various portions of the curriculum, but in his operationalized view of education all needs are ultimately met through overt activity.[6] Consequently, the kind of curriculum ordinarily developed from his rationale consists of a series of compartmentalized packages (usually called "subjects," although these may extend to the extracurriculum and then be called simply "activities"), each designed to meet a different need or cluster of needs, and each consisting of a series of suggested or required activities (usually called "learning experiences") that may or may not provide some measure of continuity—perhaps even emotional continuity—within or between various packages. The problem of how to account for the quality of the experiences of the students undertaking these activities is almost always left to the ingenuity of whichever teachers are perceptive enough to recognize the problem.

Another influential work on curriculum is *Curriculum Development: Theory and Practice* by Hilda Taba.[7] She treats the problem in much the same way as Tyler, with the exception that she is much more sensitive to its inherent difficulties and therefore much more explicit about its inherent limitations in dealing with the ordinary approaches to curriculum, including her own. One quotation from Taba ought to be sufficient to illustrate her position. In discussing the same two types of needs identified by Tyler, she writes:

the concept of social needs has moved closer to psychological meaning, and the psychological needs are interpreted in the light of their social origin. It seems also that the school's responsibility to serve student needs is neither as comprehensive as was assumed in the first flush of "discovering" the psychological needs or as limited as was assumed later.

It is clear, for example, that needs representing psychological requirements are less focal to the curriculum of the public school than are the needs representing social demands and the requirements of educational objectives. Many psychological needs lie outside the power of educational approach either within or outside the school. Yet, these psychological needs must be understood and taken into account in curriculum building, because they are a part of the constellation of conditions under which learning takes place. While schools may not be in a position to eliminate deep-seated psychological insecurity, curricula must be adjusted to the demands of security needs, and the schools need to provide learning conditions which at least do not create additional insecurities. In this sense, then, all needs are of concern to the educator, but only some of these can be provided for explicitly through the curriculum. Others may be of greater concern to the psychologist and the mental hygienist.[8]

Here Taba lays bare a number of assumptions, among them that psychological needs run throughout all portions of the curriculum and cannot be compartmentalized, and that although schools need to account for and be as consistent as possible with these needs, they are secondary to the normative instructional demands that are imposed largely by the nature of the outside society and take the form of "learning." Since learning, in Taba's view, is closely identified with overt activity, and since psychological needs and mental hygiene are closely linked with the quality of experience, her statement can be reformulated as follows: Education in general and curriculum theory in particular are primarily normative enterprises concerned first with learning overt activities imposed by contacts with the outside society and only second with the nonnormative experiential activity of assigning meaning to these contacts. Not the other way around.

Finally, in a recent issue of *Review of Educational Research* devoted to curriculum, the same contradiction that plagues Tyler surfaces again in the chapter "Forces Influencing Curriculum" by John D. McNeil.[9] Except for two passing references by John Goodlad to the "existential"[10] nature of curriculum in the closing summary of the *Review*, the two paragraphs by McNeil under the heading "The Learner as a Data Source" are the only concessions the *Review* makes to the possibility that people have psychological and experiential as well as instructional needs. Although McNeil accepts the desirability of predetermined objectives, he ponders how these are reconcilable with students' interests and concerns, and states that "taking account of learner characteristics to plan and organize instruction more effectively toward an imposed objective cannot be called self-determining."[11] Here he recognizes the possibility that imposed activities may decrease the quality of a student's experience, yet later, in his "Concluding Comment," he returns to this familiar refrain: "Curriculum is becoming more rational because researchers and practitioners are beginning to realize that the desired changes in the learner are the true 'ends' and that methods and instructional sequences used to produce those changes are the 'means,' not to be prized but appraised."[12] Clearly, what was first an "imposed objective" has ten pages later become "desired changes," and, just as clearly, McNeil's shift from a pejorative to a praiseful label to describe the same phenomenon is a result of the shift from a student's to a practitioner's point of view; it all depends on who is doing the imposing and who is doing the desiring. Somewhat perplexed by his brief foray into the psyche of the learner, McNeil concludes: "There is wide interpretation and confusion of what is meant by formulating objectives in the light of data from learners."[13] But more to the point, the question still remains whether curriculum can be at all rational when education is simultaneously acknowledged to include the broad ranges of experience, such as thinking and feeling, and operationalized to include overt activities only.

Happily, however, a growing body of recent curriculum literature is beginning to move, however tentatively, toward the problem of accounting for quality in experience. Articles by Herbert Kliebard, Robert M. W. Travers, and Elliot Eisner[14] have raised serious questions about the desirability of Tyleresque instructional objectives, not because such objectives ignore the problem of experience, but primarily because they do not meet instructional needs nearly so well as has commonly been supposed. Nonetheless, these attacks have implicitly raised doubts about how well these objectives can be consistent with psychological needs. Also, a persistent stream of publications from the Association for Supervision and Curriculum Development[15] during the 1960s has continued to raise curriculum issues about the inward experience of students, dealing with these issues in terms of mental health, psychological processes, existential situations, perceptions, and the formulation of meanings. Further, most instrumental in outlining the topography of the problem have been several papers by Dwayne Huebner, who has identified the technological bias inherent in most curriculum formulations, emphasizing that curriculum is an "environment producing" discipline and pointing out the ethical and esthetic dimensions of educational environments.[16] Finally, in the same vein are two papers by John S. Mann, further contributing to the idea of curriculum as environment and to its esthetic dimensions.[17]

The point here, however, is not to attempt to discredit completely the long-accepted notion that curriculum theory is a primarily normative discipline concerned with facilitating learning measured in overt activity, for much of what humans do and learn is overt. Nor is the point falsely to dichotomize curriculum thinkers into two irreconcilable camps. The point is that curriculum theory can quite plausibly be conceived as a primarily nonnormative discipline concerned with creating educational environments that enhance the quality of experience, and, further, this latter conception of curriculum uncovers problems that the former obscures, most notably the inevitable discrepancies between the few, impoverished, operationalized goals called "learning" and the many, rich, complex human reactions to the wider environment on which educational operations ultimately impinge.[18] I am arguing that (1) since at least the early 1950s the preponderant emphasis in curriculum thought has been on a normative conception of curriculum concerned with learning and activity, one explicated by Tyler and accepted by Taba and McNeil among many others; (2) some tendencies in the recent literature may indicate a shift toward a nonnormative conception of curriculum concerned with environment and experience; (3) this potential shift will eventually represent a salubrious return from a long-standing, generally unrecognized, and thus dangerous imbalance in curriculum thinking; and (4) since the basic material of curriculum phenomena exists in the inward experience of students reacting to their educational environments, curriculum theory needs ultimately to account for the nature of experience.

This latter conception of curriculum, however, clearly puts a heavy burden on the theorizer and somewhat restricts the way the term "theory" can be used, for the necessity of accounting for the nature of experience opens curriculum to the implications of an immense and diverse body of literature. Concern for the quality of interior experience means grappling with all manner of speculative, analytic, and empirical studies dealing with the problem, whether they be called esthetic, ethical, existential, phenomenological, psychoanalytic, or anything else. However, a fundamental concern in dealing qualitatively with experience is how students develop meanings from their educational environments, and some of the recent curriculum literature has begun to touch on this general problem.[19] Here, I think, some insights worked out in another discipline, linguistics, can be useful, for although they apply explicitly to how meanings are formed from verbal communications, they are also applicable beyond the linguistic to the general environment. They can therefore be useful both in explaining how this wider context operates in the forming of purely linguistic, or logical, meanings and in analyzing how students react to the environment in forming wide ranges of semiverbal and nonverbal, or psychological, meanings. Both these closely related areas—crucially connected with the quality of an individual's experience—have been virtually nonexistent in the traditional curriculum literature.

In a paper "Linguistics and Poetics," Roman Jakobson has identified and explicated what he calls "the six factors involved in verbal communication."[20] These factors (the addresser and the addressee; the contact, code, context, and message) form a set of linguistic coordinates within which any communication can be analyzed and which many linguists regard, in effect, as fundamental metatheoretical structure in verbal communication. A working knowledge of this set of coordinates may help the curriculum theorist deal more adequately than he has with the problem of experience, primarily because the coordinates are useful in explaining the ground for the distinction between the two conceptions of curriculum theory outlined previously in this paper.[21] If Jakobson is correct in his implicit contention that all meanings of both verbal and environmental messages are ambiguous to a greater or lesser degree (and I am thoroughly convinced he is), then a fully developed theory of curriculum must in some way account for the environmental context, including the inward reactions of students. Seen in these terms, curriculum is opened to the nonnormative conception concerned with the quality of experience, and only a small portion of what a student really learns can be considered in the Tyleresque terms of "learning." Much of the following discussion will amplify these points.

One final but integral point ought to be kept in mind in considering Jakobson's set of coordinates. A strong (although imprecise) analogy exists between the relation of poetics to linguistics and the relation of curriculum as environment to curriculum as learning. As Jakobson points out, poetics introduces concern for the "emotive elements of speech" into linguistics and thus makes theorizing much more messy—and the "science" of linguistics much less scientific—than would otherwise be the case. He continues:

> Insistence on keeping poetics apart from linguistics is warranted only when the field of linguistics appears to be illictly restricted, for example, when the sentence is viewed by some linguists as the highest analyzable construction or when the scope of linguistics is confined to grammar alone or uniquely to nonsemantic questions of external form or to the inventory of denotative devices with no reference to free variations.[22]

Similarly, the conception of curriculum as environment and experience is in some ways like introducing concern for the emotive elements of learning—experience—into the pseudoscientific conception of curriculum, which acknowledges S-R connections and overt activities only. Keeping messy human experience out of scientific theorizing is as important in curriculum as it is in linguistics, yet the restriction of the field appears equally illicit; few curriculum thinkers would appear ready to deny importance to the psychological needs of students or to their formulations of meaning.

Jakobson outlines his set of coordinates as follows:

> The ADDRESSER sends a MESSAGE to the ADDRESSEE. To be operative the message requires a CONTEXT referred to . . . , seizable by the addressee, and either verbal or capable of being verbalized; a CODE fully, or at least partially, common to the addresser and addressee (or in other words, to the encoder and decoder of the message) and, finally, a CONTACT, a physical channel and psychological connection between the addresser and the addressee, enabling both of them to enter and stay in communication. All these factors inalienably involved in verbal communication may be schematized as follows:

```
                        CONTEXT
ADDRESSER_ _ _ _ _ _ _ _ _MESSAGE_ _ _ _ _ _ _ _ _ ADDRESSEE
                        CONTACT
                        CODE
```

Each of these six factors determines a different function of language. Although we distinguish six basic aspects of language, we could, however, hardly find verbal messages that would fulfill only one function. The diversity lies not in a monopoly of some one of these several functions but in a different hierarchical order of functions.[23]

In other words, although any one of these six factors may predominate in a single verbal message, the other five are always present. As Jakobson points out:

The verbal structure of a message depends primarily on the predominant function. But even though a set . . . toward the referent, an orientation toward the CONTEXT—briefly the so-called . . . "denotative," "cognitive" function—is the leading task of numerous messages, the accessory participation of the other functions in such messages must be taken into account by the observant linguist.[24]

Even messages meant to carry information only and mercilessly purged of logical ambiguities—as in philosophic and symbolic languages—carry with them emotional, ambiguous, noncognitive overtones and, hence, psychological meanings.

According to Jakobson, both the addresser (the "emotive" function) and the addressee (the "conative" function) are involved both cognitively and emotively in verbal communication, the addresser as encoder and sender, the addressee as receiver and decoder. As he observes, regardless of the intentions of an addresser and no matter how much information his language conveys, there is always more information about his intentions and attitudes conveyed by how he uses language, and the addressee is continually engaged in a process of decoding and assimilating both these primary and secondary funds of information, as well as determining how he should act on them. In the ordinary "learning experience" encouraged by the traditional curriculum theory, the secondary fund of information, the emotive, is either unnoticed or unacknowledged, while the student is supposed to act on the primary fund, the cognitive, only. Further, the meanings—both cognitive and emotive—of the wider environment are generally ignored.[25]

Jakobson's explanations of both contact (the "phatic" function) and the code (the "metalingual" function) are reasonably straightforward. The contact is simply what physically passes between addresser and addressee, opening "a physical channel and psychological connection" for communication; it represents the only function of language shared by subhuman animals with human beings and is the first verbal function acquired by human infants. In verbal communication the contact is spoken or written words; contacts from the wider environment can include such things as gestures, signals, and spatial arrangements. The code is simply the common fund of signs and their cognitive, linguistic meanings shared by addresser and addressee, and the metalingual function of verbal communication is the checking up on whether both addresser and addressee are using the same code. "What do you mean?" is more often than not a metalingual question. Again, in terms of the ordinary "learning experience" encouraged by the traditional curriculum theory, the logical, cognitive meanings of verbal classroom languages are given high priorities, some additional contacts (such as a nod of a head or a threatening glance) may be considered and coded, but the vast majority of signals from the wider environment are left uncontrolled and are meant at best to be neutral. While it is extremely unlikely and probably undesirable that all portions of educational environments be parts of widely understood codes, a school built without windows, for instance, probably implies—for better or for worse—an attempt to isolate its interior from its exterior environment, and this kind of meaning, whether or not overtly understood, inevitably affects the experience of students.

The remaining two factors and their corresponding functions have somewhat less obvious and somewhat more important implications for curriculum theory. The context (the "referential" function) is particularly difficult, for it bears a striking, although superficial, resemblance in the code. In point of fact, it provides a kind of metacontext not only for the message but for the code itself. Unhappily, Jakobson is not at all clear in describing the context; in short, however, it appears to be what the message refers to in order to take on meaning objective enough to be comprehensible to the addressee. For instance, the highly personal and idiosyncratic musings, meanderings, and meanings within the addresser's mind will remain forever protean and private unless they can be so expressed as to refer to something public enough to make them understandable to the addressee. This is what Jakobson means when he identifies the referential function as "denotative" and "cognitive" and claims it must be capable of being verbalized. Thus, when applied to personal and idiosyncratic meanings, "What do you mean?" becomes a referential as well as a metalingual question. Yet, one other important point remains to be considered. The only way in which these points of reference, the context, can be public and objective enough for both addresser and addressee to assign similar cognitive meanings to them is for both to have had similar experiences of them. Fortunately, this is ordinarily just what happens, and communication is thus rendered possible. However, as similar as the ranges of experience may become, they can never become identical, and, therefore, communication, no matter how carefully refined, forever remains imperfect. Further, this kind of imperfection applies not only to the communication of meanings in the message but also to the communication of meanings in the metalingual sorting of the code. Both kinds of meaning can be interpreted only in the wider context of what they refer to, and what they refer to is ultimately found only in the imperfectly similar ranges of experience held by both addresser and addressee. Thus, what can be called a "theory of the context"[26] is necessary for explaining the processes of communication. Or, in terms closer to curriculum theory, this is no doubt very similar to what John Dewey meant in maintaining that education can be intelligently conducted only in light of a philosophy of experience.

This understanding of the context as experience is important because logical, linguistic meanings can be publicly assigned only in their experiential context; they do not exist by themselves. Further, an understanding of how this context operates is necessary for explaining the basis on which they are assigned. These ideas have two important implications for curriculum theory. First, the context for the intended linguistic meanings usually emphasized in the ordinary "learning experience" is the total educational environment in which the "experience" takes place; a curriculum theory which ignores the influence of this wide environment (beyond the few, atomistic, behavioristic "inputs" commonly considered as influencing "learning") on meaning will remain incomplete. Second, the context for the intended or unintended meanings—both logical and psychological—of the total educational environment is the past experiential background of the individual as he interacts with the raw materials of his immediate experience and assigns meanings to them. This process, the intelligent (although not necessarily conscious) interaction between past and present experience, is both a portion of the educational environment and the context for the educational environment. A fully developed curriculum theory must account for this last, inclusive context.

The final factor or coordinate that Jakobson identifies is the message (the "poetic" function). The important point here is that even the logical, cognitive meaning of any communication is necessarily ambiguous, not only because it depends on the imperfectly similar ranges of experience operating in the context, but also because the poetic function of the message cannot be separated from meaning. Jakobson says:

> The set ... toward the MESSAGE as such, focus on the message for its own sake, is the POETIC function of language. This function cannot be productively studied out of touch with the general problems of language, and, on the other hand, the scrutiny of language requires a thorough consideration of its poetic function. Any attempt to reduce the sphere of poetic function to poetry or to confine poetry to poetic function would be a delusive oversimplification. Poetic function is not the sole function of verbal art but only its dominant, determining function, whereas in all other verbal activities it acts as a subsidiary, accessory constituent. . . . Hence, when dealing with poetic function, linguistics cannot limit itself to the field of poetry.[27]

And later: "Ambiguity is an intrinsic, inalienable character of any self-focused message, briefly a corollary feature of poetry."[28]

In short, what Jakobson is arguing in these two brief passages and at greater length in the entire paper is that the emotive elements of communication (which I have variously called "psychological," "personal," and "idiosyncratic" meaning) found primarily in the message form the groundwork for and cannot be separated from the cognitive elements (identified with "cognitive," "linguistic," "verbal," and "logical" meaning). In this sense, psychological meaning is both psychologically and logically prior to logical meaning. Furthermore, a curriculum theory that purports to be anything more than a very narrow applied technology must expand beyond the restrictive operational confines of behavioristic "learning" to concern for the total educational environments in which both learning and the formulation of meanings occur, and finally to the portion of the environments—the highly personal experiential ranges of students—that forms the widest context for all things educational. In other words, Jakobson's paper suggests (and I am arguing) that as long as curriculum theory is concerned with normative or operationalized education only, it can be potentially either technology or metatheory, but, paradoxically, it cannot be adequate theory for the actual conduct of education.

Recognizing a similar kind of problem in linguistics, Jakobson is able to conclude:

> The poetical resources concealed in the morphological and syntactical structure of language, briefly the poetry of grammar, and its literary product, the grammar

of poetry, have been seldom known to critics and mostly disregarded by linguists but skillfully mastered by creative writers. . . . In other words, poeticalness is not a supplementation of discourse with rhetorical adornment but a total reevaluation of the discourse and of all its components whatsoever.[29]

It would be a pity if curriculum theory continued to brush aside the "poetical resources" of curriculum skillfully mastered by creative teachers simply because these phenomena have seldom been known to theorists such as Tyler and McNeil and mostly disregarded by others such as Taba. Here consideration of the coordinates identified by Jakobson can be helpful for curriculum thinkers, resulting, perhaps, in a better understanding of how a student's formulations of meanings affect the quality of his experience.

The implications in Jakobson's explanation of the message are perhaps most important in providing a damaging point against what I have been calling the "behavioristic," or "Tyleresque," or "operationalized" education and have been strongly opposing as the sole basis for curriculum theorizing. Since all messages are necessarily ambiguous in some degree and since, therefore, all addressers are necessarily involved in an emotive function, all addressees are necessarily involved in a conative function as they assign both cognitive and psychological meanings to the communications they receive. In the case of education, students, as long as they are alive, can scarcely help assigning meanings not only to the verbal communications they receive as overt portions of a "learning experience," but also to all portions of the total environment, whether all portions are meant to be communications or not. In behavioristic education, poetic, emotive, and conative functions are totally ignored.[30] The result is that the educational environment the student exists in is in fact either meaningless, or construed by the student to be meaningless, or construed by the student to mean something it does not, or construed by the student to mean that he should not assign meaning to it, or construed by the student that regardless of its state of meaning he is meant only to be controlled by it. So behavioristic education detracts from the quality of experience by becoming a gigantic source of irrationality in itself, very much like a perverse, purposeless theatre of the absurd in which activities happen without any meanings whatsoever, thus deadening the student's experiential, conative function he would otherwise and elsewhere be freely exercising as a natural part of human living.

When curriculum theory is conceived as a primarily normative discipline concerned with **facilitating** learning measured in overt activity, it almost invariably becomes too much aligned with behavioristic education, which leads to very practical problems. Only a very small portion of any educational environment is actually ever controlled; the rest happens largely by chance. Yet in behavioristic education, where control is supposed to be most precise, the greatest portions of the environment are left to chance. Seldom in practice are many of the overt portions of the environment even considered, and never, according to this view, can any overt portion be considered as modified by interaction with the student's inward, experiential context. Portions of the environment may be controlled strategically enough so that some of the student's activities become generally predictable, but these activities are not his inward experience: personal thoughts, feelings, and meanings. In this view of education, both educational activities themselves and the student's reactions to them are the tops of icebergs: only what is visible is considered, while the great mass of things beneath the surface is unknown or ignored. Jakobson's paper suggests that those deep, inward experiential things are at least as important as is what is overt, and the curriculum theorist concerned with how real education is actually conducted cannot ignore the poeticalness of the experiential context in which all education takes place.

When curriculum theory is conceived as a primarily nonnormative discipline concerned with creating educational environments that enhance the quality of experience, the narrow limits of behavioristic education are left behind. Then much of the environment is controlled, but only to the extent that it is rendered potentially meaningful to the student; in other words, he is freed to assign meanings to it consistent with his inward experiential background, to exercise his conative function as fully as the degree of potential meaningfulness makes possible, and thus to enhance the quality of his own experience by more fully interacting with a potentially more meaningful world. In this conception, curriculum theory is normative only to the extent that comparatively much less of the environment is considered as happening by chance, and, consequently, comparatively more becomes potentially meaningful communication. The ultimate task for the educator is to find ways for the total environment to communicate with the inner experiential context brought to it by each student; yet, happily, each context is, in the final analysis, idiosyncratic, private, and unique. Fortunately, however, people being people, we are all more alike than we are different, and, thus, even this kind of imperfect communication becomes possible.

Notes

1. Joseph J. Schwab comes to a somewhat similar conclusion in a recent article, "The Practical: A Language for Curriculum," in *Curriculum and the Cultural Revolution*, ed. David Purpel and Maurice Belanger (Berkeley, Calif.: McCutchan, 1972).
2. An interesting history of the twentieth-century development of curriculum theory can be written in terms of how curriculum thinkers attempted or did not attempt to conceptualize educational experience. For instance, John Dewey clearly identified the difficulties of the problem but did not resolve it, while Franklin Bobbitt wrestled with the problem for thirty years without ever clearly identifying the difficulties.
3. Ralph Tyler, *Basic Principles of Curriculum and Instruction* (Chicago: University of Chicago Press, 1950).
4. Ibid., pp. 5-6.
5. Ibid., pp. 7-8.
6. Interestingly, one of the primary "tensions" Tyler identifies is sexual. Yet what public high school, operating under the Tyler rationale, has ever presumed to meet this need by designing a course which provided overt sexual activity?
7. Hilda Taba, *Curriculum Development: Theory and Practice* (New York: Harcourt Brace & World, 1962).
8. Ibid., p. 287.
9. John D. McNeil, "Forces Influencing Curriculum," *Review of Educational Research* 39, no. 3 (1969).
10. John Goodlad, "Curriculum: State of the Field," *Review of Educational Research* 39, no. 3 (1969), pp. 369, 374.
11. McNeil, "Forces Influencing Curriculum," p. 302.
12. Ibid., p. 312.
13. Ibid., p. 313.
14. Herbert M. Kliebard, "Curricular Objectives and Evaluation: A Reassessment," *The High School Journal* 51, no. 6 (1968); Robert H. W. Travers, "Towards Taking the Fun Out of Building a Theory of Instruction," *Teachers College Record* 68 (October 1966); Elliott Eisner, "Educational Objectives: Help or Hindrance?" *The School Review* 75, no. 3 (1967).
15. Arthur W. Combs, ed., *Perceiving, Behaving, Becoming* (Washington, D.C.: ASCD, 1962); Alexander Frazier, ed., *New Insights and the Curriculum* (Washington, D.C.: ASCD, 1963); A. Harry Passow, ed., *Nurturing Individual Potential* (Washington, D.C.: ASCD, 1964); Walter B. Waetjen and Robert R. Leeper, eds., *Learning and Mental Health in the School* (Washington, D.C.: ASCD, 1966); Robert R. Leeper, ed., *Humanizing Education: The Person in the Process* (Washington, D.C.: ASCD, 1967).
16. See chapters 13, 14, 15, 16.
17. John S. Mann, "Functions of Curriculum Research," *Educational Leadership* (October 1966); also chapter 10.
18. Carl R. Rogers, in *Freedom to Learn* (Columbus, Ohio: Charles E. Merrill, 1969), indicates that enhancing experience may be the best general way not only to promote learning but also to unleash the whole range of behaviors

loosely termed *creativity*. The two conceptions of curriculum, then, may not be in as sharp opposition as might be supposed. Nonetheless, the normative conception obscures this idea as well.

19. See especially chapter 13 and Eugene T. Gendlin, "The Discovery of Felt Meaning," in *Language and Meaning*.

20. Roman Jakobson, "Linguistics and Poetics," in *Style in Language*, ed. T. A. Sebeok (Cambridge, Mass.: MIT Press, 1960). The Jakobson paper is somewhat technical, and in this essay I do not attempt either to do justice to its finer points and complexities or to treat it critically.

21. Another but peripheral reason is that what I have called the traditional curriculum theory and identified closely with the Tyler rationale has taken almost no cognizance of the analysis of linguistic structures, even in those areas—particularly academic subjects—where both the curricula themselves and the ensuing learning are preponderantly linguistic. Presumably this lack can be explained on the grounds that in the actual practice of building curricula linguistic knowledge is unimportant as long as subject matter specialists screen content to remove outright inconsistencies and to reconcile, usually intuitively, the language of the curricula with the natures of the subjects, and psychologists fractionalize content according to the best information derivable from learning theories. A better explanation, however, is that regardless of the efficacy of any practice, to be truly rigorous in theory, Tyler's panel of experts must include a linguist, even when the operationalized view of curriculum leads only to behavioristic outcomes that in no way take account of communication or meaning. In other words, the linguistic arrangement of a subject matter affects how it is learned. Even in these terms, then, Jakobson's set of coordinates should be helpful in filling another long-standing and generally unrecognized deficiency in curriculum thinking.

22. Ibid., p. 352.

23. Ibid., p. 353.

24. Ibid.

25. Some studies have taken carefully circumscribed portions of educational environments and attempted to assess their effects, usually on learning. Many studies of teacher personality are of this type.

26. I would like to thank Dr. Richard A. Macksey for first pointing out the problem to me in these terms.

27. Jakobson, "Linguistics and Poetics," p. 356.

28. Ibid., pp. 370-71.

29. Ibid., pp. 357, 377.

30. *Ignored* may be a somewhat misleading term, since these functions may be regarded simply as incorporated into a pattern of stimuli intended only to manipulate behavior. In this case, however, all stimuli have the phatic function only, and all attempts to explain behavior are given over to efforts to control it.

Francine Shuchat Shaw

I am very young in the fields of Humanities Education and the creative arts, and I am only on the brink of understanding my place here and the work I must do. For some time I have been writing educational and literary criticism, teaching, and making documentary films, trying to discover the sensibility and principles that characterize my life, and trying to make congruent the threads of my interdisciplinary studies. "Congruence" is one of those critical principles; it is simply organic harmony between one's authentic Self and one's lifework.

Francine Shuchat Shaw

Department of Film Making
Rochester Institute of Technology

26

Congruence

An authentic relationship between the self and a creative medium means feeling consanguinity with its language, having a direct involvement with the creative process and a commitment to the context and meanings it expresses. Inner languages and meanings externalize and reflect human expression through various media systems; one's center subconsciously reaches for and uses the medium with which it finds harmony and correspondence. This medium stimulates and releases what is the Self, and it makes available meanings, symbols, and modes for the expression of one's own center and commitments. Such authenticity has no equivalent; it is the development and expression of one's Self through direct, personal experience and creation of one's language and meanings over time.

So it is that the contemporary, serious student of the humanities may regard his work. The fabric of his work as a scholar and creator is threaded with his innermost being and the whole of his life-style. The substance of his work does not seem to preexist this individual; he meets the medium as if it were not an a priori reality. In touch with his center and sensitive to its relationship with his subject's language and meanings, he *becomes* the subject, has an authentic relationship with it. If he fails to attend to his work, he neglects and loses a sense of himself. The substance is relative to the consciousness and center of this individual, and all things emanate from the authenticity of his relationship with his medium. The student begins to move outward from subjective awareness toward conceptual sense, a process he values more as a means of insight into his own situation and potency than as equipment for professional accomplishment. Academic analysis labels this as emotional and intellectual growth; with an honest, pervasive absorption in the subject and skill in creatively amplifying it, this humanities student intuitively finds correspondence with his medium. He is in complete congruence with it.

Similarly, such congruence holds understandable meaning for the young and creative educator in the humanities. We have demanded it for ourselves and, theoretically, both the humanities and education demand it. Having grown up surrounded by incongruences—an educational system caught between the drifts of long-practiced tradition and the new school reform movement of the 1960s, a social system comprised of oppressed "minority" stratifications who learned and adopted their oppressors' behaviors to win humanistic causes, and a wartime economic-political system that precipitated deprivation for comfort and fighting for peace—we are particularly sensitive to the need for making authentic relationships into a pervasive moral principle of congruence. We have long lived with dialectical tension within all of our institutions and principles, and we have long sought to resolve separation and conflict between pairs such as thought and action, theory and practice, content and pedagogy, subject and methodology. If our lives are well-woven, well-balanced tapestries, we can leave no incongruent juxtaposition unattended; congruence means that threads of the Self weave a conceptual bond with and continuity between our theories and experiences, work and creative practices, our relation to students and the atmosphere we provide for them.

Our own creative expression derives from an authentic relationship with our medium; it is only this solidity that can translate into an appropriate manner of sharing and a meaningful methodology for teaching. Such strict continuity means adherence to our philosophical "highest good"; we must be in the process of growth we help our students to experience, be what we help others to become; we must *be* what we do, *live* what we do. Adhering to this highest good means allowing our own authentic relationship with our work to mature. This maturation depends entirely on continued consanguinity with the language of our medium, direct involvement with the creative process and the commitment to the subject.

Incongruently, such indulgence is often drastically undercut and distracted for us as young artists working within an educational system still filled with dialectical tension. This tension necessitates a transference of energy from personal growth through creating to preoccupations with the teaching of our medium; this transference is often too great to permit personal involvement or meaningful teaching and learning in relation to students. Try as we will to find a balance between maintaining our own authentic relationships and educating others toward establishing their own, we are often dealt a situation of incongruences that makes the fulfillment of our highest good a network of risk-taking experiences. Neglecting our own growth and losing a sense of ourselves, we may no longer belong in the educational system; the congruence between our Self and our work deteriorating, our frustrations make both self-growth and the education of others a near impossibility.

The common denominator for all humanities teachers is a theoretical relationship with their own medium, their genuine bond with its language, their direct involvement with the creative process and commitment to its meanings. We have the right to assume that every aspect of this relationship is a matter of degree, its nature a matter of capabilities and priorities. Beginning with the ultimate degree of authenticity, each progressive stage of incongruence, resulting from neglect of our highest-good principle, is a correlative of increasing imbalance of energies; dissension exists between energies directed toward the authentic relationship and energies transferred to preoccupations with teaching. If the individual who *is* what he helps others to become or finds a balance between direct involvement and teaching is the most vital of teachers, less congruent states of affairs represent risks to authenticity for both teacher and students. These risks to us are actual states of existence for others, and they might be identified as personified analogues found elsewhere in the teaching profession.

Our first risk is to become like the teacher whose less than authentic relation to a field in the humanities has always been one of interpreter-critic, rather than one of creator. The professional options for individuals excited by the humanities, but not creators of them, are admittedly narrow. It is not unusual for such persons to assume roles in teaching, criticism, and research. Certainly some authentic identity with and degree of commitment to the medium exists for these individuals, but direct involvement with the creative process is missing; this creative participation with the medium one teaches is certainly the key to one's authenticity. Artistry is the variable factor, and only if it exists is authenticity affirmed. In this first analogue of risk, the teacher of poetry reads, but he is not a

448   *Part Four: Postcritical Reconceptualists*

poet; the teacher of film views, but he is not a film maker; the teacher of curriculum observes, but he is not a theorist; the teacher of humanism believes, but he has not been through the struggle. This is not to deny the value of emotional and intellectual growth for an individual who has cognitively studied rather than creatively practiced within a field, but the situation takes its toll as an incongruence in contexts of the profession of teaching and teacher-student relationships. This sort of teacher is a degree removed from authenticity in the context of the highest-good principle; he is a generation away from the medium to begin with and two generations from it as he enters the profession of teaching.

This analogue translates easily for the creative educator who initially adheres to the highest-good principle, who originally *is* what he helps others to become. Of necessity, a certain amount of authentic energy must be diverted to the business of teaching, to the finding of methodologies. This action itself may disturb the artist's congruence with his medium. Further, his search for sustained congruence may forcibly be between the medium and the teaching methodology and no longer between the self and the medium. Surely, this situation is a risk; it may position the creative educator generations away from his authentic relationship.

Our second risk finds its analogue in the humanities education teacher. Typically, this individual is very similar to the first teacher analogue, with one additional characteristic dimension: he has chosen not to teach the medium itself, but rather to instruct others how to teach the medium, although both may occur. In practical reality, this teacher makes a drastic three-generation leap from the possibility of an authentic relationship to two separate levels of methodological concerns; energies never directed toward the creative process with regard to the subject itself are here expended to interpret the medium as a teacher of students and package these interpretations into salable methodologies as teachers of teachers.

Again, this is an analogue with frightening implications for the creative educator, who might be found in either of these situations. Both analogues represent the extreme perversions of the authentic relationship for us: becoming masters of educational methodology as a result of transferring too much energy in the direction of pedagogical packaging and too little energy in the direction of our own consanguinity, creative process and commitment. A closer translation of the analogue exposes a teacher whose pedagogy is incongruent with the medium; without a rich authentic relationship with the medium, an appropriate, meaningful pedagogy cannot evolve.

In both cases of risk, a balance of energies expended in various directions is implied and desirable. However, such a balance is often threatened by the very nature of the teaching institution. Our authenticity decreases as the imbalance of concentrations increases. While we who adhere to the highest-good principle, the principle of congruence, may be the best choice for teachers of the humanities, inevitably our positions in relation to contemporary administrations, institutions, and students often destroy what makes us so vital. Too many people involved in educational systems today oppress us with principles that comprise authenticity. They (and I use their jargon) emphasize the manageability of teachable commodities that we must package with methodologies, advertise, and sell. In turn, many students expect such salesmanship from us. Those for whom we work and teach rarely mention congruence, which connotes a manner of teaching sensitively and exclusively derived from authentic relationships with a subject. For these people, there is a great, unobjectionable separation between what is taught and the manageable way it is sold to students. In the face of this, we are hard put to maintain a sense of our centers and genuine bond with our medium, hard put to allow all that we do to emanate from those centers. Skepticism cast on the value of our authenticity, we risk professional and creative amnesia, paralysis, and deadening if we succumb to mastering the dispensable form of our subject.

Drawn as we are to the theoretically creative and scholarly milieus of the educational institution and profession, we have been disillusioned by a reality that undercuts our authentic efforts to combine self-expression as artists with sharing and facilitating as teachers. Yet these problems are not irreparable; we must not give up our efforts. It is our unique responsibility to right a profession gone wrong according to the very same principles we exemplify; we must not compromise our authentic relationships with our work; we must encourage the principle of congruence in all of its forms as a standard for teachers in the humanities; we must be leaders in the redefining of our profession and our roles in the school and university; finally, we must sustain our search for a balance of energies directed toward creating and teaching and give congruence to those dialectical tensions that have frustrated our growth and the growth of our students.

The final "must," a balance of energies, relates intrinsically to the key of the common denominator that distinguishes our high degree of authenticity from compromise: this is a direct involvement in the creative process of our medium, its language and meanings. Attaining this balance must be our immediate concern if we are to *be* what we help others to experience in a meaningful way, or, more profoundly, be in the process of becoming what we help others to become.

In an effort to concretize the relationships between our authenticity, balance, and our students, permit me to digress for the remainder of this paper and recount a chain of experiences. They represent hope and possibility.

Last July 1 I finished a documentary film on which I had been working for five months. August and September were devoted to curriculum preparations for two film-making courses, Film Production I and Scriptwriting. Quite fresh from my own experience of the creative process, I attempted to approach my task from two related states of mind, those of film maker and film teacher. I recall feeling that the process of curriculum development was more comfortable and the results more satisfying than for similar planning I had done a year ago for teaching a series of novels; the simple logic of this relates to my being a film maker rather than a novelist. Yet, more intricate logic does exist that may better explain the meaning of my comfort and satisfaction.

Intimately familiar with my own creative efforts and sensitive to my ability to learn only through doing, it seemed appropriate for both of my courses to emphasize a workshop concept rather than a lecture-discussion seminar. Having created and studied in an alternating fashion over time, I sensed my prospective students' needs would be similar; visual language learned from lectures and books would have meaning for my students only after experimentation with the visual images they had mentally tucked away through years of unexpressed accumulation. Glossaries, lectures, and models in the initial stages of visual expression would only stifle the making of film. Further, such a methodology would be incongruent with the medium itself. My belief in using visual language in order to learn how to create visual images evolved from my inherent understanding of beginners' needs and feelings, what my students would or would not need to know at a particular time, what problems would inevitably arise during the creative process, and how to help them with solutions. A visible characteristic of the workshop structure is its underlying flexibility at every stage that accounts for individual differences in relation to the pace, capabilities, and objectives of people involved in creative expression. Film scripts and visual images are not usually created according to "recommended procedures" for beginners; those not involved in the production aspects of film often misunderstand this simple fact. Most important was my sense of reality about film making; too many books and film theorists express opinions about the creative process of film that have nothing to do with reality. My priority in planning these curricula was making a completely congruent translation of my reality into authentic experiences and methodological settings. In order to express a process or concept, a teacher must make external both the developmental forms it assumes and a twin of its internal shape. My students found only this congruent authenticity credible, possible, and valuable.

With time, however, our situation grew toward incongruence. I became more preoccupied with providing experiences than with participating in them and was no longer in direct touch with the process in which my students were involved. My frustrations and discontent with vicarious experiences created a barrier to meaningful teaching and learning. I found it increasingly difficult to anticipate the needs of my students. We all suffered.

In January, I faced second-quarter continuations of my two courses with these same students. Simultaneously, I accepted the position as editor for a short theatrical film. This was my attempt to find a balance between creating and teaching, to reestablish my authentic relationship with film, to be once again in the process of becoming what I was helping my students to become. Balancing became a matter of learning to pace my energies in two directions. Ironically, my process of learning this gave forceful meaning to what I call authenticity and the creative process for my students; my initial pacing difficulties found resolution through ongoing discussion with my students of my attempt to regain a balance. My students also learned much from watching me at work, and I welcomed all interested passersby into my editing room. As I had suspected, teaching and creating simultaneously brought me back to the reality of film making and back to the reality of my students.

The counterpoint must also be well understood. Generally, my experiment was fruitful; however, several students felt neglected as a result of my personal indulgence. We must realize that our first attempts at a balance may be at the expense of several students' loss of security; this must be handled gently, and we must reassure and draw them in, give them an understanding of exactly what we are doing. We shall even find students who do not respect the intensity and authenticity with which we work; they may walk into our rooms with personal demands, regardless of our apparent involvement in something of our own. All of these students, as well as others involved in the educational system, must be made aware that we, too, are vital human beings with private and public creative needs; further, we must help them understand their own ultimate gain from our authenticity.